EQUALITY IN WATER AND SANITATION SERVICES

There is growing acceptance that the progress delivered under the Millennium Development Goal target for drinking water and sanitation has been inequitable. As a result, the progressive reduction of inequalities is now an explicit focus of the Sustainable Development Goal (SDG) targets, adopted in 2015, for universal access to drinking water, sanitation and hygiene (WASH). This shift in focus has implications for the way in which the next generation of WASH policies and programmes will be conceived, designed, financed and monitored.

This book provides an authoritative textbook for students, as well as a point of reference for policy-makers and practitioners interested in reducing inequalities in access to WASH services. Four key areas are addressed: background to the human right to water and development goals; dimensions of inequality; case studies in delivering water and sanitation equitably; and monitoring progress in reducing inequality.

Oliver Cumming is an Assistant Professor of Environmental Health at the London School of Hygiene and Tropical Medicine, UK, where he works on the epidemiology of water and sanitation-related diseases. He is currently working on multiple trials to assess the impact of water and sanitation interventions on childhood enteric infection, undernutrition and oral vaccine failure in Africa and South Asia.

Tom Slaymaker is a Senior Statistics and Monitoring Specialist in the Data and Analytics section at UNICEF Headquarters, USA. He has nearly 20 years of experience working on water and sanitation in Africa and Asia, and currently co-leads the WHO/UNICEF Joint Monitoring Programme for Water Supply, Sanitation and Hygiene (JMP).

Earthscan Water Text series
www.routledge.com/Earthscan-Water-Text/book-series/ECEWT

Equality in Water and Sanitation Services
Edited by Oliver Cumming and Tom Slaymaker

Water Stewardship and Business Value
Creating Abundance from Scarcity
William Sarni and David Grant

Water Governance and Collective Action
Multi-scale challenges
Edited by Diana Suhardiman, Alan Nicol and Everisto Mapedza

The International Law of Transboundary Groundwater Resources
Gabriel Eckstein

Reconnecting People and Water
Public Engagement and Sustainable Urban Water Management
Liz Sharp

Key Concepts in Water Resource Management
A Review and Critical Evaluation
Edited by Jonathan Lautze

Contesting Hidden Waters
Conflict Resolution for Groundwater and Aquifers
W. Todd Jarvis

Water Security
Principles, Perspectives and Practices
Edited by Bruce Lankford, Karen Bakker, Mark Zeitoun, Declan Conway

Water Ethics
A Values Approach to Solving the Water Crisis
David Groenfeldt

The Right to Water
Politics, Governance and Social Struggles
Edited by Farhana Sultana, Alex Loftus

EQUALITY IN WATER AND SANITATION SERVICES

Edited by
Oliver Cumming and
Tom Slaymaker

First published 2018
by Routledge
2 Park Square, Milton Park, Abingdon, Oxon OX14 4RN

and by Routledge
711 Third Avenue, New York, NY 10017

Routledge is an imprint of the Taylor & Francis Group, an informa business

© 2018 selection and editorial matter, Oliver Cumming and Tom Slaymaker; individual chapters, the contributors

The right of Oliver Cumming and Tom Slaymaker to be identified as the authors of the editorial material, and of the authors for their individual chapters, has been asserted in accordance with sections 77 and 78 of the Copyright, Designs and Patents Act 1988.

All rights reserved. No part of this book may be reprinted or reproduced or utilised in any form or by any electronic, mechanical, or other means, now known or hereafter invented, including photocopying and recording, or in any information storage or retrieval system, without permission in writing from the publishers.

Trademark notice: Product or corporate names may be trademarks or registered trademarks, and are used only for identification and explanation without intent to infringe.

British Library Cataloguing-in-Publication Data
A catalogue record for this book is available from the British Library

Library of Congress Cataloguing-in-Publication Data
Names: Cumming, Oliver, editor. | Slaymaker, Tom, editor.
Title: Equality in water and sanitation services /
[edited by] Oliver Cumming, Tom Slaymaker.
Description: Abingdon, Oxon ; New York, NY : Routledge, 2018. |
Includes bibliographical references and index.
Identifiers: LCCN 2018001604| ISBN 9781138203495 (hardback) |
ISBN 9781138203518 (pbk.) | ISBN 9781315471532 (ebook)
Subjects: LCSH: Sanitation—Developing countries. |
Water-supply—Developing countries. | Water security—Developing countries. |
Environmental justice—Developing countries.
Classification: LCC TD327 .E65 2018 | DDC 363.6/1091724—dc23
LC record available at https://lccn.loc.gov/2018001604

ISBN: 978-1-138-20349-5 (hbk)
ISBN: 978-1-138-20351-8 (pbk)
ISBN: 978-1-315-47153-2 (ebk)

Typeset in Bembo and Stone Sans
by Florence Production Ltd, Stoodleigh, Devon, UK

CONTENTS

Preface	ix
List of contributors	xi

PART 1
Equality as a global priority for the water and sanitation sector   **1**

1   Progress in tracking inequalities: lessons from MDG monitoring   3
    Robert Bain and Tom Slaymaker

2   The human rights to water and sanitation: challenges and
    implications for future priorities   26
    Virginia Roaf, Catarina de Albuquerque and Léo Heller

3   The potential of the SDG framework to promote equality
    through WASH initiatives   46
    Sanjay Wijesekera, Bruce Gordon and Sue Cavill

PART 2
Dimensions of inequality related to water and sanitation   **61**

4   Equality in water supply provision: beyond numbers served   63
    Alan Nicol, Lyla Mehta and Indika Arulingam

5   WASH and gender: understanding gendered consequences
    and impacts of WASH in/security   80
    Kathleen O'Reilly and Robert Dreibelbis

6 The environmental dimensions of universal access to safe water 94
Roger Calow, Alan MacDonald and Miriam Denis Le Sève

7 How international water and sanitation monitoring fails deprived urban dwellers 117
Gordon McGranahan, Anna Walnycki, Festo Dominick, Wilbard Kombe, Alphonce Kyessi, Tatu Mtwangi Limbumba, Hezron Magambo, Mwanakombo Mkanga and Tim Ndezi

PART 3
Addressing inequality in water and sanitation service provision 135

8 First a basic service for all: reducing WASH inequalities through more equitable funding and financing strategies 137
Ian Ross and Richard Franceys

9 Breaking the barriers: disability, ageing and HIV in inclusive WASH programming 157
Jane Wilbur, Louisa Gosling and Hazel Jones

10 Addressing the menstrual needs of women and girls is necessary to achieve gender equality in water and sanitation service delivery 176
Bethany Caruso and Marni Sommer

11 Interlocking inequalities related to water and sanitation, nutrition and healthcare access 196
John Anderson and Oliver Cumming

12 Inequality beyond the toilet: fecal sludge management and the community-level dimensions of sanitation 216
David Berendes and Joe Brown

PART 4
Enhanced monitoring of inequalities in water and sanitation 231

13 Monitoring inequalities in WASH service levels 233
Tom Slaymaker and Rick Johnston

14 Benchmarking progress on reducing inequalities over time 253
Jeanne Luh and Jamie Bartram

15 Counting the costs and benefits of equitable WASH service provision 286
Guy Hutton and Luis Andrés

Index 312

PREFACE

This book comes after the Millennium Development Goals (MDGs) have concluded and as we embark on a new international poverty reduction effort under the Sustainable Development Goals (SDGs). The title *Equality in Water and Sanitation Services* reflects both the opportunity and challenge of the SDG agenda for stakeholders in the water, sanitation and hygiene (WASH) sector. World leaders have agreed ambitious new global targets to achieve universal access to safe and affordable drinking water and adequate and equitable sanitation and hygiene by 2030.[1] At the same time, there are currently huge inequalities in access to these services, reflecting underlying and persistent social inequalities, that must be overcome if the vision of universal access is to be realised.

Almost two decades ago, the Millennium Development Goals (MDGs) were agreed at the United Nations General Assembly with ambitious objectives across a range of development sectors to reduce global poverty. A water and sanitation target was established to reduce by half the proportion of people without access to safe drinking water and adequate sanitation by 2015.[1] Undoubtedly, the agreement of this target has helped focus international efforts on increasing access to basic water and sanitation services. Between 1990 and 2015, some 2.6 billion people gained access to an improved source of drinking water and 2.1 billion gained access to improved sanitation facilities. Despite this impressive progress, 663 million remained without access to improved drinking water and 2.4 billion without access to improved sanitation, with these deficits concentrated within the poorest countries of the world and, within those, the poorest sections of society.[2]

The Sustainable Development Goals (SDGs) have been conceived as a universal development agenda placing equality centre stage. Beyond the more sector-specific goals, such as universal access to quality healthcare (SDG 3) and education (SDG 4), there are now cross-cutting goals which concern all development sectors, including water and sanitation. Among these, SDG 1, to 'ensure all men and women, in particular the poor and vulnerable, have equal rights to economic resources, as well as basic services', directly addresses equality. Achieving the SDG targets on water, sanitation and hygiene will require major changes in both the scale of ambition and investment among national and international actors but will also require a change in approach with regard to addressing persistent and often structural inequalities within countries. There is cause for optimism as some countries were able to reduce inequalities in water and sanitation access during the MDG era. However, in many countries, progress in extending access to water and sanitation services was unequal with marked disparities by wealth, by geography, and by other socio-economic characteristics, suggesting that new approaches will be needed.

This book is presented in four parts. Part 1 sets the scene by reviewing progress made in reducing inequalities under the MDGs (Chapter 1), considering the influence of the human rights agenda on the framing of the SDG targets for water, sanitation and hygiene (Chapter 2), and then locating the new SDG WASH targets within the broader context of the 2030 Agenda (Chapter 3). Part 2 then explores different and often over-lapping dimensions of inequality relevant to water and sanitation, from broader issues of disempowerment (Chapter 4), to gender and equity (Chapter 5), to environmental vulnerabilities (Chapter 6), and urban poverty and disenfranchisement (Chapter 7). In Part 3, the authors consider emerging policy issues with regard to financing strategies (Chapter 8), to services for people with disabilities (Chapter 9), women's and girls' rights (Chapter 10), to effective faecal sludge management (Chapter 11), and how progress in reducing inequalities might be better captured to incentivise progress (Chapter 12). In Part 4, three chapters look forward to consider how inequalities in water, sanitation and hygiene can be better monitored (Chapter 13), the clustering of inequalities or deprivation across sectors (Chapter 14), and how the costs and benefits of reducing inequality might be assessed (Chapter 15).

Amartya Sen said, 'the issue of inequality and that of poverty are not separable'.[3] 'Ending poverty in all its forms'[1] and achieving universal access to water, sanitation and hygiene services are not separate issues but one and the same. It is our sincere hope that this book will both stimulate discussion and support action on the enduring issue of inequality in water and sanitation services. And, perhaps, in 2030 it will offer a retrospective point of reference as we assess to what extent the international community were able to effectively draw lessons from the MDG era and deliver on the ambitious new SDG agenda.

Notes

1. United Nations (2015) Transforming Our World: The 2030 Agenda for Sustainable Development, UN General Assembly Resolution, A/RES/70/1, 21 October.
2. UNICEF and WHO (2015) *Progress on Sanitation and Drinking Water: 2015 update and MDG assessment*. WHO/UNICEF Joint Monitoring Programme for Water Supply and Sanitation, New York.
3. Barsamian, D. (2004) *Louder than Bombs: Interviews from the Progressive Magazine*. South End Press.

LIST OF CONTRIBUTORS

Catarina de Albuquerque is the Executive Chair of the Sanitation and Water for All Partnership and was the first UN Special Rapporteur on the right to safe drinking water and sanitation. She taught human rights and international relations in several European and American universities for 20 years. She was awarded the Human Rights Golden Medal by the Portuguese Parliament and was also honoured by the Portuguese President of the Republic with the Order of Merit, as recognition of her work on human rights.

John Anderson is a research consultant for the World Bank and PATH, whose projects include a review of chemical contaminants in drinking water and modelling global and subnational impacts of diarrhoeal disease vaccines. He recently received his Ph.D. from the University of Florida, where his research focused on water, sanitation and hygiene conditions in peri-urban Kisumu, Kenya.

Luis Andrés is Lead Economist in the Water Global Practice at the World Bank. His work at the World Bank involves both analytical and advisory services, with a focus on infrastructure, impact evaluations, private sector participation, regulation, and empirical microeconomics.

Indika Arulingam is a research consultant at the International Water Management Institute (IWMI) working with the Promoting Sustainable Growth team. She focuses on topics related to governance and political economy in water resources management at all levels.

Robert Bain is a statistics and monitoring specialist at UNICEF, based in New York.

xii List of contributors

Jamie Bartram is the Don and Jennifer Holzworth distinguished Professor of Environmental Sciences and Engineering, and Director of the Water Institute, Gillings School of Global Public Health, University of North Carolina, USA.

David Berendes is a Postdoctoral Fellow at the Georgia Institute of Technology, USA, where his research focuses on the environmental transmission of enteric pathogens in resource-poor settings where the disease burden is highest.

Joe Brown is Assistant Professor of environmental engineering at the Georgia Institute of Technology, USA.

Roger Calow is Head of the Water Policy Programme at the Overseas Development Institute, London, and an Honorary Research Associate at the British Geological Survey.

Bethany Caruso is a post-doctoral fellow in the Department of Environmental Health at Emory University's Rollins Schools of Public Health in Atlanta, USA. She is a social and behavioral scientist who uses mixed methods approaches to understand how compromised water, sanitation, and hygiene conditions impact physical and mental health, behavior, and education.

Sue Cavill has almost 20 years' experience working in the WASH sector, ranging from programme design and implementation, capacity building, programme evaluations and policy-relevant research, analysis and dissemination. Sue has a particular interest in women and WASH.

Miriam Denis le Sève is a Research Officer in the Overseas Development Institute's Water Policy Programme.

Festo Dominick is a Water and Sanitation Engineer at Center for Community Initiatives (CCI), Tanzania. His expertise lies in urban and rural water supply and treatment, low-cost sanitation and geographical information systems (GIS).

Robert Dreibelbis is an Assistant Professor at the London School of Hygiene and Tropical Medicine, UK. He researches WASH behaviours and behavioral determinants.

Richard Franceys is a water sector specialist who was previously a Senior Lecturer at the Institute of Water and Environment, Cranfield University, Bedfordshire.

Bruce Gordon coordinates WHO Headquarters work on WASH. He oversees a global portfolio of water and health-related work ranging from the development of norms on drinking water, recreational water, and wastewater through to the global monitoring of access to WASH and WASH-related burden of disease.

List of contributors xiii

Louisa Gosling is the Programme Manager for Principles at WaterAid, working in a team of sector specialists who provide support to WaterAid's country programmes.

Léo Heller is the second Special Rapporteur on the human rights to safe drinking water and sanitation since December 2014. He is currently a researcher in the Oswaldo Cruz Foundation in Brazil and previously was Professor of the Department of Sanitary and Environmental Engineering at the Federal University of Minas Gerais, Brazil, from 1990 to 2014.

Guy Hutton is a Senior Adviser in the UNICEF WASH Section based in New York.

Rick Johnston is a WASH Technical Officer for the World Health Organization, based in Geneva, Switzerland and currently co-leads the WHO/UNICEF Joint Monitoring Programme for Water Supply, Sanitation and Hygiene (JMP).

Hazel Jones (now retired) has had an illustrious career as a researcher at WEDC, focusing on ways to improve access to WASH facilities for disabled and older people, and sharing this with practitioners.

Wilbard Kombe is a Professor of land management at Ardhi University, Tanzania. His research focuses on urban governance, land management and administration; urban development and livelihoods of the poor; poverty and public services delivery; and public policy analysis.

Alphonce Kyessi is Associate Research Professor in the Institute of Human Settlements Studies at Ardhi University, Tanzania. With expertise in geographical information systems (GIS), he currently researches and consults on topics including land use planning, water and sanitation, and informal settlements regularisation.

Tatu Mtwangi Limbumba is a Senior Research Fellow at the Institute of Human Settlements Studies Ardhi University, Tanzania. Her areas of research and expertise include housing, infrastructure and urban poverty.

Jeanne Luh is a former Program Coordinator at the Water Institute at UNC, Gillings School of Global Public Health, University of North Carolina at Chapel Hill, USA.

Alan MacDonald is a principal hydrogeologist at the British Geological Survey and honorary professor at the University of Dundee, UK.

Hezron Magambo is a water and sanitation engineer with a background in environmental engineering and integrated sanitation management, and is currently working with the Center for Community Initiatives (CCI) in Tanzania. He has worked on urban and rural water and sanitation-related projects and research work for over five years.

Gordon McGranahan is a Fellow in the Cities Cluster of the Institute of Development Studies at the University of Sussex, UK. His research focuses on inclusive urbanisation, the urban land nexus and environmental burdens in and around the home, including water and sanitation.

Lyla Mehta is a Professorial Fellow at the Institute of Development Studies (IDS), University of Sussex, UK, and a Visiting Professor at Noragric, the Norwegian University of Life Sciences.

Mwanakombo Mkanga is an Urban Social Development Specialist and Program Manager at the Centre for Community Initiatives, Tanzania. She has substantial experience working with low-income communities in water, sanitation, and housing sectors, as well as social research and community organising.

Tim Ndezi is a development engineer with a background in civil, water and sanitation, and is currently working with the Center for Community Initiatives (CCI), Tanzania. He works on and researches the co-production of water and sanitation improvements in rural and urban setting, and also on land resettlement and affordable housing.

Alan Nicol leads the Strategic Program on Promoting Sustainable Growth at the International Water Management Institute (IWMI). Based in Addis Ababa, Ethiopia, his expertise lies in political economy, rural water development and transboundary river basin management in Asia and Africa.

Kathleen O'Reilly, Ph.D., is an Associate Professor of Geography and member of the faculty of the Water Management and Hydrological Sciences Program at Texas A&M University, USA. She studies the implications of changing water resource governance and the impacts of sanitation interventions for marginal groups, particularly women and the lowest castes.

Virgina Roaf is an independent consultant working on water and sanitation in development cooperation, with a specific focus on the practical implementation of the human rights to water and sanitation.

Ian Ross is currently undertaking a Ph.D. in Health Economics at the London School of Hygiene and Tropical Medicine, UK, and before that led the Water Team at Oxford Policy Management.

Marni Sommer is an Associate Professor of Sociomedical Sciences at the Mailman School of Public Health, Columbia University, New York. She is the Executive Editor of *Global Public Health*, and the Executive Director of Grow and Know, a small non-profit organisation that publishes puberty books for boys and girls.

Anna Walnycki is a Researcher at the International Institute for Environment and Development, London. Her recent research has focused on the practical and strategic challenges to extending basic services – specifically water and sanitation – into informal settlements.

Sanjay Wijesekera is Chief of Section for Water, Sanitation and Hygiene, and Associate Director of Programmes at UNICEF. He previously worked for the United Kingdom's Department for International Development (DFID), where he was responsible for managing overall policy and global programmes related to achieving the water and sanitation Millennium Development Goals. He has also worked for the Department of Water Affairs and Forestry in South Africa and on emergency programmes for Oxfam in Rwanda for UNICEF in Sri Lanka.

Jane Wilbur is a social inclusion specialist. Her experience includes developing and implementing inclusive WASH programmes and evaluation, as well as conducting, analysing, and disseminating research to influence policy and practice.

PART 1
Equality as a global priority for the water and sanitation sector

1
PROGRESS IN TRACKING INEQUALITIES

Lessons from MDG monitoring

Robert Bain and Tom Slaymaker

Introduction

As attention shifts from the Millennium Development Goals (MDGs) to the Sustainable Development Goals (SDGs), it is important to reflect on global monitoring of inequalities prior to and during the MDG period. This chapter reviews the evolving definitions of access and services used for international monitoring since the early 1990s, and the types of inequalities that have been monitored to date, with a focus on reporting of access to drinking water, sanitation and hygiene (WASH) at global level by the WHO/UNICEF Joint Monitoring Programme (JMP) for Water Supply, Sanitation and Hygiene. It describes several limitations of existing data and points to areas where inequality monitoring should be strengthened during the SDG era. The chapter provides a context within which to understand the ambition of the SDGs related to WASH (Chapter 3) and other related sectors (Chapter 11) while serving to underscore the need to go beyond access and progressively measure the levels of service (Chapter 12).

Evolving definitions of access and services used by the JMP

The WHO/UNICEF JMP has tracked progress in water, sanitation and hygiene since it was founded in the early 1990s. Mandated to monitor WASH at global, regional and national levels, the definitions of access and service levels used by the JMP have evolved in tandem with progress sector monitoring.

In its first decade (1990–2000), the JMP relied on questionnaires sent to line ministries responsible for WASH that were often completed based on administrative data. JMP questionnaires described 'safe drinking water coverage' as the proportion of population with access to an adequate amount of safe drinking water located within a convenient distance for the user's dwelling, and 'sanitary means of excreta disposal' as the proportion of population with access to a sanitary facility for human excreta disposal in the dwelling or located within a convenient distance from the user's dwelling and noted that countries should use local definitions of terms like 'safe', 'sanitary' and 'convenient'.[1]

Early reports focused on trends in national, urban and rural coverage for developing regions. However, given the diverse definitions used in different countries, a key objective was to establish a suitable common benchmark to allow for international comparison of status and trends over time. This was further underlined by the call for more robust estimates to inform international target setting. The Millennium Summit and the World Summit on Sustainable Development established new global targets for drinking water and sanitation under the framework of the Millennium Development Goals (MDGs).[2,3] No specific mention of hygiene was made in the target or declaration. Target 7C under the goal for ensuring environmental sustainability sought to 'Halve, by 2015, the proportion of the population without sustainable access to safe drinking water and basic sanitation' (source: United Nations[4]).

The JMP proposed a simple technology-based approach to classifying drinking water and sanitation facilities as 'improved' or 'unimproved' (Table 1.1). Improved drinking water sources are those designed to 'protect' the supply from outside contamination – in particular, faecal contamination. Improved sanitation facilities are those designed to prevent human contact with faeces. The improved classification was developed through a series of expert consultations and the terminology, if not the exact classification of technology types, pre-dated the MDGs.[5] It was further refined in the early 2000s to distinguish specific types of sanitation facilities such as flush/pour flush and hanging latrines, and water sources such as piped water into a dwelling, plot or yard, as well as the use of bottled water and tanker trucks.

WASH sector stakeholders rallied around the improved indicator and the comparatively small number of global MDG targets provided a renewed emphasis on progress on basic water and sanitation services. The 'improved' indicator is simple and easy to communicate, which has facilitated its use for both decision making and advocacy. By becoming a de facto global norm, however, a growing number of criticisms were raised related to reductionism (Box 1.1). A further general criticism has been the focus on average rates of progress and the formulation of the target to 'halve the proportion without' which together enable target achievement without a dedicated focus on reducing inequalities and reaching poor and marginalised groups.[7]

In 2006, the JMP published guidance for household survey programmes in the form of 'core questions' (Table 1.2). This supported the increasing harmonisation across major international survey programmes such as Multiple Indicator Cluster Surveys (MICS), Demographic and Health Surveys (DHS) and Living Standard Measurement Study (LSMS). The questions have since been promoted by the JMP and sector stakeholders and, as a result, have been adopted in many other national household surveys and a subset was also included in the 2010 round of

TABLE 1.1 MDG Improved classification

	Improved	*Unimproved*
Drinking water	Piped water into dwelling, plot or yard Public tap/standpipe Tubewell/borehole Protected dug well Protected spring Rainwater collection	Unprotected dug well Unprotected spring Cart with small tank/drum Bottled water[1] Tanker truck Surface water (river, dam, lake, pond, stream, canal, irrigation channels)

Sanitation[2]	Flush/pour flush to:
	  piped sewer system,
	  septic tank,
	  pit latrine;
	  unknown place/not known where.
	VIP latrine
	Pit latrine with slab
	Composting toilet
		Flush/pour flush to:
		  elsewhere.
		Pit latrine without slab/open pit
		Bucket
		Hanging toilet/hanging latrine
		No facilities or bush or field

Notes
1 Bottled water is considered improved only when the household uses water from an improved source for cooking and personal hygiene.
2 Shared or public facilities are not counted as improved.

Source: WHO/UNICEF (2006).[6]

BOX 1.1 THE IMPROVED DICHOTOMY

The improved/unimproved classification has proven to be readily applicable in almost all countries. It has nevertheless been criticised for being too high for low-income countries – e.g. where the majority still use 'traditional' latrines without a slab – and too low for high-income countries – e.g. with high rates of coverage with piped water and sewerage infrastructure but poor service levels. Specifically, it is widely recognised that while improved drinking water sources are less likely to be contaminated, this does not necessarily imply that they are 'safe' to drink. The use of a single threshold has also been criticised because it does not adequately reflect progress above and below the benchmark. But perhaps most importantly it is recognised that service levels vary widely among households using any given type of improved facility.[8]

TABLE 1.2 JMP core questions

Drinking water	Main source of drinking water[1]
	Time to collect drinking water per round trip
	Person primarily responsible for collecting water
	Household water-treatment practices
Sanitation	Main sanitation facility
	Sharing sanitation with other households
	Number of households sharing
	Child faeces disposal practices

Note

1 The core questions recommended recording information on the household's source for other purposes, such as cooking and hand washing if bottled water was reported as main source of drinking water.

Source: WHO/UNICEF (2006).[6]

censuses in low- and middle-income countries. The harmonisation of core questions has led to a great increase in the quality and quantity of data from households as well as comparability of survey results.

In its 2008 report, the JMP introduced a new approach to monitoring trends in the use of water and sanitation. The drinking water and sanitation service 'ladders' represented an important shift by enabling the JMP to track trends and highlight inequalities in both higher and lower levels of service. For drinking water, this ranged from the use of surface water to piped water on premises – the highest level of service monitored during the MDGs. For sanitation, rungs below improved were introduced (shared, unimproved, open defecation), but there was no equivalent higher service level. Efforts to monitor sanitation rungs below improved corresponded with increased global attention to sanitation reflected in the 2008 International Year of Sanitation and the establishment of the Sanitation and Water for All global partnership. The bottom rung in particular was important in drawing attention to the practice of open defecation, now a major focus of the sector.

The shift to the use of household surveys and censuses as the main source of data on drinking water and sanitation at the outset of the MDG period necessitated the development of new methods and in turn enabled more statistically robust comparisons of progress between and within countries.[10] Censuses are typically decadal and household surveys are usually conducted every three to five years. Moreover, sampling and non-sampling errors mean that estimates often vary between surveys. For these reasons, simply using the latest survey for all countries would have meant comparisons between data points many years apart (>5 years). Given the limited amounts of data and the need to be able to clearly articulate the methodology to the sector and government counterparts, the JMP adopted a simple method based on linear regression (Box 1.2).[9] By producing modelled estimates for any given year, it was possible to compare coverage in the same year and to compare trends for the same time periods.

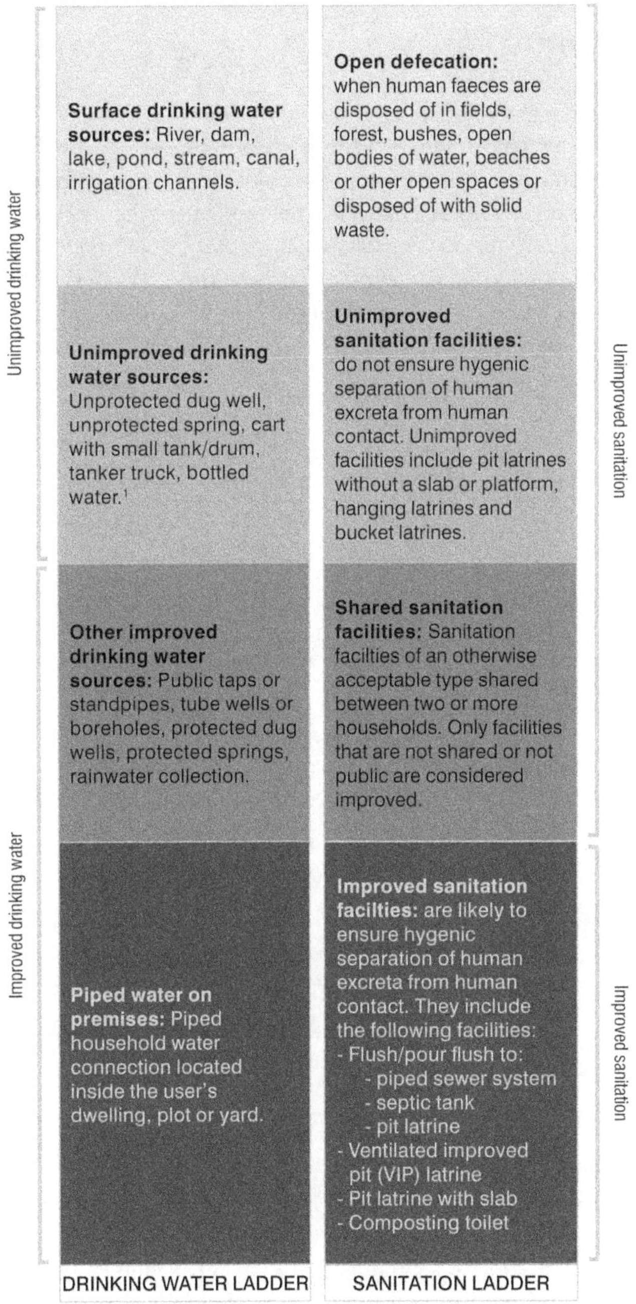

	DRINKING WATER LADDER	SANITATION LADDER	
Unimproved drinking water	**Surface drinking water sources:** River, dam, lake, pond, stream, canal, irrigation channels.	**Open defecation:** when human faeces are disposed of in fields, forest, bushes, open bodies of water, beaches or other open spaces or disposed of with solid waste.	Unimproved sanitation
Unimproved drinking water	**Unimproved drinking water sources:** Unprotected dug well, unprotected spring, cart with small tank/drum, tanker truck, bottled water.[1]	**Unimproved sanitation facilities:** do not ensure hygenic separation of human excreta from human contact. Unimproved facilities include pit latrines without a slab or platform, hanging latrines and bucket latrines.	Unimproved sanitation
Improved drinking water	**Other improved drinking water sources:** Public taps or standpipes, tube wells or boreholes, protected dug wells, protected springs, rainwater collection.	**Shared sanitation facilities:** Sanitation facilties of an otherwise acceptable type shared between two or more households. Only facilities that are not shared or not public are considered improved.	Improved sanitation

Improved drinking water	**Piped water on premises:** Piped household water connection located inside the user's dwelling, plot or yard.	**Improved sanitation facilties:** are likely to ensure hygenic separation of human excreta from human contact. They include the following facilities:
		- Flush/pour flush to:
		  - piped sewer system
		  - septic tank
		  - pit latrine
		- Ventilated improved pit (VIP) latrine
		- Pit latrine with slab
		- Composting toilet
			Improved sanitation

[1] Bottled water is considered 'improved' for drinking only when the household uses an improved source for cooking and personal hygiene.

FIGURE 1.1 JMP drinking water and sanitation ladder
Source: WHO/UNICEF JMP (2015).[9]

BOX 1.2 JMP METHOD

The JMP produces estimates using a linear regression method in order to compare estimates for different countries in a single reference year. Trends are extrapolated by at most two years and beyond this point the estimates remain unchanged for up to four years unless coverage is below 0.5 per cent or above 99.5 per cent, in which case the line is extended indefinitely. Data for urban and rural are combined using population estimates from the UN Population Division. Separate linear regressions are used for rungs in the JMP water and sanitation ladders.[9]

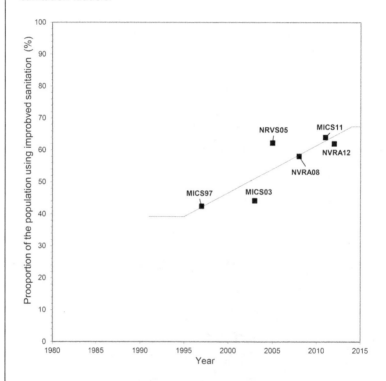

FIGURE 1.2 JMP method applied to urban sanitation coverage in Afghanistan
Source: Author's based on WHO/UNICEF JMP (2015).

With renewed focus on monitoring and international comparability during the MDGs (Box 1.3), the amount of data available to the JMP increased substantially between 1990 and 2015. Whereas in 1990 the JMP was able to report on the coverage of drinking water for 70 countries, by 2015 it had estimates for nearly all countries (over 200 countries, states and territories). The number of household survey and census datasets increased nearly sixfold from 272 to 1658.[9] This great expansion in data availability has underpinned inequality monitoring by the JMP and enables a great variety of in-depth further analysis beyond what can be achieved at the global aggregate level.

Growing attention to inequalities in international monitoring

The adoption of a global norm for access to drinking water and sanitation has enabled comparisons between regions and countries, and between urban and rural areas at a global, regional and country level. This has facilitated a greater understanding of the status and trends in absolute inequalities, and a focus on the countries and regions that have lagged farthest behind.

During the MDG period (1990–2015), 2.6 billion people gained access to improved drinking water and 2.1 billion to improved sanitation. Coverage of improved drinking water increased from 76 to 91 per cent, thereby meeting the target five years ahead of schedule.[11] In contrast, the MDG target for sanitation was not met, with coverage increasing from 54 to 68 per cent, considerably short of the 77 per cent target (Figure 1.3).

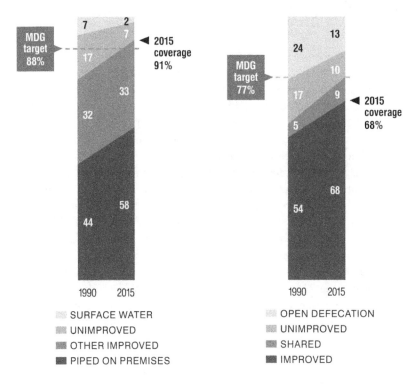

FIGURE 1.3 JMP ladders showing water and sanitation progress from 1990 to 2015
Source: WHO/UNICEF (2015).[9]

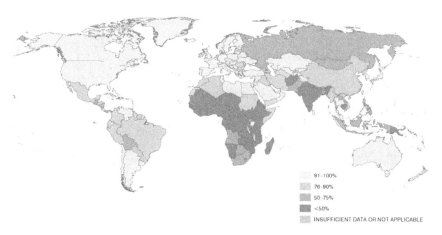

FIGURE 1.4 Sanitation coverage by country in 2015
Source: WHO/UNICEF JMP (2015).[9]

BOX 1.3 RECONCILING INTERNATIONAL AND NATIONAL DEFINITIONS

National standards are different from international standards and may use alternative classification – e.g. in parts of West Africa shared sanitation is the norm. In North Africa and the Middle East, tanker trucks are considered the norm, but both have been classified by the JMP as unimproved. Elsewhere, countries may exclude specific types classified by the JMP as improved – e.g. rainwater harvesting. There are also more subtle differences in definitions. For example, the JMP requires that pit latrines have a slab, which can be made of any material as long as it effectively covers the pit, whereas in parts of Southern Africa, countries require pit latrine slabs to be made of concrete and/or to be 'washable'.[12] While the improved/unimproved classification is sufficiently broad to cover most common types of water and sanitation facilities, further discussion is often required to determine correspondence with local definitions used in national surveys. For example, the JMP had extensive discussion with national authorities in China over the classification of 'harmless latrines', which include the following types: flush/water flush, biogas, urine diversion, two/three compartment septic tank and double pit shift use latrine. In some cases, reconciliation missions have led to countries adopting international standards, but the primary objective in all cases is to ensure that WASH sector stakeholders have a better understanding of the similarities and differences between the definitions and methods used to produce national and international estimates.[13]

Despite achieving the drinking water target and making progress towards the sanitation target, there remain large disparities in access both between and within regions and countries. The vast majority of the global population without access to improved drinking water and sanitation are concentrated in four developing regions sub-Saharan Africa, South Asia, South Eastern Asia and East Asia. Within these regions, the unserved are concentrated in rural areas: in 2015, 8 out of 10 people without improved drinking water, 7 out of 10 people without improved sanitation and 9 out of 10 people who practised open defecation lived in rural areas. At the end of the MDG period, there remained 47 countries where less than half the population used improved sanitation (Figure 1.4).

Efforts to monitor inequalities under the MDGs

The transition from use of administrative data reported by governments in aggregate form to the use of information collected from individual households through multitopic surveys greatly facilitated inequality monitoring during the MDGs. Taking advantage of the increasing availability of household survey and census data, the following approaches to monitoring inequalities were adopted during the MDGs.

Residence

In the light of the marked difference in water and sanitation coverage between urban and rural areas, the MDG targets specified that progress should be monitored separately for these two settings.[14] Disaggregated data are now available for the vast majority of countries, although there are some exceptions for countries that are either entirely urban (e.g. Singapore) or rural (e.g. Tokelau) or where information has not been collected owing to the lack of definition recognised by the national statistical offices (e.g. Lebanon). However, the definitions of 'urban' vary between countries and the use of this dichotomy can mask inequalities by residence, including between formal and informal settlements or periurban areas (Box 1.4).

The available data show that disparities between rural and urban have in most cases narrowed during the MDGs but that significant gaps remain in 2015, especially for those without any service (practising open defecation or collecting surface water for drinking) (Figure 1.5).

Wealth quintiles

Important inequalities are also observed between households in different wealth quintiles, and there is a strong correlation between access and wealth in countries with data.[16] The increasing use of household survey data for monitoring access to drinking water and sanitation during the MDG era provided the opportunity

12 R. Bain and T. Slaymaker

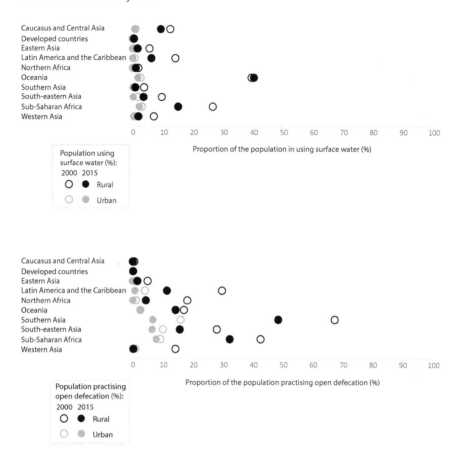

FIGURE 1.5 Rural–urban gaps in open defecation and surface water by region, 2000–2015

Source: Regional estimates from WHO/UNICEF JMP (2015).[9]

to examine inequalities along socioeconomic status. Asset-based wealth quintiles have been used extensively in the analysis of data from the DHS and MICS, and were used by the JMP to highlight the extent of inequalities between the richest and poorest.[17,18]

Visualising inequalities

In addition to the use of "ladders" to illustrate inequalities in the use of improved facilities, the JMP has developed or adapted several other ways to visualise inequalities. These have included population ladders, pie charts, equity trees and quadrant plots (Figure 1.6).

BOX 1.4 URBAN–RURAL

There is no commonly agreed international definition for urban areas.[15] Global estimates of access to water, sanitation and hygiene rely on national definitions of urban and rural that vary, often to a great degree, between countries. For example, by the definition of urban in Ethiopia ('Localities of 2,000 or more inhabitants'), almost the entire population of Bangladesh might be considered 'urban'. The urban–rural dichotomy masks a spectrum between dispersed rural populations to peri-urban and informal settlements, to densely populated formal urban areas. Urban–rural boundaries also change over time and are periodically updated by National Statistical Offices, making it difficult to estimate trends.

Progress towards MDG targets

One of the key functions of the JMP during the MDGs was to assess progress towards the MDG targets. Approaches used by the JMP included: on track/off track to meet targets based on the current rate of progress. The JMP trend estimates have been used to assess both rates of progress and the achievement of international agreed targets.[9,18] It is important to note that the JMP estimation method is not sensitive to rapid increases in rates of progress and may also mask stagnation or regression.[18,21] Such techniques have nevertheless proved useful for assessing aggregate rates of progress at country, regional and global levels.

Assessment of progress in spite of rapid population growth. Alternative indicators have been used by the JMP to capture progress in countries or regions where population growth during the MDG period made it more difficult to maintain and increase coverage. For example the population of sub-Saharan Africa nearly doubled between 1990 and 2015. Despite not meeting the MDG target, 47 per cent of the 2015 population 'gained access' to an improved drinking water source.[9] As the JMP estimates are primarily based on cross-sectional surveys, it is not usually possible to determine how much of the 'new population' is born into households with improved facilities.

Inequality monitoring in other sectors

The similarities and differences in the way in which data are collected have important implications for analysis of interlinkages between progress in WASH and other sectors and the potential for analysis of multiple overlapping dimensions of inequality. For example, while WASH monitoring to date has primarily focused at the household level, analysis of inequalities by individual characteristics such as age and sex have been more advanced in the health, nutrition and education sectors.

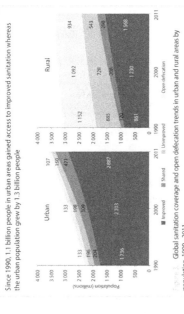

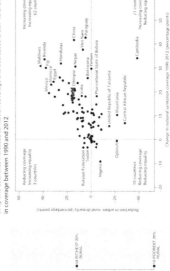

FIGURE 1.6 Illustrative examples of JMP data visualisation

Source: WHO/UNICEF JMP (2010–2014).[11,18–20]

Explore disparities in education across and within countries

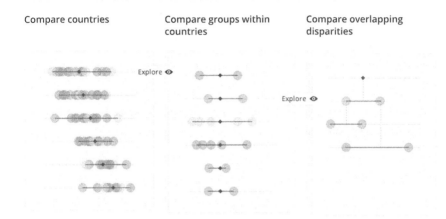

FIGURE 1.7 Data visualisation approach to show inequalities in education indicators between and within countries

Source: World Inequality Database on Education: www.education-inequalities.org

WASH monitoring is more advanced than other sectors in some other ways due to the focus on generating national estimates and the routine disaggregation of urban and rural populations, which is not always available for health indicators such as immunisation. WASH monitoring has the advantage that sample sizes are relatively high compared to indicators that relate to specific age groups (e.g. adolescents or pregnant women).

Compelling analyses of annual rates of reduction (child mortality) and the visualisation of disparities by wealth (equiplots), have provided valuable lessons and inspiration for WASH. The World Inequality Database on Education provides a good example of how online tools can enable the exploration of available data on inequalities between and within countries (Figure 1.7). On the other hand, the idea of using service ladders to benchmark progress across countries at different stages of development could be considered by other sectors for global monitoring (e.g. clean energy/fuels).

Opportunities and constraints associated with existing data sources

The harmonisation of WASH indicators collected in national household surveys and censuses affords many opportunities for cross-country comparison and in-depth analysis of inequalities between and within countries. Existing data do, however, present challenges for tracking inequalities and are not sufficient to monitor all dimensions of inequality specified in the SDGs. In this section we describe some of the progress made during the MDG period and opportunities for further analysis.

One particular challenge relates to the availability of harmonised equity stratifiers and qualifiers of service level. For example, the standardisation of methods used to create a wealth index based on household assets in the DHS and MICS international survey programmes has made it possible to generate comparable estimates of trends by wealth quintile. While these programmes now cover large parts of the world, the fact that they are not available for a number of populous countries such as China, Brazil and Russia limits the scope of global analysis. Furthermore, relatively few countries have a sufficiently long time series to generate trend estimates, and for many countries data from older surveys may not be comparable with more recent data.

Drinking water

In addition to the use of different types of drinking water source, existing data sources include information on the following, which were periodically analysed during the MDG period.

Accessibility. Data on time to collect drinking water and its gender burden or distance of the main source of drinking water from the home are often collected in surveys.[22,23] Figure 1.8 shows that many people in sub-Saharan Africa spend more than 30 minutes for a single round-trip. Harmonised surveys do not quantify the amount of time spent by individuals or collectively. A small number of surveys record the number of hours spent by adults and/or children and there is a growing interest in time-use surveys for monitoring women's economic empowerment in relation to SDG5 on gender equality.[24]

Quality. The JMP supported Rapid Assessments of Drinking Water Quality studies in 2004–2005 in several countries (including Ethiopia, Jordan, Nicaragua, Nigeria and Tajikistan) to generate information on water quality from improved sources (see: https://washdata.org/waterquality/). The studies found significant rates of contamination in some areas of the countries surveyed, but were unable to estimate the total population drinking water from contaminated sources.[25] Data on water quality were subsequently collected in a small number of nationally representative household surveys, including the Bangladesh Multiple Indicator Cluster Survey and Ghana Living Standard Survey.[26,27] Integrating water testing in existing surveys demonstrated contamination across all types of drinking water sources used by households and wide variations between rural and urban areas and other population subgroups. Subnational studies have also taken place in Peru and Liberia as part of the Demographic and Health Survey Programme.[28]

Household water treatment. Data are routinely recorded on practices including boiling, addition of chlorine or filtration of water at home. Some 1.8 billion people report practising some form of treatment, but there are concerns about the reliability of the data and evidence for effectiveness of the most common forms of treatment has also been questioned.[29,30]

More than a quarter of the population in several countries of Sub-Saharan Africa takes longer than 30 minutes to make one water collection round trip

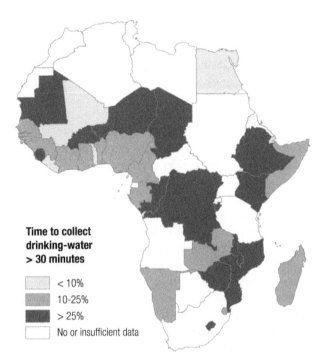

FIGURE 1.8 Map of round-trip travel times in sub-Saharan Africa
Source: WHO/UNICEF JMP (2010).[19]

Sanitation

Complementing information on the types of facilities used by households, existing data sources provide information on the following.

Child faeces disposal. Data on different practices for child faeces disposal and emphasis on the importance of ensuring appropriate sanitation solutions for all. Child faeces are considered particularly dangerous due to greater pathogen load and greater chance of exposure – for example, during play.[31]

Shared sanitation. Information on shared sanitation was available for 400 surveys/censuses at the end of the MDG period.[9] In most cases, the data sources recorded only whether facilities were shared, but in some surveys the number of people sharing and/or the nature of sharing (public vs. known neighbours) has also been recorded.

18 R. Bain and T. Slaymaker

Location of sanitation facility. Although not one of the JMP 'core questions' during the MDG period, many surveys have collected information on the location of the sanitation facility. In some cases, this is in addition to whether the facilities are shared, in others as an alternative measure. Having a facility within the dwelling or on premises may be a better proxy for privacy/dignity/personal safety than sharing.

Sewer connections networks. For the purposes of MDG monitoring, the JMP did not differentiate households using facilities connected to sewers and those using on-site sanitation facilities. However, the ability to break down the different types of sewered and non-sewered facilities used by the population will be important for future efforts to track safe management of the excreta produced.[32]

Hygiene

An analysis of combined water, sanitation and hygiene for sub-Saharan Africa found that access to basic handwashing is lower than improved drinking water and sanitation in most countries in sub-Saharan Africa and suggests that this remains an important issue of inequality.[33] The MDGs did not include an explicit target for hygiene despite its recognised importance for public health. In part, this may have been due to the lack of an agreed approach to monitoring hygiene, since it represents a diverse range of behaviours from handwashing and food hygiene to menstrual hygiene that protect health.[34] Where questions had been included in surveys, these typically asked households to report their handwashing behaviours or to list critical times. Both approaches are subject to strong biases. Towards the end of the MDG period, DHS and MICS developed a standardised module based on the observation of a handwashing facility with water and soap, with data available for over 50 countries in the end of the MDG assessment (Figure 1.9).[35]

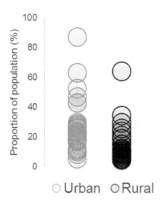

FIGURE 1.9 Proportion of the population with a handwashing facility with water and soap in urban and rural areas of Africa: each circle represents one country with data

Source: Authors' analysis based on WHO/UNICEF JMP (2015).[9]

Subnational

The types of drinking water and sanitation services used vary widely within countries and it is important to go beyond national, rural and urban to fully understand inequalities in coverage. By assessing coverage and trends at lower administrative levels, it is possible to ensure that policies and programmes target areas of lowest coverage. While essential for national planning processes, international comparison of subnational regions (e.g. provinces) can be challenging since the number of such subnational regions can range from 5 to over 40.[36] In some countries, boundaries have changed over time and harmonised population estimates may not be available for these. Whereas census data can be used at very low administrative levels, provided data can be accessed for analysis, there are limits to the spatial resolution of household surveys. Small area estimation procedures and analysis of trends based on a combination of census and household surveys are both areas of active research.[37,38] Figure 1.10 provides an example of subnational analysis for piped water on premises in Brazil.

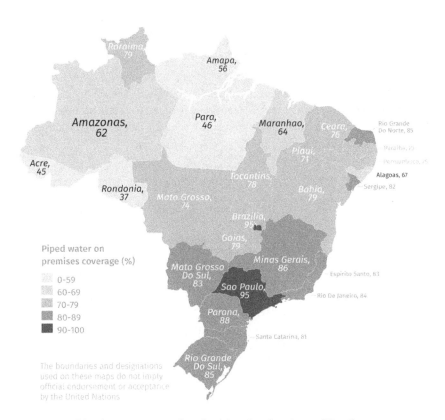

FIGURE 1.10 Piped water on premises for subnational regions of Brazil
Source: WHO/UNICEF JMP (2016).[39]

Intra-urban and intra-rural

Disparities within both urban and rural areas are also important. Slums tend to have lower coverage than 'formal' urban areas, in part by definition since slums are considered not to have access to basic services.[40,41] In most countries, slums are not recorded as a separate stratum in the census, and household surveys and cannot therefore be distinguished without special post-hoc analysis based on geospatial analysis or household characteristics. Examples include data collection for Mombassa slums in the MICS 2006 household survey and separate reporting on three types of slum (notified, registered, identified) in the India Census 2011. Inaccessible or remote rural areas can be harder to reach and are less likely to have the political influence to ensure access to basic service. Some surveys collect information on access to a paved road, which could potentially be combined with information on WASH to estimate access in remote communities. Further analysis for intra-urban and intra-rural areas will be important post-2015.

Population subgroups

In its 2014 report, the JMP provided illustrative examples of inequality analysis for population subgroups and also pointed to one of the main challenges: information is usually collected at the household, not individual level.[18]

Inequalities in access to improved drinking water and sanitation can be based on a wide range of socioeconomic variables included in surveys. These can include: education, sex, ethnicity, language and religion of the household head. Identification of disadvantaged groups is an essential first step for tracking these inequalities, and important groups vary between countries.

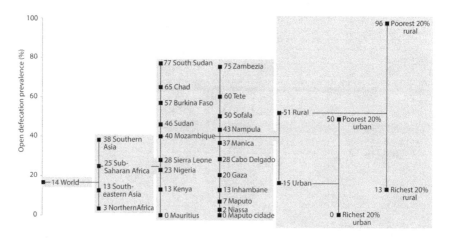

FIGURE 1.11 Equity tree with open defecation rates in Mozambique
Source: WHO/UNICEF JMP (2014).[18]

In some cases, cross-country analysis can be conducted, as is the case for indigenous groups in Latin America and the Caribbean. Important individual-level inequalities, in particular access for persons with disabilities, require dedicated surveys and would likely require questions that address the specific challenges they may face.

Composite indicators such as asset-based wealth quintiles are widely used to assess service coverage among the poorest. However, water and sanitation are among the principal determinants of wealth and therefore should ideally be excluded when analysing WASH coverage to avoid concerns related to tautology.[42] Overlapping inequalities merit further investigation and can compound disparities as illustrated for open defecation in Mozambique (Figure 1.11).

Priorities for enhanced monitoring of inequalities post-2015

Following an announcement that the drinking water target had been met and with the end of the MDG period in sight, in 2011 the JMP set up expert working groups to develop proposals for future monitoring post-2015 and ensure that the SDG indicators addressed the increasingly recognised limitations of the 'improved' classification. Four working groups were established: drinking water, sanitation, hygiene, equity and non-discrimination. The recognition of the Human Right to Water and Sanitation underpinned these efforts and was a key influence on the proposals developed by these groups and ultimately the SDG targets indicators that were adopted for the SDGs. Top priorities for post-2015 monitoring were identified as follows:

- Achieving universal access to basic water, sanitation and hygiene.
- Eliminating inequalities and progressively improving service levels.
- Extending access beyond the household, including to schools and health centres.

As described in Chapter 13,[43] new 'safely managed' indicators have been developed for monitoring the Sustainable Development Goal (SDG) targets 6.1 on drinking water and 6.2 on sanitation and hygiene. The new indicators build on the 'improved' indicator and address its limitations by addressing service levels for drinking water (accessibility, availability and quality) and sanitation (sewage/faecal sludge treated or safe disposal in situ), while expanding monitoring to include hygiene (handwashing with water and soap) and WASH in institutional settings (schools, healthcare facilities). Furthermore, the SDGs have a much stronger focus on inequalities than the MDGs. SDG 10 aims to 'reduce inequality within and among countries' and a strong emphasis has been placed on data disaggregation across all SDG indicators by 'income, sex, age, race, ethnicity, migratory status, disability and geographic location, or other characteristics'.[44]

Household surveys and censuses will remain the backbone of SDG monitoring, providing information on the types of facilities that households use. Better use of existing data from household surveys and censuses to track inequalities will be key, especially at the outset of the SDGs, as this will be the only option for assessing trends in inequalities in many countries. This should include systematic analysis of inequalities for those equity stratifiers that are already captured in existing data sources. Wealth quintiles (national, urban and rural) and subnational regions are a priority in the short term. In the medium term, analysis should be expanded to include small area estimation and targeted analysis of specific disadvantaged groups using census data. For countries with richer survey data, it may be possible to analyse inequalities in service levels that have been largely invisible in analysis to date based on facility types alone.

The new SDG indicators require the development of completely new approaches, including combining data on facility types with information on service levels (see Chapter 12). Information on the service levels will increasingly be drawn from administrative data sources, including regulators. Great efforts are needed to align monitoring instruments and address remaining data gaps, especially around water quality and availability, and the management of on-site sanitation facilities (septic tanks and latrines). There are important questions to address on how best to integrate data from different sources — household survey and utility data, census and administrative data — in order to track inequalities in both access and service levels.

Efforts to build national and subnational capacity for monitoring and reporting on inequalities in WASH need to focus on three main areas.

Data collection. Increasing the availability and quality of data relating to drinking water, sanitation and hygiene remains a high priority in many countries. In order to maximise the potential of data collected, further effort is required to harmonise the questions and indicators used to collection information across different national data sources. National Statistical Offices need to work with ministries and other agencies responsible for collecting information at different levels of government to agree standard definitions and measurement techniques in order to streamline data collection efforts and to improve the comparability and complementarity of data.

Data integration. While data availability is a challenge in some parts of the world, in almost all countries, WASH sector stakeholders could also make more and better use of existing data. First, there is a need to raise awareness of the potential of data collected in household surveys, censuses and administrative reporting to shed light on inequalities. Second, there is a need to explore opportunities to integrate information on WASH with data collected by different parts of government and to generate demand for rigorous analysis of overlapping inequalities.

Data analysis and use. Experience has shown that the availability of high-quality data and rigorous analysis is necessary but not sufficient for better informed decision making. Additional effort is required to develop tools and templates that make it easier for non-data specialists to interact with and analyse datasets in new and interesting ways, and to present analysis in a format that is easy for non-specialists to understand and to use. This requires an understanding of the data needs and priorities of different actors ranging from policy makers and practitioners to academics and to media and civil society organisations, as well as individuals interested in taking action to address inequalities in WASH.

Notes

1 WHO/UNICEF (1993) Water Supply and Sanitation Sector Monitoring Report 1993: sector status as of 31 December 1991. New York: WHO/UNICEF JMP.
2 UN (2000) Millennium Summit.
3 UN (2002) Plan of Implementation of the World Summit on Sustainable Development.
4 UN (2015) Official list of MDG indicators. Available at: https://mdgs.un.org/unsd/mdg/Host.aspx?Content=Indicators/OfficialList.htm
5 Bartram, J., Brocklehurst, C., Fisher, M.B. et al. (2014) Global monitoring of water supply and sanitation: history, methods and future challenges. *International Journal of Environmental Research and Public Health*, 11(8): 8137–65.
6 WHO/UNICEF (2006) Core questions on drinking water and sanitation for household surveys: WHO/UNICEF JMP.
7 Vandemoortele, J. (2009) The MDG conundrum: meeting the targets without missing the point. *Development Policy Review*, 27(4): 355–71.
8 Bradley, D.J. and Bartram, J.K. (2013) Domestic water and sanitation as water security: monitoring, concepts and strategy. Philosophical Transactions of the Royal Society A: *Mathematical, Physical and Engineering Sciences*, 371 (2002).
9 WHO/UNICEF (2015) Progress on sanitation and drinking water, 2015 update and MDG assessment: WHO/UNICEF JMP.
10 Bostoen, K. (2007) Measuring access and practice: designing a survey methodology for the hygiene, sanitation and water sector. London: London School of Hygiene & Tropical Medicine.
11 WHO/UNICEF (2012) Progress on drinking water and sanitation, 2012 update: WHO/UNICEF JMP.
12 Ross, I. and Bostoen, K. (2010) Data reconciliation in Southern Africa: report on a regional workshop looking at monitoring approaches in the water and sanitation sector. London: Wateraid.
13 Hucks, L. and Axwesco, F. (2011) East Africa data reconciliation workshop: WaterAid WHO UNICEF.
14 UN (2001) Road map towards the implementation of the United Nations Millennium Declaration.
15 UNSD (2015) Principles and recommendations for population and housing censuses.
16 WSP (2012) AMCOW Country status overviews: regional synthesis report: World Bank Water and Sanitation Programme.
17 Shea, R. and Johnson, K. (2004) The DHS Wealth Index. Calverton, MD: ORC Macro.
18 WHO/UNICEF (2014) Progress on drinking water and sanitation, 2014 update: WHO/UNICEF JMP.
19 WHO/UNICEF (2010) Progress on sanitation and drinking water, 2010 update: WHO/UNICEF JMP.
20 WHO/UNICEF (2013) Progress on sanitation and drinking water, 2013 update: WHO/UNICEF JMP.

21 Fuller, J.A., Goldstick, J., Bartram. J. and Eisenberg, J.N.S. (2016) Tracking progress towards global drinking water and sanitation targets: a within and among country analysis. *Science of the Total Environment*, *541*: 857–64.
22 Graham, J.P., Hirai, M. and Kim, S-S. (2016) An analysis of water collection labor among women and children in 24 sub-Saharan African countries. *PLOS One*, *11*(6): e0155981.
23 UNSD (2015) The world's women, 2015: trends and statistics.
24. UNSD (2013) Gender statistics: report of the Secretary-General.
25 Bain, R.E., Gundry, S.W., Wright, J.A., Yang, H., Pedley, S. and Bartram, J.K. (2012) Accounting for water quality in monitoring access to safe drinking-water as part of the Millennium Development Goals: lessons from five countries. *Bulletin of the World Health Organization*, *90*(3): 228–35A.
26 Multiple Indicator Cluster Survey, 2012–2013 (2014) Bangladesh Bureau of Statistics.
27 Ghana Living Standard Survey Round 6 (2014) Ghana Statistical Service.
28 Wang, A., McMahan, L., Rutstein, S., Stauber, C., Reyes, J. and Sobsey, M.D. (2017) Household microbial water quality testing in a Peruvian demographic and health survey: evaluation of the compartment bag test for *Escherichia coli*. *The American Journal of Tropical Medicine and Hygiene*, *96*(4): 970–5.
29 Rosa, G. and Clasen, T. (2010) Estimating the scope of household water treatment in low- and medium-income countries. *The American Journal of Tropical Medicine and Hygiene*, *82*(2): 289–300.
30 Rosa, G., Kelly, P. and Clasen, T. (2016) Consistency of use and effectiveness of household water treatment practices among urban and rural populations claiming to treat their drinking water at home: a case study in Zambia. *The American Journal of Tropical Medicine and Hygiene*, *94*(2): 445–55.
31 Gil, A., Lanata, C., Kleinau, E. and Penny, M. (2004) Children's feces disposal practices in developing countries and interventions to prevent diarrheal diseases: a literature review.
32 Berendes, D.M., Sumner, T.A. and Brown, J.M. (2017) Safely managed sanitation for all means fecal sludge management for at least 1.8 billion people in low and middle income countries. *Environmental Science & Technology*, *51*(5): 3074–83.
33 Roche, R., Bain, R. and Cumming, O. (2017) A long way to go: estimates of combined water, sanitation and hygiene coverage for 25 sub-Saharan African countries. *PLOS One*, *12*(2): e0171783.
34 Weinger. (2012) Report of the WHO/UNICEF JMP post-2015 expert working group on hygiene. The Hague: WHO/UNICEF JMP.
35 Ram, P. (2013) Practical guidance for measuring handwashing behavior: 2013 update: World Bank Water and Sanitation Program.
36 Hosseinpoor, A.R., Bergen, N., Barros, A.J.D., Wong, K.L.M., Boerma, T. and Victora, C.G. (2016) Monitoring subnational regional inequalities in health: measurement approaches and challenges. *International Journal for Equity in Health*, *15*(1): 18.
37 Pullan, R.L., Freeman, M.C., Gething, P.W. and Brooker, S.J. (2014) Geographical inequalities in use of improved drinking water supply and sanitation across sub-Saharan Africa: mapping and spatial analysis of cross-sectional survey data. *PLOS Medicine*, *11*(4): e1001626.
38 Gething, P., Tatem, A., Bird, T. and Burgert-Brucker, C.R. (2015) Creating spatial interpolation surfaces with DHS data: demographic and health surveys.
39 WHO/UNICEF (2016) Inequalities in sanitation and drinking water in Latin America and the Caribbean: WHO/UNICEF JMP.
40 UN-Habitat (2003) The challenge of slums: global report on human settlements. Geneva: UN-Habitat.
41 Bain, R.E.S., Wright, J.A., Christenson, E. and Bartram, J.K. (2014) Rural:urban inequalities in post 2015 targets and indicators for drinking-water. *Science of the Total Environment*, *490*: 509–13.

42 Martel, P. (2016) Review of options for reporting water, sanitation and hygiene coverage by wealth quintile. New York: UNICEF MICS.
43 Slaymaker, T. and Johnston, R. (2018) Monitoring progressive improvements in services. London: Taylor & Francis.
44 UNSD (2017) Report of the Inter-Agency and Expert Group on Sustainable Development Goal Indicators UN Statistical Commission.

2

THE HUMAN RIGHTS TO WATER AND SANITATION

Challenges and implications for future priorities

Virginia Roaf, Catarina de Albuquerque and Léo Heller

Introduction

The human rights to water and sanitation were explicitly recognised by the UN General Assembly and the Human Rights Council in 2010 and in 2015 as two interrelated but distinct rights at the UN General Assembly. These rights are also explicitly referred to in the 2030 Agenda for Sustainable Development.[1] However, recognition of water and sanitation as human rights, even at this high political level, was never going to be sufficient to put these rights into practice without significant explanation and guidance on what realising the human rights to water and sanitation entails. This requires a change in the way that decision-makers, practitioners and sector experts think and work.

In the course of their work as UN Special Rapporteurs on the human rights to safe drinking water and sanitation, both Catarina de Albuquerque and Léo Heller have committed significant time to providing guidance for policy makers and practitioners on what the human rights to water and sanitation mean when translated into practice. This has included country missions,[2] reports on topics as wide-ranging as planning, financing, waste-water management, gender, stigma and affordability, and two books that discuss putting the human rights into practice – *Good Practices on Realising the Human Rights to Water and Sanitation*[3] and *Realising the Human Rights to Water and Sanitation: A Handbook*.[4] Both of these publications have been enthusiastically received by practitioners, including governments, looking for guidance on putting the rights into practice.

The human rights to water and sanitation received a further boost with the adoption of the Sustainable Development Goals, which align with human rights principles in general and with the human rights to water and sanitation in particular.[1] Implementation of the water and sanitation-related targets under SDG 6, in particular Targets 6.1 and 6.2, will also promote the achievement of many other goals, such as those relating to poverty, hunger, health and education. The human rights framework requires that SDG 6 should be understood particularly in connection with SDG 5 and SDG 10, as these relate to achieving gender equality and reducing inequalities within and between countries respectively. Furthermore, Goals 16 and 17 focus on the cornerstones of human rights, including building effective, accountable and inclusive institutions, and establishing the means of implementation that are participatory and build on multi-stakeholder partnerships.

The legal foundations of the human rights to water and sanitation

The human rights to water and sanitation are derived from the right to an adequate standard of living, which includes other human rights, such as housing and food. They are also inextricably linked to the human right to health and should be interpreted in conjunction with the right to life.[5] The human rights to water and sanitation, as with the rights to health [6] and food,[7] demand that services are available, accessible, affordable, acceptable and safe – the normative content of other economic, social and cultural rights.

Water and sanitation are public services, which are generally, but not always, delivered by public service actors. There has been a long debate about private sector engagement in the delivery of water and sanitation services, and a strong and active anti-privatisation movement still argues that there should not be a for-profit motivation in the delivery of these essential services. Whether services are provided through public, private, community or self-managed models, or a combination of any of the above, the State has a strong role to play in regulating service provision, and ultimately has the legal obligation to and is accountable for ensuring that services meet human rights principles and standards.[8]

While food and housing are more likely to be delivered through private sector engagement, the obligation of the State remains the same. Food and housing must fulfil human rights standards. Where there is a problem with access to either food or housing, whether due to crop failure, economic depression, or other factors, the State must step in by, for example, setting fixed prices for staple foods, or in the case of housing, through the provision of public housing available at potentially below-market rates. Alternatively, the State can pay for, or supply people's housing or food directly. For water and sanitation, the State, directly or through public entities, has performed the main role in providing services, although in some contexts formal and/or informal private provision takes place. In all cases, the State has an obligation to respect, protect and fulfil the human rights to water and sanitation, and needs to ensure accountability, participation, access to information and non-discrimination and equality. These remain the same for all economic, social and cultural rights.

The legal foundations of equality and non-discrimination in the context of the human rights to water and sanitation

Equality and non-discrimination are the bedrock principles of all human rights and are linked in human rights law. States must ensure that individuals and groups do not suffer from discrimination and that they can enjoy full equality.

Article 1 of the 1948 Universal Declaration of Human Rights states that 'All human beings are born free and equal in dignity and rights', and article 2 states that 'Everyone is entitled to all the rights and freedoms set forth in this Declaration, without distinction of any kind'.

Legal obligations to ensure equality and end discrimination are central to all major human rights treaties that have come into force since the adoption of the Universal Declaration of Human Rights. The International Covenant on Economic, Social and Cultural Rights (ICESCR) specifies that the rights set out in the treaty are to be realised 'without discrimination of any kind as to race, colour, sex, language, religion, political or other opinion, national or social origin, property, birth or other status'.[9] The reference to 'other status' indicates that this is not an exhaustive list, and is inclusive of any other forms of discrimination that may evolve over time. The International Covenant on Civil and Political Rights (ICCPR) includes an almost identical guarantee.

The International Convention on the Elimination of All Forms of Racial Discrimination (ICERD) and the Convention on the Elimination of All Forms of Discrimination Against Women (CEDAW) provide protections against discrimination on the basis of race and sex. The Convention on the Rights of the Child (CRC), the International Convention on the Protection of All Migrant Workers and their Families, and the Convention on the Rights of Persons with Disabilities (CRPD) also all include guarantees of non-discrimination for these specific population groups.

Discrimination is defined as any exclusion or restriction that prevents people from exercising any of their human rights and fundamental freedoms.[10]

This principle forbids detrimental or unfavourable treatment of any individual or group due to a prohibited ground for discrimination or negative impact of actions on the basis of a prohibited ground. This principle is binding for all levels and bodies of the State at all times, and applies to all rights and benefits guaranteed by the State.[11]

Equality and non-discrimination are legal terms that have a precise legal meaning that can be invoked in a court of law, and purposefully used in legislation and in policies.

Terms such as 'equity' and 'inclusion', which are often used as proxy terms for 'equality' in discussions on development priorities, do not have the same legal weight as 'equality and non-discrimination', nor do they have the same exact definition.[12]

'Equity' is a rather imprecise and plastic concept, which can be and is interpreted differently according to one's culture, academic discipline and political preferences.

While in some instances it has the sense of an equitable sharing of wealth, or a policy process to address the most disadvantaged to ensure more equal access to services, the concept in itself does not give guarantees of what 'equity' means and how it is to be achieved. Equality has a far clearer meaning, defined in law and interpreted by the United Nations' bodies and experts. 'Equity' tends to be used in debates on public policy, but does not guarantee justiciability as 'equality' does under the human rights framework.

'Social inclusion' is another concept that is frequently heard in policy-making circles, used to denote specifically the inclusion of individuals and groups who have historically or traditionally been left out. It can refer to either individuals or groups being unable to access services for reasons of gender, religion or tribal grouping, or due to the nature of someone's work, the colour of their skin, etc. While this echoes the aim of non-discrimination, it lacks the analysis demanded by legislation that requires that practices are not discriminatory. While social inclusion is a positive step, it does not bring with it the recourse to justice if it is not achieved.

Prohibited grounds of discrimination and multiple discrimination

As stated above, non-discrimination is a central tenet of human rights law, and all human rights treaties prohibit discrimination.

There are inequalities in access to water and sanitation across the globe and within countries. Discrimination based on gender, age or disability tends to exist in some form in all countries, despite what may be seen as 'gender-neutral' policies. Ethnic, religious and caste discrimination may also exist, but will be expressed differently depending on the context.

This section highlights some of the most common forms of discrimination in access to water and sanitation that have led to inequalities. In the cases below, there is a common thread of blaming the minority or discriminated-against population for being dirty, or for not having access, rather than recognising the structural causes of the lack of access, which stem from discrimination, generally experienced not only in relation to water and sanitation services, but also with respect to access to housing, health services, education, work and other basic needs.

Marginalised groups

In some countries, indigenous peoples, those living in nominated areas, pastoralist communities and nomadic or semi-nomadic tribes may not have the same access to water or sanitation services as the majority populations.[13,14] For example, in Europe Roma or traveller populations often do not have the level of access to water and sanitation compared to other population groups.[15] In some South Asian countries, Dalits experience discrimination in access to water and sanitation and are forced to use separate (often inferior) facilities to the majority populations.[16] Furthermore, Dalits are traditionally forced into socially degrading, dirty and hazardous jobs, such as working as manual scavengers or sweepers where they must clean and empty rudimentary toilets (often just a simple concrete slab) by hand.

Sex and gender

Women and girls often experience inequalities relating to access to water and sanitation due their gender.[17] In many societies, women and girls are responsible for the domestic use of water and for keeping the home clean, and so are more negatively affected than men and boys when there is an inadequate supply. Where water is not available on the premises, women and girls tend to be responsible for the collection of water. Furthermore, when family members fall sick due to water- and sanitation-related diseases, women and girls are the ones who will generally sacrifice school and work attendance in order to care for other family members.

Women also face risks to their personal safety from people or animals if they have to leave the house to use a latrine or toilet, or to defecate in the open.[18]

Menstruation remains a taboo subject in many parts of the world, and the impact of this is that those responsible for designing sanitation systems, often men, do not take the needs of women and girls into account. Girls and women often miss school and work during their periods due to a lack of adequate sanitation.

Disability, age and health

According to the World Health Organization, over one billion people worldwide live with a physical, mental, intellectual or sensory impairment.[19] Despite this, many water and sanitation services are not accessible to people with disabilities, and people with disabilities are disproportionately represented among those without adequate access to water and sanitation.[20] States must therefore work with disability groups on policies that will address these causes of inequalities, while recognising that different disabilities will require different solutions.

States must ensure that people living with HIV/AIDS and other medical conditions that increases sanitation and hygiene needs, such as obstetric fistula and urinary tract infections, have access to adequate water and sanitation facilities.

Economic and social situation, housing

The Committee on Economic, Social and Cultural Rights has emphasised that people living in slums and homeless people should not be denied equal rights.[21] However, slums and informal settlements are often not taken into account in urban planning, and the people living there are often simply absent from official records and urban plans.

There is frequently discrimination against homeless people through the criminalisation of public urination and defecation, while states fail to provide alternative sanitation facilities for people who do not have a home. Such laws, generally intended to protect public health, impact negatively on homeless people or those living in settlements without toilets.[22]

People living in refugee or internally displaced persons (IDP) camps are often underserved when it comes to access to water and sanitation, and generally do not have the means to resolve their own service provision. States are therefore required to take special measures to ensure that refugees and other displaced persons are able to access water and sanitation.[23]

Prisoners

The human rights to water and sanitation apply equally to prisoners and people living in detention centres, but these rights are frequently violated through the provision of substandard facilities. This has been condemned by the Special Rapporteurs on water and sanitation in their mission reports,[24] as well as by the Special Rapporteur on torture and other cruel, inhuman or degrading treatment or punishment.[25]

Other prohibited grounds of discrimination

Other prohibited grounds of discrimination may have an impact on people's access to water and sanitation, including political or other opinion, marital and family status, sexual orientation and gender identity.[26]

Addressing multiple forms of discrimination

Inequalities often intersect – a woman from a minority ethnic group, for example, may suffer from various forms of discrimination, and these require different approaches to resolve.

A person with a disability and a person from an ethnic minority might both be poor and lack access to water and/or sanitation, but the reasons for their lack of access differ, and the policy responses necessary to guarantee them access are also different.

As poverty is only one basis for exclusion, a focus on inequalities due to poverty cannot address the root causes of exclusion and lack of access water and sanitation (or other service). Sometimes, the barriers to access for certain groups are not financial, but rather it is the existence of laws, policies or cumbersome administrative procedures that lead to their exclusion. Very often Roma people would like to be able to be connected to public water services and would even have the necessary money to afford paying the monthly bills. However due to the status of the land tenure, they are not allowed to do so – in such cases, poverty may not be the basis for their exclusion.

How the human rights framework defines equality in service provision

Equality in service provision implies that everyone is able to access water and sanitation services that comply with human rights. When everyone is able to access services that are available, accessible, affordable, safe and acceptable while at home as well as when outside the home, without discrimination, we will have achieved equality in service provision. This does not mean that everyone must have access to identical services. Water may come from a well that is then piped into the home, or from a municipal water provider. People may access sanitation through a latrine in the yard, or have a toilet within the household. As long as the standards of the human rights to water and sanitation are fulfilled, and there is recourse to justice should something go wrong with the service offered, there is equality in service provision.

However, there are pitfalls here. A latrine situated in a densely populated urban area may not share the same qualities as a latrine in a rural area and may also contribute to contamination of local ground or surface water sources used for drinking. Likewise, there is no equality in a city where some residents benefit from a sewerage system and others must rely on unsafe individual solutions, which may cost more to maintain and are not as reliable. Water provision through standpipes in poorer areas of a city, where the rest of the population has water connections inside the home, also does not respect the principle of equality.

Substantive equality and affirmative action

Equality does not mean that everyone has to be treated identically at all times.[27] People who are not equal may require different treatment in order to achieve substantive equality. States may need to adopt affirmative measures, giving preference to certain groups and individuals in order to redress past discrimination.

Equal access to basic services does not mean that everyone must have the same technical solutions or the same type of service, but all services must reach human rights standards. To achieve substantive equality, people who have different physical, cultural or other characteristics, or who have lower socioeconomic status, may require different, preferential, treatment. Substantive equality, therefore, may require that difference is treated differently[28] and, for example, that more resources should be put into ensuring that persons with disability are able to use a latrine. It might also mean that people with a lower economic status might need a social tariff or other type of financial support to be able to afford a service. Likewise, women may require latrines that are designed differently from those designed for men. For example, in public toilets, there is often a need for a higher number of latrines or toilets for women than for men. This is reiterated by CEDAW, which requires that states 'ensure the full development and advancement of women, for the purpose of guaranteeing them the exercise and enjoyment of human rights and fundamental freedoms on a basis of equality with men'.[29]

Affirmative action, as with other basic services, such as health and education, can also be included in legislation and in policies relating to water and sanitation.

In making decisions on how to address inequalities in access to water and sanitation, or indeed to food, education, health or other basic needs, states must examine the cause of the inequality, and attempt to address this, through affirmative measures. The solutions might vary from country to country, and even from region to region, given different social, cultural and other characteristics.

Progressive realisation and immediate equality

One of the most useful concepts for planners relating to meeting the standards required by the human rights to water and sanitation is the principle of progressive realisation. Article 2.1 of the ICESCR obliges all countries to, 'take steps . . . to the maximum of [their] available resources, with a view to achieving progressively the full realization of the rights'. This obligation recognises that states may not be able to achieve the human rights immediately, as there are many issues that need to be addressed before the rights can be made reality. This includes making sure that the right institutions are in place, that funding is available, and that there is sufficient human capacity to construct, manage, operate, rehabilitate and monitor services. Hence, the International Covenant on Economic, Social and Cultural Rights recognises that progress shall be gradual and progressive.

However, progressive realisation is not a way for states to avoid meeting their obligations by claiming that they do not have sufficient resources or the right infrastructure to comply with human rights. It is also not a justification for inaction.

States have an immediate obligation to plan how they will achieve human rights over time. They must equally be able to demonstrate that they are using the maximum available resources for the realisation of the rights.

In the case of the human rights to water and sanitation, states must also demonstrate that they are working towards the elimination of inequalities in access to water and sanitation, by identifying and prioritising services for those individuals and groups that lack access.

The requirement of immediate equality demands that states have an immediate obligation to guarantee non-discrimination in the realisation of the human rights to water and sanitation. Legislative, regulatory and policy frameworks must guarantee non-discrimination. In many cases, inequalities and discrimination are embedded in laws, policies, and practices, and addressing this takes time and resources. However, some laws, policies and practices that allow de facto discrimination should be brought to an end as speedily as possible.[30]

The Committee on Economic, Social and Cultural Rights requires that states prioritise measures that address discriminatory laws, policies and practices, as failure to do so is a violation of human rights.[31] States are responsible for demonstrating that they are doing all they can to eliminate inequalities and this can be achieved over time, but discriminatory legislation and policies must be changed immediately after ratification of or accession to the ICESCR.

In some cases, well-intentioned laws or policies will turn out to be discriminatory. An example of this would be a policy of providing the same fixed amount of water for free to all households. This would appear to be a policy based on equality. But of course, larger households would receive less free water per head, meaning that the policy in fact leads to unequal access to water. Such laws and policies must be adjusted to ensure that they are not inadvertently discriminatory.

In some countries, where there are still low levels of adequate access to sanitation, states will have to make difficult decisions on where to invest limited resources, not only in terms of which populations to target first, but also to ensure sufficient resources, both financial and human, to set up the right institutions, funding processes, regulatory and monitoring bodies that are necessary to ensure universal and sustainable access to services.

The lack of sufficient available financial resources for universal access to services will continue to be a barrier, but there is much that states can do to maximise existing funding, and to encourage investment by international development agencies and the private sector. Perhaps the most fundamental issue is for states to understand that investing in water and sanitation services will provide long-term benefits to the individuals, to the communities, and ultimately to a country's economic and social development. This means that the best systems must be put in place that enable service provision – strong institutions, multi-stakeholder dialogues and decision-making, participation of the service users, access to information on relevant policies and programmes, accountability systems. Second, given the long-term nature of the benefits, and the limited expectation of short-term profits, financing for the most marginalised and vulnerable individuals and groups must come from the public purse, or from donor finance, where short-term profits are not expected.

Countries that can provide development cooperation to countries that need it are obliged to do so, while also ensuring that the funds they provide are used to support and not violate human rights.[32] This means that development cooperation, whether from other nations, or from other sources, such as multilateral agencies or private foundations should also work to support states to eliminate inequalities in access to water and sanitation, and to prioritise those populations that do not have adequate access to services. In many cases, the best long-term investment is in supporting States to provide the right institutions and systems, which includes a focus on non-discrimination and the elimination of inequalities, for building a strong water and sanitation sector that can deliver services for all.

Human rights to water and sanitation and the SDGs

The 2015 adoption of the Sustainable Development Goals by the UN General Assembly marked a significant change in how the global community understands social and economic development. It is no longer sufficient to provide good services to a limited number of people, or to 'reduce by half the proportion of the population without access'.[33] The SDGs demand that everyone benefits from social and economic development, without exception. Principles such as equality, participation, access to information, multi-stakeholder partnership in development, sustainability and accountability embedded in the SDGs are also human rights principles.

The SDG declaration, Transforming Our World, declares in its preamble a vision of 'a world where we reaffirm our *commitments regarding the human right to safe drinking water and sanitation* and where there is *improved hygiene*'.

The synergy that exists between human rights and the SDGs is even clearer when we consider SDG 6 on water and sanitation, for which the first two targets demand universal access to water, sanitation and hygiene, with 6.2 specifically 'prioritising women, girls and vulnerable groups'. Likewise, the implementation targets 6a and 6b, which require development cooperation and participation, also reinforce human rights principles. Universal access will only be achieved through focused and deliberate targeting of services for people and communities who are vulnerable, marginalised or otherwise disadvantaged, to bring their service provision up to the level of the better-off populations. Equality in access must be measured by the human rights criteria of accessibility, affordability, safety, sustainability and acceptability.

There can be no exceptions within 'universal'. There is, however, still a somehow naive assumption that since the SDGs aim at universal access by 2030, inequalities will automatically disappear between now at the SDG deadline. This will obviously not be the case without additional deliberate efforts to reduce and eliminate inequalities. There must therefore be full awareness of the fact that universality in 2030 will not happen if all stakeholders do not start immediately to plan, budget and implement the targets contained in Goal 6 differently, by tackling the hardest to reach now, and not expecting that there will be a 'trickle-down' effect.

Obviously, universal access is a very high bar, as today no country can truly claim universal access to water and sanitation. For example, a United Nations Economic Commission for Europe (UNECE) report on Paris from 2013 acknowledges that the access rate is in fact less than 100 per cent, taking into account the individuals living in the greater metropolitan region without adequate access to water and sanitation, including homeless people and nomadic communities.[34]

Retaining universal access to water and sanitation requires adequate funding for consistent monitoring, operation, maintenance and rehabilitation programmes to ensure that there is no regression.

Universal access does not only include access to water and sanitation at the household level, but also at work, in educational and healthcare institutions, at public institutions, including detention centres and at public places, such as transport hubs and market places. People must not only have access to services outside the home, but must be able to use them – for example, people must be given time to have toilet breaks within the working day, and public conveniences must be affordable to use. This is to ensure the health and dignity of the individual, as well as public health for communities.

Water and sanitation are necessary for the realisation of many other rights, many of which are also embedded in the SDGs, such as health, food, education, work, housing and urban development. But the attainment of the human rights to water and sanitation will also support progress towards gender equality (Goal 5) and the reduction of inequalities within and between countries (Goal 10).

A human rights approach to realising Goal 6 on water and sanitation will also help progress to environmental goals and targets such as water use efficiency and the preservation of ecosystems. The human right to water demands that attention is paid to how water resources are used, to ensure that all water for domestic uses receives priority over water for other uses. Water use efficiency in agriculture and industry will simultaneously protect water resources, ensuring that more is available for domestic uses (which currently demands a minimal proportion of any country's water resources). Currently, there are many countries that charge agriculture and industry less for water from public services than domestic uses, a regressive cross-subsidy.

Investment in water and sanitation will always bring returns to individuals and households in terms of health, education and work, addressing poverty at the level of the household, which in turn will have a positive impact on the economy of the whole country, quite beyond the social benefits of better services and greater equality in access to those services.

Implications for future priorities for realising the obligation to eliminate inequalities in access to water and sanitation

There are many challenges to realising the human rights to water and sanitation and ending inequalities, not least the need to overcome political inertia and the 'business as usual' approach taken by many countries, intergovernmental bodies and professionals.

States, but also federal and municipal policy makers, are often confronted with the hard task of deciding where to invest limited financial resources – in remote rural areas, where per capita costs are higher, or in more densely populated areas, where greater numbers of people would be served at lower costs. Even though these dilemmas are real, the truth is that the question should not be posed in terms of 'either/or', and national and municipal plans should have a medium- and long-term vision of how to make sure that everyone gets access to water and sanitation services. Furthermore, inequalities will never be eliminated if policy makers fail to adopt specific and targeted measures to reach those who have been historically excluded and unserved. These population groups will often be dispersed and live in remote areas where service provision is more expensive. However, states do have a legal obligation to reach them and to prioritise them, even if the solutions found do not have to be identical to those implemented in other areas of the country.

Some governments and development partners have been making slow progress towards better access to water and sanitation, making small gains every year.

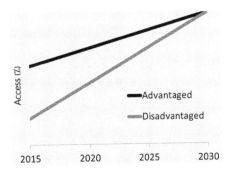

FIGURE 2.1 Closing the gap between advantaged and disadvantaged groups
Source: Created by the authors.

However, in order to achieve the human rights to water and sanitation (and to reach SDG 6 and universal access) a very different approach is required, one where those who traditionally, or through political expediency, are left to last, are brought to the fore, so that their needs are addressed first.

As can be seen in Figure 2.1, reaching the most marginalised and disadvantaged groups will require governments to prioritise these groups at a faster rate than the general population in order to reach the goal of universal access by 2030. This requires a different policy approach to that of assuming that delivering services to marginalised and disadvantaged individuals and groups will be reached using the same policies as for the general population.

Identifying the disadvantaged individuals and groups

The identification of disadvantaged groups presents a major challenge for UN member states, which have all committed to 'leave no one behind' through the SDGs and through adoption of the resolutions recognising the human rights to water and sanitation. The challenges partly relate to establishing an appropriately inclusive and participatory process to ensure that all groups and individuals have an opportunity to express their needs, but also the challenge of generating data and evidence to differentiate disadvantaged groups from the wider population. These will be unpacked further in subsequent chapters, but local definitions of disadvantage and data requirements may be highly context specific. It is important to note that these may not be amenable to standardised global WASH monitoring and may be better addressed through regional or national mechanisms.

The four disparities that could usefully be tracked are as follows.

Wealth analysis

This is the simplest measure of disparities in access, as the necessary data is already available and reported on by the WHO/UNICEF JMP. While wealth analysis is very useful for painting a broad picture of inequalities, as can be seen by the previous section on discrimination, it is only one rather crude measure of inequality in a particular country. For many countries, the data still shows that progress is being made more quickly in higher wealth quintiles, while progress is slow in the lowest wealth quintile. To address this, far more needs to be done to address the needs of the poorest individuals.

Geographic disparities

Rural–urban

There are rural–urban disparities on many counts of inequality, including access to water and sanitation services. This data is already collected and reported on by JMP (see Chapter 1).

Intra-urban

It is essential to look more closely at intra-urban disparities, specifically between formal and informal urban settlements, as these disparities are masked in the rural–urban data. Often the impact of poor services in informal settlements urban areas will have a greater negative health impact compared to rural areas due to high-density populations.

Group-related inequalities (e.g. based on race, ethnicity and migratory status)

As outlined in the previous section, inequalities can arise from group-related inequalities. Each country needs to identify the specific groups that may be discriminated against, and monitor progress in access to services.

Intra-household inequalities (e.g. based on sex, age and disability)

Even within a household, not all people are treated equally. In some cultures, particular individuals will be disadvantaged in access to services, whether women, those who have disability, older persons, children or servants. These disparities in access may be hard to monitor, but should be considered in the delivery of services (see Chapters 5 and 9).

Development co-operation[35]

The above-mentioned article 2.1 of the ICESCR, which sets out the obligation of progressive realisation within available resources, foresees that this obligation is to be implemented by states individually, but also 'through international assistance and co-operation, especially economic and technical'. This is reiterated in General Comment No. 15 on the right to water,[36] and has implications for how countries support each other in their implementation of the human rights to water and sanitation, and specifically how they plan to address inequalities in access to services.

The 2030 Agenda for Sustainable Development also demands unprecedented global commitment and co-operation between countries. Goal 17 in particular requires that developed countries increase official development assistance, building co-operation and addressing finance, technology and capacity-building needs. Goal 6a covers similar ground for water and sanitation. This obligation must also guide efforts by other international development agencies including UN agencies, regional organisations, global and regional development banks, as well as civil society organisations.

Development co-operation represents an important share of total funding for water and sanitation in the global South, and as with all programming decisions, this financing can have a negative or positive impact on inequalities. All external support agencies, including bilateral and multilateral agencies must respect recipient countries' policy space and leadership to establish and implement policies for poverty eradication and sustainable development, and must also support countries' efforts to realise all human rights.

United Nations agencies and other international organisations must also co-operate with states' parties to implement the human rights to water and sanitation in their financing, policies and development projects, as must international financial institutions and regional banks. Even when development co-operation passes through non-governmental organizations, states are still obliged to ensure that programmes are in line with human rights standards and contribute to the realisation of the human rights to water and sanitation.

Despite this, human rights have still not been well incorporated by policy makers, sector experts or practitioners in development co-operation in the water and sanitation sector.

The principle of equality and non-discrimination, for instance, requires that external support agencies and their partners work together to identify marginalised and vulnerable individuals and groups, and develop policies and programmes that prioritise those individuals and groups. However, as can be seen in the reports for the Global Analysis and Assessment of Sanitation and Drinking-Water (GLAAS), many bilateral and multilateral agencies are still financing predominantly large-scale urban programmes, that are unlikely to benefit the poorest members of society.[37] GLAAS reports also point to the need to build the capacity of funders and partners to better understand their role in realising the rights to water and sanitation.[38] A further recommendation is to improve the monitoring of the elimination of inequalities in access to water and sanitation, in order to ensure a regular update of how countries, funders and partners are managing to fulfil their obligations under the 2030 Agenda.

The affordability of services after project completion, the accountability of public authorities and contracted businesses throughout those projects, stakeholder participation, access to information and the overall sustainability of services all continue to be hard to achieve.

Some stakeholders may consider certain human rights-based approaches to divert limited funds towards areas that are not deemed necessary, restricting the flexibility of funding entities. An example of this might be the participation of stakeholders that are generally excluded from the design phase of a programme, leading to a lengthier planning process. However, strengthening participatory processes has been shown to lead to greater ownership, more involvement in operations and maintenance, and improved sustainability of sanitation and water services.[39] This is supported by Target 6b of the Sustainable Development Goals, which specifies: 'Support and strengthen the participation of local communities in improving water and sanitation management.'

Conditionalities, including policy-based, output-based and tied aid, are commonly used in development cooperation projects in the water and sanitation sector.[40] For example, a funder might require that aid provided for a collective water-supply system is dependent on the raising of tariffs paid by users, a policy of full-cost recovery or the privatisation of service provision. This may lead to human rights violations – for example, a lack of affordability of the services for certain population groups. There are therefore calls to limit conditionalities in order to allow for greater autonomy and country ownership of policies and programmes. The intergovernmental International Conference on Freshwater declared that private sector participation should not be imposed on developing countries as a conditionality for funding, and that priority should be given to catalysing other forms of financing, building capacity and targeting the poor, especially in rural areas.[41]

Government leadership and partnership with other stakeholders, including civil society, in conceptualising, implementing, monitoring and evaluating development policies, programmes and processes should be a requirement for development cooperation.[42] Project effectiveness must not be decided unilaterally by funders but must be led and fully and meaningfully endorsed by partner stakeholders.[43]

Legislative, regulatory and policy frameworks

Legislative and regulatory frameworks, budgetary priorities, policies and planning as well as specific national and local circumstances, such as corruption and levels of democracy, can affect the application of human rights principles. These frameworks can create obstacles to eliminating inequalities in access to water and sanitation, or they can have the exact opposite effect and be crucial allies in achieving equality.[4]

Legislative frameworks should enshrine the principles of non-discrimination and equality at the highest possible level, preferably in the constitution, providing individuals with the right to file legal claims. Such constitutional guarantees of equality and non-discrimination do already exist in most countries, even if not specifically in the context of access to water and sanitation. However, some laws have been put in place and are in force that discriminate against particular individuals and groups unintentionally. For example, laws or bylaws that criminalise open defecation or urination discriminate against people who do not have a toilet, or who are living on the street – generally disadvantaged individuals. Such laws can only be effective if the state ensures that everyone has access to sanitation services.

Regulatory frameworks are generally put in place for formal service providers, such as the regulation of water quality, and in some cases there will also be price regulation, but few regulators have a specific role for regulating issues relating to inequalities or to human rights more broadly. They also usually regulate service provision to persons who are considered 'clients' of a utility, leaving out all those who are not served by any formal provider. Without a specific regulatory framework for monitoring human rights, few service providers will take these into account. There are also many service providers, often informal, that do not come under any regulatory framework, and these will likewise not take human rights into account.

Policies, strategies and plans can play a specific role in achieving substantive equality through promoting affirmative action for people without access to water and sanitation services.

The monitoring of policies and plans is key, using appropriate indicators and benchmarks to assess both the steps taken and the results achieved in their attempts to eliminate discrimination. The monitoring of human rights, including inequalities, is often lacking from countries' statistics office programmes, but until this data is collected, discriminatory laws, regulations and policies will not be recognised and addressed.

Services must be universal, solutions having to be identified for everyone, including people living in informal settlements and remote rural areas. Service providers must be transparent, act in good faith, refrain from rent-seeking, and be efficient and effective. Common problems, such as a lack of democratic processes, including access to information, participation, and the corrupt practices, tend to add to the cost of water and sanitation utilities, increasing the price of utilities connections by as much as 30 per cent, and the impact tends to be most heavily felt by disadvantaged individuals and groups.[43]

An adequate institutional environment for water and sanitation services in all states is essential for development co-operation to reach those most in need and to be sustainable. It allows loans and grants to leverage national policies, making it easier for states to meet their obligations concerning the progressive realisation of human rights. The responsibility falls upon partner countries to create such an enabling environment, in which development co-operation is a fundamental part of national policies to provide water and sanitation, and the observance of human rights obligations.

Economic mechanisms

Universal access to water and sanitation will only be achieved through increased funding, and, importantly, more effective and targeted use of that funding to reduce inequalities. Increasingly, it is clear that far more funding must be spent on operation, maintenance and rehabilitation of services compared to construction – and generally this is not how financing is currently allocated. Human resources, including their capacity building, and a strong institutional framework, which includes a monitoring function, are essential for the sustainability of services.

The human rights definition of affordability is that people must be able to afford to pay for their water and sanitation services and associated hygiene, without limiting people's capacity to buy other basic goods and services, including food, housing, health and education, guaranteed by other human rights. While human rights laws do not require services to be provided free of charge, states have an obligation to provide free services or put adequate subsidy mechanisms in place to ensure that services always remain affordable for the poor.

One route for utilities and other service providers to be able to expand access to services is through collecting tariffs and user fees, which can then be used to construct new connections. However, this can have a negative impact on affordability, and must be carefully monitored and regulated. Countries may put in place affordability mechanisms, whereby users should not spend a high proportion of their income on service provision. This is notoriously difficult to establish as a universal standard – for example, as a threshold of the household incomes due to the peripatetic nature of work for many people working in the informal sector. Ensuring that access to water and sanitation is affordable remains complex, particularly where households are making investments in and paying for a variety of different services. As affordability remains a significant barrier to access to water and sanitation for many households, this requires further studies, without delaying implementation of immediate measures to protect the poorest groups in society.

Other routes for financing will include cross-subsidisation of services between richer and poorer users and general taxation.

Ensuring that everyone has access to basic services will require more than a simple increase in funds. It is necessary to look beyond the economic arguments of 'value-for-money' or 'economies of scale', which are used to justify prioritising services to particular population groups to acknowledge the human development costs of leaving people behind. We must rethink how budgets are designed, how disadvantaged population groups can be prioritised and targeted, how services are delivered and the types of services that are prioritised, in order to eliminate inequalities in access to water and sanitation.

Usually, priority for local and small-scale solutions in development and national budgetary allocations would support the realisation of the human rights to water and sanitation. Additionally, more financing for training at the local level to fund health and community workers to engage with local populations could be advisable. More money invested in operation and maintenance ensures that existing systems continue to provide essential services.

The human rights framework requires putting aside the notion of swift economic returns on investment. The cost of not being able to educate children, or having an unhealthy population, of an unproductive workforce, far outweighs the cost of ensuring access to services, and all should be done to invest in the long-term health and development of our world.

Conclusion

The human rights to water and sanitation demand that countries work towards eliminating inequalities in access to water and sanitation services. This is supported by the 2030 Development Agenda, for which the water and sanitation targets under SDG 6 require universal access by 2030, focusing on the needs of vulnerable groups.

It is imperative that 'vulnerable groups' is not only understood in terms of wealth, but in terms of a far broader range of inequalities based on stigma and discrimination, due to gender, disability, language, occupation, religion or other prohibited ground for discrimination. If countries only look towards eliminating inequalities due to income or wealth status, many people will still not be able to access water and sanitation services. Understanding the different types of discriminatory action, and the reasons for it, is an essential first step towards addressing inequalities that arise out of discrimination.

The human rights principles of equality and non-discrimination apply across the board, to all countries, and to all laws, regulations, policies, budgeting decisions and accountability mechanisms within all countries. The burden of proof that a state is complying with these principles rests with the state itself; in order to achieve this, the right systems must be put in place to be able to monitor who is receiving what level of services, and who is being left behind.

Funders must respect the principles of equality and non-discrimination – whether bilateral or multilateral, such as UN agencies or development banks – and again, the burden of proof must rest with them that they are working towards realising these principles in their funding strategies and budgeting priorities. In the case of UN agencies and development banks, therefore, the obligation to eliminate inequalities and to remove any discriminatory policies must be understood at the most senior level, and this must be carried down to the operational level. How funders support countries with development co-operation generally has a significant impact on state actions, and yet the elimination of inequalities is often underplayed in decisions of how development co-operation is prioritised.

Notes

1 Transforming our world: the 2030 agenda for sustainable development, para. 7, A/RES/70/1.
2 Annual reports of the Special Rapporteur on the human rights to water and sanitation. Available at: www.ohchr.org/EN/Issues/WaterAndSanitation/SRWater/Pages/Annual Reports.aspx
3 Catarina de Albuquerque and Roaf, Virginia (2012) Good practices in realizing the human rights to water and sanitation.

4   Catarina de Albuquerque (2014) UN Special Rapporteur on the human rights to water and sanitation. *Realising the Human Rights to Water and Sanitation: A Handbook*.
5   CESCR General Comment No. 15 on the right to water, E/C.12/2002/11, 2002.
6   CESCR General Comment No. 14 on the right to health, E/C.12/2000/4, 2000.
7   CESCR General Comment No. 12 on the right to food, E/C.12/1999/5, 1999.
8   UN Special Rapporteur on the human rights to water and sanitation (2010) Human rights obligations related to non-state service provision in water and sanitation, A/HRC/15/31, 2010.
9   International Convention on Economic, Social and Cultural Rights, Article 2(2).
10 Article 1(1), Convention on the Elimination of All Forms of Discrimination against Women (CEDAW); Article 2, Convention on the Rights of Persons with Disabilities (CPRD).
11 Human Rights Committee, General Comment No. 18: Non-discrimination, 1994 (HRI/GEN/1/Rev.1 at 26).
12 Catarina de Albuquerque, UN Special Rapporteur on the human rights to water and sanitation (2014) *Realising the Human Rights to Water and Sanitation: A Handbook*. Booklet 7, pp. 7–32.
13 UN Special Rapporteur on the human right to safe drinking water and sanitation, Catarina de Albuquerque, Mission to Costa Rica, 2009 (A/HRC/12/24/Add.1), para. 48. Also Mission to Botswana, 2016 (A/HRC/33/49/Add.3), para 61.
14 S.L. Murthy and M.K. Williams (2012) The complicated nature of stigma: realizing the human rights to water and sanitation for Bedouins in the Negev, Israel – submission to the Special Rapporteur on the human rights to water and sanitation.
15 Special Rapporteur on the human rights to water and sanitation (2016) Mission to Slovenia, 2010 (A/HRC/18/33/Add.2), para. 33. Also, Mission to Portugal.
16 Special Rapporteur on the human rights water and sanitation (2009) Mission to Bangladesh, (A/HRC/15/55), para. 25.
17 Special Rapporteur on the human rights water and sanitation (2016) Report on gender equality (A/HRC/33/49).
18 S. House, S. Ferron, M. Sommer and S. Cavill (2014) Violence, gender and WASH: a practitioner's toolkit – making water, sanitation and hygiene safer through improved programming and services (WaterAid/SHARE).
19 WHO (2011) World Report on Disability.
20 Special Rapporteur on the human rights to water and sanitation (2009) Mission to Bangladesh (A/HRC/15/55), para. 21.
21 CESCR, general comment no. 20, 2009 (E/C.12/GC/20), para.16(c).
22 UN Special Rapporteur on extreme poverty and human rights (2011) Magdalena Sepúlveda Carmona, penalization of people living in poverty (A/66/265), paras. 33–34.
23 CESCR, general comment no. 15, (E/C.12/2002/11), para. 16 (f).
24 UN Special Rapporteur on the human rights to water and sanitation (2016) Mission to El Salvador (A/HRC/33/49/Add.1). Mission to Thailand. 2013, 21/42/Add.2). Mission to Namibia, 2012 (A/HRC/21/42/Add.3). (A/HRC/24/44/Add.3). Mission to Uruguay (A/HRC/).
25 UN Special Rapporteur on torture and other cruel, inhuman or degrading treatment or punishment (2009) Manfred Nowak, note by the Secretary-General (A/64/215 and A/64/215/Corr.1), para. 43.
26 INTERIGHTS (2011) *Non-discrimination in International Law: A Handbook for Practitioners*, pp. 122–139. Available at: www.interights.org/document/153/index.html
27 Human Rights Committee (1994) General comment no. 18: non-discrimination (HRI/GEN/1/Rev.1 at 26).
28 Committee on Economic, Social and Cultural Rights (2009) General comment no. 20: non-discrimination (E/C.12/GC/20).
29 Convention on the Elimination of All Forms of Discrimination against Women, Article 3.
30 The Limburg Principles on the Implementation of the International Covenant on Economic, Social and Cultural Rights, 1987 (E/CN.4/1987/17), para 38.

31 CESCR (2009) general comment no. 20 (E/C.12/GC/20), para 13.
32 Maastricht Principles on Extraterritorial Obligations of States, Article 17.
33 Malcolm Langford and Inga Winkler (2015) Muddying the water? Assessing target-based approaches in development cooperation for water and sanitation. In *The MDGS, Capabilities and Human Rights: The Power of Numbers to Shape Agendas*, 145 (Sakiko Fukuda, Parr and Alicia Ely Yamin (eds), 2015).
34 Assessing progress in achieving equitable access to water and sanitation pilot project in the Greater Paris urban area (France) Report UNECE 2013, p. 2. Available at: www.unece.org/fileadmin/DAM/env/water/activities/Equitable_access/Country_report __Pilot_project_Greater_Paris_urban_area_rev.pdf
35 Based on the 2016 report to the United Nations General Assembly of the Special Rapporteur on the human rights to safe drinking water and sanitation (A/71/302).
36 CESCR general comment no. 15, E/C.12/2002/11 (2002), para 38.
37 GLAAS 2017 Report: Financing universal water, sanitation and hygiene under the sustainable development goals, p. 31.
38 GLAAS 2016 Report: Investing in water and sanitation: increasing access, reducing inequalities, p. 14.
39 WHO, UN-Water Global Analysis and Assessment of Sanitation and Drinking-Water (GLAAS) (2012) Report: The challenge of extending and sustaining services. WHO: Geneva.
40 Svea Koch (2015) A typology of political conditionality beyond aid: conceptual horizons based on lessons from the European Union. *World Development*, 75 (November).
41 Summary of the International Conference on Freshwater, held in Bonn, Germany, 3–7 December 2001. Available at: www.iisd.ca/crs/water/SDH20/sdvol66num5.html
42 InterAction (2011) Country ownership: moving from rhetoric to action (Washington, DC).
43 World Bank. Comprehensive development framework: country ownership. Available at: http://web.worldbank.org/archive/website01013/WEB/0__CON-5.HTM

3
THE POTENTIAL OF THE SDG FRAMEWORK TO PROMOTE EQUALITY THROUGH WASH INITIATIVES

Sanjay Wijesekera, Bruce Gordon and Sue Cavill

Background

The 2030 Agenda for Sustainable Development was adopted by the UN member states in September 2015 (UN, 2015b). The vision in Agenda 2030 as well as the Sustainable Development Goals (SDGs) was agreed after a three-year participatory process with civil society groups, which involved face-to-face as well as on-line consultations, in more than 100 countries. The 2030 Agenda is made up of the 17 SDGs and 169 targets. Taken together, the SDGs represent a roadmap for advancing global sustainable development in three dimensions: the economic, the social and environmental.

The SDGs replace the Millennium Development Goals (MDGs). In 2000, the UN Millennium Declaration set a target for 2015 to halve the 1.2 billion people without sustainable access to adequate quantities of affordable safe water. The World Summit on Sustainable Development later set the target of halving the 2.4 billion people who lacked improved sanitation by 2015. Increasing access to drinking-water and sanitation became targets under MDG 7 to 'ensure environmental sustainability'. Target 7.C was to halve, by 2015, the proportion of the population without sustainable access to safe drinking water and basic sanitation. The drinking water target was met in 2010, albeit with significant differences between and within countries, regions and disadvantaged groups, while the world fell well short of achieving the sanitation MDG target (WHO and UNICEF, 2015). The MDG targets under 7°C were critiqued for being too modest in their ambition as well as for benefiting the relatively better-off countries and people, rather than the most vulnerable and marginalised (Cavill *et al.*, 2016). Agenda 2030 and the SDGs represent a much more transformative agenda applicable to all countries and with a commitment to 'leave no one behind'.

Under Agenda 2030, SDG 6 is a dedicated goal for the sustainable management of water and sanitation with eight targets, including universal access to safe water, sanitation and hygiene, and eliminating open defecation. The global indicator for monitoring SDG target 6.1 is the 'Proportion of population using safely managed drinking water'. The global indicator for monitoring SDG target 6.2 is the 'Proportion of population using safely managed sanitation services, including a handwashing facility with soap and water'. The indicators refer to 'safely managed' drinking water and sanitation services, meaning drinking water at home that is free from contamination and available when needed, and toilets from which excreta are treated and disposed of safely (WHO and UNICEF, 2017). Other SDG 6 targets encompass water quality and wastewater treatment, water use, integrated water resource management, and water-related ecosystems. The WHO and UNICEF Joint Monitoring Programme have produced baseline estimates and will continue to publish global monitoring reports for targets 6.1 and 6.2, as well as facilitating the development of international norms and standards to strengthen monitoring systems. The Joint Monitoring Programme also report on access to basic WASH services as a contribution to SDG target 1.4. The WHO, through the UN-Water Global Analysis and Assessment of Sanitation and Drinking-Water Report (GLAAS), together with the UNEP and OECD, will monitor the 'Means of Implementation' for targets 6.a.1[1] and 6.b.1[2] (UN Water, 2017).

Lack of access to WASH is not only a technical concern. Fundamentally, lack of access is a result of poverty, inequality and unequal power relationships (Human Development Report, 2006). Agenda 2030 explicitly states that the SDGs should be met for all people, and all countries, and for all segments of society. Leaving no one behind means that inequalities are tackled (such as those affecting girls and women, people at different stages in the life course, people with a disability or of a minority race, ethnicity, religion, or economic group, or 'other status') and that governments will endeavour to reach the furthest behind first so that marginalised groups make progress more quickly than the average (UN, 2015b, 2015c). Access to and use of WASH services and behaviour change can have a transformative impact on inequalities, addressing a range of social and economic goals simultaneously (Willetts et al., 2010). It is estimated tht investment in WASH infrastructure has a global average rate of return on investment of between US$3–6 gains annually for every dollar investment (Hutton, 2015). The case for investment is even more compelling for those in vulnerable situations.

This chapter outlines two key principles for action – universality and interconnectedness – before illustrating how these can be applied in the context of three challenges to accelerating progress: inequalities, urbanisation and climate change. An assessment is made of what is needed to put this rhetoric into practice, through national plans, policy changes, data, financing and political will.

The principles of universality and interconnectedness

Universality

The 2030 Agenda for Sustainable Development offers a universal set of goals applicable to all countries, in all contexts and at all times. The UN General

Assembly recognised the human rights to water and sanitation in 2010, acknowledging that safe, affordable, acceptable, available, and accessible drinking water and sanitation services for all without discrimination are essential to the realization of human rights.

The establishment of a rights-based principle in the SDGs makes them universal, applying to all people, everywhere and always. The targets for SDG 6 are universally applicable and therefore present a universal challenge, cutting across countries, contexts (from households to institutions), and across time. Pockets of the unserved can be found in rich and poor countries alike, as well as in subnational regions. A large number of middle- and high-income countries may have large sections of their populations (such as indigenous people) who have not benefited from progress on improved access to WASH (Hall et al., 2016; Bradford et al., 2016; UNDP, 2009; Jiménez et al., 2015) or else people suffer from poor quality services – for instance, those with piped water supplies may have an unreliable supply of inconsistent quality (Franceys and Jalakam, 2010). Attention to household- level services is accompanied by a concern for WASH in extra-household settings – i.e. schools, prisons, health facilities and public spaces (Kendall and Snel, 2016). Area-wide approaches, covering entire districts, municipalities or administrative areas require further consideration of different contexts (Agenda for Change, 2015). Sustainability of WASH services are a challenge: non-functional water points and reversion to open defecation is more likely among those communities and people least able to build and maintain WASH facilities by themselves (Cavill et al., 2015).

Government is the ultimate duty-bearer for the rights to water and sanitation and implementation of the SDGs, an obligation that should be reflected in policies, strategies, guidelines and training materials. A range of good practices on the human right to water and sanitation have been documented to inform policy and decision-makers, practitioners, activists and civil society (de Albuquerque, 2012). National WASH programmes will likely require a combination of approaches and support mechanisms to reach the most vulnerable with WASH (UNICEF, 2016a).

The human rights to water and sanitation, and Agenda 2030, call upon states and partners to provide financial resources, capacity building and technologies to advance access to safe, clean, accessible and affordable drinking water and sanitation for all (de Albuquerque, 2012; UN-Water, 2014). It is possible to accelerate the provision of WASH, but for that to be sustained, attention to the long-term funding of efficient operating costs, capital maintenance costs and any costs of capital is necessary, through a combination of user charges, national taxes and international transfers as well as subsidies, direct to consumers and indirect to the supporting institutions and the enabling environment (Franceys et al., 2016).

Interconnectedness

The interconnectedness across the SDGs promotes a more integrated approach to development. Actions to achieve one goal or target have the potential to reinforce the achievement of others, showing the link between WASH and other dimensions of sustainable development. WASH underpins many of the 169 targets and over 230 indicators, including those related to nutrition, health, education, poverty and economic growth, urban services, gender equality, resilience and climate change, reduce inequality. Integrated approaches thus have the potential to improve the effectiveness and sustainability of WASH. Examples of interconnectedness include the role of WASH in education (SDG 4), health (SDG 3) and gender (SDG 5) (UNICEF, 2016a).

As an example, and with regard to SDG 3, a global review (WHO and UNICEF, 2015) found that a third of health facilities in low- and middle-income countries lack a water source, and a similar proportion lack water and soap for handwashing. Approximately one-fifth do not have improved sanitation and over half lack adequate systems for the safe disposal of healthcare waste; anti-microbial resistance is a more recent challenge in this context (WHO, 2015). A joint WHO and UNICEF Global Action Plan aims to ensure that all healthcare facilities in all settings have adequate WASH services by 2030, contributing directly to several SDG targets, including Goal 3 targets on reducing maternal mortality, ending preventable newborn deaths, and providing quality universal health coverage (Velleman et al., 2014) as well as Goal 2 targets on improving nutritional status (Freeman et al., 2017).

Advancing SDG implementation requires cross-sectoral coordination between levels of government (central as well as regional and local), aligning policy objectives and strategies with the SDGs and integrating targets into the national strategies or plans. National government has a role in setting out the mechanisms by which stakeholders (private sector, PPPs, civil society organisations and academia) can contribute to 2030 Agenda and the SDGs. Government has responsibility for catalyzing partners in the implementation of the action plans, regulation, monitoring and harmonizing sector approaches, and maintaining oversight of national implementation. Knowledge sharing, advocacy and capacity building are necessary to inform integrated policy development and resource allocation (IWA, 2014) – for instance, by ensuring that the voices of marginalized people inform policy and evaluations of the effectiveness of policies aimed at mainstreaming equity.

A challenge for governments is to create the 'architecture' necessary to work across sectors, actors, governance levels and time horizon, in addition to enhancing coherence across policy areas in implementing the SDGs (in terms of time, human resources, expertise and financial resources). Further evidence is needed on how to ensure that progress achieved in one goal (e.g. water) contributes to progress in other goals (food security or health) (UNICEF, 2016a).

Addressing universality and interconnectedness in WASH services

The two principles of universality and interconnectedness are discussed below in the context of three key challenges affecting the provision of WASH services with regard to other SDGs: inequalities between and within countries (SDG 10), sustainable cities (SDG 11), and environmental protection and climate change (SDG 13).

SDG 10: inequalities between and within countries

UN-Water (2015) provides a typology of inequalities relating to the use of WASH: 1) geographic inequalities (e.g. residence in urban or rural settings, or remote areas); 2) group-based inequalities (e.g. ethnic or religious groups); 3) individual-based inequalities (e.g. gender, age, or disability). Implicit in the SDGs is recognition that these inequalities intersect: that frequently a person will be a member of two or more marginalised groups. 'Leave no-one behind', with its implication that no target can be met if it is not met for all, provides a new opportunity for ensuring access for all those experiencing multiple and overlapping disadvantages, including women and girls, people with disabilities, children, youth and older people, migrants, refugees, internally displaced people as well as indigenous groups, isolated communities, the urban poor and slum dwellers (Willetts et al., 2010).

A range of WASH organisations focus on women, adolescents, older people, people with disabilities and transgender people in their work (House et al., 2012; Jones, 2013; Roose et al., 2015; Wilbur and Danquah, 2015; Danquah, 2014; Halcrow et al., 2014; House et al., 2017; FANSA and WSSCC, 2015; Toubkiss, 2016; Boyce et al., 2018). It has been taken for granted that community-based WASH approaches will reach and include the poorest and most vulnerable. However, recent evidence and experience shows that more deliberate attention is needed to strengthen approaches and introduce support mechanisms to reach these 'last mile' groups (Myers et al., 2017). In particular, achieving Target 6.2 of the SDGs means addressing gender inequality. Women and girls are affected disproportionally by poor access to WASH (Fisher, 2008; Fisher et al., 2017; Carrard et al., 2013): in 7 out of 10 households, in 45 developing countries, the burden of collecting water falls to women and girls (UNICEF website). When schools cannot provide clean, safe toilets, as well as a safe space to manage their menstrual hygiene (van Eijk et al., 2016), girls' attendance is reported to drop (Sclar et al., 2017). One survey found that less than half of primary schools in developing countries have access to safe water and adequate sanitation (UNICEF, 2015). Approximately one in seven people globally have disabilities (around one billion people), and they and their families are disproportionately affected by poverty. Designing WASH for people with disabilities improves accessibility (UNICEF, 2016a). Considerations such as the design and siting of facilities with safety in mind can reduce the vulnerability of women and girls to the risk of violence (House et al., 2014). Gender relations at both household and community levels can be influenced by WASH policies and programming that promote equality (Kilsby, 2012).

Policies can address the specific barriers that marginalized people face in using WASH, as well as ensuring that marginalized people and their representative organizations are meaningfully consulted in decision-making processes. Thus, a consultation mechanism can strengthen the voice and participation of disadvantaged and vulnerable groups. Policies and plans can also promote knowledge sharing and good practices in the adoption of SDG-related standards and policies.

Government systems for identifying those in poverty are not necessarily designed to identify those who are not able to construct, access and maintain a latrine themselves (Myers et al., 2017). Additional efforts are then required to determine who requires extra support including: how to identify and target people for support, the sequencing of support, the roles and responsibilities of stakeholders, and the comparative advantages of different support mechanisms (Myers et al., 2017).

There are still a range of sector knowledge gaps to reach those facing multiple 'layers' of marginalization or disadvantage – for instance, the needs of those who face multiple deprivations are often insufficiently understood and inadequately addressed through WASH (such as women and girls with disabilities, older women, transgender people and intersex people).

Collaboration with vulnerable and marginalized people (and their representative organisations) is important, so that such people and groups can identify their own priorities, following the 'nothing about us, without us' principle (Myers et al., 2017). Where groups and people are deliberately marginalized, advocacy organisations are required to ensure that the rights of marginalized people to water and sanitation needs are prioritized, creating the space for civil society to advocate for more progressive and fair policies.

SDG 11: Sustainable cities and communities

Approximately 55 per cent of the world's population live in urban areas; rural-to-urban migration together with population growth mean that existing urban areas are growing and many small towns are rapidly becoming urban centres. By 2050, urban dwellers may account for 70 per cent of the world's population. Nearly 60 per cent of all refugees in the world – and more than half of all Internally Displaced Persons – live in urban areas (IIED, 2016). Some of the world's largest cities will be in Africa by 2100, many with over 40 million residents (IIED, 2016). As urban populations grow, so too have rates of urban poverty and numbers of people living in informal settlements or on marginal land. Achieving citywide sanitation requires attention to equality.

In 2015, 85 per cent of people living in urban areas used safely managed water, compared to 55 per cent in rural areas. 43 per cent of urban dwellers had access to safely managed sanitation, compared to 35 per cent of rural dwellers (JMP, 2017). Informal settlements are characterized by shared arrangements for sanitation, challenges in accessing toilets safely, erratic water supplies and poor drainage (Parkinson et al., 2014), all of which have implications for SDG 6 and SDG 11.

Public toilets are needed for those in transit, away from home or without facilities of their own (Scott et al., 2017). Personal safety and the perception of security is also a critical factor in the use of public toilets: often men and boys lurk around toilet entrances intimidating women away from access (House et al., 2014; Sahoo et al., 2015). While open or public urination is more common for men and boys, there are often fewer physical public toilet facilities available for women (Scott et al., 2017). Pregnancy, menstrual hygiene management or incontinence call for a more frequent use of accessible sanitation facilities (House et al., 2012). Vulnerable groups such as women with disabilities, Gender and Sexual Minority groups and homeless/street sleepers need specific attention: 'Women living on the pavement often carry a mat to make a shield around themselves if they need to defecate or urinate in the open. They go together in groups at night to use the disused dilapidated latrine' (Joshi and Morgan, 2007).

A number of cities (such as in India and Nigeria) have included ending open defecation and urination in their citywide strategies for achieving Open Defecation-Free (ODF) status. Local governments, particularly in small cities and towns, require regulatory and institutional arrangements for planning, budgeting and capacity for implementing WASH services (Parkinson et al., 2014). Integrated WASH programming in urban settings has the potential to address a range of issues, including employment, skills development, governance issues (including gang control of services) and empowerment through involving organisations of the urban poor in participatory planning (Kohlitz et al., 2018). Integrated approaches need to be multisectoral and multi-institutional. Following the 'new urban agenda', set out in Habitat III, and the Paris Agreement (2015) on climate change adaptation and mitigation, it will be necessary to build resilience into national WASH sector plans, policies and programmes. Partnerships between those with expertise and programmes in urban WASH, as well as with municipal government, and the private sector are one pathway to address the challenges of urban WASH service provision (Kohlitz et al., 2018). Policy, governance and institutional frameworks are necessary to support entrepreneurship with the (micro, small and medium) private sector (Mason et al., 2015). Innovative financing (sustainable subsidy models, voucher systems or cash transfers) as part of a broader national financing policy can support affordable access to all (Myers et al., 2017). Disaggregated data collection and monitoring is a prerequisite to targeting national and municipal resources for the urban poor and unserved populations (WHO and UNICEF, 2017). Evidence, experience and lessons from different contexts can be used to identify policies, programmes or projects that are innovative, sustainable and scalable.

A study of 12 cities in low- and middle-income countries found that while 98 per cent of households used toilets, only 29 per cent of faecal waste was safely managed (Blackett et al., 2014). Addressing the bottlenecks to effective delivery of sanitation services is imperative, requiring policy and regulation, funding (e.g., including access to credit), technical options and WASH business viability (e.g. business and technical skills) (Mills et al., 2018). Diverse approaches are needed for the variety of urban environments such as for settlements located in marginal areas prone to flooding (Parkinson et al., 2014). Strategic planning requires working with the urban poor and their organisations, and investing time and resources to build their capacity and the capability to engage (Luethi et al., 2011). Integrated plans and programmes require a multidisciplinary approach (including town planning, economics, municipal finance, governance, health, education and social development), as well as long-term predictable support.

SDG 13: Environmental protection and climate change

SDG 6 integrates targets on water resource management and ecosystem conservation together with targets on access to water and sanitation. Climate change and its impacts (primarily addressed in SDG 13) are an increasing threat to WASH systems, and contribute to both disparities in access and safe, reliable and continuous service delivery (UNICEF, 2016a). Extreme storm events, El Nino and la Nina weather patterns, flooding, droughts, salt-water intrusion and changes to groundwater availability threaten existing water supplies and sanitation systems (Howard et al., 2016). The impacts include disease outbreaks, food insecurity and coastal erosion, especially in poor countries and vulnerable communities, with fewer resources available for response and adaptation (UNICEF, 2016b).

The most vulnerable populations are most affected by climate change and have the least resilience to deal with its effects (Carrard and Willetts, 2017). For instance, women and girls experience climate change in ways that are distinct from men and boys, particularly women-headed households, older women and women with a disability. Non-functional water and sanitation systems mean that women and girls once again have to walk further distances for water collection or else revert to open defecation, with implications for convenience, physical discomfort and insecurity for women and girls (House et al., 2014). Programmatic responses include integrating 'no regret' adaptations into existing WASH programmes – for instance, designing and constructing water supply infrastructure to take account of the variability of water levels/flows, sewerage, stormwater drainage and solid waste management to cope with vulnerability to higher flood flows (Mason and Mosello, 2016), selecting sustainable water-lifting technologies like solar power water pumps such as in Kenya and Uganda (UNICEF, 2016c), and raising latrines to reduce the likelihood of collapse during floods in Ghana (UNICEF, 2016d). In coastal areas and the Pacific Islands, programmatic responses to sea level rise, variable rainfall and temperature, floods as well as droughts include Water Safety Plans to identify and address threats to drinking-water safety, adoption of preventive risk-management approaches and the implementation of risk- management control measures – for example, in Vanuatu and Fiji – as well as rainwater harvesting and behaviour changes for water conservation (UNICEF, 2016e). These are intended to build the resilience of communities and support the creation of enabling environments for climate change mitigation, especially if implemented in a way that integrates equity considerations into the water safety planning process (WHO, 2014).

Climate-resilient risk assessment and action plans are necessary for the WASH sector to protect water resources, adapt to water scarcity, avoid deteriorating water quality, and promote disaster-resilient WASH technologies and systems (Carrard and Willetts, 2017). Innovative approaches such as drinking-water safety and security planning mean that communities can safely manage their water resources during short-term or slow-onset disasters (UNICEF, 2016e). Including risk-informed programming in strategies and action plans enables managers to strengthen planning processes for identifying, prioritising and managing risk (UNICEF and GWP, 2015a, b; UNICEF, 2016b). Strengthening national policy frameworks for addressing climate change requires building the resilience of vulnerable groups such as women, people with disabilities, the elderly, youth and those in remote geographical locations (Kohlitz, Chong and Willetts, 2017). Adaptations to policies and guidelines should be coupled with training for staff on climate change and building the resilience of communities.

There are a number of challenges and opportunities for preparing for climate change within the WASH sector. Inequalities are an integral part of the causes of and responses to climate change (Kohlitz, Chong and Willetts, 2017). Given that the impacts of climate change are projected to increase in severity, this potentially makes WASH services more difficult to sustain in those countries and communities that have fewer resources available for response and adaptation (UNICEF, 2016b). Further technological innovation is important together with more research to inform national strategies on how best to integrate climate resilience into the management of WASH services (Carrard and Willetts, 2017). Further integration of the development and emergency WASH programming can improve both the effectiveness of humanitarian response and the long-term sustainability of national WASH systems (Mason and Mosello, 2016).

Conclusions

In this chapter, we considered the potential of the 2030 Agenda to advance equality in WASH. We argued that WASH interventions can and do successfully contribute to equality outcomes and that the 2030 Agenda has the potential to further amplify this through its focus on universality and interconnectedness. The design, implementation, and monitoring of WASH programmes can be an entry point to attaining a range of SDG targets, reduce inequalities within and between countries; deliver sustainable services in small towns and informal settlements; and in adapting to climate change. Achieving this requires that WASH practitioners develop their capacity to work in an integrated way in support of government leadership, strengthened institutional arrangements (coordination, service delivery arrangements, accountability and regulation), sustainable WASH budgeting and financing, planning, monitoring and review.

Notes

1   Indicator 6.a.1: The amount of water- and sanitation-related activities and programmes that is part of a government-coordinated spending plan.

2 Indicator 6.b.1: The percentage of local administrative units with established and operational policies and procedures for the participation of local communities in water and sanitation management.

References

Agenda for Change. Available at: www.washagendaforchange.net/

Blackett, I. and Hawkins, P. (2014) The Missing Link in Sanitation Service Delivery: A Review of Fecal Sludge Management in 12 Cities. Water and Sanitation Program Research Brief. World Bank: Washington, DC.

Boyce, P., Brown, S., Cavill, S., Chaukekar, S., Chisenga, B., Dash, M., Dasgupta, R.K., Brosse, N.D.L., Dhall, P., Fisher, J. and Gutierrez-Patterson, M., (2018) Transgender-inclusive sanitation: insights from South Asia. *Waterlines*, 37(2):102–117.

Bradford, L., Bharadwaj, L., Okpalauwaekwe, U. and Waldner, C. (2016) Drinking water quality in Indigenous communities in Canada and health outcomes: a scoping review. *International Journal of Circumpolar Health*.

Carrard, N.J., Crawford, G., Halcrow, C., Rowland, C. and Willetts, J. (2013) A framework for exploring gender equality outcomes from WASH programmes. *Waterlines: International Journal of Water, Sanitation and Waste*, 32(4): 315–333. doi: 10.3362/1756-3488.2013.033

Carrard, N. and Willetts, J. (2017) Environmentally sustainable WASH? Current discourse, planetary boundaries and future directions. *Journal of Water Sanitation and Hygiene for Development*, 7(2): 209–228.

Cavill, S. with Chambers, R. and Vernon, N. (2015) Sustainability and CLTS: Taking Stock, Frontiers of CLTS: Innovations and Insights 4, Brighton: IDS. Available at: www.communityledtotalsanitation.org/sites/communityledtotalsanitation.org/files/Frontiers4_Sustainability_0.pdf

Cavill, S., Roose, S., Stephen, C. and Wilbur J. (2016) Putting the hardest to reach at the heart of the SDGs. In P. Bongartz, N. Vernon and J. Fox (eds) *Sustainability for All: Experiences, Challenges and Innovations*, Rugby: Practical Action.

de Albuquerque, C. with Roaf, V. (February, 2012) On the right track: good practices in realizing the rights to water and sanitation. UN Special Rapporteur on the human right to safe drinking water and sanitation. Available at: www.ohchr.org/Documents/Issues/Water/BookonGoodPractices_en.pdf

FANSA and WSSCC (2015) Voices of women, adolescent girls, elderly and disabled people, and sanitation workers. FANSA and WSSCC.

Fisher, J. (2008) Women in water supply, sanitation and hygiene programmes. Proceedings of the ICE: *Municipal Engineer*, 161(4): 223–229.

Fisher, J., Cavill, S. and Reed, B. (2017) Mainstreaming gender in the WASH sector: dilution or distillation? *Gender and Development: Water, Sanitation and Hygiene*, July.

Franceys, R. and Jalakam, A. (2010) The Karnataka Urban Water Sector Improvement Project: 24 × 7 water supply is achievable. WSP field note. Available at: www.wsp.org/sites/wsp.org/files/publications/WSP_Karnataka-water-supply.pdf

Franceys, R., Cavill, S. and Trevett, A. (2016) Who really pays? A critical overview of the practicalities of funding universal access. *Waterlines*, 35(1).

Freeman, M., Garn, J., Sclar, G., Boisson, S., Medlicott, K., Alexander, K., Penakalapati, G., Anderson, D., Mahtani, A., Grimes, J., Rehfuess, E., and Clasen, T. (2017). The impact of sanitation on infectious disease and nutritional status: a systematic review and meta-analysis. *International Journal of Hygiene and Environmental Health*, 10.1016/j.ijheh.2017.05.007.

Halcrow, G., Rowland, C., Bond, M., Willets, J. and Carrard, N. (2014) Working from strengths: plan and SNV integrate gender into community-led sanitation and hygiene approaches in Vietnam. Case study 15: Towards inclusive WASH: Sharing experience from the field. WaterAid, Australia.

Hall, N.L., Shannon, C. and Jagals, P. (2016). It's a fallacy that all Australians have access to clean water, sanitation and hygiene. Available at: http://theconversation.com/its-a-fallacy-that-all-australians-have-access-to-clean-water-sanitation-and-hygiene-61436

House, S., Ferron, S. and Cavill, S. (2017) Research study: scoping and diagnosis of the Global Sanitation Fund's approach to equality and non-discrimination. Water Supply and Sanitation Collaborative Council (WSSCC): Geneva.

House, S., Mahon, T. and Cavill. S. (2012) Menstrual hygiene matters: a resource for improving menstrual hygiene around the world. London: WaterAid/SHARE.

House, S., Ferron, S., Sommer. M. and Cavill, S. (2014) Violence, gender and WASH: A practitioner's toolkit – making water, sanitation and hygiene safer through improved programming and services. London: WaterAid/SHARE.

Howard, G., Calow, R., Macdonald, A. and Bartram, J. (2016) Climate change and water and sanitation: likely impacts and emerging trends for action. *Annual Review of Environment and Resources*, 41: 253–276.

Human Development Report (2006) Beyond scarcity: power, poverty and the global water crisis. Published for the United Nations Development Programme (UNDP).

Hutton, G. (2015) Benefits and costs of the water sanitation and hygiene targets for the post-2015 development agenda. Post-2015 consensus. Manchester Business School, Working Paper, 26 January.

Hutton, G. (2016) Editorial: Can we meet the costs of achieving safely managed drinking-water, sanitation and hygiene services under the new sustainable development goals? Published June. 6(2): 191–194. DOI: 10.2166/washdev.2016.037

IIED (2016) Available at: www.iied.org/towards-humanitarians-handbook-for-cities-crisis

IWA (2014) An avoidable crisis: wash human resource capacity gaps in 15 developing economies. Available at: www.iwa-network.org/wp-content/uploads/2015/12/1422745887-an-avoidable-crisis-wash-gaps.pdf

Jiménez, A., Cortobius, M. and Kjellén, M. (January 2015) Recommendations for working with indigenous peoples in rural water and sanitation. Stockholm International Water Institute (SIWI). Available at: http://watergovernance.org/resources/working-with-indigenous-peoples-in-rural-water-and-sanitation/

Jones, H. (2013) Mainstreaming disability and ageing in water, sanitation and hygiene programmes A mapping study carried out for WaterAid. WEDC and WaterAid.

Joshi, D. and Morgan, J. (2007) Pavement dwellers' sanitation activities – visible but ignored. *Waterlines*, 25(3). DOI: 10.3362/0262-8104.2007.007.

Kendall, L. and Snel, M. (April 2016) Looking at WASH in non-household settings: WASH away from the home information guide. Available at: www.ircwash.org/sites/default/files/literature_review_wash_away_from_home_web_0.pdf

Kilsby, D. (2012) Now we feel like respected adults: positive change in gender roles and relations in a Timor-Leste WASH programme. ACFID Research in Development Series, Report No. 6, Deakin, ACT: International Women's Development Agency, WaterAid and Australian Council for International Development.

Kohlitz, J.P., Chong, J. and Willetts, J. (2017) Climate change vulnerability and resilience of water, sanitation, and hygiene services: a theoretical perspective. *Journal of Water Sanitation and Hygiene for Development*, 7(2): 181–195. DOI:10.2166/washdev.2017.134.

Kohlitz, J.P., Rostiani, R., Indarti, N., Murta, J. and Willetts, J. (2018) Sludge removal enterprises in Indonesia: factors affecting entrepreneurial success. *Journal of Water Sanitation and Hygiene for Development,* p.washdev2018085.

Mason, N. and Mosello, B. (2016) Making humanitarian and development WASH work better together. August. Available at: www.odi.org/sites/odi.org.uk/files/resource-documents/10823.pdf

Mason, N., Matoso, M. and Smith, W. (2015) Private sector and water supply, sanitation and hygiene, October. UNICEF and the UN Foundation. Available at: www.odi.org/publications/10023-private-sector-and-water-supply-sanitation-and-hygiene

Mills, F., Willetts, J., Petterson, S., Mitchell, C., and G Norman (2018) Faecal pathogen flows and their public health risks in urban environments: a proposed approach to inform sanitation planning. *International Journal of Environmental and Residential Public Health, 15*(2): 181. DOI:10.3390/ijerph15020181.

Myers, J., Maule, L. Gnilo, M., Chambers, R. and Cavill, S. June, 2017. Supporting the least able throughout and beyond CLTS. CLTS Knowledge Hub Learning Brief.

Nauges, C. and J. Strand (2011) Water hauling and girls' school attendance: some new evidence from Ghana. Available at: water.care2share.wikispaces.net/file/view/Water+hauling+and+Girls+school+attendance_Ghana_2011.pdf

Parkinson, J., Lüthi, C. and Walther, D. (2014) Sanitation 21—*A Planning Framework for Improving City-Wide Sanitation Services.* GIZ: Eschborn, Germany

Sahoo, K.C., Hulland, K.R., Caruso, B.A., Swain, R., Freeman, M.C., Panigrahi P. *et al.* (2015) Sanitation-related psychosocial stress: a grounded theory study of women across the life-course in Odisha, India. *Social Science & Medicine, 139:* 80–89.

Sclar, G.D., Garn, J.V., Penakalapati, G., Alexander, K.T., Krauss, J., Freeman M.C., Boisson, S, Medlicott, K.O. and Clasen, T. (2017) Effects of sanitation on cognitive development and school absence: a systematic review. International Journal of *Hygiene and Environmental Health, 220*(6): 917–927, August.

Scott, P., Sohail, M. and Cavill, S. (2017) Urination needs and practices away from home: where do women go? 40th WEDC International Conference, Loughborough.

The Paris Agreement (2015). Available at: http://unfccc.int/files/meetings/paris_nov_2015/application/pdf/paris_agreement_english_.pdf

Toubkiss, J. (2016) Equity, scalability and sustainability in UNICEF wash programming: evidence from UNICEF evaluations 2007–2015. Evaluation Report, UNICEF, New York. Available at: www.unicef.org/evaluation/files/WASH_evaluation_synthesis_(ExBoard_summary)_-_Final_at_25_July_to_OSEB(1).pdf

United Nations (2000) UN Millennium Declaration. Available at: www.un.org/millennium/declaration/ares552e.htm/ (accessed 13 December 2015).

United Nations (2015a) Millennium Development Goals Report 2015, New York. Available at: www.un.org/millenniumgoals/2015_MDG_Report/pdf/MDG%202015%20rev%20%28July%201%29.pdf (accessed 13 December 2015).

United Nations (2015b) Transforming Our World: the 2030 Agenda for Sustainable Development, New York. Available at: https://sustainabledevelopment.un.org/content/documents/21252030%20Agenda%20for%20Sustainable %20Development%20web.pdf (accessed 13 December 2015).

United Nations (2015c) Addis Ababa Action Agenda of the Third International Conference on Financing for Development, New York. Available at: www.un.org/esa/ffd/wp-content/uploads/2015/08/AAAA_Outcome.pdf (accessed 13 December 2015).

UN Special Rapporteur on the human right to safe drinking water and sanitation (2014). *Realizing the Human Rights to water and Sanitation: A Handbook.* Available at: www.ohchr.org/EN/Issues/ WaterAndSanitation/SRWater/Pages/ Handbook.aspx

UN-Water (2015) Eliminating discrimination and inequalities in access to water and sanitation (Policy and Analytical Briefs). New York. Available at: www.unwater.org/publications/publications-detail/en/c/340177/

UN-Water (2017) Financing universal water, sanitation and hygiene under the sustainable development goals. UN-Water Global Analysis and Assessment of Sanitation and Drinking-Water (GLAAS) Report. Geneva: World Health Organization. Available at: http://apps.who.int/iris/bitstream/10665/254999/1/9789241512190-eng.pdf?ua=1

UNDP GoAL WaSH Programme (2009) Governance, advocacy and leadership for water, sanitation and hygiene country sector assessments, Vol. 1, Paraguay. Available at: www.undp.org/content/undp/en/home/librarypage/environment-energy/water_governance/goal-wash.html

UNICEF website. Available at: www.unicef.org/wash/3942_43106.html

UNICEF (2015) Advancing WASH in schools monitoring. Available at: www.unicef.org/wash/schoolsfiles/Advancing_WASH_in_Schgools_Monitoring(1).pdf

UNICEF (2016a) Strategy for water, sanitation and hygiene 2016–2030. Available at: www.unicef.org/wash/3942_91538.html

UNICEF (2016b) The ripple effect: Climate change and children's access to water and sanitation. Available at: www.unicef.org/wash/files/Climate_change_WASH_Brief.pdf (accessed December 2016).

UNICEF (2016c) Scaling up solar powered water supply systems: a review of experiences. UNICEF.

UNICEF (2016d) Sanitation technology options manuals provided for urban and flood-prone environments (Ghana).

UNICEF (2016e) Community drinking water safety and security planning in Pacific Island countries. UNICEF Office for Pacific Island Countries. UNICEF.

UNICEF and GWP (2015a) WASH climate resilient development strategic framework. Available at: www.unicef.org/wash/files/Strategic_Framework_WEB.PDF (accessed December 2016).

UNICEF and GWP (2015b) WASH climate resilient development: technical briefs for implementation (UNICEF WASH Climate Resilient Development Series). New York: UNICEF, Global Water Partnership. Available at: www.unicef.org/wash/files/GWP_UNICEF_Tech_B_WEB.PDF (accessed December 2016).

United Nations (2010). Resolution 64/92: The human right to water and sanitation, A/RES/64/292 (2010). Available at: www.un.org/es/comun/docs/?symbol=A/RES/64/292&lang=E

United Nations (13–16 July 2015) Addis Ababa Action Agenda of the Third International Conference on Financing for Development (Addis Ababa Action Agenda). General Assembly resolution 69/313 of 27 July 2015. Available at: www.un.org/esa/ffd/wp-content/uploads/2015/08/AAAA_Outcome.pdf

United Nations (2015) Transforming our world: the 2030 Agenda for Sustainable Development A/RES/70/1. Available at: www.un.org/ga/search/view_doc.asp?symbol=A/RES/70/1&Lang=E

van Eijk, A.M., Sivakami, M., Thakkar, M.B., Bauman, A., Laserson, K.F, Coates, S., Phillips-Howard, P.A. (2016) Menstrual hygiene management among adolescent girls in India: a systematic review and meta-analysis. *BMJ Open*, *6*(3), March: e010290. doi: 10.1136/bmjopen-2015-010290.

Velleman, Y., Mason E., Graham., W, Benova, L., Chopra, M., Oona, M.R., Campbell, B., Wijesekera, S. Hounton, S., Esteves Mills, J., Curtis, V., Afsana, K., Boisson, S., Magoma, M., Cairncross, S. and Cumming, O. (2014) From joint thinking to joint action: a call to action on improving water, sanitation, and hygiene for maternal and newborn health December. *PLOS Medicine.* Available at: http://journals.plos.org/plosmedicine/article?id=10.1371/journal.pmed.1001771

WHO (2014) *Equity in Water Safety Planning: A guide to integrating equity considerations into the water.* Draft Version 27 September 2017. Prepared for the World Health Organization by the Institute for Sustainable Futures, University of Technology Sydney. Available at: https://www.uts.edu.au/sites/default/files/article/downloads/Water_Safety_Planning_Equity_Study_Synthesis_Report_DRAFT.pdf

WHO and UNICEF (2015) Water, sanitation and hygiene in health care facilities: status in low- and middle-income countries and way forward. Geneva: WHO. Available at: www.who.int/ water_sanitation_health/publications/wash-health-care-facilities/en/

WHO and UNICEF (2017) Progress on sanitation and drinking water – update and MDG assessment. New York, Geneva: JMP.

Wilbur, J. and Danquah, L. (2015) Undoing inequity: water, sanitation and hygiene programmes that delivers for all in Uganda and Zambia – an early indication of trends. Presented at the 38th WEDC International Conference, Loughborough, 7pp.

Willetts, J., Halcrow, G. Carrard, N., Rowland, C. and Crawford, J. (2010) Addressing two critical MDGs together: gender in water, sanitation and hygiene initiatives. *Pacific Economic Bulletin,* 25(1): 162–176.

World Health Organization (2015) UN-Water GLAAS Trackfin Initiative. Guidance Document. Available at: www.who.int/water_sanitation_health/publications/trackfin_guidance_document/en/

World Health Organization (2015) Antimicrobial resistance: An emerging water, sanitation and hygiene issue. Briefing note.

World Health Organization, UNICEF and USAID (2015) Improving nutrition outcomes with better water, sanitation and hygiene: practical solutions for policies and programmes. Available at: www.unicef.org/media/files/IntegratingWASHandNut_WHO_UNICEF_USAID_Nov2015.pdf

PART 2
Dimensions of inequality related to water and sanitation

4

EQUALITY IN WATER SUPPLY PROVISION

Beyond numbers served

Alan Nicol, Lyla Mehta and Indika Arulingam

Introduction

Achieving equality in water and sanitation delivery has been practically the goal of the water and sanitation world since the UN 'Water Decade' of the 1980s. This goal has been tracked and measured largely through indicators of numbers with access to a safe drinking water supply, reducing achievement to a physical measure of success against a fairly limited understanding of domestic water use. Recently, achieving equality in access has been further underscored through the setting of Sustainable Development Goal 6, target 6.1, which is: 'By 2030, achieve universal and equitable access to safe and affordable drinking water for all'.[1]

The aim of this chapter is to examine critically notions of equality embedded in such goals and targets, and to assess in more depth what achieving 'equality' may in fact mean, particularly with respect to the concept of 'drinking water' – a complex category when understood at a household level. We take water supply as our focus because, although the picture is bleaker for sanitation – 2.3 billion people still lacked access to basic sanitation in 2015[2] – and we recognize the many interlinkages between sanitation and water issues, at the same time they contain different logics, politics and disciplinary underpinnings. These include the role that water plays in livelihoods, sustainability and diversity more widely, and the relationship of water as a service to its wider natural resource base, associated with which are a host of ownership, management and environmental issues. These factors alone determine a different and unique set of institutional and development pathways compared to issues of equality in sanitation service provision.

Challenges and issues surrounding achievement of equality in water supply are embedded in wider global development processes relating to poverty and growth in inequality(ies) observed since the 1990s. These factors are well known and dealt with elsewhere by different authors.[3,4,5] The global response to these challenges has been a constant refrain, focusing on achieving equality in access to drinking water for all, but without a great deal of analysis of what this actually means both at a more philosophical level and in terms of practice. As a result, huge volumes of financing inevitably go into provisioning clean (drinking quality) supplies of water for households that may only use a proportion for drinking, while the rest is put to other uses, including washing, cleaning, small gardens, and household industry.

Beyond expanding access, moreover, there is also the need to ensure that systems and services remain sustainable. Mehta and Movik[6] argue that the long-term sustainability of systems and services for accessing water has not received the emphasis it deserves in debates. They attribute this to the globalized and generalized nature of the discourse, which is not easily translated into meeting the specific requirements of localized systems, coupled with inadequate consideration of the dynamic interplay among social, technical, and ecological/hydrological dimensions of water across scales. In addition, the financial and technological sustainability of a water supply system may not always complement equitable access, as in the case of policies of cost recovery for water supply, where systems based on the ability to pay could lead to low-income households being locked into using low-quality and inconvenient services over time.[7]

Global policy on water supply delivery since the 1977 Mar del Plata UN World Water Conference and subsequent International Drinking Water Supply and Sanitation Decade (IDWSSD, see note 8) has driven action. The 'World Water Decade' kicked off a surge in new institutions of civil society, networks and innovative campaigns that have focused on achieving equality and mobilizing resources to deliver services and bridge the 'equality gap'. Sanitation and Water for All (SWA) is the largest contemporary global undertaking, and describes itself as a 'global partnership to achieve universal access to clean water and adequate sanitation'. Its unique success lies in combining both WASH and financial communities in seeking solutions.

Coupled with these efforts at improving service delivery levels, there has been a push to recognize universal access to drinking water as a human right. This qualitative change was formally acknowledged by 122 countries in UN General Assembly Resolution 64/292 on 28 July 2010 and reaffirmed in Resolution 70/169 of 2015 in response to the SDGs. The Resolution stated: 'that the human right to safe drinking water entitles everyone, without discrimination, to have access to sufficient, safe, acceptable, physically accessible and affordable water for personal and domestic use' (see Chapter 2).

In spite of such global efforts and continued technical and political inputs, the more nuanced and variegated challenges involved in addressing water supply gaps that are sustainable and support poorer and marginalized people remain largely unsolved (see note 6). Domestic water use is not a simple category and differences can mask hugely important factors in addressing inequalities. A major challenge is that the number of those 'covered' by the provision of services can mask serious inequalities both in the reach of any level of service and in the type and quality of services provided. This particular challenge reflects at a more philosophical level the wider and more complex meanings of 'equal' and 'equality' in different social and economic contexts.

At the outset, what is equal or equivalent is a difficult concept to pin down philosophically. The global community of institutions has struggled to answer this question effectively at the level of practice. What is emerging seems to be two types of equality: the first is equality in access (capacity to, all other things being equal, achieve a level of domestic water availability); the second is equality in use (based on relative costs of the resource in different contexts, as well as rules and regulations surrounding usage volumes). The core challenge for governments and others tasked with supporting the delivery of greater equality in access is how to translate these types into nationally meaningful policy actions. Further, even when this can be achieved in some measure, there continues to persist a disconnect between the rhetoric of universality and the ability of states to provide services, with the 'financing gap' frequently posited as the major impediment, although more serious structural and institutional issues may lie as root causes.

The primary policy response at an international level to address the challenge of 663 million people receiving drinking water from unimproved sources[9] has been to push out the provision of low-cost services to communities, including, in some cases, self-supply by households themselves.[7,10,11] These options have been chosen, particularly where access to water and sanitation has been either very costly or simply inaccessible due to social, economic and physical access barriers. The rush to 'scale up' and meet targets – at the forefront of UN-spearheaded efforts – frequently drives unsustainable provision in which are embedded assumptions about technical and financial sustainability, as well as disregard for local and cultural preferences that may be important determinants of social acceptability.[6,7,10,12] This approach also frequently places a large burden on communities as 'resource managers', including an expectation that they will bear some of the financial burden.

It could also be argued that the recognition of the human right to safe drinking water and sanitation contradicts the current approach to push low-cost community-managed services. A right cannot be implemented if it is not clear who would assume responsibility, who would be held accountable and how the right would be enforced.[13] With community-managed systems, the State's role in providing this right could become ambiguous, thereby absolving the State from its responsibility as the duty bearer in enforcing it.

Since the 1980s, the search for greater 'equality' has traversed a spectrum of development ideologies, including increased emphasis on democratic decentralization, new institutional economics and notions of market-based preferences under the influence of neoliberal theory.[14,15,16] An overly technical focus on the challenge of achieving more equal water provision is reflected in 'technological optimist' policies. Driven by conventional engineering paradigms, technological choices in water are often portrayed as providing solutions that transcend politics, yet in reality they are often embedded in the value systems that determine acceptable or unacceptable levels of equality. Pumps in villages break down not just due to technological issues, but also to intra-village conflicts and local politics.

In building up new ways of addressing equality, the dynamic interplay between society, technology, economy and ecology needs to be reflected in more integrated approaches, including a greater emphasis and importance placed on how water is embedded in various uses, and in livelihood practices and development outcomes.[17,18] Indeed, embedded in the 'water for all slogan' are two dimensions: first, the right water in quality and quantity for a complex range of demands manifested by the heterogeneity of any one system user group; and second, water access that is consistent and sustainable over time so that measurement of 'success' is not measurement of a practical chimera. We now turn to a deeper examination of the policy and theoretical landscape surrounding service provision in the last three decades.

Policy landscapes and equality debates

The policy landscape

In 1990, after Mar del Plata, the UN held a global consultation in New Delhi under the slogan 'Some for All Rather than More for Some'. The emergent New Delhi Statement set a global course for the international community during the 1990s, with the drafters mindful that progress had been unsatisfactory in the preceding 'water decade'. The guiding principles in the New Delhi Statement related to the protection of the environment and safeguarding of health and institutional reforms, promoting an integrated approach that would embed the participation of women, community management of services, sound financial practices and the use of appropriate technologies.

Co-sponsored by the UN Steering Committee for the International Drinking Water Supply and Sanitation Decade, and the Water Supply and Sanitation Collaborative Council (WSSCC), the New Delhi consultation was expected to lead to national-level action plans for water and sanitation, incorporating the New Delhi principles which the Indian Government would present to the 45th Session of the United Nations General Assembly in October 1990. These principles and the wider statement were rapidly overshadowed by Dublin, the product of the January 1992 meeting held under the auspices of the World Meteorological Organization (WMO). The fourth 'Dublin Principle' established a major divergence between the two meetings by privileging economic valuation of the resource over social constructions of water supply delivery. This was further pushed in emerging policy discourse by key institutions such as the World Bank and became embedded in more neoliberal and market-oriented development approaches. These envisaged a shrinking state role, enabling greater adherence to free-market capitalism and the commoditisation of resources,[19] a consensus within which water as an 'economic good' sat comfortably.[17]

Castro[20] argues that the impact of these neoliberal reforms continues to linger in efforts at achieving universal water supply provision. The basic elements of the dominant water supply and sanitation policies promoted in the 1990s by the

World Bank and similar institutions were towards reversing universalization, and instead providing services under commercial, profit-making private enterprises. With the failure of these policies now widely recognized, Castro suggests that they continue to reinforce structural inequalities that prevent equitable access to water supply and sanitation services. This occurs through the continued treatment of water and sanitation services as commercial commodities – even the use of the term 'service' itself – under which those who use them are consumers, instead of citizens with rights to access, and under which the public utilities that provide them place more emphasis on commercial efficiency than universal provision.

The discourse around the human right to water which emerged in parallel to the process of neoliberal reforms described above has not had much success in providing a moderating influence. According to Bakker,[21] the international campaign for the human right to water fell short in many countries due to the adoption of an individualistic Eurocentric approach to human rights, enabling the concept to sit comfortably within capitalist and private property rights systems. Private sector participation is therefore fully compatible with this approach, not requiring water supply to be free, although an affordable basic threshold could be required. While South Africa was the first country to provide constitutional recognition to the right to water, the government's water policies have been influenced by the dominant paradigms in water management at the time, including cost recovery, user fees and cut-offs.[6] The Free Basic Water Policy provides a basic water supply, where the lowest tariff block is free of charge and the highest tariff is set at a rate that is expected to discourage consumption. The 6,000 litres per household per month, which is the basic supply provided free of charge, has faced criticism from civil society groups for being too little to adequately meet the daily needs of an individual, particularly in larger households,[22] let alone the wider needs of household use for livelihood activities. The basic notion of per capita supply qua equality (as in the case of the block tariff system implemented in South Africa) failed to account for differences in the reliability and quality of supplies, and for substantial differences in circumstance between communities and households. This 'equal share' came predetermined from above and frequently on the basis of political decision making.

To address and tackle the meaning and challenges of these inequalities, it is important to ask what does equality of provision actually mean and how can (and should) it be measured? Next, we review the emergence of theoretical debates on equality and, specifically, the philosophical basis by which a principle for a basic amount or minimum standard of a basic good such as water can be set. This is followed by discussion of water as a human right and productive resource, in which resource use is seen as intrinsic to people's lives – and their livelihoods.

Philosophical terrain

Rawls[23] is a useful point of departure. He focuses on 'primary goods', which refers to the resources that people are entitled to, both income and the 'general-purpose means' that help anyone to promote his or her ends. The latter includes 'rights, liberties and opportunities, income and wealth, and the social bases of self-respect' (24: p. 72). For Rawls, there are different individual 'conceptions of the good'. Primary goods refer to the individual advantage in terms of opportunities to pursue their own objectives. Rawls focuses on the poorest groups and how the poorest groups can be made better off. He uses a heuristic device – the 'veil of ignorance' – allowing him to derive his 'difference' or 'maximin principle'. This fits well with the notion of a basic entitlement to water, in that all persons, irrespective of their standing under a veil of ignorance, would likely agree to a minimum amount of this basic necessity. The difference principle, or the 'maximin principle' focuses on equality or distributive justice, stating that any gap between the poor and the non-poor in terms of wealth and income can only be justified if – and only if – that gap serves the benefit of the least advantaged, and is associated with positions open to all – that is, conditions of fair equality of opportunity.[23]

This could take the form that the greater consumption of water by some people – for example, irrigation – is justified if that consumption generates proportionate employment and therefore income for the least advantaged (or provision of another good for distribution – e.g. food), but under the condition that the least advantaged would have had the same opportunity of accessing and using that same amount of water had they wished to. The principle would only hold, therefore, if given the choice between water-generated employment and taking up water use for their own productive means, the least advantaged people would prefer the former (*ceteris paribus*).

Sen goes beyond Rawls's primary goods to focus on the characteristics that govern the conversion of commodities 'into the person's ability to promote her ends' (24, p. 75). In other words, it is not just interest in the means, but also in the ends. Central to Sen's approach are the conversion factors (personal, social and environmental), as these influence the relation between a good and the level of functioning. People in different places will need varying amounts for the same capability and the same good will translate into different freedoms for different people, depending on how it can be converted. For example, entitlements to safe water could for one person mean freedom from thirst, but for another person may also go beyond the domestic only to involve livelihood uses such as brick-making, thereby enhancing livelihood outcomes in terms of household income – in short, a kind of 'domestic plus'. This links closely at a service-delivery level to arguments made for water provision to take into account wider livelihood needs[17] under so-called multiple-use systems.[25] This also speaks to more recent debates on the right to water and emerging concerns around economic and social rights embedded in water for food production; it further illustrates the complexities involved in the notion of 'universal access' and equality, when universal ends will not be achieved through the great spectrum of ways in which individuals use water as a resource provided in different quantities and qualities.

In Gujarat, for example, before displacement caused by the construction of the Narmada Dam, tribal groups used the river not just for domestic purposes, but also for productive activities (lift irrigation, fishing, transport and riverbed cultivation), leading to better and more varied diets and livelihood diversification. Individual achievement of these conversions depends, therefore, on a range of issues such as physical condition, knowledge and skills, gender, age and geographical location.

Sen has not provided any specification regarding priority, quantity or implementation regarding capabilities. This is interpreted by others as an unwillingness to put forward a substantive theory of justice (see note 26). In his capabilities approach, the focus is not on the quantity of the bundles of entitlements, but instead on the principle of equality and finding a framework for egalitarian concerns. In fact, it could even be argued that women and men differ within and between societies, and the ability to function on the basis of the same allocation of any one resource varies – indeed, may vary dramatically. It therefore makes little sense to give everyone equal amounts of something (in this case, water), rather to see equality as each according to her needs, as far as one person's needs do not impinge significantly on the needs of others.

Sen suggests the notion of basic capabilities, a subset of all capabilities encompassing the freedom to do 'basic' things. As Sen says, basic capabilities help in 'deciding on a cut-off point for the purpose of assessing poverty and deprivation' (see note 27, p. 109). They provide a kind of threshold or the minimum standard required for basic functioning. When translated to water, this would mean that a basic amount of water is required for human functioning (drinking, washing, and to be free of disease). At a higher level, one could also argue that this minimum requirement for human functioning should also capture livelihood uses and subsistence, relative to needs in particular contexts (e.g. the difference between a drylands context where groundwater or other storage may need tapping into, versus a wetlands context where the emphasis may be more on available water of sufficient quality – or between farm household use and and urban household where the main income is employment in the industrial sector).

Robeyns[28] builds on the idea of basic capabilities, which she subsequently called 'general capabilities' in order to present the idea of fundamental capabilities referring to the deeper, foundational, more abstract and aggregated capabilities (not over persons but over different capabilities in one person). In the water realm, basic or general capabilities would include having the right to access a minimum amount of water required to survive. By contrast, non-basic capabilities would mean having enough to water one's livestock or to grow commercial crops.

The philosopher Martha Nussbaum has developed Sen's work to advance a Central Human Capabilities List. This is considered a cross-cultural evaluation tool free from cultural biases.[29] She tries to address upfront Sen's reluctance to make commitments about a substantive theory of justice and the level of fundamental entitlements a 'just' society should deliver to all its citizens. She proposes a concrete list of capabilities comprising ten categories: life; bodily health; bodily integrity; senses, imagination and thought; emotions; practical reason; affiliation; other species; play, and control over one's environment. Water is not explicitly mentioned, but would probably feature at the top end of the list –

namely, under 1) life or 2) bodily health.[29] For Nussbaum, even though the body may be culturally influenced, some human physiological attributes are completely universal, including hunger, thirst, and so on, and cannot therefore vary between different races and cultures. Nussbaum's list, however, has been critiqued for making contested metaphysical assumptions and priorities, and for being too Western liberal in orientation, paternalistic and lacking in legitimacy (see notes 26 and 28).

In spite of these critiques, it is useful to ask what are the implications of interpreting this list with respect to water? It would be valuable for all governments to prioritize safe and secure water access for their citizens. However, it is not easy to have a universal cross-cultural evaluation tool around water requirements and needs, and hence the physical equality inherent in supplying a measurable resource. Evidence from the water sector in setting up standards around what constitutes a 'basic water requirement' varies greatly by country, highlighting that a basic need is, in many senses, a constructed notion. Basic water requirements have been suggested by various donor agencies, ranging from 20 to 50 litres a day, regardless of culture, livelihood system, climate, or technology, even though their separate attributes do matter. The WHO prescribes between 20 and 100 litres a day,[30] but recognizes that below 50 litres can only reach a 'low' level of impact and that 100 litres is the minimum required for cooking basic food and personal hygiene (this amount completely excludes water for productive or survival activities such as growing food). In emergency situations, the SPHERE minimum standard is lower still, at 15 litres per person per day.[31]

The threshold level of what counts as 'hygienic' or 'safe' is also culturally determined, and therefore what equates with 'safe access' can vary widely. The amount of water people use to wash themselves, for example, can vary widely across societies and geographies. The UNICEF/WHO Joint Monitoring Programme's definitions of what constitutes 'improved' water supply and sanitation are, again, highly contested, not least because international definitions may not be in tune with local preferences and realities. Nussbaum's moral-legal and philosophical perspective on capabilities argues for governments to incorporate her principles into their constitutions, and her list is supposed to provide citizens with a justification to have a right to make demands on their governments.

Political and economic drivers of inequality

To be implemented effectively, principles of equality and sustainability must overcome a host of political, economic, social and cultural barriers. According to the Human Development Report by UNDP,[32] water scarcities seen around the world arise mainly from power, poverty and inequality, rather than from issues of physical barriers to access. Inequitable access to water supplies persists because those who are most highly affected are also often those with the least power to shape and influence national priorities and implementation strategies. Even in wealthy, industrialised countries where financially, technically and institutionally sustainable water supply and sanitation systems are in place, access can be limited for certain groups as a result of structural social inequalities.[20] For example, when the affordability of water supply services was evaluated using the UK Government's criteria, it was estimated that up to 2–4 million people in England and Wales from low-income households were living in a state of 'water poverty'.[16]

Mehta[33] uses unequal and invisible power systems to explain how inequalities in access to water and sanitation are caused and naturalized around the world. Invisible power is one of three levels or forms of political power, the other two being visible and hidden forms of power. Of the three forms, invisible power is considered to be the most insidious as it can lead to marginalized and disempowered groups – including those with disabilities[34] – accepting their place in the system as the norm, without questioning their disadvantaged positions. Injustices faced by such groups can be excluded from decision-making processes, as invisible power can obstruct such injustices from being viewed and their change being envisaged.[35,36]

Invisible power can also operate in the context of structural violence.[33] Structural violence can be viewed as 'social arrangements that put individuals and populations in harm's way'.[40,41,42] This can be further worsened by elite biases, democratic deficits (and distortions), jurisdictional ambiguities and market-based mechanisms.[33] Water is vital for human life, and thus such structural violence can harm and endanger people's lives and human development in multiple ways. Such harm can materialize through inequalities faced both when attempting to access water and sanitation systems, as well as when the water and sanitation facilities that can be accessed are not of acceptable quality. As a result of structural violence, based on racial discrimination, nearly 12 million largely Black South Africans were denied access to water in apartheid South Africa, while the white minority was provided by the state with water infrastructure. Military and other rulings prohibit the Palestinians from digging wells or collecting water from rooftops, resulting in the Palestinians having access to only a third of the amount of water that the Israelis do.[33] These multiple harms and contributors to inequality can have severe consequences on the health, education, productivity and human dignity of those affected.

Equality and the new goals in water and sanitation

In 2012, the WHO/UNICEF JMP announced that the world had met the Millennium Development Goal (MDG) target of halving the proportion of people without sustainable access to safe drinking water, well in advance of the 2015 deadline.[43] Arguably, in terms of equality, however, the water MDG was flawed on many counts. The target of halving by 2015 the proportion of people without sustainable access to safe drinking water and basic sanitation failed to address universality and left almost 800 million people using poor sources of drinking water with 40 per cent of this population living in sub-Saharan Africa. Rural dwellers, including some of the poorest of the poor, were by-passed in the

BOX 4.1 CASE STUDY: NEW DELHI

Delhi's peri-urban poor, many of whom live in what are considered illegal and unplanned settlements, are estimated to be roughly one third of the city's population. Often, these settlements have origins tied to the development of the city. The planned development of the city in the past created employment for large numbers of workers who took up residence within and around Delhi, with their presence largely tolerated for this reason. However, recent efforts to rationalise and modernise the city space has led to these settlements being increasingly viewed as illegal. Many people have been forcefully relocated elsewhere.[36,37]

The majority of those in such illegal and informal settlements lack access to the city's piped water infrastructure, for reasons including the lack of legal rights to do so and proximity, and therefore have to rely on other means, some illegal. They also lack proper sewerage and sanitation services. As the pipe borne water is subsidized by the state, those who cannot access it usually pay much higher prices to obtain it through other means. When access is provided by the state, the water is often of inferior quality and the supply of inadequate quantity and irregular.[37,38]

As is the case elsewhere, it is the women on whom responsibility falls for collecting water, and in this case making up for defects in the state's responsibility to deliver. Apart from the physical hardships and dangers faced when collecting water, the missed opportunities connected to education and employment, accessing water sources often brings these women into the realm of what is considered illegal activities. For example, as Truelove[36] illustrates, slum-dwelling women pay tanker drivers extra money to deliver water more frequently, or may attempt to tap into water sources that have been provided for the use of more affluent neighbourhoods. When doing so, they are often harassed and abused, and face the risk of being caught by the police.

Such practices are gaining increasing prominence in state discourses on how the water that is lost from the city's supply can be regulated – so-called 'unaccounted for' water. Illegal connections and specifically those associated with illegal residence are singled out, with the water accessing methods of the urban poor being the main target.[39] According to Truelove,[37] in reality, there are a wide variety of reasons for this loss, including defects in the water supply infrastructure and extra legal efforts made by citizens from all classes to increase their access. Further, such attention on the urban poor as the main culprits is contradicted by the fact that it is the poor who consume the least amount of water in Delhi.

While the constitution of India does not explicitly provide for a fundamental right to water, it has been interpreted through several court rulings as being

> implied in other provisions, including the right to life and the right to a clean
> environment.[38] However, most of the poor are ignorant of their right to
> water,[38] which is an example of how invisible power systems normalize the
> deprivation of a fundamental right.

achievement of this target, with frequent technical malfunction.[44] The limitations of the indicators used to measure progress meant that achieving gender equality, social equity and sustainability tended to be overlooked in an effort to extend coverage.[45] Regional variations and variations between socioeconomic groups or by gender were not adequately captured (see, for example, box below), including in peri-urban and slum areas, which are some of the fastest-growing areas in the world. These categories were not included in official MDG statistics. It is important to note that commitments to the rights to water and sanitation had no influence on the original MDG formulation, and many were made after the MDGs were established (see note 6).

The Sustainable Development Goal (SDG) on water and sanitation is a huge improvement on the MDG targets, and the impact of subsequent discourse on the human rights to safe drinking water and sanitation is reflected in the formulation of the targets and indicators. The SDG target seeks by 2030 to achieve universal and equitable access to safe and affordable drinking water for all, as well as access to adequate and equitable sanitation and hygiene for all and an end open defecation, paying special attention to the needs of women and girls and those in vulnerable situations. In addition, water quality concerns that were missing from the MDGs are addressed, including a commitment to reduce the number of people suffering from water scarcity and support, and to strengthen the participation of local communities in improving water and sanitation management. The importance of strengthening the wider water management environment, as well as immediate supply access, recognizes that equality in supplies may be hindered significantly if the resource base itself is inadequately managed and maintained, both in terms of the availability of quantities and the overall quality of the resource.

Still, like the other SDGs, there is a risk that there are too many indicators and hence problems with monitoring and tracking, and the risk of an SDG monitoring industry emerging in each country, with an over-emphasis on tracking numbers of beneficiaries and an under-emphasis on tracking qualitative differences in access. In common with the MDGs, there is also a lack of clear mechanisms of accountability and similarly a definition of each goal and target at more specific national and subnational levels. These will always be different and need to be locally defined. Also generalized, globalized arguments that underpin policy debates tend to remain disconnected from the everyday experiences of local people. The 'service ladder' used for monitoring target 6.1 (see Chapter 12) is far more nuanced than the binary improved/unimproved classification used for MDG monitoring.

BOX 4.2 CASE STUDY: SRI LANKA

The 'Indian Tamils' or Estate Tamils of Sri Lanka largely reside in the central mountainous region of the country, where much of the tea – the most valuable export commodity of the country – is cultivated. The Indian Tamils are the major source of labour for the tea industry, a practice that dates back to the days of British rule in Sri Lanka when the Indian Tamils were brought to the island to work in plantations as indentured labourers. Those who thus migrated did so under the promise of a better life, as in Southern India they had been part of the lowest castes in the social hierarchy. The major ethnic groups of the country, the Sinhalese and the second largest minority, the 'Sri Lankan Tamils' have long considered the Indian Tamils to be interlopers. They were stripped of their citizenship rights after Sri Lanka's independence from colonial rule, an issue that was only fully resolved recently in 2003.[46]

In terms of general human development, Sri Lanka has done well. The human development index level is far higher than other countries in the region. Island-wide, the majority of the 27 MDG targets were met, an achievement attributed to long-running free education, health and other welfare programmes.[47] However, regional disparities persist. Areas that have lagged behind mainly fall into two categories: those that were the seat of groups engaged in a 30-year-old civil war and the estate sector.[48] With regard to water and sanitation, the water supply coverage for 2012 was 100 per cent, 82 per cent and 62 per cent in urban, rural and estate areas; that for sanitation was respectively 100 per cent, 82 per cent and 55 per cent.[49]

Many of the estate workers still live in 'line houses' (barrack-type rows with single rooms), constructed almost 150 years ago, many of which are heavily dilapidated. Living conditions are congested and unhygienic. Almost half of these populations depend on public taps for drinking water with difficulties in access, and pollution of the water sources used to supply pipe-borne water has been recorded. Challenges in accessing proper water and sanitation facilities, combined with low investments in health services result in illnesses that lead to absenteeism from work.[50] The prevalence of soil-transmitted helminth parasite infection, which is strongly associated with the presence of good sanitation facilities, is higher in school-going children in the estate sector when compared to the rest of the country.[51] Decades of political marginalization and denial of citizenship, together with the geographical isolation of the estates and cultural differences with the other ethnic groups, have resulted in the Estate Tamil community being excluded from the development and welfare activities of the government. This community continues to live in a state of low socioeconomic development with little access to basic services.

However, as Welle[52] has demonstrated, there is a large gap between the way in which global agencies, national agencies and local people understand, define and measure water access and inequality, reflecting different levels of knowledge and understanding of local contexts. This is vastly different from how sector performance monitoring was often depicted during the MDG period as being a rational and objective basis on which decisions can be made.

There is also a lack of explicit recognition in policies and programmes of the power imbalances that create water and sanitation crises in the first place, linked to a tendency to ignore critical issues concerning the social, institutional and financial sustainability of water services. The hardware or project-oriented approach has led to neglect in focusing on the sustainable provision of a service. Nevertheless, despite the continued prevalence of approaches focused on aggregate, technical aspects of water supply, there have been important moves towards a greater recognition of distributional issues. For example, the need to share limited water resources equitably is the logic behind the water allocation reform processes underway in many parts of the world, including South Africa. But merely enhancing access is not enough. There is also a need to look at what we might term the 'use value' of water access in this case defined as the particular services that people derive from water from survival to diverse livelihoods needs, and how these are rooted in particular socioeconomic and cultural contexts.

This calls for greater attention to diverse local settings and the meanings and values that people attach to water in their everyday lives. At the same time, the sustainability of this use value is key, referring to the extent to which water equitable access enables people, communities and regions to use water services in a way that is resilient and robust over time, and in the face of shocks and stresses that may occur and impinge on equitable access that goes beyond mere water for human survival.

For example, when dam building on the Narmadha River relocated the Vasava and Tadvi, so-called 'tribal people' in Gujarat, India, from their ancestral settlements on the river, they experienced mostly detrimental changes to their livelihood options, health and access to a safe and assured supply of water. The main source of water in the new settlement were standpoints fed by wells, operated by outsiders. Thus, the villagers did not have control over these sources, and experienced irregular supply of low quantity and quality. The uncertainty around accessing water meant that the villagers had less time for other tasks and had to experience increased social friction due to competition in accessing this water.[53]

These challenges establish again that water is so central to understandings of development that go beyond physical benefits and that notions of equality related to water supply alone as a physical measure will not suffice as a real understanding of progress, including the iconic use of images of water flowing from tap stands as a marker for development progress. This is not to deny the importance of water supply improvements, rather to underscore that 'improved' and 'coverage' are not easily reconciled with broader notions of equality.

Conclusions and policy directions: beyond equality, towards empowerment?

In conclusion, there are significant challenges in taking equality as a starting point for the achievement of universal access to water supply and sanitation. As noted above, the meaning of equal access varies widely across different social, economic, cultural, religious and economic dimensions. How does a measure of equality take into account non-survival needs, and how are these needs met relative to other livelihood strategies and systems? We have identified how the measures of equality need to transcend the simple physical realm and address wider elements of human capabilities and capacities.

In particular, as the global community continues to track and trace progress against SDG target 6.1, notions of equality need to become more nuanced and our satisfaction levels with 'coverage' need to be reduced, particularly where intra-household inequalities are stark and have significant drag on the development potential of women and girls.

We do not suggest that measures of inequality that exist – including SDG target 6.1 – are challenged (they are far too important as markers of progress). We do, however, conclude that follow-up analysis and understanding of what inequality outcomes are observed needs to be more clearly assessed and recorded as well as just beneficiary numbers alone. The fact that 663 million people were estimated to lack access to an improved drinking water source in 2015 is largely meaningless if serious inequalities continue to persist among a large proportion of those who do have access to an improved supply.

Taking this further, and at a more challenging level, are we content to leave our measure of success at a minimum standard of access to drinking water quality supplies in terms of a generalized per capita figure? There are multiple benefits and uses accruing from water usage that go beyond human consumption, and have direct and indirect benefits and development impacts.[17,18]

As the world continues to strive for progress – and to attract funds to drive forward tangible improvements in water supply services – ways of measuring different types of inequalities will become more significant in future, including tackling the thorny question of relative inequalities in existing service levels and the complex notion of context-specific inequality related to the needs and capabilities of individuals.

The concept of 'relativeness' suggests the need for contextualization of need and demand, and the tailoring of service provision to more local-level targets based on specific social, environmental and/or economic conditions. Particular effort should be made to establish useful ways of measuring equality in non drinking-water consumption and to add these to global indicator sets over time. These more complex 'relative inequalities' are perhaps even more central to the broader goal of poverty reduction and help link water supply to a wider objective of the sustainable development goals.

Notes

1 United Nations (2015). Transforming our world: the 2030 agenda for sustainable development. Geneva: United Nations, Department of Economic and Social Affairs.
2 WHO and UNICEF (2017). Progress on drinking water, sanitation and hygiene: 2017 update and SDG baselines. WHO/UNICEF Joint Monitoring Programme for Water Supply, Sanitation and Hygiene. Geneva.
3 Chaplin, S.E. (1999). Cities, sewers and poverty: India's politics of sanitation. *Environment and Urbanization*, *11*(1), 145–158.
4 Ahmad, Q.K. (2003). Towards poverty alleviation: the water sector perspectives. *International Journal of Water Resources Development*, *19*(2), 263–277.
5 Stephens, C. (1996). Healthy cities or unhealthy islands? The health and social implications of urban inequality. *Environment and Urbanization*, *8*(2), 9–30.
6 Mehta, L. and Movik, S. (2014). Liquid dynamics: challenges for sustainability in the water domain, *Wiley 54 Interdisciplinary Reviews: Water*, *1*(4), 369–384
7 Cleaver, F. and Toner, A. (2006). The evolution of community water governance in Uchira, Tanzania: the implications for equality of access, sustainability and effectiveness. In *Natural Resources Forum*, 30(3), 207–218. Blackwell Publishing.
8 Nicol, A., Mehta, L. and Allouche, J. (2011). Editorial: Some for all rather than more for some? Contested politics and pathways in water and sanitation since the 1990 New Delhi Statement, *IDS Bulletin*, 43.2, 1–9.
9 UNICEF and WHO (2015). Progress on sanitation and drinking water: 2015 update and MDG assessment. WHO/UNICEF Joint Monitoring Programme for Water Supply and Sanitation, New York.
10 Harvey, P.A. and Reed, R.A. 2006. Community-managed water supplies in Africa: sustainable or dispensable? *Community Development Journal*, *42*(3), 365–378.
11 Whittington, D., Davis, J., Prokopy, L., Komives, K., Thorsten, R., Lukacs, H., Bakalian, A. and Wakeman, W. (2009). How well is the demand-driven, community management model for rural water supply systems doing? Evidence from Bolivia, Peru and Ghana. *Water Policy*, *11*(6), 696–718.
12 Ademiluyi, I.A. and Odugbesan, J.A. 2008. Sustainability and impact of community water supply and sanitation programmes in Nigeria: an overview. *African Journal of Agricultural Research*, *3*(12), 811–817.
13 Mehta, L. (2000). Water for the twenty-first century: challenges and misconceptions. Brighton: Institute of Development Studies. IDS Working Paper 111.
14 Spronk, S. (2010). Water and sanitation utilities in the Global South: re-centering the debate on "efficiency". *Review of Radical Political Economics*, *42*(2), 156–174.
15 Prasad, N. (2006). Privatisation results: private sector participation in water services after 15 years. *Development Policy Review*, *24*(6), 669–692.
16 Castro, J.E. (2008). Neoliberal water and sanitation policies as a failed development strategy: lessons from developing countries. *Progress in Development Studies*, *8*(1), 63–83.
17 Nicol, A. (2000) A sustainable livelihoods approach to water projects: policy and practice implications. ODI Working Paper 133, Overseas Development Institute, London.
18 Loevinsohn, M., Mehta, L., Cuming, K., Nicol, A., Cumming, O. and Ensink, J.H. (2015). The cost of a knowledge silo: a systematic re-review of water, sanitation and hygiene interventions. *Health Policy and Planning*, *30*(5), 660–674. DOI: 10.1093/heapol/czu039.
19 Finger, M. and Allouche, J. (2002) *Water Privatisation: Transnational Corporations and the Re-regulation of the Water Industry*. London: SPON Press.
20 Castro, J.E. (2007). Systemic conditions affecting the universalisation of water and sanitation services: a sociological exploration. *Journal of Comparative Social Welfare*, *23*(2), 105–119.
21 Bakker, K. (2007). The "commons" versus the "commodity": alter-globalization, anti-privatization and the human right to water in the global south. *Antipode*, *39*(3), 430–455.

22 Muller, M. (2008). Free basic water—a sustainable instrument for a sustainable future in South Africa. *Environment and Urbanization*, 20(1), 67–87.
23 Rawls, J. (1971). *A Theory of Justice*. Cambridge, MA: Harvard University Press.
24 Sen, A. (1999). *Development as Freedom*. Oxford: Oxford University Press.
25 Smits, S., van Koppen, B., Moriarty, P. and Butterworth, J. (2010). Multiple-use services as an alternative to rural water supply services: a characterisation of the approach. *Water Alternatives*, 3(1),102–121.
26 Srinivasan, S. (2007). No democracy without justice: political freedom in Amartya Sen's capability approach, 8(3).
27 Sen, A. (ed. Hawthorne, G.) *The Standard of Living* (1987). Cambridge: Cambridge University Press.
28 Robeyns, I. (2005). The capability approach: a theoretical survey. *Journal of Human Development*, 6(1), 93–117.
29 Nussbaum, M.C. (2003). Capabilities as fundamental entitlements: Sen and social justice. *Feminist Economics*, 9, 33–59.
30 WHO (2003) The right to water. Health and Human Rights publication series 3. Geneva.
31 *The Sphere Handbook, Humanitarian Charter and Minimum Standards in Humanitarian Response* (2000). Available at: www.SphereProject.org
32 UNDP (2006). Human Development Report: Beyond scarcity: power, poverty and the global water. Available at: http://hdr.undp.org/en/content/human-development-report-2006 (accessed 10 November 2016).
33 Mehta, L. (2016). Why invisible power and structural violence persist in the water domain. *IDS Bulletin*, 47(5).
34 Clement, F., Nicol, A. and Cordier, S. (2017). Water justice, gender and disability, *SAWAS Special Issue*, 5(4), June. SaciWaters.
35 VeneKlasen, L. and Miller, V. (2002) *A New Weave of People, Power and Politics: The Action Guide for Advocacy and Citizen Participation*. Oklahoma City, OK: World Neighbors.
36 Gaventa, J. (2006). Finding the spaces for change: a power analysis. *IDS Bulletin*, 37(6), 23–33.
37 Truelove, Y. (2011). (Re-)Conceptualizing water inequality in Delhi, India through a feminist political ecology framework. *Geoforum*, 42(2), 143–152.
38 Mehta, L., Allouche, J., Nicol, A. and Walnycki, A. (2014). Global environmental justice and the right to water: the case of peri-urban Cochabamba and Delhi. *Geoforum*, 54, 158–166.
39 Truelove, Y. and Mawdsley, E. (2011). Discourses of citizenship and criminality in clean, green Delhi. In I. Clark-Decès (ed.) *A Companion to the Anthropology of India*. Oxford: Wiley-Blackwell, pp. 407–425.
40 Farmer, P. (1996). On suffering and structural violence: a view from below. *Daedalus*, 125(1), 261–283.
41 Farmer, P. (2004). An anthropology of structural violence. *Current Anthropology*, 45(3), 305–325. doi:1.
42 Farmer, P.E., Nizeye, B., Stulac, S. and Keshavjee, S. (2006). Structural violence and clinical medicine. *PLOS Medicine*, 3(10), e449.
43 UNICEF and WHO (2012). Progress on drinking water and sanitation, 2012 update. New York.
44 IIED (2009). Where every drop counts: tackling rural Africa's water crisis. IIED Briefing. IIED Global Water Initiative, London.
45 UNICEF and WHO (2011). Drinking water equity, safety and sustainability: JMP thematic report on drinking water.
46 Deori, N. (2013)The Indian origin Tamils in Sri Lanka: a study of their socio-economic-political plight. *A Biannual Journal of South Asian Studies*, 77.
47 United Nations, Sri Lanka (2015). Sri Lanka millennium development goals county report: 2014.

48 UNICEF, Sri Lanka (2016). Water, sanitation and hygiene: UNICEF in Sri Lanka fact sheet. Available at: www.unicef.org/srilanka/WASH.pdf (accessed 10 November 2016).
49 International Water Association (2013). Mapping human resource capacity gaps in the water supply and sanitation sector. Country briefing note Sri Lanka. Available at: www.iwa-network.org/wp-content/uploads/2015/12/1422744575-Briefing-Note-Sri-Lanka-final.pdf (accessed 10 November 2016).
50 Aheeyar, M.M.M. (2006). Preliminary investigation on the issues related to poverty and marginalization of estate sector communities in Badulla and Nuwara Eliya districts. Final report: practical action consulting.
51 De Silva, N. (2012). Can we eliminate soil-transmitted helminth infections in Sri Lanka? *Ceylon Medical Journal*, 57(1).
52 Welle, K. 2013. Performance monitoring or monitoring performance? Access to rural water supply in Ethiopia. Unpublished Ph.D. thesis, University of Sussex.
53 Mehta, L. and Punja, P. (2006). Water and well-being: explaining the gap in understandings of water. In A. Baviskar (ed.) *Waterscapes: The Cultural Politics of a Natural Resource*. Delhi: Permanent Black, pp. 188–210.

5

WASH AND GENDER

Understanding gendered consequences and impacts of WASH in/security

Kathleen O'Reilly and Robert Dreibelbis

Introduction

The Sustainable Development Goals have outlined a broad set of objectives for building a "sustainable and resilient future for people and the planet," including Goal 6—Ensure access to water and sanitation for all, with a specific gender-related target: "By 2030, achieve access to adequate and equitable sanitation and hygiene for all and end open defecation, paying special attention to the needs of women and girls and those in vulnerable situations."

Missing is an articulation of the "needs of women and girls", which are contextually bound, dynamic, and multifaceted. In this chapter, we discuss the WASH needs of women and girls from the perspective of water, sanitation, and hygiene (WASH) security and its correlary insecurity. We define gendered WASH security to mean sufficient access to clean water and the ability of women and girls to secure sustainable, appropriate sanitation such that they can meet their hygiene needs. We provide a broad overview of how addressing WASH insecurity is central to meeting multiple aspects of the Sustainable Development Goal agenda and how WASH in/security is created and maintained through gendered power relationships. We provide an overview of the gendered impacts of WASH access and WASH insecurity on physical health, well-being, and development. We suggest that WASH policy moves beyond technical interventions to consider the complex social realities that hinder gendered WASH security[1].

Water, sanitation, gender, and the Sustainable Development Goals

In addition to the Goal 6 Targets, discussed above, gender, WASH (water, sanitation, and hygiene), and WASH in/security intersect with the SGDs in multiple ways. Ensuring inclusive and quality education for all—Goal 4—requires that schools address the specific WASH needs of girls (see Chapter 10). WASH insecurity can force women into locations and activities that compromise their personal safety, compounding both the fear of and risk of violence,[2-4] central to Goal 5 (Eliminate all forms of violence against all women and girls in the public and private spheres, including trafficking, and sexual and other types of exploitation) and Goal 16 (Significantly reduce all forms of violence and related death rates everywhere).

Within the domestic sphere, women's roles and contribution to household productive activities are marginalized and negatively impacted by WASH insecurity. Targets for Goal 5 include: "Recognize and value unpaid care and domestic work through the provision of public services, infrastructure and social protection policies and the promotion of shared responsibility within the household and the family as nationally appropriate." Increasing access to improved sources of drinking water is one of the great success stories of the MGD period[5]—over 2.6 billion people gained access to improved drinking water sources since 1990. However, 33 per cent of the world's population—2.4 billion people±lack access to water piped into the home, and the vast majority of these households are in low- and middle-income countries. Multiple analyses have shown that when water supplies are located away from the home, water collection and transport is primarily the responsibility of women.[6,7] Multi-country data also suggests that as water collection becomes more difficult and labor-intensive, the likelihood that it will be a woman's responsibility also increases.[8] So, recognizing water collection as constitutive of gender inequalities can assist planners in avoiding reproducing them.

WASH in/security

Water security is defined as "the capacity of a population to safeguard sustainable access to adequate quantities of acceptable quality water for sustaining livelihoods, human well-being, and socio-economic development."[9] Recent additions to the standard definition of water security and proposed definitions of sanitation security have drawn attention to the lived experience of users—reflecting both availability to adequate resources and services and the individual, social, and cultural factors that determine both the need and capacity to access them.[10,11] We combine these concepts of both sanitation and water security and define WASH security as the capacity of populations and individuals within those populations to access necessary water resources and safeguard sustainable access to sanitation that meets basic requirements of dignity, privacy, and safety, while protecting health and the resources and supplies necessary for adequate hygiene. WASH security means that women have access to sufficient, safe water supplies for their needs, and a hygienic toilet facility with adequate access to water for hygiene as they understand it. It means being able to use that facility, and have sufficient water, time and safety for hygiene purposes.

Our discussion of WASH insecurity and gender is based on the concept that WASH in/security can be viewed as a product of gendered relations of power—power relations that are manifested in gendered norms, gendered responsibilities, and gendered differences in access to resources. This chapter explores WASH and gender with attention to gender as a relational system that creates men and women as distinctly separate and unequal.[12] While sex is considered a biologically determined factor about an individual, gender includes social expectations about the physical and mental capabilities and characteristics of men and women—and establishes a shared cultural meaning about the relationship between them. The inherent inequalities associated with socially constructed meanings of gender is key to understanding the relationship of WASH and gender.[13] Put simply, the inequalities of gender relationships disadvantage women and girls, and negatively impact their WASH security.

As an example—a woman is collecting water for use in the home. Gendered roles and responsibilities have shaped the fact that she is responsible for the physical labor associated with water collection for the entire family. Her water needs are further shaped by gendered expectations within the household and community—she may have specific cooking and cleaning responsibilities in the home that require water or culturally defined bathing and hygiene practices. The time of day when she fetches water will be shaped by the nature and scope of her other domestic responsibilities and can potentially be dictated by the times when she—as a woman—is allowed to leave the home and in whose company she is allowed to be seen while in public. Her ability to access specific water resources within her community may be shaped further by gendered power relations—she may be barred from access to certain water points in the community, other sources may require her to travel longer distances than she can physically manage, other sources may place her in areas that will compromise her safety and security. If she cannot secure sufficient water for the home, she may be blamed and punished by male members of her household or face social isolation based on others' perception regarding her ability to provide for her family.

Research suggests that experiences of insecurity are highly gendered. Intra-household gender differences in experiences of water insecurity identify that men and women hold different perceptions of water insecurity, with men perceiving water insecurity as less severe than women,[14] although these differences may be less pronounced during acute emergency periods.[15] That women do not experience WASH security as men is due in part to gender norms including gendered responsibilities, standards of conduct, and opportunities. The gender norms that produce WASH insecurity must be addressed alongside the provision of WASH security.[11]

Women, adolescent girls, and young children are more vulnerable than men to environmental risk and violence in both urban and rural settings.[16] The needs of women and girls are often the reason behind toilet building campaigns. But toilets can also be deployed as a reason to limit women's mobility,[12] an important aspect of women participating in public life and demands for rights—in short, a denial of women's freedom that might lead to enhancing their capabilities.[17]

Gender norms change over time and place, and their relationship with WASH in/security changes throughout women's lives. For example, among young girls there is some evidence that reduced time and involvement of children in household water collection—due to increased availability—can result in increased attendance in schools after accounting for other factors.[18] Separate sanitation facilities, privacy and access to water may increase girls' attendance in school, although this relationship has yet to be tested empirically.[19-21] While easy access to water and sanitation facilities is expected to save time and reduce work burdens, that does not necessarily mean that time saved will be spent as girls would wish, that their overall work burden will be reduced, or that social norms will shift to address women and girls' many concerns and questions regarding WASH and their bodies.[1,22]

We focus our discussion of WASH security to the domestic sphere—the ability to access water in sufficient quantities and of quality that is safe for drinking, cooking, and personal hygiene, and to safeguard sanitation facilities acceptable to the women and girls who use them. In the home, women are the traditional managers, cooks, and caregivers. Water is also necessary for gendered sanitation and hygiene behaviors, ranging from anal cleansing, menstrual hygiene management, bathing, and ritual bathing.[2] We recognize that WASH in/security extends far beyond the household scale.

Intersectionality

The intersection of WASH insecurity and gender must be understood within the broad, overlapping networks of social and power dynamics that result in exclusion and marginalization. Intersectionality refers to the ways in which social privilege or disadvantage is shaped by overlapping and dynamic social categories, such as race, class, gender, socioeconomic status, education, ethnicity.[23] While public health and development typically focus on singular attributes of a person or group, the intersectionality perspective attempts to understand how multiple social categories combine within a single individual. As discussed above, gender is a social relationship that determines specific access to power and expectations within a given society. However, the lived experience of these gender dynamics may differ considerably between women from different classes, life stages, or ethnicities. Gender norms and experiences of WASH insecurity are different between women and within communities—gender intersects with religion, class, caste, color, ethnicity, dis/ability, life stage, and geography in ways that mean that women living in the same communities, and even households, experience WASH insecurity differently.[24] Gender is one among many unequal social relations.

In India, for example, the interwoven relationship of water, caste, and purity in Hindu society created a distinct difference, by caste, in water that was available for women's practical needs.[25] After completion of a project that delivered water to rural communities through public taps, the taps were manipulated such that water flowed to the individual households of upper-caste and upper-class households, leaving the poor and lower-caste households to seek alternative supplies. The poor's WASH insecurity was gendered, as the collection of water was done by women, meaning that it was poor, lower-caste women who begged, borrowed and traveled in order to secure water for their households.[26,27]

The Indian project also demonstrates how interventions designed to improves the lives of women and girls can reinforce and perpetuate gendered power dynamics. The project expected that women, as 'traditional' household water managers, should give their free time and labour for cleaning public taps, serving on water management committees, and promoting the payment for water.[28] The project intended to alter gender relations through women's participation, although it followed established patterns. Thus, women were discouraged from attending public meetings by their community, and collecting payment for water was quickly assumed by men. Women's participation goals reinforced gender dynamics, as ultimately, women's participation meant women taking responsibility for cleaning the new public taps.

The connections between WASH security, gender, and other social categories are multiple.[29] Research on sanitation access among the urban poor provides a compelling example of how gender and WASH insecurity intersect with a range of social categories. In many informal settlements, women have constrained choices when finding places to safely and privately (if possible) defecate due to a lack of available sanitation and water services.[30] For women in cities, toilets symbolize male privilege, as males have access or do not 'need' access, while women plan their travel and activities throughout the day to accommodate constrained sanitation choices. Middle-class or professional women in the city have opportunities to use the sanitation facilities of hotels and restaurants or their places of employment, options that poor urban women are excluded from.[31]

Interventions to improve access among the urban poor, such as the provision of block or communal toilets, are often implemented without attention to community beliefs or gendered, daily experiences.[24] Built without adequate access to water resources, latrines remain filthy and do not provide sufficient water for hygienic purposes. Placed in public areas where men can and do congregate, use of these communal toilets can result in harassment or violence from men. Across religions, women are unenthusiastic about sharing toilets with men. Filthy, unsafe toilet blocks drive women to defecate in the open, compounding the risks of physical violence, harassment and stress.[32]

Gendered health impacts associated with WASH and WASH insecurity

With WASH insecurity following generally gendered lines, the health impacts of this insecurity can compound health outcomes among women and girls, or create negative consequences for overall health and well-being. These health topics have mostly gone under-acknowledged and under-researched within the global community.

Caloric expenditure and injuries

The physical labor required for water collection has a direct impact on time and energy costs[33] and comes at a cost of high caloric expenditures. Carrying water from the point of collection to the household is also associated with increased rates of physical injuries and musculoskeletal disorders; however, data on physical health impacts is limited. One study in South Africa found that among women who carry water, the prevalence of self-reported spinal pain was 69 per cent.[34,35] The risk of long-term impacts on musculoskeletal function and pain of carrying water are potentially exacerbated by the practice of head-loading, common in resource poor settings.[36]

Urogenital infections

Urogential infections—including bacterial vaginosis, urinary tract infections, and reproductive tract infections—are increasingly identified as a public health priority worldwide, particularly in low-income countries.[37,38] Infections have been associated with an increased risk of sexually transmitted infections (such as HIV), pain and incontinence, and adverse pregnancy outcomes.[39] Menstrual hygiene management practices have been linked to urogenital infections in a number of studies[39]—specifically, the reuse of absorbent material for menstruation (cotton cloths, rags, etc.). While the links are plausible, there is limited data available on the links between water and other hygiene practices during menstruation and urogenital infections. WASH insecurity is an important determinant of a woman's menstrual hygiene practices. In India, women without access to a sanitation facility reported not washing and cleaning during menstruation to their own satisfaction.[2] In a case-control study of laboratory-confirmed bacterial vaginosis, access to a private, personal space for menstrual hygiene management was associated with lower rates of bacterial vaginosis.

Maternal and child health outcomes

The links between WASH and maternal health outcomes were established as early as the mid-1800s with the pioneering work of Semmelweis and his studies linking improved hand hygiene during labor with reductions in maternal deaths. More recently, Campbell and colleagues identified 77 different linkages between water, sanitation and hygiene, and maternal and reproductive health outcomes. A UNICEF-commissioned review of the impact of WASH on health and social outcomes[40] identified studies linking infectious diseases transmission due to inadequate water and sanitation to anemia, infection, spontaneous abortion and maternal death, and that the physical and caloric expenditures associated with water collection can further contribute to adverse pregnancy outcomes.

Robust data on the association between water and sanitation security, and maternal and child outcomes are limited. A recent systematic review limited to observational studies[41] found that women living in homes without access to toilet facilities were over three times as likely to die during pregnancy or childbirth than women who live in homes with appropriate facilities. Individual studies have also found links between maternal mortality and adverse pregnancy outcomes, and constrained access to water and sanitation in the home.[42,43]

With a global increase in the number of births that happen in health facilities, it is important to understand the links between WASH insecurity and maternal outcomes not only at the household, but also at the facility level. An assessment of water and sanitation in healthcare facilities in low- and middle-income countries found that over a third of facilities lacked access to basic water supply.[44] Insecure water access may impact proper infection-prevention and control strategies at hospitals, contributing to high rates of hospital-acquired infections during labor and delivery.

Stress, distress, and quality of life

Current WHO definitions of health encompass not only the absence of disease, but the complete physical, emotion, and social well-being of individuals. WASH insecurity has been linked both qualitatively and quantitatively with stress, distress, and reduced quality of life generally.[45,46] Gender-specific studies have further explored these links. In Bolivia, water insecurity and female gender were both associated with higher rates of self-reported emotional distress.[15,47] A series of studies in Ethiopia found that water insecurity was associated with higher levels of emotional distress among women and that community-level improvements in water supply could improve mental well-being by reducing scarcity experiences.[48,49] A robust body of observational studies, primarily focused on India, have found associations between sanitation access, sanitation in/security, and self-reported quality of life and self-reported stress.[2,50,51,52] Factors that shaped experiences of psychosocial stress related to sanitation access included social constraint on when women could leave the home for defecation, adopting maladaptive behaviours to reduce the need to utilize inadequate facilities (i.e., eating or drinking less), navigating natural and man-made barriers in the physical environment, and fear of harassment, physical violence, and sexual assault.

Conflict and violence

The role of WASH insecurity in community and individual conflict has been under-explored. However, there is compelling evidence that insecurity can compound existing social and gendered tensions. In a study in rural Kenya, contested access to limited water resources was the focal point of a cascade of social conflicts that followed along social and gendered lines.[53] Among women who prioritized water supply for domestic purposes (per their socially defined rolls), limited resources resulted in conflict with male members of the society who prioritized water access for livestock production. Among women, constrained access led to conflict between community members with a different social standing, forcing poorer and more marginalized women to use less reliable and distant sources. It is critical to examine the gendered, contested values of water (e.g., meeting basic needs or use for cash-generating activities).

Rigorous data on the relationship of insecurity with violence are limited. A 2014 review of practice-based solutions[3] documented the various ways that violence against women can be considered and incorporated into water and sanitation programming. In a study of secondary data in urban Kenya,[4] women without access to adequate sanitation facilities had 38 per cent greater odds of experiencing non-intimate partner sexual violence in the past 12 months than women with a sanitation facility in their compound.

Participatory solutions and problems

Multiple SDG goals and targets focus on inclusive, participatory management of local resources and support for gender and social equality:

- Support and strengthen the participation of local communities in improving WASH management.
- Undertake reforms to give women equal rights to economic resources, as well as access to ownership and control over land and other forms of property, financial services, inheritance and natural resources, in accordance with national laws.
- By 2030, empower and promote the social, economic and political inclusion of all, irrespective of age, sex, disability, race, ethnicity, origin, religion or economic, or other status.
- Ensure responsive, inclusive, participatory and representative decision-making at all levels.

Studies have shown that women's involvement—beyond tokenism—in the improvement and management of local WASH services can improve the sustainability and equity of access, but not necessarily for all women, given intersectionality.[54,55,56] WASH interventions are frequently unsuccessful, in part because the participation of those on the margins in WASH—including women—is undertaken without supporting their participation as citizens of the state—citizens who have the right to make claims on the state. As governments are the ultimately duty bearer for providing WASH services, participation in WASH programs as full citizens is essential. Without this participation, feelings of ownership, desire to participate in planning and cost recovery are absent. Approaches that view the plight of those on the social margins as helplessness perpetuate notions of specific communities as 'problems', instead of seeing them as partners in the development of their effective participants in state-sponsored solutions.[57,58,59]

It is also important to move beyond deploying gender in an instrumental way—e.g., using women's participation (i.e., unpaid labor) – to increase the efficiency of projects. It remains critical to understand WASH insecurity as gendered norms, gendered responsibilities, and gendered differences in access to resources—everyday unequal gender relations that appear 'normal' but must be questioned. Arrangements between external donors and local implementing organizations can mean that NGOs are under pressure to hit targets for women's participation. In their efforts to meet these targets, implementing partners control women's participation in a top–down approach, since bottom–up approaches to women's participation introduce uncertainties that can slow or derail women's participation achievements and programs in general. The result is that women's participation is managed by NGOs, instead of women assuming ownership of projects.[60]

An additional challenge facing attainment of the SDGs through gendered participation is the ideological basis from which WASH programs often spring. Almost universally, neoliberal approaches to drinking WASH service provision (e.g., payment for services, decentralized governance, privatization of state resources) are rolled out, despite significant criticism of the ways in which neoliberal approaches may have severe impacts for the most socially marginal, including poor women.[61] A feminist approach championing local control of WASH is directly at odds with a neoliberal approach and logic, meaning that women's WASH needs are subsidiary to cost recovery.[62] Ideological foundations of programs deserve scrutiny for their potential positive and negative impacts on women and girls, with due consideration for additional cross-cutting inequalities that may exacerbate negative impacts.

Policy implications

The complexities and socially constructed nature of gender and the realities of WASH service provision make it difficult to develop programs and policies that respond to both WASH needs while remaining cognizant of gender. There exist a variety of tools available for addressing and understanding gendered WASH insecurity in policy and practice. However, these tools have rarely been employed consistently within the sector, and even fewer programs and intervention models—for example, the widely deployed Community Lead Total Sanitation and its variants—incorporate or demonstrate awareness of the gendered complexity we described above.

Understanding the ways in which programs target and address the needs of women is a critical and necessary component for policy development. The UN-Women Training Center offers a comprehensive Gender Equality Glossary[63]—from 'gender blind' to 'gender transformative'—through which gender sensitivity of WASH policies may be assessed. The WASH Poverty Index[29] has an application in identifying geographic and programming priorities related to multiple facets of WASH conditions, many of them directly related to the concept of gendered WASH insecurity.

In addition, measurements of water in/security would include an assessment of institutions and the power of subordinate groups to influence those institutions. It would also include a way to capture a process of moving in and out of water in/security, or as used in sanitation, moving up and down the sanitation ladder. Metrics of WASH in/security like access, quantity, and quality—measures codified and utilized within the international monitoring systems—are inherently about social difference and control of resources, between and within communities. The control of WASH infrastructure is usually men's domain; however, women often act to maintain social difference through their roles as the managers of domestic water (also used for sanitation and hygiene practices). These gendered relationships deserve attention when examining entrenched patterns of WASH insecurity.

Tools also exist for understanding how the WASH programs impact underlying gendered power relationships. A framework for exploring gender equality outcomes in WASH programs based on both individual and relationship changes at multiple scales (e.g., household or community level) has been proposed by Carrard and colleagues.[22] This dual consideration enables an assessment of situational advancements in women's quality of life due to WASH, and whether these improvements have resulted in changes in gender relations. As we have argued above, gender relationships are key to mitigating WASH insecurity, as too much focus on 'gender roles and responsibilities' and not on relationships of power can mean that gender equality goals have not been met, despite improvements in WASH security for individual women.

Scholars and practitioners, however, have cautioned against burdening gender and WASH programming with unreasonable expectations.[11,62] As stated by O'Reilly, 'Sanitation is not inherently gender transformative.' A policy focused on changing technology alone has not, and cannot, eliminate the practices that lead to poor health outcomes for women.[11] Nor is it able to overcome other social inequalities tied to WASH insecurity.[30] One promising approach to addressing gendered dimensions of WASH insecurity is the use of Strengths Based Approaches (SBA) to development planning. In response to traditional development approaches that focus on what communities are lacking, SBA focus on what communities have.[64] With regard to gender, SBA approaches incorporate what men and women value of existing gender roles and their vision for ideal (or improved) gender relationships. The focus moves away from 'women's problems' to engaging men and women in constructive ways. Furthermore, men are not blamed for gender inequality, but brought into the conversation about a shared vision, although both men and women in many communities may not prioritize a shift in gender relations compared to other concerns.[8] As such, outsider interventions in gender inequality that are attached to WASH programs face an uphill battle. What is more, if gender is determined to be a key indicator of the success of WASH programs, then it may be extremely difficult to engage communities on gender when WASH insecurity at the community scale is their priority.

Conclusions

An examination of gender illustrates the ways in which women's subordination to men is created and reproduced across a variety of structures and behaviors. Importantly, as gender is a social construction, it is capable of changing, and of being changed through sustained efforts directed at social norms and institutional shifts that promote gender equity. The subordination of women manifests itself in WASH insecurity—insecurity that has resulted in various gendered impacts on health and well-being. The relationships that have established the current unequal distribution of WASH services (at any scale) may be examined critically for the ways that women—generally and within specific groups—are differentially impacted by the provision or lack of WASH services and should be integrated centrally into WASH programs and policies. Gender analysis is key to successful and sustained WASH security for all.

Notes

1. Joshi, D., Buit, G., and González-Botero, D. (2015) Menstrual hygiene management: education and empowerment for girls? *Waterlines*, 34(1): 51–67.
2. Sahoo, K.C., Hulland. K.R., Caruso. B.A., et al. (2015) Sanitation-related psychosocial stress: a grounded theory study of women across the life-course in Odisha, India. *Social Science & Medicine*, 139: 80–9.
3. Sommer, M., Ferron, S., Cavill, S., and House, S. (2014) Violence, gender and WASH: spurring action on a complex, under-documented and sensitive topic. *Environment and Urbanization*, 0956247814564528.
4. Winter, S.C. and Barchi, F. (2015) Access to sanitation and violence against women: evidence from Demographic Health Survey (DHS) data in Kenya. *International Journal of Environmental Health Research*, 1–15.
5. World Health Organization, UNICEF (2015) Progress on sanitation and drinking water—2015 update and MDG assessment: World Health Organization.
6. Graham, J.P., Hirai, M., and Kim. S.-S. (2016) An analysis of water collection labor among women and children in 24 sub-Saharan African countries. *PLOS One*, 11(6): e0155981.
7. Sorenson, S.B., Morssink, C., and Campos, P.A. (2011) Safe access to safe water in low income countries: water fetching in current times. *Social Science & Medicine*, 72(9): 1522–6.
8. Willetts, J., Asker, S., Carrard, N., and Winterford, K. (2014) The practice of a strengths-based approach to community development in Solomon Islands. *Development Studies Research: An Open Access Journal*, 1(1): 354–67.
9. UN Water (2013) UN-Water Analytical Brief on Water Security and the Global Water Agenda.
10. Caruso, B.A., Clasen, T.F., Hadley, C., et al. (2017) Understanding and defining sanitation insecurity: women's gendered experiences of urination, defecation and menstruation in rural Odisha, India. *BMJ Global Health*, 2(4): e000414.
11. O'Reilly, K. (2016) From toilet insecurity to toilet security: creating safe sanitation for women and girls. *Wiley Interdisciplinary Reviews: Water*, 3(1): 19–24.
12. O'Reilly, K. (2010) Combining sanitation and women's participation in water supply: an example from Rajasthan. *Development in Practice*, 20(1): 45–56.
13. Wallace, T. and Coles, A. (2005) *Gender, water and development*: Oxford: Berg.
14. Tsai, A.C., Kakuhikire, B., Mushavi, R., et al. (2015) Population-based study of intra-household gender differences in water insecurity: reliability and validity of a survey instrument for use in rural Uganda. *Journal of Water and Health*, wh2015165.

15 Wutich, A. (2009) Intrahousehold disparities in women and men's experiences of water insecurity and emotional distress in urban Bolivia. *Medical Anthropology Quarterly*, 23(4): 436–54.
16 Desai, R., McFarlane, C., and Graham S. (2015) The politics of open defecation: informality, body, and infrastructure in Mumbai. *Antipode*, 47(1): 98–120.
17 Sen, A. (2001) *Development as Freedom*. New York: Alfred A. Knopf.
18 Dreibelbis, R., Greene, L.E., Freeman, M.C., Saboori, S., Chase, R.P., and Rheingans, R. (2013) Water, sanitation, and primary school attendance: a multi-level assessment of determinants of household-reported absence in Kenya. *International Journal of Educational Development*, 33(5): 457–65.
19 Birdthistle, I., Dickson, K., Freeman, M., and Javidi, L. (2011) What impact does the provision of separate toilets for girls at schools have on their primary and secondary school enrolment, attendance and completion? A systematic review of the evidence. Social Science Research Unit, Institute of Education, University of London, 6.
20 Garn, J.V., Greene, L.E., Dreibelbis, R., Saboori, S., Rheingans, R.D., Freeman, M.C. (2013) A cluster-randomized trial assessing the impact of school water, sanitation, and hygiene improvements on pupil enrollment and gender parity in enrollment. *Journal of Water, Sanitation, and Hygiene for Development: A Journal of the International Water Association*, 3(4).
21 Sommer, M., Kjellén, M., Pensulo, C. (2013) Girls' and women's unmet needs for menstrual hygiene management (MHM): the interactions between MHM and sanitation systems in low-income countries. *Journal of Water Sanitation and Hygiene for Development*, 3(3): 283–97.
22 Carrard, N., Crawford, J., Halcrow, G., Rowland, C., and Willetts, J. (2013) A framework for exploring gender equality outcomes from WASH programmes. *Waterlines*, 32(4): 315–33.
23 Larson, E., George, A., Morgan, R., and Poteat, T. (2016) 10 Best resources on . . . intersectionality with an emphasis on low- and middle-income countries. *Health Policy and Planning*, 31(8): 964–9.
24 Joshi, D. (2011) Caste, gender and the rhetoric of reform in India's drinking water sector. *Economic and Political Weekly*, 56–63.
25 Moser, C. (1993) *Gender Planning and Development: Theory, Practice and Training*. New York: Routledge.
26 O'Reilly, K. and Dhanju, R. (2012) Hybrid drinking water governance: community participation and ongoing neoliberal reforms in rural Rajasthan. *Geoforum*, 43: 623–33.
27 Birkenholtz, T. (2013) "On the network, off the map": developing intervillage and intragender differentiation in rural water supply. *Environment and Planning: A*, 31(2): 354–71.
28 O'Reilly, K. (2006) "Traditional" women, "modern" water: linking gender and commodification in Rajasthan, India. *Geoforum*, 37(6): 958–72.
29 Garriga, R.G. and Foguet, A.P. (2013) Unravelling the linkages between water, sanitation, hygiene and rural poverty: the WASH Poverty Index. *Water Resources Management*, 27(5): 1501–15.
30 McFarlane, C., Desai. R., and Graham, S. (2014) Informal urban sanitation: everyday life, poverty, and comparison. *Annals of the Association of American Geographers*, 104(5): 989–1011.
31 Phadke, S. (2011) Constructing sexuality in the new spaces of consumption: middle class women in Mumbai. Tata Institute of Social Sciences.
32 Kwiringira, J., Atekyereza, P., Niwagaba, C., and Guenther, I. (2014) Gender variations in access, choice to use and cleaning of shared latrines: experiences from Kampala Slums, Uganda. *BMC Public Health*, 14(1): 1–11.
33 Mehretu, A. and Mutambirwa, C. (1992) Time and energy costs of distance in rural life space of Zimbabwe: case study in the Chiduku communal area. *Social Science & Medicine*, 34(1): 17–24.

34 Geere, J.-A.L., Hunter, P.R., and Jagals, P. (2010) Domestic water carrying and its implications for health: a review and mixed methods pilot study in Limpopo Province, South Africa. *Environmental Health*, 9(1): 52.
35 Page, B. (1996) Taking the strain—the ergonomics of water carrying. *Waterlines*, 14(29–31).
36 Porter, G., Hampshire, K., Dunn, C., et al. (2013) Health impacts of pedestrian head-loading: a review of the evidence with particular reference to women and children in sub-Saharan Africa. *Social Science & Medicine*, 88: 90–7.
37 Groen, S. (2005) The course of recurrent urinary tract infections in non-pregnant women of childbearing age, the consequences for daily life and the ideas of the patients. *Nederlands tijdschrift voor geneeskunde*, 149(19): 1048–51.
38 Wasserheit, J.N., Harris, J.R, Chakraborty, J., Kay, B.A., and Mason, K.J. (1989) Reproductive tract infections in a family planning population in rural Bangladesh. *Studies in Family Planning*, 20(2): 69–80.
39 Sumpter, C. and Torondel. B. (2013) A systematic review of the health and social effects of menstrual hygiene management. *PLOS One*, 8(4): e62004.
40 Esteves Mill, J. and Cumming, O. (2016) Impact of water, sanitation, and hygiene on key health and social outcomes: review of evidence: SHARE research and UNICEF.
41 Benova, L., Cumming, O., and Campbell, O.M. (2014) Systematic review and meta-analysis: association between water and sanitation environment and maternal mortality. *Tropical Medicine & International Health*, 19(4): 368–87.
42 Gon, G., Monzon-Llamas, L., Benova, L., Willey, B., Campbell, O.M. (2014) The contribution of unimproved water and toilet facilities to pregnancy-related mortality in Afghanistan: analysis of the Afghan Mortality Survey. *Tropical Medicine & International Health*, 19(12): 1488–99.
43 Padhi, B.K., Baker, K.K., Dutta, A., et al. (2015) Risk of adverse pregnancy outcomes among women practicing poor sanitation in rural India: a population-based prospective cohort study. *PLOS Medicine*, 12(7): e1001851.
44 UNICEF and World Health Organization (2015) Water, sanitation and hygiene in health care facilities: status in low and middle income countries and way forward.
45 Henley, P., Lowthers, M., Koren, G., et al. (2014) Cultural and socio-economic conditions as factors contributing to chronic stress in sub-Saharan African communities. *Canadian Journal of Physiology and Pharmacology*, 92(9): 725–32.
46 Gruebner, O., Khan, M.H., Lautenbach, S., et al. (2011) A spatial epidemiological analysis of self-rated mental health in the slums of Dhaka. *International Journal of Health Geographics*, 10(1): 36.
47 Wutich, A. and Ragsdale, K. (2008) Water insecurity and emotional distress: coping with supply, access, and seasonal variability of water in a Bolivian squatter settlement. *Social Science & Medicine*, 67(12): 2116–25.
48 Stevenson, E., Ambelu, A., Caruso, B., Tesfaye, Y., and Freeman, M. (2016) Community water improvement, household water Insecurity, and women's psychological distress: an intervention and control study in Ethiopia. *PLOS One*, 11(4): e0153432.
49 Stevenson, E.G., Greene, L.E., Maes, K.C., et al. (2012) Water insecurity in 3 dimensions: an anthropological perspective on water and women's psychosocial distress in Ethiopia. *Social Science & Medicine*, 75(2): 392–400.
50 Hirve, S., Lele, P., Sundaram, N., et al. (2015) Psychosocial stress associated with sanitation practices: experiences of women in a rural community in India. *Journal of water sanitation and hygiene for development*, 5(1): 115–26.
51 Hulland, K.R., Chase, R.P, Caruso, B.A., et al. (2015) Sanitation, stress, and life stage: a systematic data collection study among women in Odisha, India. *PLOS One*, 10(11): e0141883.
52 Caruso, B.A., Clasen, T., Yount, K.M., Cooper, H.L., Hadley, C., and Haardörfer, R. (2017) Assessing women's negative sanitation experiences and concerns: the development of a novel sanitation insecurity measure. *International Journal of Environmental Research and Public Health*, 14(7): 755.

53 Yerian, S., Hennink, M., Greene, L.E., Kiptugen, D., Buri, J., Freeman, M.C. (2014) The role of women in water management and conflict resolution in Marsabit, Kenya. *Environmental Management*, 54(6): 1320–30.
54 Hirai, M., Graham, J.P., and Sandberg, J. (2016) Understanding women's decision making power and its link to improved household sanitation: the case of Kenya. *Journal of Water Sanitation and Hygiene for Development*, 6(1): 151–60.
55 Cleaver, F. and Hamada, K. (2010) 'Good' water governance and gender equity: a troubled relationship. *Gender & Development*, 18(1): 27–41.
56 Prokopy, L.S. (2004) Women's participation in rural water supply projects in India: is it moving beyond tokenism and does it matter? *Water Policy*, 6(2): 103–16.
57 Padawangi, R. (2010) Community-driven development as a driver of change: water supply and sanitation projects in rural Punjab, Pakistan. *Water Policy*, 12(1): 104–20.
58 Bapat, M. and Agarwal, I. (2003) Our needs, our priorities; women and men from the slums in Mumbai and Pune talk about their needs for water and sanitation. *Environment & Urbanization*, 15(2): 71–86.
59 McFarlane, C. (2014) The everywhere of sanitation: violence, oppression and the body. *Open India*, June 14.
60 Beck, E. (2016) Repopulating development: an agent-based approach to studying development interventions. *World Development*, 80: 19–32.
61 Harris, L. (2009) Gender and emergent water governance: comparative overview of neoliberalized natures and gender dimensions of privatization, devolution, and marketization. *Gender, Place, and Culture*, 16(4): 387–408.
62 Corbett, H. and Mehta, L. (2013) Ensuring women and girls' rights to water and sanitation post-2015. IDS Policy Briefing 38.
63 UN-Women Training Centre (2017) Gender Equality Glossary. Available at: https://trainingcentre.unwomen.org/mod/glossary/view.php?id=362017
64 Cunningham, G. (2008) Stimulating asset based development: lessons from five communities in Ethiopia. In G. Cunningham, A. Mathie and G. Cunningham (eds) *From Clients to Citizens: Communities Changing the Course of Their Own Development*. Practical Action Publishing, pp. 263–89.

6

THE ENVIRONMENTAL DIMENSIONS OF UNIVERSAL ACCESS TO SAFE WATER

Roger Calow, Alan MacDonald and Miriam Denis Le Sève

Introduction

The world faces a major challenge in adapting to a future where demand for water is accelerating, but supply remains essentially fixed and increasingly variable. Meeting this challenge is central to achieving the Sustainable Development Goals (SDGs) as water is a common denominator linking health, food security and nutrition, clean energy, sustainable cities, climate action, gender equality and the protection of ecosystems. The overall framing of the SDGs, and Goal 6 specifically, marked a desire to unite the hitherto polarised spheres of environment and development, recognising the need to both develop water resources for domestic and productive uses, and to protect them for current and future generations.[1,2]

Against this background, Goal 6 – Ensuring availability and sustainable management of water and sanitation for all by 2030 – represents a hard-won marriage of environmental and developmental objectives. But can we 'have our cake and eat it?' Unlike energy, where trade-offs between energy expansion and environmental degradation can be negated through renewables, extending access to water without a commensurate increase in 'efficiency', or reallocation from another use/user, may increase pressure on a finite resource. In a 2050 world of almost 10 billion people (based on the latest UN medium-variant projections estimating a 2050 global population of 9.8 billion)[3] requiring food, energy and drinking water, demands and trade-offs will increase.

In this chapter we attempt to answer this question in the context of a more ambitious SDG target for achieving 'universal and equitable access to safe and affordable drinking water for all' (Target 6.1). More specifically, we address two key questions:

1. What are the likely environmental constraints to meeting a much more ambitious SDG drinking water target, alongside other goals that have a bearing, or claim, on the use of water resources?

2   What steps can be taken to safeguard both existing gains in access to safe drinking water (water with no microbial or chemical contamination), and secure future entitlements as pressures on water resources increase?

We begin with a brief review of the status of global water resources. We then turn our attention to Africa, and sub-Saharan Africa (SSA) in particular, the SDG region with the greatest drinking water challenge (of the 159 million people still using unimproved surface water sources in 2015, 147 lived in rural areas, with over 50% living in SSA),[4] and highlight the growing importance of groundwater as a source of supply. We then review key pressures and trends affecting water resources and drinking water services. Finally, we set out three priorities for extending and protecting poor people's access to safe water.

Although the focus of this chapter is on drinking water, we note some of the obvious connections between extending and sustaining access to safe water and sanitation. Excreta that are not safely disposed of in situ, or transported and treated offsite, pose a threat to water resources, water sources and the wider environment, with well-rehearsed health risks.[5]

Water resource status

Interpreting the global arithmetic: what does the balance sheet look like?

Future water availability to meet the goal of universal access cannot be assumed. To date, however, sector strategies in most countries have operated in a silo, disconnected from wider concerns about water availability, water quality and competing demands from other sectors.[6]

In part, this reflects the fact that domestic supply accounts for only a minor component of total water withdrawals, albeit with significant local variation. However, it also reflects the dearth of data on resource conditions and patterns of use, particularly for groundwater. Globally, monitoring records have been in decline for decades, with under-investment leading to the collapse of established networks and a reduction in the quantity and quality of data available for decision-making.[7,8] The result is that

> few countries know about how much water is being used and for what purposes, the quantity and quality of water that is available and can be withdrawn without serious environmental consequences, and how much is being invested in water infrastructure.[9]

On the supply side, we know that the resource base is essentially fixed but highly variable over space and time. We also know that humans have little control over the majority – saltwater in oceans, freshwater in glaciers, and water in the atmosphere. Most public investment and attention has focused on rivers and lakes

– providing the images used for water messaging – and the dams, reservoirs and distribution systems that receive the bulk of investment.[8,10] However, groundwater accounts for roughly 96 per cent of freshwater, excluding that locked in glaciers.[11]

In view of its significance, we might expect to see groundwater figure prominently in the assessments of global, regional and national water availability. Surprisingly, it does not. As Taylor[12] and Gleeson et al.[13] note, most assessments of global resources have focused on surface water only, or have failed to differentiate between the fraction of freshwater that is well distributed as groundwater with long residence times (years to decades or longer), or which is relatively ephemeral and concentrated in rivers. Crucially, this means that while groundwater may implicitly be included in freshwater assessments through its contribution to surface water baseflow (e.g. see note 14), the significance of groundwater storage is overlooked. This is a major oversight; many countries designated 'water scarce' in terms of annual flows have significant groundwater reserves that could be developed for domestic use.[15,16]

On the demand side, of the water that is withdrawn for human use, roughly 69 per cent is used for irrigation, 19 per cent for industry (including energy generation) and 12 per cent to meet municipal (largely domestic) needs.[17] Global averages again conceal major variation, however. Throughout much of the low rainfall areas of the Middle East, North Africa and Central Asia, for example, irrigation accounts for 80–90 per cent of total withdrawals (ibid.).

Globally, groundwater abstraction accounts for around one-quarter of total water withdrawals.[8] An estimated 1.5–2.8 billion people rely on groundwater as their primary source of domestic water supply;[18,19] in Africa, probably 50 per cent or more of the population rely on groundwater for drinking.[20] Large-scale and intensive groundwater use has also provided the springboard for many Asian countries to transform from agrarian to industrialised economies, helping millions of poor farmers escape poverty.[10,21]

Although water abstractions or withdrawals are often equated with consumption, more than 60 per cent of withdrawals flow back to local hydrological systems via return flows to rivers and aquifers. The distinction between consumptive and non-consumptive use helps explain why efficiency 'savings' in major water-using sectors often fail to translate into downstream gains for others, since the 'saved' water was never lost in the first place.[22,23] That said, the impact of return flows is not always positive. Where these are of poor quality, the effect may be to degrade water resources and reduce the availability of safe drinking water.

Digging deeper: regional trends and hot spots

Looking a little deeper at the relationship between supply and demand, we know that water scarcity[24] in broad terms is increasing. Population growth is a major factor, but water withdrawals have been growing faster than population for decades; between 1990 and 2000, the world's population grew by a factor of four, but freshwater withdrawals grew by a factor of nine.[25,26] This trend is set to continue, driven by economic transformation in the fast-growing economies of Africa, Asia and South America.[27]

On the supply-side, while desalination will likely grow in importance in some richer (coastal) countries with secure energy supplies, low-cost desalination will not be scaled in the short to medium term. And while climate change is also influencing freshwater availability (see below), over the next 30 years or so global warming will have only a modest effect on future water scarcity relative to demand-side drivers.[14,28,29]

More than 1.6 billion people now live in river basins where water withdrawals are estimated to approach or exceed sustainable limits, typically defined in terms of abstraction rates at or above 70–80 per cent of total annual renewable (river) flows. Over the next two decades, the numbers of people living in such 'water-stressed' basins may double.[30] The symptoms of unsustainable use are most visible in river, lake and wetland systems – in the intermittent failure of the Yellow River in China to reach the sea, for example, or the shrinking of the Aral Sea in central Asia. However, the fastest growth in water withdrawals is for groundwater, with abstraction at least tripling over the last 50 years.[19]

Over the ten-year period 2003–2013, water levels reportedly fell in 21 of the world's 37 largest aquifer systems.[8,31] These include the North China Plain, the Guarani aquifer in South America, the western Sahara and Nubian sandstone aquifers of North Africa, aquifers of the Arabian peninsula and the Levant, and the aquifers of the Indus and Ganges basins, as well as those in central and southern India (ibid.). Nearly all underlie some of the world's most important agricultural regions, with over-pumping for irrigation the primary culprit. While the 'domestic' sector's contribution has been relatively minor, and confined largely to urban areas, the consequences extend to rural and urban drinking water in terms of both reduced availability and quality. In its latest 2016–2030 strategy, UNICEF argues that unsustainable water withdrawals associated with drying rivers, depleting aquifers and deteriorating ecosystems put safe and sustainable drinking water at risk.[32]

While the problem of aquifer-scale water level decline assumes prominence in the literature, the direct monitoring evidence remains thin. Over the last ten years or so, remote sensing techniques using GRACE[33] datasets have been used to indirectly assess the extent of groundwater 'overdraft'.[34] However, the dominance of publications using GRACE data has arguably skewed much of the recent debate on aquifer depletion. Gravity data from the GRACE mission are gathered at a coarse scale of 400 x 400 km. Trends in resource conditions at a finer scale can only be confidently resolved with careful interpretation of in situ measurements.[36] This is illustrated in northern India, where repeated GRACE studies have warned of widespread depletion across the Indo-Gangetic aquifer. However, a careful analysis of water well measurements in the region shows a much more nuanced situation, with rapid depletion limited to smaller zones, and larger areas with stable or rising groundwater levels.[36] Findings indicate that deteriorating water quality rather than widespread depletion is the principal concern for drinking water and sustainable agriculture (ibid.).

Water quality: a neglected but growing concern

The availability of water is also linked to water quality, as the pollution of water resources can compromise different types of use, especially for drinking. The symptoms of water quality degradation are evident in the data we have on waterborne disease, primarily from faecal contamination. Many of the poorest people rely on untreated water from either improved or unimproved sources, so maintaining the quality of the 'raw' resource remains vital. Local groundwater is often preferred as it is better protected from pathogens.[37] That said, with only 39 per cent of the global population using a safely managed sanitation service and nearly 900 million people still defecating in the open,[4] risks to water quality are a widespread concern.

Risks are amplified in fast-growing cities where the subsurface acts as both a source of water and a receptor of waste. A recent 12-city study by the World Bank found that two-thirds of households relied on on-site sanitation facilities and, on average, faecal waste from only 22 per cent of households using such systems was safely managed.[38] In flood-prone cities such as Dhaka, Bangladesh, almost all faecal sludge ends up in drains or the wider environment, with the result that floodwaters mix with raw sewage, water supplies become contaminated, and outbreaks of typhoid and cholera are commonplace.[39]

Less well documented are the risks associated with a range of organic and inorganic chemical agents from agricultural and industrial sources, and those associated with the salinisation of water bodies. Inorganic industrial pollutants linked to disease include arsenic, copper and lead; in agricultural areas, elevated concentrations of nitrate and high salinity can be a concern. Organic pollutants linked to health impacts include pesticides, chlordane, phenol, endocrine-disrupting compounds and pharmaceuticals.[40, 41]

The experience of rapidly urbanising and industrialising economies that have failed to address the pollution threat offer lessons on the costs – in economic and health terms – of inaction. China, for example, faces one of most serious water pollution crises ever documented, with official data indicating that over 30 per cent of monitored river reaches are unfit for potable use or human contact.[42] In the densely populated North China Plain, less than 30 per cent of shallow and deep groundwater sources are classified as drinkable (ibid.).

Two natural constituents in groundwater, arsenic and fluoride, are of particular concern to health. One of the most dramatic demonstrations of this is the arsenic crisis in South Asia (notably Bangladesh and West Bengal), where shallow boreholes constructed to supply safe drinking water turned out to have naturally high arsenic concentrations.[43,44] Arsenic in drinking water is responsible for significant morbidity and mortality through a wide range of health problems, including skin and other cancers, Type 2 diabetes, and higher rates of fetal loss and infant death. Natural fluoride in groundwater also poses a significant health risk in some areas, particularly in hard-rock formations. Around 200 million people may be at risk,[45] with over 60 million affected with dental, skeletal and non-skeletal fluorosis in India alone.[46]

The problem of under-utilisation and inequitable allocation

While the problem of unsustainable use is a growing problem in some locations, it would be wrong to assume that the world is 'running out of water' in any meaningful sense. As the authors of the Human Development Report pointed out in 2006, 'The scarcity at the heart of the global water crisis is rooted in power, poverty and inequality, not in physical availability'.[47] More recently, an analysis of resource conditions and trends across ten of the world's major river basins concluded that while there was scarcity in certain areas, inefficient and inequitable use – essentially a political challenge – was a more widespread concern than physical scarcity.[48] This brings us back to the question of who gets what – discussed further on pp. 101–113.

In addition, while much of the research on water resources management focuses on overuse and abuse, there are also areas of major untapped potential that could support multiple uses. While the untapped potential of groundwater in parts of Africa is well known[15] – see below – even in India, where groundwater resources are under greater pressure, there are significant opportunities. Recent work has focused on mapping out differences in water resource resilience, with the large Indo-Gangetic aquifer divided into a series of typologies, each responding in a different way to external pressures.[36] In eastern India, there is still vast groundwater potential that remains largely untapped.[10]

A regional perspective: Africa's hydrology and what it means for drinking water

Uneven distribution between areas and over time

Contrary to popular myth, Africa is not short of water, at least when assessed with conventional 'averaging' metrics. Water availability in sub-Saharan Africa (SSA) compares favourably with other regions of the world, having 9 per cent of the world's water resources and roughly 6,000 cubic metres of annual renewable water resources per capita. This compares with Asia's 4,000 cubic metres and the Middle East and North Africa's 1,500 cubic metres per capita.[49] However, the regional average conceals major problems with mobilising and managing water for lives and livelihoods, and the challenge of uneven distribution across and within countries.

Water in Africa is distributed very unevenly between areas and over time. Inter-annual rainfall variability, especially in eastern and southern Africa, is extremely high and will likely increase with climate change. These areas experience year-on-year variations exceeding 30 per cent around the mean – much greater than in the temperate climates of Europe and North America.[19] High seasonal variability compounds these effects, causing droughts and floods.[50] Runoff is also very low. This, coupled with high rainfall variability, helps explain the unpredictable and relatively low seasonal and annual flows in many African rivers, and the growing importance of groundwater as a source of supply – for agriculture, industry and domestic supply.

The advantages of groundwater for secure water supply

In rural areas with dispersed populations, the relative ubiquity and higher quality of groundwater compared with surface water alternatives means that groundwater development often provides the only cost-effective way of meeting demand. Moreover, the storage aquifers offer a hugely valuable buffering or stabilisation effect, allowing groundwater sources to provide more reliable dry season or drought supply and, in the Asian context especially, supplementary or full irrigation for millions of farmers.

Storage or, more specifically, large storage volume per unit of inflow, makes groundwater less sensitive to annual and inter-annual rainfall variation and longer term change.[15,16,51] Storage potential varies significantly between different hydrogeological environments, but the emerging evidence suggests that groundwater storage in SSA is substantial – perhaps 20 times the water stored in the continent's rivers and lakes (Figure 6.1).

As elsewhere, areas of the largest groundwater storage occur in sedimentary basins – both renewable and non-renewable. In North Africa, for example, water is stored in extensive 'fossil' aquifers (e.g. the Nubian sandstone aquifer beneath Chad and Egypt) that receive no contemporary recharge but offer significant development potential. Aquifers with less storage occur in the basement rocks that cover roughly 3 per cent of the continent.[37] However, research using environmental tracers has shown that even these lower potential aquifers can store water from several decades (20–70 years), with reserves that are effectively decoupled from more recent rainfall.[52]

Implications for meeting drinking water targets

What does this mean for the ambition of achieving universal access to safe drinking water in Africa? On the plus side, evidence suggests that modest yields of groundwater (0.1–0.3 litres per second) are widely available at accessible depths, sufficient to sustain hand-pump abstraction and with enough storage to sustain use through inter-annual variations in rainfall[15] – see Figure 6.2. Moreover, the long-term reductions in average rainfall and runoff projected for much of southern Africa by the end of the century will not necessarily translate into less groundwater; much will depend on the timing and intensity of rainfall events, and on changes in land use (see pp. 104–106).

In terms of risks and uncertainties, the implication is that higher levels of service associated with on-plot access may be difficult to achieve, either from networked sources, or from household-developed (self-supply) sources of the kind seen in south Asia. Although the safely managed indicator does not specify the quantity of safe water that should be supplied, the clear implication is that households with on-plot access will use significantly more water than those with only 'basic' or 'intermediate' levels of service.[5] Moreover, there is at least some evidence to suggest that easy-to-reach areas and groups of people have already been targeted, leaving more difficult environments still to be tackled. For example, MacDonald and Calow[37] discuss the 'gravitational pull' of easier hydrogeological areas where drilling success rates are higher and unit costs lower.

A key conclusion is that the higher yields (>5 litres per second) needed for more intensive groundwater use – for multi-village schemes, more intensive urban development or major agricultural abstraction – are unlikely beyond the major sedimentary terrain, or achievable only when accompanied by in-depth hydrogeological investigation. The availability and accessibility of groundwater over much of Africa is therefore favourable to rural development, but there are limits to the levels of service that can potentially be provided by groundwater alone.

Some African cities will continue to rely heavily on groundwater for utility supply because of their favourable hydrogeological location (e.g. Addis Ababa, Lusaka). Across a much wider range of environments, however, household self-supply within urban areas will likely grow in importance, not least because of rapid urban growth and the limited reach of piped networks. This poses a risk to health in circumstances where shallow aquifers are contaminated, and where households use this water for drinking (rather than as a source of supplementary, non-potable supply) in the absence of safe and affordable alternatives.[54]

Global pressures and trends: key issues affecting water resources and services

Although the discussion above points broadly to a world of increasing water stress, irrespective of the precise metrics employed, it tells us little about what is driving change, and the specific pressure points or constraints that might impact on SDG attainment. In this section, we therefore briefly review some of the main drivers of change and global projections, before looking specifically at two converging trends: climate change as a driver affecting the availability and quality of freshwater, and urbanisation as a driver affecting water demand and pollution loads.

Drivers of change: decadal projections

Population growth and economic transformation in developing countries will account for almost all growth in water demand.[26] While agricultural withdrawals will continue to dominate the overall share, manufacturing, energy and domestic demands will account for a larger proportion of the overall take in those countries experiencing rapid growth.

The drivers of demand are interconnected and complex to model. The need to raise agricultural output, for example, will substantially increase demand for the water needed to grow crops, and for the water needed to generate the energy required to produce and process food. And rising living standards will increase domestic demand, energy-water demand, and further shift diets from predominantly starch-based to more water-intensive meat and dairy products.

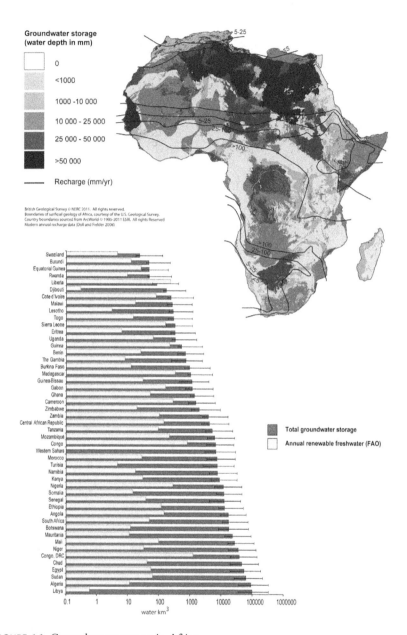

FIGURE 6.1 Groundwater storage in Africa

Note: Groundwater storage based on effective porosity and saturated aquifer thickness (see note 15). The map of Africa (left) shows groundwater storage expressed as water depth in millimetres with modern annual recharge (contour lines) for comparison. The graph on the right compares groundwater storage volume for each country with annual renewable freshwater availability (FAO data for 2005).

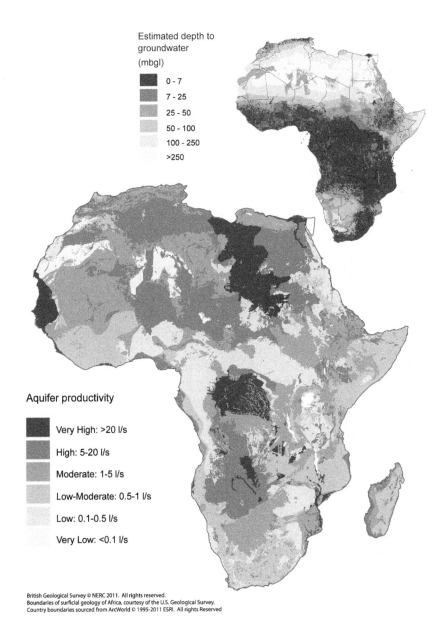

FIGURE 6.2 Aquifer productivity map of Africa[15]

Note: aquifer productivity based on likely interquartile range for boreholes drilled and sited using appropriate techniques and expertise. The inset map shows an approximate depth to groundwater.[53]

On the supply-side, we know that climate change will alter the timing, amount and intensity of rainfall, while changes in evaporative demand resulting from the combined effects of shifts in temperature, radiation, humidity and wind speed will modify surface and groundwater availability. Specific outcomes are difficult to predict, particularly for rainfall and its secondary impacts on runoff and recharge (see below) but, in broad terms, water availability is expected to increase at high latitudes and in some wet tropical areas, and decrease over some dry regions at mid-latitudes and in the dry tropics. At the same time, overall variability is expected to increase, with more droughts and floods.[28,55]

Bringing the demand and supply-side together, what can we deduce about the combined effects of these major global changes, and what does this begin to tell us about the opportunities and constraints affecting the 'domestic' sector? Drawing on recent high- resolution modelling by the Water Resources Institute (WRI) to 2040[28] and on assessments carried out by the Intergovernmental Panel on Climate Change (IPCC),[29] we highlight the following:

- Rapid increases in water stress[56] across many regions, including North and Southern Africa, the Middle East, northern China, western Asia and Chile, as well as the (much richer) North American West, eastern Australia and Mediterranean.
- The relative dominance of changes in demand over changes in supply, with projected increases in irrigation withdrawals (and consumptive use) dominating the demand side.
- The large numbers of people moving across categories of water stress because of climate change. Demand-side pressures tend to dominate the picture over the next three decades. Beyond that point, climate change begins to dominate other factors because global population and economic growth stabilise in the 2050s.
- Significant relative increases in demand in developing countries (e.g. in central Africa) where baseline water demand is very low. Indeed, many poorer countries remain at low stress levels for the next few decades despite a rapid acceleration in water use, highlighting significant scope for resource mobilisation.

As with all such projections, major uncertainties are associated with both the climate models used to derive water availability and the assumptions linking demographic and economic change with water demand. The role of groundwater storage is also overlooked (see p. 100). Nonetheless, findings are useful in highlighting hotspots of water stress where competition for water is likely to be intense, and where the entitlements of domestic users – urban and rural – will need to be defended against other claims (see below).

Climate variability and change: impacts on water resources and services

The impacts of climate change on water-dependent services will be felt through a complex mix of slow onset trends (e.g. warming), changes in variability (daily to seasonal and decadal), fluctuations in mean conditions (places may become wetter or drier), and changes in the frequency and intensity of extreme events (droughts and floods). However, we also know that climate models typically fail to show how key elements of the hydrological cycle will evolve at the spatial and temporal scales needed for planning.[55] This is partly because of the difficulties of downscaling global and regional models to the local level, but also about attribution. Untangling the climate signal from what the IPCC term 'confounding' factors (e.g. land-use change, water withdrawals) is hampered by the shortage of observational data in developing countries needed to establish baselines and project impacts. The climate-observing system for Africa, in particular, is in a worse state than in any other continent and is deteriorating.[57]

So what can we say about likely impacts on water availability, quality and services? Table 6.1 provides a summary of water-related hazards and risks to drinking water services, both urban and rural.

Where rainfall decreases, we might expect to see a reduction in renewable freshwater resources and vice versa. Reductions in water availability pose a particular risk to more basic water supply systems unable to draw on significant storage (e.g. rooftop rainwater harvesting, springs, shallow dug wells). Increases in water availability may be broadly positive, though the risk of microbial contamination will likely increase if groundwater levels rise – for example, by reducing the distance (and hence travel time for pathogens) between the base of pit latrines and the water table.

Impacts are by no means certain, however, and much will depend on local conditions, and specifically the relationship between evapotranspiration, soil moisture and land-use change. Moreover, climate model projections based on average rainfall years do not adequately capture the interannual and interdecadal variability that can positively or negatively affect water resources and water services. The West African Sahel provides a case in point. Here, groundwater recharge and storage increased in the latter part of the 20th century despite a multidecadal drought. The reason was a shift from deep-rooted savannah to crop land that increased surface runoff and aquifer recharge.[16]

In terms of variability, climate models are broadly consistent in projecting increases in the proportion of total rainfall that falls in heavy events, increasing flood hazards.[28,58] As exposure to floods goes up – a clear trend over the last 50 years – socioeconomic losses will increase, especially in smaller catchments with high population densities.[28] Flood damage already accounts for around one-third of the economic losses inflicted by natural hazards worldwide (ibid.), and even localised flooding can damage water supply infrastructure and expose water sources and distribution systems to serious contamination.

The flip side is an increase in the frequency and/or duration of droughts, at least in those areas where rainfall is already low, such as southern Africa.[28] Droughts remain Africa's most significant natural hazard, though over the last 50 years there is no evidence that the frequency of surface and groundwater droughts has changed.[50]

The combination of changes in streamflow and rising temperatures is also expected to have broadly negative impacts on freshwater ecosystems and water quality.[28] Higher water temperatures encourage algal blooms and increase risks from cyanotoxins and natural organic matter in water sources. Increased runoff results in greater loads of fertilisers, animal wastes and particulates; in semi-arid areas, heavy rainfall events may contribute around half of total soil erosion (ibid.). Low flows, meanwhile, reduce the capacity of rivers to dilute, attenuate, and remove pollution and sediment. Reductions in raw water quality pose risks to drinking water quality, even with conventional treatment, though the extent and nature of changes remain uncertain, and very dependent on rainfall seasonality, land cover and soil management practices (ibid.).

While the longer term impacts of climate change on WASH are a clear concern, a preoccupation with projections can divert attention away from existing threats, particularly in areas with high seasonal and interannual variability. Indeed, there is little value scrutinising climate projections to the end of the century for rural WASH programmes that prioritise household or community-based system with a design life of 10–20 years.[60] For major investments in storm drains, sewerage or other long-term infrastructure, the situation is clearly different.

The impact of 'normal' seasonality on the reliability and level of services that people receive is frequently overlooked, and not captured in the most often quoted binary (functional/non-functional) data on performance. Yet discontinuity of supply can lead to households spending more time and covering additional distances to reach an alternative source, if available. And since rural users in particular may collect water on a daily basis, even short duration failures impose hardship. If unimproved sources are used in the interim, even for short periods, many of the benefits associated with continuous access to safe water are jeopardised.[41]

In Sierra Leone, up to 40 per cent of water points either fail completely towards the end of the dry season, or provide insufficient water for basic needs.[61] In Ethiopia, detailed water audits have shown how even in 'covered' communities, households can struggle to meet water requirements recommended for emergency situations, particularly in the dry season.[62] Increasing (seasonal) collection times affected the poorest households most severely, as they had the least labour to release, the fewest assets to collect and store water, and the least cash to pay for it. They were also more likely to forego income-generating activities in favour of water collection, and more likely to see the condition of their livestock deteriorate because of poor water access (ibid.). The recent El Niño-triggered drought of 2015–16 has also raised questions about the resilience of existing water services. In Ethiopia alone, around nine million people were affected by acute water shortages.[63]

Changes in water demand and load: the urbanisation challenge

Globally, 54 per cent of the population now reside in urban settlements. By 2050, 66 per cent of the world's population is projected to be urban, with nearly 90 per

TABLE 6.1 Water-related climate hazards and impacts on drinking water services

Climate trend	Hydrological changes	Impacts on domestic supply
Declining rainfall	Reductions in renewable surface and groundwater resources, though locally specific.	Threats to water supply, especially rainwater storage, ephemeral streams, shallow wells. Reduced raw water quality because of less dilution – health threats, higher treatment costs. Increased demand for surface water storage and groundwater to bridge surface water deficits. Growing competition between domestic and others uses, especially at the urban-rural interface.
Increasing rainfall	Increases in renewable surface and groundwater resources, though locally specific.	Potentially more water available for domestic use, though short-term shortages due to more variable streamflow still possible. Rising groundwater levels may flood onsite sanitation and drainage – health risks – e.g. contamination of water supply.
Variability of rainfall – frequency, intensity, duration	Increases in flood and drought hazards.	Floods cause damage to infrastructure, disrupt supply and treatment, and reduce raw water quality (sediment, nutrient, pollution loads). Droughts threaten less resilient sources (e.g. ponds, shallow wells, rainwater storage). Droughts reduce dilution of pollutants – health risks, higher treatment costs.
Higher temperatures	Higher rates of evapotranspiration affect water balance. Rise in temperature of rivers and lakes.	More algal blooms and increased risks from cyanotoxins and natural organic matter in water sources – threat to water quality even with conventional treatment. Higher ambient temperature increases domestic water demand.
Rising sea levels	Intrusion of brackish or salty water into coastal aquifers. Coastal surges and inundation of sea water.	Groundwater supply in coastal areas negatively affected. Coastal storms damage and/or contaminate water supply systems and treatment works.

Source: notes 5, 59, 60.

cent of the increase concentrated in Africa and Asia.[62] Moreover, most of the growth will occur not in the world's mega-cities, but in smaller towns and cities of less than one million people, where close to half of the world's urban dwellers reside (ibid.).

Some of the key environmental risks associated with rapid urban growth are illustrated in Figure 6.3, showing the evolution of water supply, and wastewater and excreta disposal in a growing settlement underlain by shallow groundwater. As the settlement expands, water supplies originally obtained from shallow aquifers may no longer be sufficient, either because the available resource is too limited or because of pollution. Public supply may then be tapped from deeper aquifers or, more often, drawn from aquifers or surface water sources in the city's hinterland at increasing distance and cost. However, such sources usually have a competing prior use – typically, agricultural.

Further city expansion may then lead to encroachment on peri-urban well fields, leading to a new wave of pollution risk.[54,65] While public utilities may again seek to develop new, more costly supplies or invest in treatment, households may continue to self-supply increasingly polluted water from within the city. Widespread groundwater contamination by petroleum products, chlorinated hydrocarbons and other synthetic compounds is common; contamination by pathogenic bacteria and viruses may be more localised because of die-off, but can be similarly widespread where on-site excreta disposal via septic tanks, cesspits and pit latrines occurs in high-density settlements. Many of the people using onsite sanitation in urban areas have neither connections to sewerage networks, or access to systems of faecal sludge management, particularly those that include treatment of waste before disposal.[5]

The scale and pace of urban growth in Asia and Africa is such that the development of infrastructure lags behind city expansion. Smaller towns are particularly disadvantaged. While large utilities have the potential to draw on significant human and financial capital to address vulnerabilities and invest in infrastructure, fast-growing towns typically do not. They are effectively trapped in a transition zone where (rural-style) community management is stretched beyond its limits and larger, professionalised utilities have yet to emerge.[66]

In India, many better-off urban households self-supply groundwater as a coping response for dealing with poor municipal supply.[67,68] Poorer households, on the other hand, have no option but to rely on unregulated private vendors or, if more fortunate, standpipes. Meanwhile, the water (and pollution) footprint of cities extends out into rural areas, bringing rural and urban users and sometimes adjacent states into conflict.[69,70]

In China, city planners in the water-scarce north are experimenting with trading systems designed to reallocate agricultural water along the Yellow River to thirsty towns and cities downstream.[71] As in India, environmental stresses have taken on a political hue. Widespread water degradation has fuelled civil unrest, threatening the legitimacy of the party-state.[72]

Universal access to safe water **109**

The resource challenges affecting growing towns in SSA are less well documented. However, recent research in Ethiopia[73] shows how local and basin-scale conflicts can arise in a relatively water-abundant country. In the Awash Valley, for example, the claims of urban, industrial, energy and irrigation users are increasingly interdependent. The combined annual diversions for upstream sugar cane irrigation account for over 75 per cent of water releases from the Koka Dam and schemes are expanding. At the same time, rapidly growing downstream towns

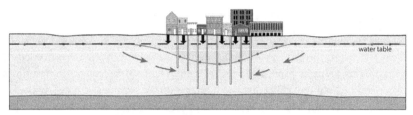

(a)
Town becomes a city
- water table lowered beneath city, wells deepened
- waste water discharged to ground
- shallow groundwater in city centre becomes polluted
- subsidence can occur if aquifer is unconsolidated and interbedded
- expansion of pluvial drainage to ground and local watercourses

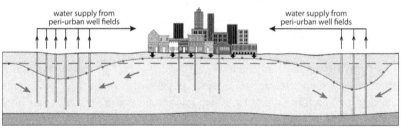

(b)
City expands
- aquifer beneath city largely abandoned because of contamination
- water table begins to rise beneath city due to cessation of pumping and high urban recharge
- significant water table decline in city periphery due to heavy abstraction from well fields
- incipient contamination of urban well fields by groundwater recharged beneath city centre

(c)
City expands further
- well fields unable to cope with increased demand and threatened by outward growth of city
- expensive water imports from distant sources or conjunctive use schemes necessary
- water table rises beneath city nucleus — problems of flooding, waste-water disposal etc.
- scope reduced for (low cost) pluvial drainage to ground

FIGURE 6.3 Evolution of water supply and wastewater disposal in a growing settlement
Source: (note 65) BGS © NERC (2003).

are struggling for water, with utilities unable to deliver more than a few hours of service per day (ibid.).

Adjustment pressures in each case are proving difficult to resolve, although China is making progress through its 'command and control' bureaucracy.[71,72] Shared concerns over climate change may present an opportunity for different sector actors, including those involved in WASH, to make the case for investment in water resources management.

Managing for sustainability and equity: three priorities for the new development era

In this concluding section, we turn our attention to some of the steps needed to safeguard both existing gains and future entitlements as pressures on resources accelerate. A key contention is that the higher levels of service associated with on-plot access will not be achieved with a business-as-usual approach to delivery that treats WASH as a distinct 'sector', and assumes that quantity and quality needs can be met in isolation from other demands. Neither can many hard-to-reach areas and groups, unserved or poorly served at present, be reached without much better information on resources than most countries currently have.

Priority 1: Invest in water resource assessment and monitoring. In most parts of the world, water resources remain poorly understood, and monitoring systems are unable to track the impacts of economic, demographic and climate change.

Global metrics of the kind reviewed in this chapter can be a useful starting point for talking about pressures and trends. In particular, they can draw attention to the range of pressures affecting water availability (less so quality), and likely 'hot spots' where adjustment pressures between users and uses may be particularly acute. In the African context, they have also allowed us to highlight the development potential of groundwater – at least up to a point.

But what exactly is that 'point'? When it comes to local planning and investment decisions, global or national metrics are no substitute for more granular basin and/or aquifer scale information on development potential, sustainability and risks. And although much can be done on the back of individual water supply programmes and projects to collect data, incentives for data collection, synthesis and use are often lacking. Yet we know that more systematic assessment and monitoring of resources is needed to guide decisions. For example, we still do not know enough about where groundwater resources could provide at-house levels of supply, or how multi-village schemes could be developed from higher yielding sources supporting discrete areas of a network, with the potential to supply others to avoid network-critical failures. Nor do we know enough about how intensive water development to support commercial agriculture or the growth of towns might impact smaller (rural) domestic users, or the ecosystem services that poorer households, in particular, are dependent on.

We also note that there is at least some evidence to suggest that geographical disparities in access to water services can reflect 'easier' and more 'difficult' environments, at least in more complex hydrogeological and meteorological contexts. In short, easier environments are cherry-picked in an effort to bump up results and demonstrate value for money, a risk that may increase with results-based financing modalities. Difficult areas are avoided because of high costs and low drilling success rates, irrespective of demand. Here again, even modest investment in resource assessment can pay dividends in terms of higher drilling success rates and in locating higher yielding, more resilient sources.

Priority 2: Recognise that degrading water quality poses at least as great a risk to drinking water as over-exploitation. In rapidly growing and transforming economies, the nature of pollution risk changes; resources can easily be 'written off' if industrial discharges, in particular, are not controlled.

While the global conversation on water tends to fixate on scarcity and over-exploitation, the pollution of drinking water sources – or potential sources of drinking water – may be a more significant problem. While data are scarce, we know that water resources can become too contaminated to safely use or economically treat long before abstraction even begins, or the symptoms of pollution are first detected. Even in the intensively developed Indo-Gangetic basic, new research points to the much more widespread threat of salinisation (from irrigation returns) and urban–industrial pollution to current and future users, including domestic.

For rivers, streams and lakes, water quality degradation often occurs through direct discharge of waste to the river. This can take the form of sewerage or industrial effluent. These point sources of pollution are relatively easy to identify, but require regulation and enforcement measures to control, and sufficient environmental flows to dilute and disperse remaining contaminants. Diffuse pollution (which also impacts groundwater) can be more difficult to identify and manage, and requires a catchment-wide approach to mitigate. Intensive agriculture in particular can present risks, releasing nutrients and sediment to water resources that can lead to a rapid decline in ecological status. Controlling the use of fertilisers and pesticides, in combination with 'buffer strips' in the landscape that intercept sediments and contaminants, can be effective – with monitoring and enforcement. In Europe, the introduction of point source and diffuse control measures has led to improvements in the quality and status of many highly degraded rivers.

Groundwater is at risk of pollution if the natural capacity of the soil, unsaturated zone, or confining layers of an aquifer are insufficient to contain and attenuate contaminant loads. Since the movement of water in the ground is generally slow, pollution of groundwater may not be detectable for decades, but may remain a problem for decades after the polluting activity has stopped.[74] How seriously groundwater is polluted depends on the nature of the aquifer and overlying unsaturated zone and soil – hence, control measures typically rely on land-use planning linked to vulnerability mapping, together with systematic programmes for identifying polluting activities and monitoring water sources.

Looking ahead, we know that on-site sanitation will remain the norm in most developing countries. The adoption of risk-based approaches (e.g. water safety plans) to the siting of drinking water sources and latrines can be effective in preventing microbial contamination of water supplies, as can relatively simple adaptations to latrine and sanitation design. As economies and populations grow, however, new threats will emerge linked to agricultural intensification, industrialisation and urbanisation. One of the biggest challenges facing planners will likely be service delivery and pollution control in rapidly expanding 'rural' towns. Effective faecal sludge management will grow in importance alongside the control of industrial activities, to avoid the massive costs of resource degradation now faced in large parts of China and India.

Priority 3: Engage in the wider conversation about water resources management – who gets what as pressures on resources increase and climate change accelerates. Weak governance will exacerbate existing inequalities and undermine progress towards universal access.

The SDGs set a high bar of 'safely managed' water and sanitation services. For drinking water, the clear implication is that households with on-plot access will use significantly more water than those with only 'basic' or 'intermediate' access. This is obviously good for health and livelihoods – if water is available on a sustainable basis and if the claims of poorer domestic users can be defended against other interests.

Our review of global trends has highlighted hot spots, where basins are (or may be) over-exploited or approaching closure, but also major development opportunities. For water-stressed areas, adjustment pressures within and between sectors may be intense, and while climate change may exacerbate problems, the main drivers of change will likely be socioeconomic. Even in these areas, it would be wrong to assume that scarcity is simply a 'natural' phenomenon: indicators of water stress offer little insight into why, for example, people living in the slums of Mumbai face shortages of clean water while their neighbours in high-income suburbs irrigate their lawns.

Our main argument here, however, is about avoiding some of the more damaging inequalities in access to water that can emerge through a combination of growing demand and weak governance. Take sub-Saharan Africa. Here, the mobilisation of water for power, food production, industry and domestic use is a clear priority. But building the hard infrastructure of storage and conveyance needs to be matched with investment in the 'soft plumbing' of rights, rules and incentives. Without it, there is a risk that water will be captured by powerful interests – in commercial agriculture or industry, for example. The result may be good for headline GDP, but not for the livelihoods of poorer people with a stake but no voice in water allocation. For mainly fast-growing economies, progression up the water service ladder and the ability to sustain hard-won gains will increasingly depend on an ability to manage water resources for a range of competing interests, with domestic use a clear priority.

Building robust institutions and frameworks for managing water remains a long-term goal in most countries, not always helped by a preoccupation with idealised forms of 'integrated' management. So what needs to change? Perhaps the main priority is for those working on WASH to play a much more active role in wider policy and planning debates around water allocation and protection – in short, it is about how and for whom water resources are developed and managed, beyond wistful visions of 'water security for all'. There will be few quick wins. Investment in institution building – registration systems, water accounting, rights, allocation licensing, pollution control – does not generate the kind of short-term, measurable results that many now favour, but will be essential in realising the goal of universal access.

Notes

1 Melamed. C., Scott, A. and Mitchell, T. (2012) Separated at birth, reunited in Rio? A roadmap to bring environment and development back together. ODI Background Note, May.
2 Mason, N. and Calow, R. (2012) Water security: from abstract concept to meaningful metrics – an initial overview of options. ODI Working Paper 357. London: Overseas Development Institute.
3 UNDESA (2017) World population prospects: The 2017 revision, key findings and advance tables. Working Paper No. ESA/P/WP/248. Department of Economic and Social Affairs, Population Division. New York: United Nations.
4 WHO/UNICEF (2017) Progress on drinking water, sanitation and hygiene. Update and SDG baselines. Geneva: World Health Organization and the United Nations Children's Fund (UNICEF).
5 Howard G., Calow, R.C., MacDonald, A.M., Bartram, J. (2016) Climate change and water and sanitation: likely impacts and emerging trends for action. *Annual Review of Environment and Resources, 41*: 253–276.
6 Calow, R. and Mason, N. (2014) The real water crisis: inequality in a fast changing world. London: Overseas Development Institute.
7 Robins, N.S., Davies, J., Farr, J.L. and Calow, R.C. (2006) The changing role of hydrogeology in semi-arid southern and eastern Africa. *Hydrogeology Journal, 14*: 1483–1492.
8 Smith. M., Cross, K., Paden, M. and Laban, P. (eds) (2016) Spring – Managing groundwater sustainably. Gland, Switzerland: IUCN.
9 World Water Assessment Programme (WWAP) (2009) The United Nations World Water Development Report 3: Water in a changing world. Paris: UNESCO.
10 Giordano, M. (2009) Global groundwater? Issues and solutions. *Annual Review of Environment and Resources. 34*: 153–178.
11 Gleick, P.H. (ed.) (1993) *Water in Crisis: A Guide to the World's Fresh Water Resources*. New York: Oxford University Press.
12 Taylor, R. (2009) Rethinking water scarcity: the role of storage. *EoS, 90*: 237–238.
13 Gleeson, T., Wada, Y., Biekens, M.F.P. and van Beek, L.P.H. (2012) Water balance of global aquifers revealed by groundwater footprint. *Nature, 488*: 197–200.
14 Vorosmarty, C.J., McIntyre, P.B., Gessner, M.O. et al. (2010) Global threats to human water security and river biodiversity. *Nature, 467*: 555–561.
15 MacDonald, A.M., Bonsor, H.C., Ó Dochartaigh, B.E. and Taylor, R.G. (2012) Quantitative maps of groundwater resources in Africa. *Environmental Research Letters, 7*: 024009.
16 Taylor, R., Scanlon, B., Doll, P. et al. (2013) Ground water and climate change. *Nature Climate Change. 3*: 322–329.
17 FAO. FAO-AQUASTAT database. Last updated November 2016 (accessed August 2017).
18 Döll, P. et al. (2012) Impact of water withdrawals from groundwater and surface water on continental water storage variations. *Journal of Geodynamics, 59–60*: 143–156.

19 Margat, J. and van der Gun, J. (2013) *Groundwater Around the World: A Geographic Synopsis*. London: CRC Press.
20 Carter, R.C. and Parker, A. (2009) Climate change, population trends and groundwater in Africa. *Hydrological Sciences*, 54: 676–689.
21 Shah, T., Burke, J., Villholth, K. et al. (2007) Groundwater: a global assessment of scale and significance. In D. Molden (ed.) *Water for Food, Water for Life: A Comprehensive Assessment of Water Management in Agriculture*. London: Earthscan.
22 Molden, D. (ed.) (2007) *Water for Food, Water for Life: A Comprehensive Assessment of Water Management in Agriculture*. London: Earthscan.
23 Perry, C. (2007) Efficient irrigation: inefficient communication: flawed recommendations. *Irrigation and Drainage*, 56: 367–378.
24 Defined broadly here to indicate a difference between water availability and demand. Some authors have used thresholds of available water per person per year to define different categories or levels of water scarcity; others have defined 'economic' water scarcity to describe situations where water is abundant but access is constained by lack of infrastructure, finance or other factors. For a detailed review of water metrics, see Mason and Catlow (note 2).
25 Waughray, D. (ed.) (2013) Water security: the water–food–energy–climate nexus. The World Economic Forum Water Initiative. Washington: Island Press.
26 World Water Assessment Programme (WWAP) (2015) The United Nations World Water Development Report: Water for a sustainable world. Paris: UNESCO.
27 ERD (2012) Confronting scarcity: managing water, energy and land for inclusive and sustainable growth. European Report on Development 2011/12. Brussels: European Union.
28 Luck, M. and Gassert, F. (2015) Aqueduct water stress projections: decadal projections of water supply and demand using CMIP5 GCMs. Technical note. Washington, DC: World Resources Institute.
29 Cisneros, J., Oki, T., Arnell, N. et al. (2014) Freshwater resources. In *Climate Change 2014: Impacts, Adaptation and Vulnerability. Part A: Global and Sectoral Aspects. Contribution of Working Group 11 to the Fifth Assessment Report of the Intergovernmental Panel on Climate Change*. IPPC. Cambridge: Cambridge University Press.
30 World Bank (2015) A water secure world for all. Water for development: responding to the challenges. Washington, DC: World Bank.
31 Gravity Recovery and Climate Experiment (GRACE) data are collected by two NASA satellites that have flown in low-earth orbit since 2012.
32 Famiglietti, J.S. (2014) The global groundwater crisis. *Nature Climate Change*, 4: 945–948.
33 UNICEF Strategy for Water, Sanitation and Hygiene, 2016–2030 (2016) UNICEF, New York, August.
34 Richey, A.S., Thomas, B.F., Lo, M.H. et al. Quantifying renewable groundwater stress with GRACE (2015) *Water Resources Research*, 51: 1–22.
35 Alley, W.M. and Konikow, L. (2015) Bringing GRACE down to earth: ground water, 53: 826–829.
36 MacDonald, A.M., Bonsor, H.C., Ahmed, K.M. et al. (2016) Groundwater quality and depletion in the Indo-Gangetic basic mapped from in situ observations. *Nature Geoscience*, 9: 762–766.
37 MacDonald, A.M. and Calow, R.C. (2010) Developing groundwater for secure rural water supplies in Africa. *Desalination*. 248: 546–556.
38 World Bank (2014) The missing link in sanitation service delivery: a review of faecal sludge management in 12 cities. Washington, DC: World Bank.
39 Ross, I., Scott, R. and Josep, R. (2016) Faecal sludge management: diagnostics for service delivery in urban areas. A case study in Dhaka, Bangladesh. World Bank Water and Sanitation Programme. Washington, DC: World Bank.
40 Foster, S.S.D. and Chilton, P.J. (2003) Groundwater: the processes and global significance of aquifer degradation. Philosophical Transactions of the Royal Society B, 358: 1957–1972.

41 Hunter, P., Zmirou-Navier, D. and Hartemann, P. (2009) Estimating the impact on health of poor reliability of drinking water interventions in developing countries. *Science of the Total Environment*, 407: 2621–2624.
42 Han, D., Currell, M.J. and Cao, G. (2016) Deep challenges for China's water on pollution. *Environmental Pollution*, 218: 1222–1233.
43 Heikens, A. (2006) Arsenic contamination of irrigation water, soils and crops in Bangladesh: risk implication for sustainable agriculture and food safety in Asia. Bangkok: FAO Regional Office, Asia-Pacific.
44 Argos, M., Kalra, T., Rathouz, P.J. et al. (2010) Arsenic exposure from drinking water, and all-cause and chronic-disease mortalities in Bangladesh (HEALS): a prospective cohort study. *The Lancet*. 376: 252–258.
45 Edmunds, W.M. and Smedley, P.L. (2005) Fluoride in natural waters. In O. Selinus (ed.) *Essentials of Medical Geology*. London: Elsevier Academic Press, pp. 301–329.
46 Susheela, A.K. (1999) Fluorosis management programme in India. *Current Science*, 77: 1250–1256.
47 UNDP (2006) Human Development Report 2006: Beyond scarcity: power, poverty and the global water crisis. New York: United Nations Development Programme.
48 Cook, S., Fisher, M., Tiemann, T. and Vidal, A. (2011) Water, food and poverty: global and basin scale analysis. *Water International*, 36: 1–16.
49 Foster, V. and Briceno-Garmendia, C. (2010) Africa's infrastructure: a time for transformation. Washington, D.C. Agence Française de Development and World Bank.
50 Niang, I., Ruppel, O.C. and Abdrabo, M.A. (2014) Africa. In *Intergovernmental Panel on Climate Change. Climate Change 2014 – Impacts, Adaptation and Vulnerability: Regional Aspects*. Cambridge: Cambridge University Press.
51 Calow, R., MacDonald, A., Nicol, A. and Robins, N. (2010) Ground water security and drought in Africa: linking availability, access and demand. *Ground Water*, 48: 246–256.
52 Lapworth, D.J., MacDonald, A.M., Tijani, M.N. et al. (2013) Residence times of shallow groundwater in West Africa: implications for hydrogeology and resilience to future changes in climate. *Hydrogeology Journal*, 21: 673–686.
53 Bonsor, H.C. and MacDonald, A.M. (2011) An initial estimate of depth to groundwater across Africa. British Geological Survey Open Report OR/11/067.
54 Foster, S.S.D. (2017) Urban groundwater dependency in tropical Africa: a scoping study of pro-poor implications. UPGro Working Paper. Swindon: UPGro.
55 Conway, D. (2013) Water security in a changing climate. In B.A. Lankford, K. Bakker, M. Zeitoun and D. Conway (eds) *Water Security: Principles, Perspectives and Practices*. London: Earthscan, pp. 81–100.
56 Defined by WRI (see note 30) as the ratio of water withdrawals to available freshwater on an average, annual basis, excluding storage. Average freshwater was calculated as flow-accumulated runoff minus upstream consumptive use computed over hydrological catchments.
57 Conway, D. (2011) Adapting climate research for development in Africa. *Wiley Interdisciplinary Reviews: Climate Change*, 2: 428–450.
58 Allan, R. and Soden, B. (2008) Atmospheric warming and the amplification of precipitation extremes. *Science*, 321: 1481–1484.
59 Howard, G. and Bartram, J. (2010) The resilience of water supply and sanitation in the face of climate change. Technical report. Geneva: World Health Organization.
60 Calow, R., Bonsor, H., Jones, L., O'Meally, S., MacDonald, A. and Kaur, N. (2011) Climate change, water resources and WASH: a scoping study. London: Overseas Development Institute.
61 MWR and WSP (2014) Technical guidelines for the construction and maintenance of hand dug wells. Sierra Leone: Ministry of Water Resources and WSP.
62 Tucker, J., MacDonald, A.M., Coulter, L. and Calow, R. (2014) Household water use, poverty and easonality in Ethiopia: quantitative findings from a highland to lowland transect. *Water Resources and Rural Development*, 3: 27–47.

63 FDRE (2016) Ethiopian Humanitarian Response. Federal Democratic Republic of Ethiopia. *WASH Cluster Bulletin*, 1.
64 UNDESA World Urbanization Prospects (2014) The 2014 revision, highlights. New York: United Nations Department of Economic and Social Affairs. Available at: http://esa.un.org/unup/
65 Morris, B.L., Lawrence, A.R., Chilton, P.J., Adams, B., Calow, R.C. and Klinck, B.A. (2003) Groundwater and its susceptibility to degradation: a global assessment of the problem and options for management. Early Warning Assessment Report, Series RS, 03–3. Nairobi, Kenya: UNDP.
66 Mason, N., Denis Le Seve, M. and Calow, R. (2017) Future flows: global trends to watch on water and sanitation. ODI Working Paper 520, August.
67 Briscoe, J. and Malik, R.P.S. (2006) *India's Water Economy: Bracing for a Turbulent Future*. World Bank, Washington, DC: Oxford University Press.
68 Shah, M. and Kulkarni, H. (2015) Urban water systems in India. *Economic and Political Weekly. 50*: 57–60.
69 Van Rooijen, D.J., Turral, H. and Wade-Biggs, T. (2005) Sponge city: water balance of mega-city water use and wastewater use in Hyderabad, India. *Irrigation and Drainage, 54*: S81–S91.
70 Molle, F. and Berkoff, J. (2006) Cities versus agriculture: revisiting intersectoral water transfers, potential gains and conflicts. Comprehensive Assessment Research Report 10. Colombo, Sri Lanka: International Water Management Institute.
71 Calow, R.C., Howarth, S.E. and Wang, J. (2009) Irrigation development and water rights reform in China. *Water Resources Development, 25*: 227–248.
72 Doczi, J., Calow, R. and d'Alancon, V. (2014) Growing more with less: China's progress in agricultural water management and reallocation. ODI Development Progress: Case Study Report – Environment. London: ODI.
73 Parker, H., Mosello. B., Calow, R., Quattri, M., Kebede, S. and Alamirew, T. (2016) A thirsty future? Water strategies for Ethiopia's new development era. London: Overseas Development Institute.
74 MacDonald, A.M. and Foster, S.S.D. (2016) Groundwater systems. In M. Smith, K. Cross, M. Paden and P. Laban (eds) Spring – managing groundwater sustainably. IUCN, Gland, Switzerland.

7
HOW INTERNATIONAL WATER AND SANITATION MONITORING FAILS DEPRIVED URBAN DWELLERS

Gordon McGranahan, Anna Walnycki, Festo Dominick, Wilbard Kombe, Alphonce Kyessi, Tatu Mtwangi Limbumba, Hezron Magambo, Mwanakombo Mkanga and Tim Ndezi

How international water and sanitation indicators overestimate coverage and sacrifice local relevance in low-income urban settings

The United Nations Water Conference of 1977 called for national governments to commit to providing all people "with water of safe quality and adequate quantity and basic sanitation facilities by 1990" (United Nations, 1977, p. 68). Soon thereafter, the United Nations officially declared the 1980s the International Drinking Water Supply and Sanitation Decade (with somewhat lower ambitions). Statistics gathered to monitor coverage throughout the decade were led by the World Health Organization (WHO) and showed the vast majority of the population lacking access to adequate sanitation and water supplies to be rural (WHO, 1992). That WHO was chosen to lead the monitoring reflected the widespread belief that health was the overarching concern. The rural focus reflected a desire of key international practitioners, including at the World Bank, to shift attention and international funding in the sector away from cities and costly piped systems towards rural settlements and low-cost alternative technologies (Black, 1998). This was at a time when concerns about the urban bias in development policies were beginning to attract a lot of attention (Lipton, 1977). Both the health emphasis and the rural–urban distinction remain central to the presentation of water and sanitation statistics, which still show enormous rural–urban discrepancies (WHO/UNICEF, 2017a).

Justification for proclaiming the progressive realisation of universal coverage to be a global goal lies more in human rights and solidarity than in preventing adverse global consequences of local water and sanitation deficiencies. In contrast to a global public good like climate change mitigation, the public impacts of inadequate water and sanitation coverage now mostly occur in or around the areas where the deficiencies are concentrated. In these circumstances, the perceptions and priorities of those without adequate water and sanitation are of more obvious relevance, and those of international experts and institutions less so. Health is only one of many concerns people have about water and sanitation facilities they consider inadequate. Cost-benefit analysis suggests that most of the value from achieving universal water and sanitation coverage comes from users' time savings, not their health benefits (Hutton, 2015). Moreover, living with or being exposed to the inadequate water and sanitation of others can be socially degrading and extremely unpleasant, and not just unhealthy and time-consuming. Nevertheless, international monitoring has tended to focus on the technical qualities of water and sanitation facilities and their health risks. In the latest monitoring system, there is some allowance for national variation in indicators, but no provision for adjusting the criteria to reflect rural and urban differences or variations in the priorities and values of local users (WHO/UNICEF, 2017a; WHO/UNICEF, 2017b).

As described in Chapter 1, the Joint Monitoring Programme of WHO and UNICEF (JMP) identifies certain technologies as "improved", and used "ladders" to assess progress towards the Millennium Development Goals (MDGs) (Figure 1.1). Information used to classify facilities has primarily been collected through household surveys and censuses. The higher rungs added for the Sustainable Development Goal (SDG) era, described as safely managed water and sanitation (WHO/UNICEF 2017a), require new data on the availability and quality of water supplied and the treatment and disposal of wastewater and faecal sludge. Universal provision of safely managed water and sanitation services is part of the sixth SDG ensuring "availability and sustainable management of water and sanitation for all" (United Nations, 2015). An adapted version of "improved" water and sanitation is still being used to monitor progress towards universal coverage with "basic" services, as part of the first SDG on eliminating poverty.

Underestimating the urban deficiencies

The water target for MDGs referred explicitly to "safe water" and it seems likely that the "basic sanitation" target added to the MDGs at the World Summit on Sustainable Development in 2002 was also meant to be safe. From the beginning of the MDG era, it was acknowledged that indicators of improved provision did not ensure safe provision (WHO/UNICEF, 2000). However, discrepancies between targets and indicators, and the resulting upward bias in coverage estimates, were rarely mentioned.

This subsection is mainly concerned that improved water and sanitation indicators are misleading because they assume that the same technologies are equally adequate or inadequate in different locations, and particularly between rural and urban areas. Yet, one would expect technically similar shallow wells and pit latrines to be less safe, more unpleasant, and socially degrading when used by a given population share in large, dense urban settlements than by a similar population share in dispersed rural locations.

Defining features of urban settlement – larger settlements with higher population densities – make simpler water and sanitation technologies less safe, and not just for immediate users but for the local public (McGranahan, 2015). Given otherwise similar geographies, groundwater contamination and depletion are likely to be more rapid when the pit latrines and wells are spatially concentrated, even with similar shares of people using the technologies. Population density is also likely to make similar open defecation rates more of a public hazard. In effect, comparable technologies do not have comparable consequences in urban and rural settings. This is one of the reasons the 19th-century sanitary movement started in cities.

The move to "safely managed" provision, with its emphasis on water quality and the treatment of faecal sludge, sets up a more comparable target of universal coverage, when everyone in rural and urban areas has good access to high quality water and faecal sludge is all safely managed. However, where coverage rates are low, rural–urban comparability can also be expected to be low. There is a dearth of information to assess fully how much the shift to estimating "safely managed" rather than just "improved" provision will affect coverage estimates, but preliminary results suggest they depress coverage rates substantially. In 2015, an estimated 62% of rural populations in the Least Developed Countries (LDCs) had access to a basic drinking water service, while only 33% had access to safely managed water services (WHO/UNICEF, 2017a). In LDC urban populations, both basic water coverage and safely managed water coverage were higher, at 83% and 53% respectively. Similar figures are not available for sanitation coverage in LDCs, but global coverage estimates for safely managed sanitation are very low even in urban areas. Based on very limited data, an estimated 35% rural and 43% urban populations have access to safely managed sanitation. But for reasons given above, even if these figures turn out to be accurate, they say little about the population shares facing the consequences of the unsafe management, particularly of sanitation.

It is also misleading to use coverage rates and then to treat "equitable" access as one that "implies progressive reduction and elimination of inequalities between population sub-groups" (WHO/UNICEF, 2015 and 2017b). If everyone has a right to acceptable water and sanitation, that right holds equally for rural and urban populations. The many rural dwellers deprived of their rights are a poor excuse for giving less priority and moral gravity to helping deprived urban populations. In terms of power, privilege and well-being, deprived urban dwellers have more in common with their rural counterparts than with better served urban dwellers. Moreover, while urban agglomeration amplifies the adverse consequences of bad sanitation, it reduces the costs of networked technologies like piped water systems, making equal coverage rates a particularly doubtful benchmark for equal treatment. Even ignoring this, using coverage rates to assess water and sanitation burdens across groups is inappropriate: much of the inequality derives from enormous differences in qualities of provision among those who are not "covered" (and the smaller differences among those who are), which JMP ladders are only beginning to reveal, and comparisons of coverage rates do not capture at all. There may well be a policy bias against poor rural groups, but comparing rural and urban coverage rates is not the way to identify this.

Failing to support urban solutions

Urban water and sanitation challenges in low- and middle-income countries are bound up with local demographics, population movements, processes of exclusion and the challenges of informal settlements (McGranahan et al., 2016). In order to increase coverage, local authorities, utilities and civil society groups need to locate existing deficiencies and understand where and why deficiencies are increasing. National coverage rates and rural/urban differentials are at most marginally useful in supporting local action. Ideally, the international system monitoring progress towards global water and sanitation targets would be rooted in statistics that also inform local actors, who are responsible for most efforts to improve water and sanitation (UCLG 2014), or can contribute to local pressures favouring improvements.

Unfortunately, existing statistics are primarily based on household surveys with sample frames and sizes designed to allow rural–urban comparisons (albeit misleading ones), but not coverage estimates for individual urban centres, let alone for the smaller units of concern to local actors working to extend provision. They often focus on internationally comparable technological features, neglecting location-specific technological issues and local conditions affecting the desirability of the technologies (e.g. saline groundwater, flooding, aquifer depletion, land subsidence, cultural prohibitions and practices, economic constraints, gender relations, and many other geographical, social and economic features). Moreover, they neglect how water and sanitation improvements are perceived, prioritised and pursued locally, including by the intended beneficiaries.

In any case, even good indicators for estimating coverage rates do not necessarily reflect the qualities that local improvement efforts should prioritise. Even if having a slab is closely associated statistically with better quality latrines, and hence is a good indicator, this does not imply that adding slabs to latrines is a good way to improve sanitation. Similarly, when people get water from tanker trucks (not treated as coverage under the MDGs), this may be a reasonably good indicator of water supply problems, but does not imply that water provision will be improved if the tanker trucks are stopped and a borehole is provided instead.

The question of whether shared sanitation should be considered coverage illustrates some of the contradictory logics that apply, and how even good indicators of coverage are not necessarily indicators that action should target. Even if sharing reflects inadequate or unsafe sanitation, it should not necessarily be discouraged. The problem needs to be met with more facilities, not less sharing of the same facilities. If 50% of households in a given city are sharing improved toilets with one other household (and hence 50% are not 'covered'), one could in principle increase coverage rates to 75% simply by stopping this sharing, and leaving 25% without any access to toilets at all. But few would argue that this was a sanitary improvement. Moreover, some efforts to promote shared facilities have led to substantial sanitation improvements (Mara, 2016).

The working group JMP convened actually recommended "accepting sharing by a limited number of people (5 households or 30 people) who know each other" (WHO/UNICEF, 2015, October draft). The JMP's principal reason for not accepting the recommendation allowing limited sharing is revealing: "Having reviewed available data the JMP concluded that differentiating between limited sharing and any sharing is extremely difficult" as only about a quarter of recent surveys allow sufficient differentiation (p. 19). The implicit argument is that the insights from the quarter of surveys that do allow differentiation should not be used because even if they improve local estimates, these better estimates would no longer be constructed in the same way as estimates in places where such differentiation is not possible – in effect, international comparability trumps local relevance.

Finally, while there is some mixed evidence that even low levels of sharing are associated with diarrhoea among young children, this could be because shared latrines are driving children towards open defecation (Baker et al., 2016), which is again a better argument for more latrines than for less sharing. Moreover, recent evidence strongly suggests there is significant local variation (Heijnen et al., 2014) and in some circumstances sharing may even be safer (Exley et al., 2015). When it comes to designing improvements, there are good reasons to think that local relevance should trump international comparability.

International indicators and the challenge of universal coverage in Dar es Salaam

This section uses the situation in Dar es Salaam to elaborate on the points made above. It starts with a review of the role of informal settlement in Dar es Salaam's water and sanitation challenges. It then considers the difficulties of using existing international indicators and "ladders" to guide local water and sanitation improvement efforts – difficulties that are exacerbated by the informal settlement patterns. It ends with an overview of some community-based water and sanitation "climbing frames" that suggest a somewhat different approach to local monitoring.

Informal settlements and the local challenges of water and sanitation provision

Between the censuses of 2002 and 2012, Dar es Salaam's population grew at an annual rate of 5.8 per cent, reaching 4.4 million in 2012 (Andreasen, 2013). Much of the city's existing population is located in older informal developments, where homeowners have extended their structures and rental markets have developed along with the sale of structures. Population growth has declined or even reversed in the most central areas, however. The largest absolute increments in the number of people per unit of area are in somewhat newer informal settlements in the near periphery. And the highest percentage growth rates are in somewhat more distant peripheral settlements.

Like many cities in rapidly urbanising countries, Dar es Salaam is expanding largely through informal development, with most newly settled land being divided into residential plots and sold independently of the city's formal plans and procedures, and much densification also unplanned (Kombe, 2005). Formally, people are expected to wait to move into already constructed and serviced homes on centrally registered plots. In practice, people usually move in when the shelter and services are rudimentary, and they work to incrementally improve both the shelter and services, many eventually adding in rental accommodation (Andreasen, 2016). Informal development gives upwardly mobile tenants a means to secure property, benefit from urban consolidation (Andreasen & Agergaard, 2016) and provides a large share of the more affordable rental accommodations. However, its unplanned nature also amplifies the challenges of improving water and sanitation provision (Kyessi, 2002; Kombe et al., 2015) and designing useful indicators of coverage. The effects of informal expansion and densification play out somewhat differently for water and sanitation.

As informal areas are consolidated, formal water services may become available (Andreasen & Møller-Jensen, 2016). However, groundwater quality often declines due to pollution, including from the growing concentration of latrines (Gomme, 2016; Walraevens et al., 2015). The unplanned nature of informal development reduces both the capacity and the incentive of the authorities and the utility to provide services. While piped water may eventually become available, the initial extension of services into informal settlements tends to involve complex combinations of private enterprise, local organisation and lobbying, with varying levels of negotiated formal service delivery. Meanwhile, in rapidly developing peripheral areas, clustering around boreholes and trucks delivering water to more distant homes often accompany the initial residential development (McGranahan et al., 2016).

Water resource supply problems compound the challenges of securing sustainable water services for Dar es Salaam's informal settlements, whether through the piped water system or independent boreholes. Over-extraction and groundwater depletion are a major threat, including demand from informal borehole operators supplying informal settlements. Borehole users have little reason to be concerned about depleting the aquifer, as their individual contributions are minimal, but the rough estimates available suggest that their collective usage already exceeds recharge rates, putting future supplies at risk (Gomme, 2016; McGranahan et al., 2016), and complicating the interpretation of coverage rates.

The piped water system in Dar es Salaam depends on both groundwater and surface water from the Wami/Ruvu Basin. With inadequate investment and poor accounting of water and infrastructure deficiencies, supply problems within the piped water network have significantly contributed to the limited network expansion, and to rationing in some parts of the network. Recent investments in storage capacity and new dams mean these constraints are now easing, but water deficits are still likely to occur in dry years and deficits may again become more pronounced in the absence of improved demand management (Nobert & Skinner, 2016).

The benefits of sanitation improvements are more public than those of water, which mostly accrue to the using household (McGranahan, 2015). In the absence of collective action or social capital, good sanitation is likely to be underprovided. The risks from poor sanitation, or even the use of reasonably well-built pit latrines, is higher in dense informal settlements, with greater consequences of contaminating the ambient environment. Land pressures in the centre can also make it difficult to find alternative locations for new pits, even as small lanes in the most densely settled informal settlements complicate pit emptying. Moreover, even in the more central parts of Dar es Salaam, piped sewers are costly and only provided to a small minority (Kjellén & Kyessi, 2015). Thus, sanitary conditions in the more central informal settlements are likely to be worse than in the periphery, though there are few current statistics that demonstrate this relationship.

The challenge associated with the ultimate disposal of faecal sludge is somewhat analogous to that of managing water resources. Just as governments need to take some responsibility for preventing excessive water withdrawals from threatened underground aquifers or water-scarce river basins, they have a similar responsibility for preventing excessive release of hazardous faecal sludge into aquifers and waterways. Cities have historically been inclined to displace their faecal sludge by releasing it untreated in the waterways. A recent "Shit Flow Diagram" for Dar es Salaam (Brandes *et al.* 2015) estimates that only 7% of faecal sludge is treated, while 36% is contained in onsite facilities. The remaining 57% finds its way into the ambient environment, posing a potential health risk. This faecal sludge treatment challenge is not just from informal settlements: only 66% of wastewater transported through sewers is treated, with the remainder discharged into the ocean or environment as a result of overflows (Brandes *et al.* 2015). There are decentralised means of on-site treatment, including "ecological" sanitation (Simha & Ganesapillai, 2017), but currently, none of the existing technologies have managed to overcome the barriers to widespread use, in either low- or high-income settings.

In these circumstances, water and sanitation targets monitored with internationally comparable indicators cannot contribute much to government water and sanitation strategies. Complex politics and decentralised processes undermine centrally orchestrated solutions that ignore them. Information and indicators have important roles to play, but existing international indicators do not inform local action except to a very limited degree. The more detailed statistics are difficult to compare, even across different parts of the city.

The limited applicability of international water and sanitation ladders in Dar es Salaam

Water and sanitation coverage estimates in Tanzania usually come from large surveys undertaken through the National Bureau of Statistics or smaller efforts of independent researchers as well as organisations involved in water and sanitation provision. Most large-scale household surveys that include modules on water and sanitation have adapted their questions to fit the international criteria as closely as possible (McGranahan *et al.*, 2016). However, few sample surveys are able to provide average coverage rates for Dar es Salaam, let alone for smaller settlements. The exception is the census, undertaken every ten years. The core census data is as comprehensive as possible since it attempts to include everyone. Water and sanitation questions were included in a longer survey administered to 30% of the population, which is still an extremely large survey. Privacy and related concerns preclude releasing the data in a fully disaggregated form. Nevertheless, the census provides a data source far more relevant to local decision-making than conventional sample survey, though it is not readily made available in a suitable form.

Water and sanitation access indicators from the 2012 census in Dar es Salaam (Tables 7.2 and 7.3) are slight variants on the JMP ladders (though they do not include sanitation sharing). Both imply higher coverage rates in urban than rural settlements, and, in the case of sanitation, higher rates still in Dar es Salaam. Does this reflect reality? It almost certainly reflects a real tendency for more per capita to be invested in improving water and sanitation in urban than rural settlements, and for most to be invested in Dar es Salaam. The extent to which more costly services yield better outcomes is less clear. It is not clear that the "protected" wells and springs in Dar es Salaam really provide better and more reliable water supplies than the "unimproved" sources in rural areas or, for that matter, than "unimproved" water from tankers in Dar es Salaam.

Adding information on latrine sharing would change the sanitation coverage estimates considerably. The 2010 DHS survey estimated that 57% of urban households in Tanzania, as opposed to 20% of rural households, shared their sanitation facilities (NBS Tanzania & ICF Macro, 2011). Particularly in densely settled urban areas, it is important to know how faecal sludge is disposed of, and whether it is contaminating the groundwater. These technological profiles are potentially useful, but on their own do not provide the basis for estimating coverage with safe or acceptable water and sanitation services, or what problems users experience with these different facilities. Indeed, each of the technologies can be associated with a wide range of overlapping service levels (Tables 7.1 and 7.2).

Several articles on water and sanitation in Dar es Salaam claim that the technology-based classifications do not capture the inadequacies, complexities and unequal qualities of household and individual services in the city (Nganyanyuka *et al.*, 2014; Pastore, 2015; Rugemalila & Gibbs, 2015; Smiley, 2013, 2016). Across communities within Dar es Salaam, the same technologies provide different and often unfavourable outcomes. For example, pit latrines that operate reasonably well in one community become dangerous sources of neighbourhood pollution in a flood-prone areas. Current national statistics omit factors that undermine technologies considered basic or improved, including poor pit-latrine emptying practices (Jenkins *et al.*, 2015), environmental pollution from faecal sludge (Brandes *et al.* 2015), groundwater salinity and contamination where wells are used (Elisante

TABLE 7.1 Percentage distribution of households by main drinking water source for Dar es Salaam based on 2012 census

Facilities	Rural (%)	Urban (%)	Dar es Salaam (%)
Piped water into dwelling	6.0	22.7	20.1
Piped water to yard/plot	3.4	16.9	12.9
Public tap/standpipe	16.6	19.0	18.8
Tube well/borehole	6.9	9.8	18.9
Protected dug well	7.0	9.0	7.6
Protected spring	2.7	1.2	0.3
ALL IMPROVED	**43**	**79**	**79**
Bottled water	0.1	0.6	1.2
Tanker truck	0.4	3.3	8.4
Cart with small tank/drum	1.4	4.7	7.0
Unprotected dug well	25.2	7.0	4.2
Unprotected spring	14.0	2.3	0.2
Surface water	14.9	2.8	1.2
Other	1.4	0.7	0.3
ALL UNIMPROVED	**57**	**21**	**21**
TOTAL	**100**	**100**	**100**

Note: These are the "main" sources of drinking water, but households and often use multiple water sources.

Source: United Republic of Tanzania (2015).

TABLE 7.2 Percentage distribution of households by main sanitation facility for Dar es Salaam from 2012 census

Facilities	Rural (%)	Urban (%)	Dar es Salaam (%)
Flush/pour water to piped sewer system	0.3	4.5	5.7
Flush/pour water to septic tank	0.6	10.8	15.2
Flush/pour water to covered pit	2.2	17.0	14.0
Ventilated improved pit latrine	0.8	2.9	2.1
Pit latrine with washable slab with lid	4.5	16.8	22.9
Pit latrine with washable slab without lid	6.4	19.8	29.3
Other improved	0.2	0.1	0.0
ALL IMPROVED	**15**	**72**	**89**
Flush/pour water to somewhere else	0.5	2.9	3.1
Pit latrine without washable/soil slab	38.1	14.0	4.5
Pit latrine without slab/open pit	35.1	10.2	3.0
No facility/bush/field/beach	11.3	0.9	0.2
ALL UNIMPROVED	**85**	**28**	**11**
TOTAL	**100**	**100**	**100**

Note: As with water, these are the main sanitation facilities, and household members may use different or multiple facilities. For example, such statistics can hide open defecation by children.

Source: United Republic of Tanzania (2015).

& Muzuka, 2015; Walraevens *et al.*, 2015), electric outages, and the rationing system of the piped water network (Smiley, 2016). Similarly, they omit the complex strategies that households have to adopt, many involving multiple sources and facilities (Nganyanyuka *et al.*, 2014).

In any case, publically available water and sanitation statistics are not widely used in planning for water and sanitation provision. To take the most obvious example, Dar es Salaam's Water and Sewerage Authority (DAWASA) and its Water and Sewerage Corporation (DAWASCO) rely heavily on their own limited data on the piped water and sewerage systems that are their primary responsibility. Just 20% of the population of Dar es Salaam uses water piped into the dwelling (Table 7.2) and 6% uses sanitation facilities connected to a sewer (Table 7.3).

Community-based water and sanitation climbing frames and locally driven water and sanitation improvement

A large number of actors in Dar es Salaam are involved in water and sanitation provision, including in informal settlements, many of whom could benefit from better indicators of the extent and quality of coverage. This subsection is particularly concerned with people and groups more rooted in the informal communities themselves. The Tanzania Urban Poor Federation (TUPF) and its support NGO the Centre for Community Initiatives (CCI) are active in a number of informal settlements in Dar es Salaam and try to work towards city-wide improvements (Banana *et al.*, 2015). They are affiliated with Slum Dwellers International (SDI), an umbrella organisation for a network of federations of the urban poor and their support NGOs, active in around 30 countries of Latin America, Asia and predominantly Africa (Satterthwaite & Mitlin, 2014, pp. 159–172).

The federations have been built up around savings groups, including mostly women, in low-income neighbourhoods. Groups work in their communities, forming larger federations that work together to address their collective challenges, which often include water and sanitation deficiencies. The federations are supported by local NGOs, providing technical and project management expertise meant to drive improvement initiatives, including developing citywide strategies and engaging with local authorities. SDI provides an important international link, and sometimes a strong international steer. It has a Council of (mature) Federations as its highest authority, and an SDI Board of seven community leaders and two professionals (http://knowyourcity.info/governance).

Enumeration and local data collection have long been central to the strategies of local SDI alliances (Patel & Baptist, 2012). When alliances in Dar es Salaam, Kitwe (Zambia), Blantyre (Malawi) and Chinoye (Zimbabwe) worked together with the International Institute for Environment and Development in London on action research to explore ways of addressing sanitation needs at scale (Banana *et al.*, 2015), one of the first stages involved geo-referencing and mapping housing and sanitary conditions in selected informal settlements. Mapping and enumerations served multiple purposes including assessment of existing conditions, mobilising concerned residents, and eventually facilitating engagement between the federation and local authorities around possible solutions.

As part of the research, TUPF and CCI developed their water and sanitation mapping methodology in Mtoni, Kombo and Tungi informal communities in Dar es Salaam (Walnycki & Skinner, 2017). Maps and survey data were then used in workshops facilitated by CCI and TUPFI. Workshops focused on water and sanitation provision and perceptions of progress, with the aim of developing community-based water and sanitation ladders, comparable to JMP ladders more familiar to government officials (Tables 7.3 and 7.4).

Local participants were unfamiliar with the JMP ladders for water and sanitation. First, they felt that technological categories did not reflect the diversity of provision in low-income and informal urban settlements, either in terms of the facilities, risks and hazards they encounter. Second, discussions around provision focused on the diverse range of formal and informal actors involved in water and sanitation provision, and associated challenges and opportunities inherent to improving different types of provision in a settlement.

The categorisations that were eventually developed were based on community perceptions, capable of supporting a CCI-TUPF citywide strategy for pursuing water and sanitation improvements. Results from the three communities resembled a climbing frame more than a ladder. While discussions started by describing different technologies, it ended in identified qualities that were only partially dependent on the type of technology. Participants identified eight different dimensions for water (e.g. collection time, water quality, cost, reliability) and nine for sanitation (e.g. cleanliness, structure, waste removal, privacy).

Dimensions identified by the communities and the perceptions of progress attached to each reflect the lived experience of water and sanitation conditions in informal settlements. The extent to which households are willing to share sanitation facilities reflect the common living arrangements in low-income settlements in Dar es Salaam. Ideally, participants agreed that each family should share one toilet. However, given that informal settlements in Dar es Salaam are characterised by compound living, where several households might share one toilet, communities agreed that it would be acceptable for two to four households to share a toilet. Responses reflect a spectrum of acceptability from community to community, and the fact that household sizes vary. Shared public toilet blocks were always deemed unacceptable as the principal facility for a household. The physical and cultural realities of living in an informal settlement means that the acceptability of sharing sanitation varies within, and presumably between, cities.

During discussions of ideal and acceptable water sources, all communities agreed that a source would be acceptable if treated and tested by the water utility in Dar es Salaam. This is not quite the same as saying that the water must be of the same quality as piped water, which does not always pass the tests, and is quite similar to the international criterion for safely managed water. Groundwater is a common source in these communities, but its quality and salinity varies enormously. Communities perceive local groundwater sources provided through local vendors

TABLE 7.3 Community-based water ladder/climbing frame

	Unacceptable	*Acceptable*	*Best possible*
Proximity to house/user	More than 30 minutes	No more than 5 minutes from the house	Ideally, taps in kitchen and bathroom (particularly important for women); at least tap at yard level
Time to collect	Daily water collection takes 1.5–2 hours	Not more than 15 minutes to collect daily water	Negligible as in house/yard
Treated	Not treated	Treated to water utility standards	Treated to the level of the water utility (for cooking and drinking, might boil)
Tested	Not tested	Tested to water utility standards	Tested to water utility standards
Cost	1 bucket for TSh300; more than TSh30,000 monthly per house; more than TSh10,000 monthly per HH	HH connection no more than TSh350,000; affordable monthly cost per house TSh15,000–30,000 (TSh7,000–10,000 per HH)	TSh200,000–250,000 to get HH connection; TSh15,000–20,000 monthly per house with multiple HHs sharing (TSh3,000–4,000 monthly per HH); some prefer metered, others flat rate
Reliability	Frequent rationing (up to twice a week)	Water available 6–12 hours per day; morning and evening availability important	Safe water available 24/7
Source	Shallow untreated well; piped network through drainage channels; borehole near toilets	Dar es Salaam Water and Sewerage Corporation, wells, boreholes (if treated and tested); accessing multiple sources for different uses acceptable; people prepared to walk further/take more time to collect drinking water	Utility water, but also deep boreholes

continued . . .

TABLE 7.3 Continued

	Unacceptable	Acceptable	Best possible
Storage	None or near toilets	Yes	Storage of approximately 100l for emergency situations – e.g. power cut
Quantity	Less than 15l per person per day; water for sanitation is additional	60l for small family; 110l for large family (15–20l per person per day); water for sanitation is additional	80–100l per HH per day (20–30l of water per person per day); water for sanitation is additional

Note: HH – household ; l – liter.

Source: Adapted from McGranahan et al. (2016).

to be acceptable if tested and treated. This has implications for plans to extend water services in informal settlements, specifically for identifying water sources that could be used if sustainably managed, treated and tested, and the role that informal vendors might be able to play in extending provision. In practice, many of the participants relied on multiple water sources for different purposes. In Mtoni, shallow wells are widespread and the water is used for washing and considered unacceptable sources of drinking water without treatment.

When discussions shifted focus on criteria as opposed to technologies, the scope widened to an exploration of what could be achieved by families, households and communities, and what required support from the utility and local government. The climbing frame not only captures physical characteristics, but also explores strategic and political processes that facilitate water and sanitation improvements, many of which are not captured by international ladders. It is not clear how effective locally created climbing frames will actually be in overcoming challenges in Dar es Salaam, which go well beyond the lack of locally relevant indicators or how replicable these water and sanitation climbing frames are in different contexts. However, this example illustrates that while communities and international experts may see things differently, there is potential for improved cooperation, with local perceptions having a greater influence on international monitoring systems that include information more supportive of local initiatives.

Conclusions

It is perhaps inevitable that those involved in international monitoring seek out indicators that can be constructed in a comparable way in different countries. As illustrated above, however, the prioritisation of such comparability in international water and sanitation monitoring has inadvertently crowded out more locally

TABLE 7.4 Community-based sanitation ladder/climbing frame

	Unacceptable	*Acceptable*	*Best possible*
Environment	Wastewater flows to immediate environment	No impact on immediate environment	Toilet is well constructed; wastewater does not flow to neighbours, or contaminate environment/ground water sources
Cleanliness	Full pit, causes back flow; dirty toilet, poor ventilation, damp, fungus and mould	Clean inside and easy to keep clean	Cleanable floor and tiles, with tools and products available for cleaning; handwashing facility
Structured	Uses cloth, sacks, tree branches, etc.	Needs a roof, walls and door; lined	Brick construction; well built, with opening for ventilation; door for privacy
Waste removal	Manual emptying; opening and flooding of pit during the rainy season; abandoning pits	Safe emptying without polluting the environment; no manual emptying	Waste removal safe, affordable and appropriate to local context—e.g. sewers, simplified sewerage or vacuum tankers
Sharing	More than five families sharing	2–4 HHs sharing; 8–20 people	No more than one family or 5–6 people sharing
Cost	Usually more than TSh2 million (excessive cost); lower than TSh400,000 indicates poor quality toilet	For HHs to build new toilet: TSh1–1.5 million (high cost due to need to dig pit and buy tank)	For HHs to build new toilet. TSh600,000–800,000
Water	Men should use between 20 and 5l; women between 30 and 10l	Water needed, same as for ideal (20–30l)	Men approximately 20l; women 20–30l
Privacy	No door, no privacy	Lockable door	Men: toilet can be inside or outside of house but tank/pit should be outside; women: inside toilet preferred unless plot is fenced

continued . . .

TABLE 7.4 Continued

	Unacceptable	Acceptable	Best possible
Typical facilities	Unlined and poorly lined pit latrines (using barrels, tyres, etc.)	Soak-away pit/pit latrine with Asian squatting pan, which does not transmit diseases	Sewer connections (including simplified) septic tank/vacuum tank emptying

Source: adapted from McGranahan et al. (2016).

tailored and action-relevant indicators. It has supported particularly misleading rural–urban comparisons, indicator systems poorly suited to tracking changes in rapidly developing urban informal settlements, and a tendency to neglect the concerns of those in need of water and sanitation improvements. It is difficult to imagine locally generated information systems on water and sanitation feeding seamlessly into international statistics on coverage, or an internationally generated indicator system prioritising information relevant to local action. The costs of such integrated systems would almost certainly be prohibitive. Much could be done, however, to support locally tailored monitoring systems, rooted more firmly in the views and capacities of those without adequate provision, and more directly supportive of local action by government actors and others. The knowledge that such local systems could generate would also be of value to international monitoring, and be used to make that international monitoring more relevant to local action.

References

Andreasen, M.H. (2013). *Population Growth and Spatial Expansion of Dar es Salaam: An Analysis of the Rate and Spatial Distribution of Recent Population Growth in Dar es Salaam.* Copenhagen: University of Copenhagen.

Andreasen, M.H., & Agergaard, J. (2016). Residential mobility and homeownership in Dar es Salaam. *Population and Development Review,* 42(1), 95–110. doi:10.1111/j.1728-4457.2016.00104.x

Andreasen, M.H., & Møller-Jensen, L. (2016). Beyond the networks: self-help services and post-settlement network extensions in the periphery of Dar es Salaam. *Habitat International,* 53, 39–47. doi:http://dx.doi.org/10.1016/j.habitatint.2015.11.003

Andreasen, M.H., Agergaard, J., & Møller-Jensen, L. (2016). Suburbanisation, homeownership aspirations and urban housing: exploring urban expansion in Dar es Salaam. *Urban Studies.* doi:10.1177/0042098016643303

Baker, K.K., O'Reilly, C.E., Levine, M.M., Kotloff, K.L., Nataro, J. P., Ayers, T.L., . . . Mintz, E.D. (2016). Sanitation and hygiene-specific risk factors for moderate-to-severe diarrhea in young children in the global enteric multicenter study, 2007–2011: case-control study. *PLOS Medicine,* 13(5), e1002010. doi:10.1371/journal.pmed.1002010

Banana, E., Chikoti, P., Harawa, C., McGranahan, G., Mitlin, D., Stephen, S., . . . Walnycki, A. (2015). Sharing reflections on inclusive sanitation. *Environment and Urbanization,* 27(1), 19–34. doi:10.1177/0956247815569702

Black, M. (1998). Learning what works: a 20 year retrospective view on international water and sanitation co-operation. Washington: UNDP-World Bank Water and Sanitation Program.

Brandes, K., Schoebitz, L., Kimwaga, R., & Strande, L. (2015). Shit flow diagram report for Dar es Salaam, Tanzania. Dübendorf, Switzerland: Eawag/Sandec.

Elisante, E., & Muzuka, A.N.N. (2015). Occurrence of nitrate in Tanzanian groundwater aquifers: a review. *Applied Water Science*, 1–17. doi:10.1007/s13201-015-0269-z

Exley, J.L., Liseka, B., Cumming, O., & Ensink, J.H.J. (2015). The sanitation ladder, what constitutes an improved form of sanitation? *Environmental Science & Technology*, *49*(2), 1086–1094.

Gomme, J. (2016). Availability and sustainability of groundwater in Dar es Salaam and its potential role in meeting SDG 6. London: ESI Environmental Specialists.

Heijnen, M., Rosa, G., Fuller, J., Eisenberg, J.N.S., & Clasen, T. (2014). The geographic and demographic scope of shared sanitation: an analysis of national survey data from low- and middle-income countries. *Tropical Medicine & International Health*, *19*(11), 1334–1345. doi:10.1111/tmi.12375

Hutton, G. (2015). Benefits and costs of the water sanitation and hygiene targets for the post-2015 development agenda. Copenhagen: Copenhagen Consensus Center.

Jenkins, M.W., Cumming, O., & Cairncross, S. (2015). Pit latrine emptying behavior and demand for sanitation services in Dar es Salaam, Tanzania. *International Journal of Environmental Research and Public Health*, *12*(3), 2588–2611. doi:10.3390/ijerph120302588

Kjellén, M. and Kyessi, A. (2015). Dar es Salam: the development of water supply and sewage systems. In: Tvedt, T. & Oestigaard, T. (eds) *A History of Water: Water and Urbanization*. London: I.B. Tauris, pp. 550–574.

Kombe, W. (2005). Land use dynamics in peri-urban areas and their implications on the urban growth and form: the case of Dar es Salaam, Tanzania. *Habitat International*, 29(1), 113–135.

Kombe, W., Ndezi, T., & Hofmann, P. (2015). Water justice city profile: Dar es Salaam, Tanzania. London: Development Planning Unit, University College London.

Kyessi, A.G (2002). Community participation in urban infrastructure provision: servicing informal settlements in Dar es Salaam. Dortmund: SPRING Research Series no. 33.

Lipton, M. (1977). *Why Poor People Stay Poor: A Study of Urban Bias in World Development*. London: Temple Smith.

Mara, D. (2016). Shared sanitation: to include or to exclude? *Transactions of the Royal Society of Tropical Medicine and Hygiene*, *110*(5), 265–267. doi:10.1093/trstmh/trw029

McGranahan, G. (2015). Realizing the right to sanitation in deprived urban communities: meeting the challenges of collective action, coproduction, affordability, and housing tenure. *World Development*, *68*, 242–253. doi:http://dx.doi.org/10.1016/j.worlddev.2014.12.008

McGranahan, G., Schensul, D., & Singh, G. (2016). Inclusive urbanization: can the 2030 agenda be delivered without it? *Environment and Urbanization*, *28*(1), 13–34.

McGranahan, G., Walnycki, A., Dominick, F., Kombe, W., Kyessi, A., Limbumba, T. M., ... Ndezi, T. (2016). Universalising water and sanitation coverage in urban areas: from global targets to local realities in Dar es Salaam, and back. London: International Institute for Environment and Development.

NBS Tanzania, & ICF Macro (2011). Tanzania demographic and health survey 2010. Dar es Salaam, Tanzania: NBS and ICF Macro.

Nganyanyuka, K., Martinez, J., Wesselink, A., Lungo, J. H., & Georgiadou, Y. (2014). Accessing water services in Dar es Salaam: are we counting what counts? *Habitat International*, *44*, 358–366. doi:http://dx.doi.org/10.1016/j.habitatint.2014.07.003

Nobert, J., & Skinner, J. (2016). Meeting future demand for drinking water supply in Dar es Salaam Hydrological modelling of the Ruvu River and assessment of flow. London: International Institute of Environment and Development.

Pastore, M.C. (2015). Reworking the relation between sanitation and the city in Dar es Salaam, Tanzania. *Environment and Urbanization*, 27(2), 473–488. doi:10.1177/0956247815592285

Patel, S., & Baptist, C. (2012). Editorial: documenting by the undocumented. *Environment and Urbanization*, 24(1), 3–12. doi:10.1177/0956247812438364

Rugemalila, R., & Gibbs, L. (2015). Urban water governance failure and local strategies for overcoming water shortages in Dar es Salaam, Tanzania. *Environment and Planning C: Government and Policy*, 33(2), 412–427. doi:10.1068/c1324

Satterthwaite, D., & Mitlin, D. (2014). *Reducing Urban Poverty in the Global South*. New York: Routledge.

Simha, P., & Ganesapillai, M. (2017). Ecological sanitation and nutrient recovery from human urine: how far have we come? A review. *Sustainable Environment Research*. doi:http://doi.org/10.1016/j.serj.2016.12.001

Smiley, S.L. (2013). Complexities of water access in Dar es Salaam, Tanzania. *Applied Geography*, 41, 132–138. doi:http://dx.doi.org/10.1016/j.apgeog.2013.03.019

Smiley, S.L. (2016). Water availability and reliability in Dar es Salaam, Tanzania. *The Journal of Development Studies*, 52(9), 1320–1334. doi:10.1080/00220388.2016.1146699

UCLG (2014). *Basic Services For All in an Urbanizing World*. Milton Park: Routledge.

United Nations (1977). Report of the United Nations Water Conference, Mar del Plata, 14–25 March 1977. New York: United Nations.

United Nations (2015). Transforming our world: the 2030 Agenda for Sustainable Development. New York: United Nations.

United Republic of Tanzania (2015). Thematic report on housing condition, household amenities and assets, 2012 population and housing census (Vol. V). Dar es Salaam, Tanzania: National Bureau of Statistics.

Walnycki, A., & Skinner, J. (2017). Connecting cities to basins – meeting the water and sanitation SDG targets at scale: a focus on Dar es Salaam. Retrieved from: www.iied.org/connecting-cities-basins (accessed 27 April 2017).

Walraevens, K., Mjemah, I.C., Mtoni, Y., & Van Camp, M. (2015). Sources of salinity and urban pollution in the Quaternary sand aquifers of Dar es Salaam, Tanzania. *Journal of African Earth Sciences*, 102, 149–165. doi:http://dx.doi.org/10.1016/j.jafrearsci.2014.11.003

WHO (1992). The international drinking water supply and sanitation decade: end of decade review. Geneva: World Health Organization.

WHO/UNICEF (2000). Global water supply and sanitation assessment 2000 report. Geneva and New York: World Health Organization and United Nations Children's Fund.

WHO/UNICEF (2015). Methodological note: proposed indicator framework for monitoring SDG targets on drinking-water, sanitation, hygiene and wastewater. Geneva/New York: WHO/UNICEF Joint Monitoring Program.

WHO/UNICEF (2015 October draft). JMP Green Paper: Global monitoring of water, sanitation and hygiene post-2015. Geneva/New York: WHO/UNICEF Joint Monitoring Program.

WHO/UNICEF (2017a). Progress on drinking water, sanitation and hygiene: 2017 update and SDG baselines. Geneva: World Health Organization and the United Nations Children's Fund.

WHO/UNICEF (2017b). Safely managed drinking water – thematic report on drinking water 2017. Geneva: World Health Organization and the United Nations Children's Fund.

PART 3
Addressing inequality in water and sanitation service provision

8
FIRST A BASIC SERVICE FOR ALL

Reducing WASH inequalities through more equitable funding and financing strategies

Ian Ross and Richard Franceys

Introduction

The sixth sustainable development goal (SDG) aims for access to water, sanitation and hygiene (WASH) services to be universal. When taken alongside the high levels of "safely managed" service in its definition of access, this has significant implications for funding and financing WASH infrastructure and ongoing services.

Universal access means that the hardest-to-reach should now be reached. What is more, they should be reached with higher levels of service than were aimed at under the Millennium Development Goals (MDGs). Both of these will involve higher costs per person than were experienced in the MDG era. Funding and financing strategies focus on how to cover those costs. The focus of this chapter is how the goal of equality in WASH service use can be achieved via more equitable funding and financing strategies.

Overall, this chapter aims to:

- Examine the implications of new SDG targets and indicators for funding and financing strategies.
- Consider how achieving equality in outcomes in sanitation, as opposed to water, may require different funding and financing approaches.
- Give a broad overview of key issues, while going into depth on three specific issues with detailed country examples.

In doing so, synergies with the rest of this volume are sought, in particular two chapters. Chapter 15 focuses on costs and affordability of equitable WASH service provision, as well as benefits. Covering those costs is a key focus of funding and financing strategies, so care has been taken to avoid overlap. Second, Chapter 13 describes the new SDG targets. Since the targets and indicators have implications for costs and therefore funding and financing, some discussion of them is essential in the present chapter.

The chapter is structured as follows. Pages 138–146 address key definitions and concepts, the implications of SDG indicators for equitable funding and financing, and a framework for thinking about WASH funding and financing decisions. Pages 146–154 then go into detail on three specific issues, each illustrated with an in-depth country example. The final section concludes the chapter.

Key definitions and concepts

As set out in Chapter 13, SDG targets 6.1 (water) and 6.2 (sanitation) include the notions of "equitable" access to safe WASH "for all".[1] This implies that equality in outcomes is the goal, with equity, or more equitable interventions, as a means of achieving equality. More equitable interventions are considered as those that tackle differences in well-being that are seen to be unfair. Whether interventions are equitable can be considered at various levels: in funding and financing of services; in access to or utilisation of services; or in higher level outcomes such as health status. The present chapter considers mainly the goal of equality via more equitable funding and financing.

The SDGs are global goals that provide every country with an aspirational level of service for their citizens. Few lower-income countries already have 100% safely managed services.[2] Those that do face challenges in maintaining this universal coverage. The user group of primary interest in this chapter is people in low- and middle-income countries (LMICs) and, within those countries, the poorest quintiles. The World Bank's focus on the "bottom 40%" (B40) of the income distribution provides a clear focus that will be used in this chapter.[3] It is beyond the scope of this chapter to discuss whether the WASH SDG targets are achievable at the national level in most LMICs. However, it will be argued that "first get a basic service for all" is likely to be a financially necessary "stepping stone" (that is an equitable interim target), on the way to the equality of "safely managed for all".

A distinction is drawn throughout this chapter between funding and financing, building on the approach used by the Infrastructure Finance Working Group.[4] Funding is broadly defined as providing money which is not expected to be repaid. In the WASH context, funding usually comes from three sources: tariffs (including self-supply expenditure or user charges such as connection fees), government tax revenue, and donor transfers. Together, these are known as the "3Ts" framework, popularised by the OECD.[5] In contrast, financing is defined as providing money as a loan or equity in the expectation that it will be returned in full and with interest, in the case of debt, or dividends from profits, in the case of equity. In other words, funding is the provision of non-repayable money, and financing is the provision of money that is repayable to the financiers.

A distinction can also be made in the way this money can be used. Both funding and financing can be used to build new assets, but financing is most commonly used when the high capital expenditure on new assets cannot be funded directly through revenues. Funding is more often used to pay for the costs of ongoing services – e.g. operational expenditure, depreciation charges for capital maintenance and the interest or dividends cost of repayable capital.

Implications of SDG indicators for funding and financing

The ambitious scale of the new WASH SDG poses major cost implications. New funding and financing strategies will be needed to meet the costs of achieving universal basic access and extending access to "safely managed" services. Several key implications are discussed below.

Implications of higher service levels for costs

The biggest challenge for water supply is that on-plot services are now the target level of service, implying piped networks rather than point sources. For sanitation, it is that excreta must be safely managed across the service chain from containment, through emptying and conveyance, to treatment and disposal. Ensuring the continuity of water services (so they are "available when needed"), that drinking water is treated and that toilets are not shared have major cost implications but, by comparison to getting an on-plot supply in the first place, these are generally second-order cost implications.

In rural areas, for example, there is a significant difference between the per person costs of infrastructure and ongoing services to deliver an off-plot handpump service no more than 250m away and delivering an on-plot piped service. Fonseca et al. (2011) explore the different costs of WASH services based on the following cost categories, which will be discussed further in this chapter: Capital expenditure (CapEx), Operation and minor maintenance expenditure (OpEx), Capital maintenance expenditure (CapManEx), Cost of capital (CoC), Expenditure on direct support (ExpDS) and Expenditure on indirect support (ExpIDS).[6]

Implications of higher service levels for willingness to pay

Willingness to pay (WTP) for an on-plot supply (that is a supply direct to the place of residence), is likely to be greater than for off-plot services. In many cases, an off-plot handpump may only offer small marginal benefits from the user's perspective over an unimproved source. Water still has to be hauled so quantities used are likely to remain similar, it may be no closer than before and it may not taste as good. So WTP for improved off-plot supplies may not be high since the tariff for off-plot unimproved services is usually zero.

An on-plot tap, however, represents a significant increase in level of service over off-plot, which potentially allows per person consumption to increase markedly, which is beneficial for hygiene and women's time.[7] This costly service enhancement is more likely to be associated with a rise in average WTP. However, the higher level of service may not be affordable – in others words, ability to pay (ATP) may be insufficient. The challenge then is to ensure a financial management approach that allows the B40 to benefit from a higher service level when their ATP becomes the overriding factor. For example, connection fees are often effective barriers to entry to the often subsidised tariff.[8] This class of consumer may not be able to connect until the fees are reduced, with costs of connection absorbed into the other fixed asset costs of supply. These issues of affordability are not discussed in detail here, but are returned to in Chapter 15.

For sanitation, the same idea holds but with a key difference. The infrastructure and services to ensure effective faecal sludge management (FSM) cost more than abandoning a pit latrine or emptying it unsafely.[9] The key difference, compared to water, is that the implications of unsafe FSM are an externality not experienced directly by the household, but are a burden that affects everyone. The move to a safely managed sanitation service therefore is not as strongly associated with an increase in willingness to pay as for on-plot water. This is because a higher proportion of the benefits accrue to society as a whole rather than the household.

Implications of targeting universal access for costs

Universal access means reaching everyone. Reaching the hardest to reach means higher per person costs than funders and governments are used to. Delivering programmes in areas with low population density drives up per person costs for both sanitation and water interventions.

Even where per person costs are not higher, the poorer the user, the lower the proportion of costs they will be able to cover from their own resources. Given the public good element in WASH services, subsidy of assets or services will play a role, as it has done for many years.[10] The question often comes down to what is the best use of limited public funds.

The service mix as a political decision

Even with an ultimate goal of universal access to a minimum level of improved infrastructure, the question of who gets access to what level of service, and who gets it first, is still fundamentally a political one. Consider two countries with the same 2015 starting point and budget constraint. By 2030, they have achieved the following combination of levels of access across the service ladder (Chapter 14): country A, which has a safely managed water service for 50% of the population, a basic service for 30% and a limited service for the remaining 20%; and country B, which has a safely managed service for 30% and a basic service for the remaining 70%.

Both outcomes involve 100% access to improved infrastructure, though neither has reached the SDG, which implies 100% safely managed.[11] However, the country B outcome is arguably more equal since, even though it has a lower proportion using safely managed water, nobody remains on a limited service whereas 20% do in country A. This example aims to illustrate that the service mix is a political decision with equality implications. Key questions for funding and financing strategies therefore include: How will public finance be targeted across territories? What is the ambition for direct cost recovery and will this differ across population groups? How will subsidies be used to progressively reduce inequalities?

The answers to these questions are often contained in various existing policies and practices, rather than existing as a consolidated WASH funding and financing strategy. This is a missed opportunity. Resources might be more effectively used and better coordinated if these political decisions were laid out for scrutiny and their implications for improving equity were debated. In the health sector, for example, it is quite common to have a "health financing strategy" as a specific document, so that these policy decisions are made more explicit and coherent.[12] What is key is to identify the greatest deficits in access, and then identify a package of WASH services appropriate to that need.

A sector funding and financing framework for WASH

Three core objectives of effectiveness, equity and efficiency (the "3Es") are common to most social sectors. In the health sector, for example, the World Health Organization has identified equity (in utilisation and resource distribution), efficiency, quality/effectiveness and transparency as the four core objectives in health financing policy.[13] WASH sector strategies also commonly incorporate the 3Es, with some suggesting additional objectives in the 'EEVERT' acronym (effectiveness, equity, viability, efficiency, replicability and transparency).[14]

A framework for WASH funding and financing strategies, showing key potential steps in their development, and how these link to the 3Es, is shown in Figure 8.1. WASH funding and financing strategies should be based on an overall assessment of needs in the sector (step 1), linked to existing sector policies and strategies and associated targets (step 2). With sector targets agreed, the costs of achieving them can be estimated (step 3), which enables the development of a comprehensive WASH funding and financing strategy to cover those costs (step 4). Finally, the uptake and quality of services can be analysed to assess whether their outcomes improve equity (step 5).

With key concepts and frameworks now explained, the rest of this chapter focuses on three critical issues with respect to improving equity: the use of repayable finance, the level of tariffs and the way in which urban sanitation investments are made. Each is accompanied by a detailed country example to illustrate the point made.

The role of repayable finance

The "3Ts" framework of tariffs, taxes and transfers[4] was mentioned earlier. However the levels of funding obtainable through the 3Ts might not allow for the capital-intensive nature of WASH investment requirements. Very large, but occasional, investments are required to pay for fixed assets such as new reservoirs and pipelines, whether at village or city scale. These assets can then deliver services over many years through affordable tariff funding.

Sanitation services are similarly capital-intensive – a latrine or treatment plant is a significant upfront capital cost at the scale of the purchaser. Repayable finance can therefore act as the link between what is affordable in the short-term to what is affordable over the long-term life of the WASH assets.

The main difference between repayable finance and the flows of the 3Ts is that the debt has to be serviced (with interest and dividends paid over the life of the loan) and the principal borrowed has to be paid back. This may seem obvious but it is often forgotten. It can have equity implications, particularly if poorer households are expected to foot the bill through tariffs, as an example, for the high cost of capital implied by commercial bank interest rates.

Despite the recent increased focus on repayable finance in the WASH sector, it still represents a small proportion of the money flowing into the sector in most LMICs. This is shown in recent data presented in the UN-WATER GLAAS report as shown in Figure 8.2 below.

Most of those countries featured in Figure 8.2 are middle-income countries (MIC); only Mali and Nepal are low-income countries (LIC). Among the countries shown, Nepal is the only LIC where repayable finance, which included

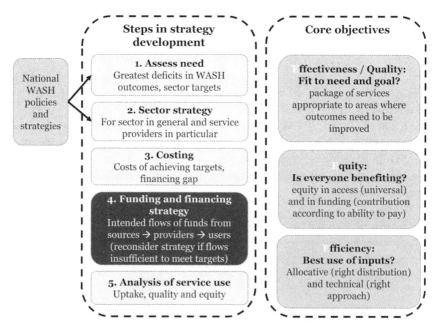

FIGURE 8.1 Framework for WASH funding and financing strategies

Source: Author's own.

A basic service for all 143

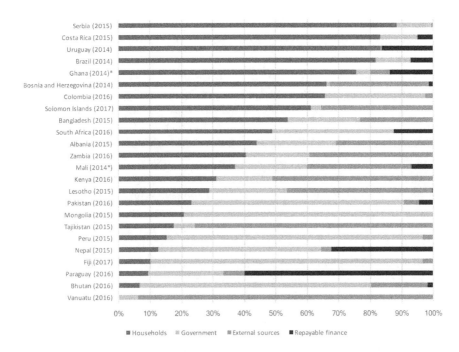

FIGURE 8.2 Sources of funding and financing contributing to total WASH expenditure

Source: UN-Water (2017).[15]

concessional loans according to GLAAS questionnaire guidance, constitutes more than 15% of sector funding.

These data may be open to question, since resources available within water ministries for filling in the GLAAS survey are low. Detailed information on funding and financing for the whole WASH sector is not easily available. This is one reason why various stakeholders (e.g. WHO, World Bank, USAID) are investing in studies to produce WASH accounts. TrackFin is a framework for WASH accounts developed by WHO to provide a basis for disaggregating expenditure by subsectors, sources of funding and service providers.[16] Countries with TrackFin data are asterisked in Figure 8.2, such studies currently being undertaken in more than ten other countries.

An example from Kenya, illustrating the role which repayable finance can play, is given in the next section.

Commercial finance for water: improving equity in the Kenya case

Kenya's sector reforms in recent years have set the scene for increased use of "blended" finance, defined as the use of concessional finance or grants to mobilise private capital flows.[17] This provides a useful case study for improving equity in the context of commercial finance. The context and recent changes are explained, with information coming from Advani (2011),[18] then several equity-related issues are drawn out.

With blended finance, "cheap" (i.e. concessional) finance or grants are used to leverage commercial finance, which is more "expensive" from an interest rate perspective. This aims to secure the necessary asset investments while still generating a market rate of return for private investors. In other words, blended finance can be used to make investments happen which otherwise would not have happened because the commercial finance on offer was too expensive for the borrower. At the same time, since each investment is not 100% grant-funded, more investments can be enabled from the same pot of money. With national commercial finance being more readily accessible than international concessional money, it is hoped that the hybrid approach will facilitate future access to commercial-only loans, paid for by the higher efficiency that "market discipline" demands.

Maji ni Maisha (MnM) is a loan programme in Kenya, which began in 2007 as a partnership between the World Bank and K-Rep Bank, now Sidian Bank. K-Rep had up until that point specialised in microfinance. MnM aimed to deliver enhancement and extension (E&E) of small piped water systems in peri-urban and rural Kenya, by incentivising service providers to access commercial finance. In most cases, service providers were legally registered community associations who had managed the schemes for many years. The underlying objective was to overcome the fact that this type of small provider is seen as a credit risk, which makes banks reluctant to lend at realistic rates.

MnM is essentially a financing product. Loans could be between US$60,000 and $115,000 for up to five years. Market rates of interest were charged, which at the time of the pilot were around 16–18% annually. The community had to fund 20% of the total project cost as equity – i.e. a down-payment commitment and a declaration of community ownership.

The key ingredient that made the finance affordable was an output-based aid (OBA) grant of up to 40% of costs, provided by the Global Partnership on Output-Based Aid (GPOBA), with the outputs being new connections and revenue targets. This ensured that taking on commercial finance was more attractive, since interest payments only had to be made on the remaining CapEx. Five years later in 2012, 35 communities had invested US$1.2 million of their own equity in E&E. Service providers had borrowed US$3.4 million from K-Rep Bank, serving an estimated 190,000 people.[19]

There are several equity angles to this. One key issue is that MnM can enable the extension of SDG-compliant on-plot connections to those unserved. This is a critical way to improve service levels to those more likely to be poor, not to mention support long-term financial viability of the service provider and therefore ensure reliability of the service for all. However, this approach may have implications for tariffs and therefore equity, which is best illustrated through a numerical example.

Making some simple assumptions about OpEx, CapManEx, population, consumption and other factors, we estimated the cost-reflective tariff it would likely be necessary to charge under a scenario of a $275,000 project cost.[20] Based on these estimates, fully grant-funded CapEx with no loan might require a cost-reflective tariff of US$0.48 per m^3. An MnM scenario where 40% of CapEx is borrowed at commercial costs of capital might require this to be raised to US$0.87 per m^3. However, a third scenario without subsidy would mean that 80% of CapEx, after the 20% community down-payment, would need to be borrowed at commercial rates. This would require a cost-reflective tariff of US$1.16.

The positive effect of the blended financing approach is to enable new connections to the unserved, who are more likely to be poor. It does still mean, however, that the service provider will most likely have to raise tariffs to cover the CoC, with potentially negative effects on equity. Nonetheless, the positive effect of the OBA grant is to enable the same investment alongside a cost-reflective tariff increase of only US$0.39 instead of $0.68.

This example should make service providers think twice about the implications for inequalities of borrowing at commercial rates. Furthermore, it should make sector stakeholders consider the risks for financial viability if managers baulk at increasing tariffs to the cost-reflective level and opt to lose money instead. Nonetheless, this example does show the benefits of schemes that leverage more available, though more risk-averse, private capital into the sector which would otherwise have been unavailable. Judicious use of such blended finance in ways that extend domestic connections to poorer households, and in ways that don't require steep tariff increases, can be an important financing mechanism for supporting the achievement of safely managed drinking water in densely populated rural areas and small towns.

The role of water tariffs

Many countries report having inadequate funds to meet sector targets. This was also established by a recent World Bank costing of the SDGs.[21] This leaves an investment gap, at the sector level, between the desired service level implied by targets and what is affordable now. However, there is a more important gap in recurrent costs at the service provider level. This second gap is between service providers' costs and their revenue. Here, "costs" include not only what is being spent, but also what should be spent on OpEx and CapManEx, as well as enhancement and expansion (E&E). Most water utilities in poor countries do not even cover required OpEx from their revenue.[22]

This service provider funding gap is key for improving equity. It has implications for present levels of service since it is common that intermittency and water quality are worse than they should be, which could be due to underspending on OpEx or CapManEx. However, it also has intergenerational equity implications. Franceys *et al.* (2016) propose a qualifying fourth "T" to the 3Ts, which is "timing", meaning that many service providers invest lower than the optimal level of capital maintenance for decades by postponing key repairs.[23] Future users then have to foot the bill when the infrastructure eventually fails, what Gasson (2017) calls "accelerated depreciation".[24] During this failing period the poorest tend to be paying the price of low-quality service, usually being at the tail end of any pipe network, and therefore most vulnerable to service level reductions.

The OECD has developed a useful framework for considering the gap between service providers' revenue and costs, as shown in Figure 8.3 below.[25] They recommend that, in the short and medium term, repayable finance can bridge the gap, as discussed in the Kenya example above.

However, in some places it is the case that tariffs could be raised to help reduce the gap, sometimes with limited affordability and equity implications. Getting tariffs right, with respect to price gradation (e.g. volumetric) and absolute levels, is critical since they are the main sustainable funding source for service providers, governmental support through taxes being as unpredictable as donor transfers. The Tunisia case given below illustrates one example where tariff increases could be used to bridge the service provider funding gap, without big implications for equity.

Equity in funding for water: the Tunisia case

Tunisia's recent tariff reforms and debates over territorial allocation of public funds provide a useful example of equity challenges in funding water services.

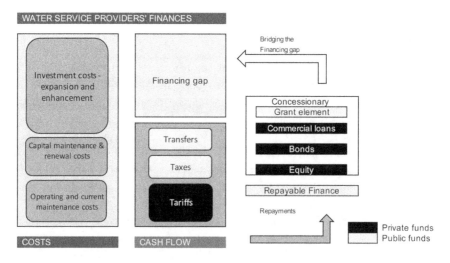

FIGURE 8.3 Service provider financing framework
Source: Adapted from OECD (2010).

The context and recent changes are explained, with information coming from a World Bank study.[26] Subsequently, several equity-related issues are drawn out.

Tunisia is a country of 11 million people, a third of whom live in rural areas, which has achieved near universal access to basic services. Between 1990 and 2015, access to improved drinking water rose from 83% to 98% of the population, while access to improved sanitation rose from 73% to 92%.[27]

The main water service provider is the state-owned utility SONEDE (Société Nationale d'Exploitation et de Distribution des Eaux), which serves 95% of the urban population and 51% of the rural population. Most of the remaining rural population is served by GDAs (Groupements de Développement Agricole), which are community-based organisations in charge of distributing water. Nonetheless, around 250,000 people rely on unimproved drinking water, mostly unprotected wells and springs.

SONEDE uses an increasing block tariff (IBT) design for pricing water services, explicitly designed to deliver affordable services to the poor, through the initital "lifeline" block, who are directly connected to the distribution system. However, in this case, like many others, all consumption is implicitly subsidised, since the utility falls short of cost recovery, with a financial gap of around US$50 million, which is covered by the government. Since the richest 20% of households consume four times more water than the poorest 20%, they capture far more of the subsidy.

As part of the World Bank study, reforms to reduce these implicit subsidies by raising tariffs were modelled, based on analysis in 2016 of household survey datasets, including WASH and welfare variables and SONEDE data.[28] This aimed to model the distributive effects of tariff reforms. The analysis concluded that even a 25% increase in tariffs would only increase poverty by 0.1%, and an almost imperceptible change (Table 8.2). This would free up much of the US$50 million, which could be invested in targeting the pockets of poor WASH access that remained. This should be caveated by the fact that Tunisia is a middle-income country where water expenditure accounts for a very small share of total household expenditure – only 0.5% on average. Such increases in tariffs in low-income countries would have more significant effects on poverty.

TABLE 8.1 Estimations on the effect of the elimination of water subsidies in Tunisia

	7% tariff increase	15% tariff increase	25% tariff increase	Full elimination of subsidies
On total per capita expenditure (TND)	−1.7	−3.5	−5.6	−10.7
On SONEDE revenues (TND million)	13.1	27.0	42.7	149.5
On poverty rates (percentage points)	0.06	0.09	0.12	0.22
On inequality Gini (0–100 scale)	0.01	0.02	0.03	0.10

Source: Trémolet et al. (2017).[26]

Such assessments are called benefit incidence analysis and aim to measure the distribution of the benefit of a public service or subsidy across the population. They are a powerful tool for assessing equity in funding and financing, and the WASH sector would do well to increase the use of such tools.

In Tunisia, two-thirds of WASH expenditures are on water. Private sources of funding make up the lion's share, particularly tariffs and self-supply expenditure. On average, over 2013–15, these sources made up 75% of total WASH expenditure. Nonetheless, domestic taxation remains an important source of funding in the sector – in 2015 domestic public transfers comprised 21% of WASH sector expenditure. These results were established by a TrackFin study, which also looked at the allocation of public funds between Tunisia's 24 governorates.[29]

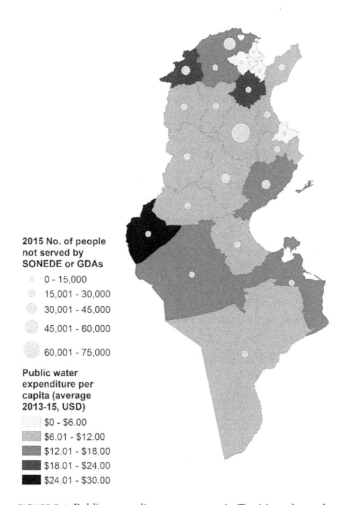

FIGURE 8.4 Public expenditure per person in Tunisia and people unserved by formal providers

Source: Trémolet et al. (2017).[26]

However, public expenditure allocations do not always appear to be linked to deficits in access, as shown in Figure 8.4. The correlation coefficient between per person public water expenditure and people without a formally provided water service is only 0.19. The allocation of public resources is more correlated to other socioeconomic criteria such as poverty or to likely O&M requirements. For example, government resources for water do tend to be more targeted to the poorest governorates, with a correlation of 0.32.

Trémolet et al. (2017) argue that, on the whole, public finance for water is well targeted to reduce regional disparities, although it raises more concerns regarding sanitation.[28] More could nonetheless be done to target funds at areas where the most formally unserved people live, especially the areas where the 250,000 people using unimproved sources are concentrated.

This case study shows how subsidies may not always be progressive, and regular assessment of whether tariffs are set at an optimal level is advised. There may not necessarily be big implications for reducing inequalities if tariffs need to be raised. In many countries, they are kept artificially low for political reasons. It is better that people pay a cost-reflective tariff in the present, rather than "accelerated depreciation" or inter-generational transfer of required funding through suboptimal OpEx and CapManEx.

Funding and financing sanitation as distinct from water

Sanitation is about far more than the private good of a latrine. Sanitation services include latrine construction services, faecal sludge management (FSM) services (e.g. emptying and conveyance), sewerage services, treatment services and more. Funding and financing sanitation offers very different challenges to water supply.

First, in situations with low baseline coverage, demand for sanitation is usually less established than for water. The prevalent orthodoxy in this situation, in rural sanitation at least, is that it is necessary to fund stimulation of that demand, either through behaviour change communication, sanitation marketing or both. The funding and financing implications of this have led to a significant debate over the best way to facilitate demand as well as supply.

Second, sanitation is arguably a public good. While a household toilet can be seen as a private good, and therefore a "household responsibility", a clean environment is certainly a public good. Since open defecation, or discharge of untreated faecal sludge, by one household affects the health of others in the community, sanitation has significant externalities. At the beginning of the chapter, sanitation was proposed as a reason why the move from a basic to a safely managed service is not likely to be as strongly associated with a big increase in willingness to pay, as would be the case for water. In public economics, both public goods and externalities are strong justification for the use of public funds.

Third, sources of funding and financing are used in quite different ways from water. For a non-networked service at the household level, whether urban or rural, the cost profile over time seems similar to water. For example, there is an upfront CapEx investment (e.g. latrine, septic tank), which then has to be sustained

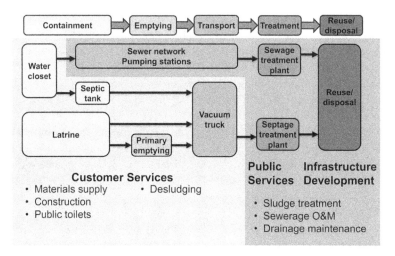

FIGURE 8.5 Urban sanitation as a suite of services
Source: Ross et al. (2016).[9]

through OpEx (e.g. cleaning, minor maintenance) and CapManEx (e.g. pit emptying or redigging).

However, the key differences to water on the funding and financing side are: 1) there is rarely a recurring charge or tariff (except for sewerage); 2) for toilets, most or all of the CapEx is usually funded by the household (i.e. self-supply), not by the government or an external source; 3) if repayable financing is used, then it is usually in the form of a small loan taken on by the household. However, if the extra-household links in a typical non-networked sanitation chain are considered, then different funding and financing questions emerge. This can be explored through Figure 8.5 with respect to urban sanitation.

Figure 8.5 illustrates how, for sewerage service chains, the piped network and pumping stations are generally seen as public services that require public finance and only in high-income countries can be financed wholly through user charges. However, for the FSM service chain, the stages of emptying and conveyance are generally seen as private or "customer" services that should be viable on a commercial basis through user charges alone. Municipalities therefore often implicitly see FSM as a private good and sewerage as a public good, even though they provide essentially the same benefits, usually resulting in under-investment in FSM services.[29] These issues are explored through a case study from Kenya.

Equity in funding for urban sanitation: the case of Nakuru, Kenya

Nakuru, Kenya, provides an interesting example of equity challenges in urban sanitation funding and cross-subsidy. The current situation is set out, with information coming from Edwards *et al.* (2015),[31] and several possible funding scenarios are discussed. Nakuru is a city of 400,000–600,000 people, with population data uncertain. Use of improved sanitation is unknown, but is likely to be very low in poorer areas. There are 14,000 sewer connections. Given the uncertainty around total population, and assuming an average household size of 5, that suggests sewerage coverage of around 10–20%. The rest of the population, then, relies on non-networked sanitation, so will eventually require FSM services when their pit latrine or septic tank fills. Household water connections provided by the utility NAWASSCO serve 30–50% of the population.

Kenya recently decentralised a number of responsibilities to county level, equivalent to district level. For household sanitation, county-level ministries have a role with respect to building sewer networks, while publicly owned utilities maintain sewer systems and wastewater treatment plants, of which Nakuru has two. Households are responsible for toilet construction and on-site waste management. The private sector runs all pit and tank emptying services.

In terms of funding and financing, the sewerage system is cross-subsidised from water tariffs. There is a "sanitation charge" comprising 75% on the customer's water bill, regardless of whether they are connected to the sewer network – hence, a regressive tax on those not able to access sewerage. The exact details of its present and future application remain unconfirmed, but it presents a useful case study for debates around reducing inequalities through cross-subsidising different kinds of WASH services.[30]

Table 8.2 presents some scenarios for use of the charge in the Nakuru context, considering in each case what the charge might fund and who might be expected to pay. The possible equity implications of that are also considered, following the principle of equity in funding – i.e. relative to their ability to pay, the poor should not pay more than the rich.

Table 8.2 is not intended to be exhaustive in setting out all the options – there are far more possible models. The question of how much revenue each would generate is also important. A conceptual framework for most types of sanitation surcharge is shown in Figure 8.6. Furthermore, a charge could be used to cover a mix of two or three of the uses in the table above, or could even be used to fund new infrastructure. All models above could likely be made more equitable if the charge was higher for those with a sewer connection.

If the charge is not linked to the service being directly provided, or if it does not cover the OpEx, CapManEx and CoC costs, then these costs will need to be covered from elsewhere. WSUP (2012) argue that such charges "can be considered pro-poor if it forms part of a system which directs a net subsidy to low-income communities [or anti-poor] if the services provided are of lower value than the charge applied".[32] Put differently, in a context where a sewer network exists, is spending on services which benefit non-sewered customers higher than revenues raised from those customers?

FSM services for low-income areas are the most challenging service to subsidise, although they arguably deserve subsidy, being more likely to be used by the poor

TABLE 8.2 Some hypothetical funding options for the sanitation charge in Nakuru

Use of charge	Who pays	Possible equity implications
Fund sewerage O&M	Only sewerage users	**Fairly equitable** – only the users of the sewerage service are being charged for its upkeep. However, these households are likely to be richer and able to afford to also cross-subsidise services used by poorer households such as FSM services of public toilets.
	All water bill payers	**Not equitable** – even non-connected households (likely to be poorer) are expected to cover costs of sewer users.
Fund FSM O&M	Only sewerage users	**Very equitable** – sewerage users are likely to be able to afford this charge. Even though they do not directly benefit from FSM services, they benefit indirectly from a cleaner environment.
	All water bill payers	**Fairly equitable** – water bill users represent 30–50% of urban dwellers and are likely the richer half of teh city. 50–75% of water bill payers are likely to be users of FSM services themselves, and would also benefit indirectly from a cleaner environment.
Fund public toilets O&M	All water bill payers	**Very equitable** – those relying on public toilets are more likely to be poor, so a cross-subsidy to them from either group is likely to be fair.

Source: Authors, based on information in Edwards *et al.* (2015).[31]

around the world.[9] The aim should be to increase uptake of the services by reducing the cost to poor households, but the challenge lies in how that should be done. Emptying services are often provided by the private sector, which may be preferable since publicly operated vacuum truck services have a chequered record. What, therefore, should be subsidised?

In Nakuru, existing financial flows in the FSM service chain include: 1) user fees from households to private operators; 2) private operators paying an annual US$170 charge to empty at the treatment plant; 3) NAWASSCO funding of treatment plant O&M via water tariff revenue. There is not an obvious way to subsidise user fees without providing funds to private operators which, without price regulation and other mechanisms, could be difficult to police. If the emptying charge were subsidised, then savings could only be passed on to households through some form of price control mechanism. One option could be to fund an NGO or small business to provide low-tech emptying services in poorer neighbourhoods that vacuum trucks found hard to access, implicitly provided by a part-subsidy for the user fee. Sewerage connection fees could also be reduced, but this would be unlikely to reach the poorest households.

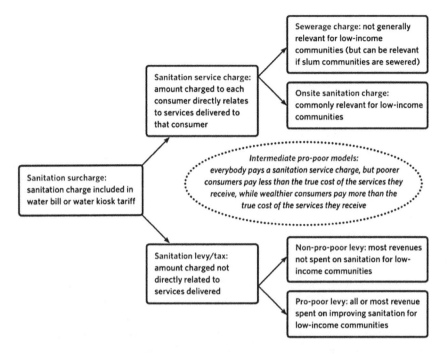

FIGURE 8.6 Main types of sanitation surcharge system
Source: Reproduced from WSUP (2012).[32]

Conclusion

This chapter has examined the implications of new SDG targets and indicators for funding and financing strategies, with a view to reducing inequalities in WASH access. In particular, the implications for the costs of service provision and how they should be covered, have been considered.

It has been argued that "first a basic service for all" is likely to be a more realistic and equitable interim goal than "safely managed for all". However, since those without basic access are the least able to pay, sources of funding beyond tariffs will remain critically important for reducing inequalities. Service levels will need to be appropriate to prevalent levels of demand and willingness to pay. Without sufficient demand, levels of service uptake required to cover costs will not be achieved, and the sustainability of services will be threatened. When that happens, the poorest tend to pay the price of low-quality service, usually being at the tail end of any pipe network, and therefore most vulnerable to service level reductions.

The Kenya water case study illustrates that innovative mechanisms such as blended finance can unlock new investment. However, care needs to be taken around the implications for affordability for the B40, so that inequalities are not widened. The Tunisia case study shows that subsidies may not always be progressive, and regular assessment of whether tariffs are set at an optimal level is advised. There may not necessarily be big equity implications if tariffs need to be raised. It is better that people pay a cost-reflective tariff in the present, rather than "accelerated depreciation" through suboptimal OpEx and CapManEx. The Kenya sanitation case study shows that the equity implications of cross-subsidies need to be carefully considered. The B40 are far more likely to use FSM services than to have a sewerage connection, so FSM services are equally, if not more deserving of subsidies to ensure affordability and thereby reduce inequalities.

Very few countries have an explicit "WASH funding and financing strategy", whereas it is quite common in the health sector. This is a missed opportunity. Resources might be more effectively used and better coordinated if these political decisions were laid out for scrutiny and their implications for reducing inequalities were debated. Governments need to carefully consider the service levels they are aiming for as part of the SDGs and, having undertaken a costing of those targets, they need to work out how those costs can be covered.

However, the inescapable conclusion has to be that international transfers will be required, at a significant level, if the desired equalities in WASH outcomes are to be achieved by 2030. Tariffs can be, and have to be, cost-reflective at the operational expenditure level, but accepting that affordability limit means that governments have to support capital maintenance through taxes for a generation. Similarly, accepting below-cost tariffs means that private capital cannot be a significant financing stream. Significantly increased levels of donor grants and support to concessional finance will be required for lower-income countries to deliver the SDG-desired improved access to WASH. This, is how, in effect, high-income countries achieved the equality of universal service.

Notes

1 WHO/UNICEF (2017) Progress on drinking water, sanitation and hygiene.
2 WHO/UNICEF (2017) Safely managed drinking water: 1–56.
3 World Bank (2016) Poverty and shared prosperity 2016: taking on inequality. World Bank. DOI:10.1596/978–1-4648–0958–3.
4 Infrastructure Finance Working Group (2012) Infrastructure finance and funding reform: 1–43.
5 OECD (2009) Strategic financial planning for water supply and sanitation: 94.
6 Fonseca, C., Franceys, R., Batchelor, C., et al. (2011) Life-cycle costs approach. Costing sustainable services. IRC .
7 Evans, B., Bartram, J.K., Hunter, P. et al. Public health and social benefits of at-house water supplies: final report: 53.
8 Franceys, R.W.A. (2005). Charging to enter the water shop? The costs of urban water connections for the poor. *Water Science and Technology: Water Supply*, 5: 209 LP-216.
9 Ross, I., Scott, R., Blackett, I.C., Hawkins, P.M. (2016). Fecal Sludge Management: Diagnostics for Service Delivery in Urban Areas Summary Report – Diagnostic Tools for Fecal Sludge Management Services in Urban Areas. Available at: http://documents.worldbank.org/curated/en/909691468338135561/Fecal-sludge-management-diagnostics-for-service-delivery-in-urban-areas-summary-report
10 The classic arguments for subsidising basic social services hold true for both water and sanitation. Subsidies for WASH services can be economically efficient. This is because

both sanitation and water supply have externalities, in the form of social benefits which would not be fully taken into account if prices were set entirely by the market. Subsidies can also be equitable, because public funds can help ensure access to services considered as human rights and which may be difficult for the poor to access.

11 Universal basic WASH services for all should be achievable for all countries by 2030. However, achieving universal access to safely managed services by 2030 is probably unachievable for many countries, given likely institutional and funding constraints.
12 As examples, links to the health financing strategies for Ghana and Côte d'Ivoire are available below: www.moh.gov.gh/wp-content/uploads/2016/02/Health-Finance-Strategy-160203045304.pdf www.coopami.org/fr/countries/countries/cote_ivoire/social_protection/pdf/social_protection05.pdf
13 WHO (2008) Health financing policy: a guide for decision-makers.
14 Viability means ability to access ongoing funding sources, replicability means not being dependent on a particular leader or donor, and transparency relates particularly to financial management.
15 UN-Water (2017) UN-Water Global Analysis and Assessment of Sanitation and Drinking-Water (GLAAS). World Health Organization. DOI:CC BY-NC-SA 3.0 IGO.
16 TrackFin has established standard classifications so as to facilitate comparison across countries. Crucially, it includes not only public finance allocated to WASH but also contributions from households, service providers, donors, etc.
17 OECD (2015) *Blended Finance Vol. 1: A Primer for Development Finance and Philanthropic Funders, ReDesigning Development Finance Initiative.*
18 Advani, R. (2011) Financing small piped water systems in rural and peri-urban Kenya. *Water and Sanitation Program Working Paper*, WSP. Washington, DC: World Bank.
19 Other important design aspects included a partial credit guarantee for K-Rep to cover themselves for 50% of the loan value in case of default, as well as technical assistance in the form of consultants to help develop a bankable proposal and oversee the project.
20 The calculation assumes a 20-year asset lifetime (i.e. depreciation of US$ 13,750 per year), OpEx at 3% of CapEx a year (i.e. US$ 8,250 per year), 100% bill collection efficiency, and a population of 3,500 using 40 litres per capita per day. Furthermore, it is based on 'rolling-over' the loan at the end of the tenor – i.e. borrowing the same amount again.
21 Hutton, G. and Varughese, M. (2016) The costs of meeting the 2030 Sustainable Development Goal targets on drinking water, sanitation, and hygiene – summary report. Available at: www.worldbank.org/en/topic/water/publication/the-costs-of-meeting-the-2030-sustainable-development-goal-targets-on-drinking-water-sanitation-and-hygiene?CID=WAT_TT_Water_EN_EXT.
22 Danilenko, A., van den Berg, C., Macheve, B., Moffitt, L.J. (2014) The IBNET Water Supply and Sanitation Blue Book 2014: The International Benchmarking Network for Water and Sanitation Utilities Databook. Washington, DC: The World Bank, DOI:10.1596/978–1-4648–0276–8.
23 Franceys, R., Cavill, S. and Trevett, A. (2016) Who really pays? A critical overview of the practicalities of funding universal access. *Waterlines*, 35: 78–93.
24 Gasson, C. (2017) A new model for water access: a global blueprint for innovation. 1–40.
25 OECD (2010) Innovative financing mechanisms for the water sector. DOI:10.2166/wp.2008.149.
26 Trémolet, S. *et al.* (2017) Tunisia WASH and poverty diagnostic: Phase 3 report: synthesis and policy recommendations.
27 WHO/UNICEF (2015) Progress on sanitation and drinking water: 2015 update and MDG assessment. World Health Organization: 90.
28 Trémolet, S., Ross, I., Mnif, M., Mujica, A. and Said F. (2017) Tunisia – WASH and poverty diagnostic: Phase 2 report – WASH accounts.
29 Ross, I., Scott, R., Blackett, I. and Hawkins P. (2016). Fecal sludge management: diagnostics for service delivery in urban areas – tools and guidelines, 66.

30 WSUP commissioned a follow-up study in Nakuru and Kisumu of factors affecting the willingness (or no willingness) of non-poor consumers and businesses to pay a pro-poor sanitation surcharge added to their water bill. The report was available in autumn 2017.
31 Edwards, B., Nagpal, T., Mohammed, A., Uandela, A., Wolfsbauer, M. and Norman, G. (2015) Municipal finance for sanitation in three African cities.
32 WSUP (2012) Sanitation surcharges collected through water bills: a way forward for financing pro-poor sanitation? Available at: www.wsup.com/resource/sanitation-surcharges-collected-through-water-bills-a-way-forward-for-financing-pro-poor-sanitation/

9

BREAKING THE BARRIERS

Disability, ageing and HIV in inclusive WASH programming

Jane Wilbur, Louisa Gosling and Hazel Jones

Introduction

Progress on the Millennium Development Goals (MDGs) drinking water and sanitation targets has been uneven, with the hardest to reach largely left out, including the poorest and particularly disadvantaged groups.[1] This inequitable progress has led to a stronger emphasis in the Sustainable Development Goals (SDGs) on reducing inequalities, and a commitment to 'leave no-one behind'.[2] Among the groups who are most vulnerable to being left behind are people with disabilities, older people, and people living with chronic illnesses like HIV. These facets of vulnerability are cross-cutting and often result in multiple disadvantages especially when compounded by poverty.

This is not a small minority of the population. WHO and the World Bank (2011)[3] estimate that 15% of the global population – over 1 billion people – have some kind of disability, and are more likely to be poor than the general population.[4] In 2015, 901 million (12.3%) of the world's population were aged 60 or over; by 2050 this number is expected to grow to 2.1 billion, of whom 8 out of 10 will live in developing countries.[5] In 2014, there were 36.7 million people living with HIV.[6] This chapter focuses on disability, ageing and HIV (as an example of chronic illness) because the barriers to accessing water, sanitation and hygiene (WASH) services faced by these people, and the potential solutions to address them are similar. Most of the experience on which this chapter is based relates to disability and ageing, but the barriers and solutions to WASH access are often similar for people living with chronic illnesses.

People with disabilities and older people

People with disabilities and older people are disproportionately affected by lack of access to WASH and face many similar barriers. As people age, they are more are likely to experience health conditions that lead to impairments.

When water is only available from a distant water point or difficult to fetch, where a pump is heavy to operate or where stored water is hard to access, disabled and older people often rely on others and may restrict their fluid intake so as not to be a burden, with the attendant risk of urinary infections.[7]

Where sanitation and hygiene facilities are available, they are often difficult for older and disabled people to access and use. As a result, they may continue open defecation, or need assistance from a family member, thereby increasing the workload on the family. People with visual impairments may need someone to guide them to the toilet, or, if they make their own way, they risk stepping in the faeces of others.[8] Unhygienic toilets affect everyone, but if the floors are soiled, it is much harder for disabled people to keep themselves clean, especially if they are blind, or have a mobility impairments and are forced to crawl on a wet and soiled floor.[9] Bathing, hygiene and menstrual hygiene management also present a range of difficulties for people with different impairments and for those looking after them,[10] especially for those who experience incontinence. People with intellectual disabilities may have additional difficulties communicating their needs and understanding information about hygiene. For disabled and older people, the dangers of getting dirty affect their health, degrade their self-esteem and can affect how others see and treat them. This can undermine their confidence, make them unwilling to express their needs and further perpetuate their exclusion or disadvantage.

People living with HIV

WASH is particularly important for people living with chronic illnesses like HIV (PHLIV) to ensure that they continue to live healthy and productive lives. It is estimated that PLHIV need more than the average amount of water per person per day to have sufficient water for drinking, food preparation, laundry and personal hygiene.[11] Access to WASH can help prevent opportunistic infections and diarrhoea, which affects 90% of PLHIV,[12] and there is growing evidence that WASH interventions are cost-effective in reducing morbidity associated with HIV.[13]

Unfortunately, a lack of access to safe WASH and high rates of HIV often converge. For example, in the Southern Africa region, an estimated 12.7 million people have HIV. In the same region, 174 million people, almost two-thirds of the population, do not have access to basic sanitation; more than 100 million do not have safe water.[14]

Poor access to safe water, sanitation and waste-disposal facilities can pose significant challenges to PLHIV or those caring for them. Physical barriers are exacerbated by reduced energy levels, side effects from medication or symptoms of opportunistic infections, and may be compounded by stigma and discrimination where PLHIV are prevented from using community services due to misconceptions about the routes of transmission of HIV.[14]

Equality and non-discrimination in human rights

People who are older, with disabilities or living with HIV are entitled to the Human Rights to Water and Sanitation as explained in Chapter 2. Their rights are reinforced through the principle of equality and non-discrimination.[15]

Article 28 of the Convention on the Rights of Persons with Disabilities (CRPD) also specifically mentions the right to safe water, and Article 9 to 'access, on an equal basis with others, to the physical environment ... and to facilities and services'. States parties are required to take measures that 'include the identification and elimination of obstacles and barriers to accessibility'.[16]

Many countries have now enshrined these rights in their legal frameworks, but much more work is needed to advocate for their progressive realisation. A human rights-based approach seeks to ensure that even the most marginalised rights holders can hold duty-bearers accountable for the realisation of their rights to water and sanitation. This means supporting duty bearers to fulfil their responsibilities to make WASH accessible to all, as well as supporting rights holders to claim their rights.[17]

What are the barriers that prevent access?

Disabled and older people and PLHIV experience numerous barriers preventing their access to and use of WASH services.

Physical barriers in the natural and built environment tend to be obvious, such as distance to facilities, heavy hand pumps or stiff taps, lack of support rails and seats, and narrow entrances.[7,20,21]

Social and cultural barriers tend to be deep-rooted and harder to identify and address, such as negative attitudes and discriminatory practices experienced by PLHIV and people with disabilities.[22]

Institutional barriers relate to the way that programmes and services are planned, delivered and resourced. Barriers include inadequate policies, inadequate funding for inclusion, lack of staff awareness and training, lack of information about appropriate designs, consultation procedures that ignore marginalised groups and individuals, and a lack of effective integration across sectors (i.e. HIV and WASH[8,14]).

Most marginalised groups face a combination of all these barriers and therefore face multiple and diverse disadvantages.[21,23,24]

Intersectionality

Analyses of 'multiple aspects of identity and status in a society are critical to understanding the power imbalances that exist within cultures leading to inequality'.[10] The concept of intersectionality describes the interaction of multiple dimensions of discrimination – for instance, a disabled woman with HIV who is also disadvantaged due to her gender, her disability and her health status.

BOX 9.1 THE SOCIAL MODEL OF INCLUSION

The UN Convention on the Rights of Persons with Disabilities[16] states that 'disability is an evolving concept [...] ... disability results from the interaction between persons with impairments and attitudinal and environmental barriers that hinders their full and effective participation in society on an equal basis with others'. Traditional 'charity' or medical approaches often focus on treating the different and 'special' needs of excluded groups. In contrast the 'social model'[18] asserts that diversity is part of any society, and the lack of opportunities, independence and participation experienced by excluded groups is the result of social, institutional and environmental barriers. WASH services can be designed to be more inclusive by finding ways to overcome these barriers.

While the focus on dismantling barriers in society is empowering, individuals' impairments do also affect their WASH needs. For instance, incontinence, pain, and an inability to communicate WASH needs are also significant barriers to WASH access.[10] Understanding how to meet individual needs as well as address the societal barriers is one of the core challenges for the WASH sector.

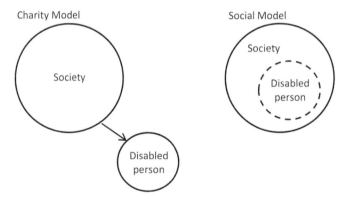

FIGURE 9.1 The charity and social model
Source: Coe and Wapling (2010).[19]

A study in Papua New Guinea (WaterAid et al., 2017[25]) showed that age, disability, gender and social status intersected to increase the barriers to WASH access and use. Disability had a greater impact on women than on men, in terms of the physical burden of water collection and an increased risk of violence when performing WASH-related tasks. There was also a difference in the WASH support provided to older men and women. Women were only supported when their functional limitations were severe. Men were supported much earlier.

Other dimensions of inequality are also important. There are often disparities between urban and rural populations; and improved WASH access appears to be strongly associated with higher levels of education and wealth.[10]

Intersectionality shows that disability, ageing and chronic illness cannot be addressed in silos. WASH practitioners attempting to address inequalities need to recognise this complexity in programme design and policy. For example, the Australian Government invested in a national political economy analysis in Indonesia that incorporated gender and disability to help understand the drivers and barriers, policy, budgetary and implementation arrangements that ensure that everybody is guaranteed access to WASH services.[26]

What do we know about solutions?

Solutions to make WASH inclusive for these groups are still evolving. There is growing experience in the sector of the following approaches, of their potential for success as well as challenges in implementation.

Legal requirements for accessible WASH services

An obvious starting point is infrastructure solutions that improve the physical accessibility of facilities, such as ramps to WASH facilities, wider entrances to latrines, hand-rails in latrines, water-point resting stands and markers for paths.[7,27,28]

National laws and building regulations often set out standards that include accessibility. For example, in India the Persons with Disabilities (Equal Opportunities, Protection of Rights and Full Participation) Act 1994, states: non-discrimination in the built environment [means] that 'the appropriate Governments and the local authorities shall, within the limits of their economic capacity and development, provide for [. . .] adaptation of toilets for wheel chair users.[29]

Laws are further specified through regulation. In England, Building Regulations require that all people, regardless of disability, age or gender are able to access public buildings and use their facilities, both as visitors and people who live or work in them. It sets out detailed guidance for accessible toilets and mechanisms for enforcing compliance with regulations.[30] It is the responsibility of governments to have and enforce such standards for accessibility, particularly in public buildings, but compliance is weak in many countries. Advocacy and campaigning are often necessary to pressurise governments and service providers to make services accessible to all.

Guidelines on design and construction of accessible WASH services

Many countries have accessibility standards that exist on paper but are not implemented or enforced. One reason is a lack of capacity and clear guidelines on the design and construction of accessible facilities, but the body of resources on how to construct accessible institutional WASH services in low- and middle-income settings is growing. Similarly, low-cost WASH solutions for households are increasingly available. The following examples have been grouped into three types:

- Guidance for constructing accessible WASH services in institutional settings, such as in schools, healthcare centres and market places: Developed in collaboration with relevant government officials, Disabled Persons' Organisations (DPOs) and disabled end users, these set out technical standards to improve the physical accessibility of facilities, such as ramps, hand-rails and raised toilet seats, wider doorways and additional space inside cubicles. Examples include:
    - Technical options for school water sanitation and hygiene (United Republic of Tanzania, 2015).[31]
    - National standards for designs of child-friendly school WASH facilities, including units for children with disabilities (MOET Vietnam, 2011).[32]
    - Technical manual on community water supply, hygiene and sanitation facilities (WaterAid Madagascar, 2010).[33]

- **Manuals for accessible household latrine options:** Developed for different geographic contexts, these include technical drawings of different designs that household members and service providers can adapt to suit needs and budgets. The adaptations include options for doorways, pathways, ramps, hand-rails, raised toilet seats, water-dispensers, handwashing and bathing arrangements. Examples include:
    - Disability Friendly-Latrine: Removing Sanitation Barriers of Persons with Disabilities (ADD International Bangladesh, 2015).[34]
    - The Compendium of Accessible WASH Technologies (Jones and Wilbur, 2014).[27]
    - The Handbook on Accessible Household Sanitation for Persons with Disabilities (Ministry of Drinking Water and Sanitation & WaterAid India, 2015).[35]
    - The Handbook on Toilet Options for Rural Households in Bhutan, Rural Sanitation and Hygiene Program (Public Heath Engineering Division, 2011).[36]
    - Water and Sanitation for Disabled People and Other Vulnerable Groups: Designing Services to Improve Accessibility (Jones and Reed, 2005).[37]

- **Individual solutions for marginalised groups and individuals**: These include incremental infrastructure improvements for greater access to WASH at the household level, tailored to individual needs. For example:
    - The Living with Dignity Program in Papa New Guinea (Layton and Atchison, 2012).[23]
    - Small doable actions: a feasible approach to behaviour change (WASHplus, 2015).[38]

BOX 9.2 INCLUSION IS NOT A TECHNICAL FIX: ADDRESS ALL BARRIERS

Even when physical barriers have been addressed, marginalised individuals may still be excluded by social, cultural and institutional barriers. For instance, it is quite common to find carefully designed accessible school toilets located in an inaccessible part of the school grounds, or to find that no disabled children attend the school because they are afraid of being teased. Research in Uganda and Zambia revealed that 19% of people with disabilities in the target population were told by non-disabled people not to touch water because they thought them unclean or that their condition was contagious.[39]

Strengthening the ability of excluded groups to claim rights to WASH

Civil society organisations, at global, national and local levels, have always played a critical role in fighting for laws and policies against discrimination and for their enforcement. For example, the International Disability Alliance advocates globally, while the likes of the Madagascar National Platform for people with disabilities (PFPH) is engaging their government on disability rights, with a focus on the national inclusion plan for people with disabilities, which includes WASH.[40]

While Disabled Persons' Organisations are key stakeholders, they often have limited capacity and funding, and may be limited in whom they represent. People who have had more opportunities, often physically disabled men who live in urban areas, are more likely to be members than people with an intellectual, hearing or communication impairment, or those living in rural areas. WASH practitioners need to work with DPOs, but be aware that the DPO's agenda may only represent a limited section of people with disabilities living in the country. For example, collaboration with organisations of disabled persons in several countries has helped raise awareness of water and sanitation as human rights. In Cambodia, WaterAid collaborated with the inclusive arts organisation 'Epic Arts' to raise awareness of government laws and guidelines on accessible WASH through films, drama and song.[41] During the 2014 uprising in Burkina Faso, disabled people were closely involved with other civil society organisations in calling for changes in governance, including for more equitable, sustainable and accountable WASH services.[42]

Practical checklists and guidelines for inclusive processes

Community mobilisation processes, hygiene behaviour change and the development of community structures for managing and maintaining services should be as inclusive. Promoting the participation of marginalised groups in these processes and programme design phases is key, as is using situation analysis, baseline surveys and planning procedures to assess barriers to WASH experienced by different groups in specific contexts. Finally, inclusive approaches are needed to monitor and evaluate access and use of services.

A number of good practice guidelines have been developed including:

- The Inclusive WASH checklist[43] and Disability: making CLTS fully inclusive.[27] These highlight possible modifications to a 'standard' community-based WASH programme to make it more inclusive.
- CLTS+:[44] Further modifications to Community Led Total Sanitation (CLTS) processes were made in an action-research project in Malawi. CLTS implementers introduced additional triggering activities and paid more attention to households with disabled and older people post-triggering. It resulted in increased awareness of the community and implementers of the access needs of older and disabled people, and in adaptations to improve accessibility of some household latrines.
- A Field Guide for Integrating WASH and HIV programmes in Southern Africa[45] provides advice on HIV-sensitive approaches to WASH programmes and ways of working with communities to dispel myths around HIV and reduce stigma.
- The Minimum standards for age and disability standards in humanitarian action[46] includes a section on WASH.

These experience-based guidelines provide practical ideas that can be further developed, although taking them to scale remains a challenge and further evidence is needed to promote them. For example, 'Undoing Inequity'[39] was a collaboration between NGO, academic and disability actors in the UK, Uganda and Zambia. Baseline surveys gathered evidence about barriers faced by disabled, older and chronically ill people when accessing WASH services.[47] Solutions were developed and tested[39] and the process was monitored.[48] The research helped to influence national WASH plans and standards in Uganda,[49] and the DFID Disability Framework in the UK.

Promoting participatory approaches

Effective participatory processes can improve the accessibility and sustainability of services and empower marginalised groups. However, if people participate without being able to influence decisions, it can be a disempowering experience and reinforce inequality.

People who are socially marginalised or stigmatised often need support to participate in a meaningful way. They may face a negative reaction from others and it is often a challenge to convince non-marginalised groups that including marginalised groups adds value and can benefit the whole community.

Participation can also be constrained by stigma in the private sphere. Research in Timor-Leste[50] found that due to the perception of stigma, households rarely include their disabled family members in community decision-making about WASH.

The Special Rapporteur on Human Rights to Water and Sanitation set out the following essential elements for ensuring active, free and meaningful participation at various levels of decision-making, after an extensive consultation with stakeholders.[51] These 'nothing about us without us' principles apply at every stage of policy and programme design.

- Involve people in setting out the terms of engagement.
- Create space for participation; enable people to access the participatory process by addressing barriers (such as language, meeting venues, time, and information). Raise awareness among others of the value of their participation.
- Guarantee free and safe participation.
- Ensure access to information in a form and language they can understand. Provide a real opportunity to influence decision-making and make sure people understand the process.
- Use a variety of methods that work at different levels. For example, a national DPO federation may contribute most effectively to policy-making decisions, while at the community level it is important to have direct participation of individuals who will be using the facilities.

BOX 9.3 ACCESSIBILITY AND SAFETY AUDITS

Accessibility and safety audits of WASH facilities are an excellent way to increase service usability and promote the participation of marginalised groups in design and programming.[52,53]

These are carried out collaboratively with implementers and users - women and men of different ages, girls and boys, including disabled people with different impairments. Different members of the team try to use the facility to see if this can be done as independently as possible, with ease and without feeling unsafe. With facilitation, the group then suggests what improvements can be made. These feed into new designs or adaptation of existing facilities and the way they are managed and maintained. For example, lighting at night can have a big impact on ease of use and feelings of safety for users, especially women.[54]

The process enables marginalised individuals to express their challenges and contribute to the development of their community. Practitioners gain a direct and practical understanding of the design barriers and their impact on some users.

Bilateral agency and development partners' policies and strategies

Funding agencies' priorities and policies can help effect inclusive implementation. For example, the Australian Government's strategy for strengthening disability inclusive development in Australia's aid programme[55] is supplemented by its Design Principles[56] for the design of public infrastructure. The UK Department for International Development (DFID)'s disability framework includes commitments to hold implementing partners to account for disability sensitive programmes in the WASH sector, and to make partner governments aware of their responsibility to deliver on their United Nations CRPD commitments through policy dialogue and programme design.[57] DFID is also pushing for disaggregation of data by disability status in the global monitoring system for WASH.[58] Both DFID and DFAT are promoting a 'twin-track' approach (Box 9.4).

The World Bank's policy framework makes a strong case for inclusive development in its operations to end extreme poverty and promote shared prosperity. The Environmental and Social Framework,[59] set to be operational in 2018, makes several references to safeguarding the interests of 'the elderly' and persons with disabilities. The Bank has produced a Guidance Note on including persons with disabilities in Water Sector Operations that provides practical advice.[60] Such frameworks aim to mainstream disability-inclusive development at scale. For example, the PAMSIMSA AF Project in Indonesia, co-financed by the Government of Indonesia, World Bank and DFAT, has introduced a disability-inclusive approach into its operations since November 2016. CBM Australia has conducted training on disability inclusion to community facilitators that has now reached about 4,200 individuals. After pilot projects in 200 villages, the project has developed practice guidelines, design specifications and monitoring indicators to help institutionalise the inclusive approach.[60]

Coordination, collaboration and integration with stakeholders from other sectors

A significant reason for the lack of attention to WASH for disabled and older people, or PLHIV is the poor integration between the sectors. A gap and needs assessment carried out in four countries in Southern Africa by SAfAIDS[45] showed that PLHIV have specific WASH needs, but there is limited integration of WASH in national HIV policies, guidelines and frameworks; nor is HIV adequately integrated into WASH frameworks. The study concludes that the WASH and HIV integration process should involve stakeholders at all levels, led by national governments. A bi-directional field guide for integrating WASH and HIV programmes in Southern Africa was produced after the study.[61]

There are some examples where WASH and HIV have been integrated in national policy and programmes. In Lesotho, health extension workers are raising awareness on HIV and WASH in communities and healthcare centres, as well as providing advice to primary caregivers on effective WASH practices when caring for people who are sick. In Swaziland, Rural Health Motivators are integrating WASH with HIV in their community work. In Mozambique, Water & Sanitation for the Urban Poor has mainstreamed HIV in WASH interventions in urban slums.[61]

Mainstreaming inclusive approaches

The mainstreaming continuum

Jones[63] identified a continuum that shows how institutions can mainstream disability and ageing in their work (Figure 9.2). This continuum is a useful way for institutions to conceptualise the stages along the journey to mainstream equality and inclusion. It can be used to help plan, resource and monitor progress, regardless of where on the continuum an institution finds itself.

BOX 9.4 THE TWIN-TRACK APPROACH

The twin-track approach to disability in development aims to ensure that marginalised groups or individuals are included and benefit equally from all development activities. The approach mainstreams disability issues in programmes and policies, while at the same time supporting disability-focused programmes, with the two tracks complementing each other.[62]

The approach has been widely adopted by development agencies, although there is a risk that more emphasis is placed on disability specific programmes with less emphasis on mainstreaming which requires changes in attitudes and entrenched practices.

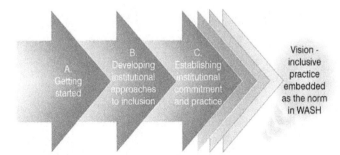

FIGURE 9.2 A continuum towards WASH organisations mainstreaming disability and ageing in the work

Source: Jones (2013).[64]

BOX 9.5 INCLUSIVE BUDGETING

Budget is needed to cover the administrative and operational costs of mainstreaming equality and inclusion comprehensively within an organisation and its work.[63]

Administrative budget items:

- Awareness of staff on equality and inclusion.
- Workplace adaptations permitting recruitment of people marginalized on the basis of gender, disability, health condition, age, race, ethnicity.

Operational budget items:

- Awareness on equality and inclusion among different stakeholders involved in programmes.
- Ensuring infrastructure constructed is fully accessible.
- Ensuring information is accessible for all including persons with a hearing or visual impairments, as well as with mental health, intellectual and psychosocial impairments.

Mobility International broadly recommends allocating 5 to 7% of the operational costs, and between 1 to 3% of the administrative costs to disability inclusion.[64] This will vary depending on the type of activities the organisation is implementing.

The final goal of the mainstreaming continuum is to have inclusive practices embedded as standard in all policies, practices and procedures and in all aspects of WASH programmes and services,[63] which no WASH organisation has yet achieved. It takes a long time to progress through the continuum, and it is important not to underestimate the long-term investment needed. It is important to celebrate achievements along the way and to keep refreshing the commitment to continue moving forward.

Monitoring

There is currently a lack of routine data collection on disability, ageing, chronic illness and WASH at national level, although more effort is being focused on developing methodologies and indicators. There is also growing experience of monitoring inclusion in programmes. At programme level, it is possible to monitor inputs, process, outputs and outcomes to assess progress towards reaching people with accessible and acceptable services.

Inputs

Organisations can monitor the processes and programme inputs that help make WASH services more inclusive, such as institutional policies and standards on inclusion, training for staff and partners, and plans and budgets for inclusion.

Processes

Process monitoring is useful for learning how to strengthen inclusive approaches. At institutional level, the mainstreaming continuum (described above) was used to analyse progress in mainstreaming equality and inclusion in WaterAid[66] showing what progress has been made and what further steps are needed.

At community level, qualitative tools can be used to monitor aspects of inclusive WASH programming[48] such as the attendance and participation of more marginalised community members at meetings, the developing capacity of WASH staff to understand and implement inclusive approaches, and what stakeholders consider to be the most significant changes.

Process monitoring is invariably qualitative and does not provide rigorous or comparable findings. It is important to treat this type of monitoring with caution, but the tools can provoke illuminating insights among participants that can help to inform and deepen inclusive approaches.

Outputs

It is relatively easy to monitor what accessible facilities have been constructed. Public facilities can be monitored using a checklist of observable features, such as a ramp, wider cubicle, hand-rail and raised toilet seat, accompanied by specifications on details like ramp slope and door width. An Accessibility and Safety Audit (see Box 9.3) can be used to check whether intended users of the facility can actually use it independently, safely and in comfort.

Accessible facilities in households are less standardised as they are tailored to meet the requirements of individual users. Monitors could use a checklist of accessibility features, but it is more important to ask users directly whether the adaptations really meet their needs.

Outcomes

The main measure of outcomes is the increased use of WASH services by older people, people with disabilities and PLHIV. This is best measured by accessibility audits or in-depth interviews that take time, but if carried out on a sample basis by practitioners can provide important insights to guide programme design. Survey questions, such as 'can/does everyone in this household use this latrine/handwashing unaided, or as independently as possible?', have been used for baseline studies to provide quantitative information on the quality of WASH access.

If incorporated into evaluation or monitoring questionnaires, these could also be used to assess programme outcomes.

National monitoring

The in-depth monitoring of individual and group-based inequalities is costly, but can nevertheless be done in a targeted manner where relevant to provide a proxy measure of progress. A small number of questions can be included in national surveys to enable disaggregation of specific groups such as people living with disabilities (Box 9.6), while more detailed and selective studies can be carried out to stimulate discussion and diagnosis of the specific challenges faced.

The WHO/UNICEF JMP Task Force on Monitoring Inequalities for the 2030 Sustainable Development Agenda recommends the use of subnational sample surveys and perception surveys to see whether the barriers to WASH, including physical, social and cultural and institutional barriers, have actually been addressed.[67]

It is easier to measure the accessibility of institutional facilities. The JMP expanded WASH questions for school surveys[68] now include questions on whether drinking water, toilets and handwashing facilities are accessible to those with limited mobility or vision.

As more people begin to collect data about accessibility in schools, it will increase state accountability to make WASH services inclusive.

Disaggregating data

There are strong arguments for collecting disaggregated data for WASH programmes to better understand the nature and scale of inequalities, and to advocate for strengthening of political and policy commitments to invest in reaching everyone.

However, identifying people who are older, disabled or ill in a community can highlight differences, increase stigma and make members of marginalised groups feel as though they are part of a stocktake every time a new organisation comes to a community. Disaggregating data can be tokenistic and not produce any benefits for those groups unless it is clear how the information will be used.

The method for disaggregation is important. It is widely accepted that simply asking whether someone is disabled or HIV positive is potentially stigmatising and unlikely to get reliable results. The terms are not understood consistently, and affected individuals are very often unwilling to identify themselves.

Two tools have been developed to capture information about disability from household surveys: the Washington Group (WG) questions[69] and the WHO's Model Disability Survey (MDS). Both are based on the psycho-social model of disability that informs the International Classification of Functioning, Disability and Health (ICF).[70]

The MDS is a more comprehensive dedicated survey that would be implemented once every five years or so, and a WASH module has recently been developed. On the other hand, the WG short set of six questions can be added to any existing national household survey or census. For this reason, many stakeholders consider that the WG questions are better suited for monitoring the SDGs, and they have been recommended as such by UN Department of Economic and Social Affairs Disability Data Experts Group.[71]

BOX 9.6 THE WASHINGTON GROUP QUESTIONS

The WG short set of six questions focuses on levels of difficulty due to health problems across six domains and assesses the level of difficulty in each domain. For each question the answer choices are:

- No, no difficulty.
- Yes, some difficulty.
- Yes, a lot of difficulty.
- Cannot do it at all.

The short set is as follows:
1. Do you have difficulty seeing, even if wearing glasses?
2. Do you have difficulty hearing, even if using a hearing aid?
3. Do you have difficulty walking or climbing steps?
4. Do you have difficulty remembering or concentrating?
5. Do you have difficulty (with self-care such as) washing all over or dressing?
6. Using your usual language, do you have difficulty communicating – for example, understanding or being understood?

The restriction on functioning can be due to any cause, including ageing or chronic illness. In its Disability Framework, DFID states that asking these six questions in existing surveys and registration processes is known to add 1 minute 15 seconds per person to the data-collection process.[57]

Nevertheless, it is important to train enumerators carefully to use the questions without any changes and ask the questions without using the word 'disability' to prevent any stigma, discrimination or bias that this can incur.

Experience in using the tool is gradually growing, and although it has not yet been tested at scale in relation to WASH, it has helped surveys focus on the specific impacts and needs of people experiencing particular difficulties.

Conclusion

This chapter has set out key concepts of inclusive practice in relation to disability, ageing and HIV and WASH; and how these principles can be applied in practice through national policy, programme design, resourcing and monitoring. We have argued that social exclusion is caused by a lack of power and voice, and by barriers in society, and that the identification and removal of those barriers is required for more inclusive societies and access to WASH services. Although the social model of inclusion has its limitations, it offers a practical way of identifying barriers and possible solutions. The physical barriers are easier to identify and address than others, but the social, cultural and institutional barriers must also be addressed to ensure WASH services are accessible and used by everyone. As more organisations are trying and learning how to mainstream inclusive practice they need to share experiences freely and transparently to help avoid common pitfalls and progress.

It is the government's responsibility to progressively realise their citizen's rights to water and sanitation. However, where resources and capacities are limited, civil society must support the development of the government's capabilities as well as lobby them to prioritise these basic services. WASH practitioners should seek to collaborate with groups of marginalised individuals to drive an agenda of change and not speak on their behalf, and promote the integration of inclusive programming approaches across sectors for a greater positive impact on the lives of marginalised groups and individuals. And efforts to monitor the reduction of inequalities in access due to disability, age and chronic illness must continue. There are promising tools and monitoring frameworks, but these need to be urgently tested and applied at scale so that progress towards the reduction and elimination of inequalities can be tracked within the SDGs.

Notes

1 WHO & UNICEF (2015) Progress on drinking water and sanitation: 2015 update and MDG assessment. Joint Monitoring Programme (JMP).
2 UN (2015) Sustainable Development Goals: Goal 6: Ensure access to water and sanitation for all.
3 WHO and the World Bank (2011) World Report on Disability. WHO: Geneva.
4 Hosseinpoor, A.R., Stewart Williams, J., Gautam, J., Posarac, A., Officer, A., Verdes, E., Kostanjsek, N. and Chatterji, S. (2013) Socioeconomic inequality in disability among adults: a multicountry study using the world health survey. *American Journal of Public Health.* 103(7): 1278–1286, July.
5 HAI (2015) Global AgeWatch Index 2015. Insight Report. HelpAge International: London.
6 UNAIDS (2015) Fact Sheet 2015.
7 Jones, H. & Reed, R.A. (2005) Water and sanitation for disabled people and other vulnerable groups: Designing services to improve accessibility. WEDC, Loughborough University, UK.
8 Wilbur, J. & Jones, H. (2014) Disability: making CLTS fully inclusive. Frontiers of CLTS #3. IDS: Brighton. Available at: www.communityledtotalsanitation.org/resources/frontiers/disability-making-clts-fully-inclusive
9 Wilbur, J. (2011) Principles and practices for the inclusion of disabled people in access to safe sanitation: a case study from Ethiopia.

10 White, S., Kuper, H., Itimu-Phiri, A., Holm, R. and Biran, A. (2016) A qualitative study of barriers to accessing water, sanitation and hygiene for disabled people in Malawi.
11 USAID/Hygiene Improvement Project and WB/Water and Sanitation Programme (2007) Research and resources linking water, sanitation and hygiene with HIV/AIDS home-based care.
12 Katabira, E.T. (1999) Epidemiology and management of diarrheal disease in HIV infected patients. *International Journal of Infectious Diseases*, 3(3):164–7, Spring.
13 Yates, T., Lantagne, D., Mintz, E. and Quick, R. (2015) The impact of water, sanitation, and hygiene interventions on the health and well-being of people living with HIV: a systematic review.
14 WaterAid & SAfAIDS (2014) An integrated approach to HIV and water, sanitation and hygiene in Southern Africa. Briefing note.
15 De Albuquerque, C. and Roaf, V. (2012) *On the Right Track, Good Practices in Realising the Rights to Water and Sanitation* (1st edn). Lisbon: UN Special Rapporteur on the Human Right to Safe Drinking Water and Sanitation.
16 UN (2006) Convention on the Rights of Persons with Disabilities (CRPD). United Nations: New York.
17 Gosling, L. (2014) Moving along the right track? The experience of developing a rights-based approach at WaterAid. *Waterlines*, 33(4).
18 Shakespeare, T. and Watson, N. (2002) The social model of disability: an outdated ideology? *Research in Social Science and Disability*, 2: 9–28.
19 Coe, S. and Wapling, L. (2010) Travelling together. How to include disabled people on the main road to development. World Vision UK.
20 Smith, N. (2010) Disability and Rural Water, Sanitation and Hygiene (RWASH) in Timor Leste. BESIK: Dili: Timor Leste.
21 WSSCC and FANSA (2015) Leave No One Behind: Voices of women, adolescent girls, elderly, persons with disabilities and sanitation workforce.
22 Mugambe, R.K., Tumwesigye, N.M. and Larkan, F. (2013) Barriers to accessing water, sanitation and hygiene among people living with HIV/AIDS in Gomba and Mpigi districts in Uganda: a qualitative study. *Journal of Public Health*, 21: 29–37.
23 Layton, S. and Atchison, B. (2012) The Living with Dignity Program in Papua New Guinea. Available at: www.ircwash.org/resources/living-dignity-program-papua-new-guinea
24 WaterAid (2012) Towards Inclusive WASH: sharing evidence and experience from the field. WaterAid: Australia.
25 WaterAid, Burnet Institute, International Development Agency (2017) The last taboo, research menstrual hygiene management in the Pacific: Solomon Islands, Fiji, and Papua New Guinea. Available at: https://washmatters.wateraid.org/
26 Australian Government AusAID (2012) Australia–Indonesia partnership for pro-poor policy: the knowledge sector initiative.
27 Jones, H., Fisher, J. and Reed, R.A. (2012) Water and sanitation for all in low-income countries. Proceedings of the Institution of Civil Engineers: *Municipal Engineer*, 165(3):167–174.
28 Jones, H. and Wilbur, J. (2014) Compendium of accessible WASH technologies. WaterAid, WEDC and SHARE: London and Loughborough University.
29 De Alburquerque, C. (2014) Participation in the realisation of the human rights to water and sanitation. Report of the Special Rapporteur on the human right to safe drinking water and sanitation to the General Assembly, July.
30 HM Government (2015) Access to and use of buildings: approved document M: Building regulations 2010. Available at: www.planningportal.gov.uk/uploads/br/br_pdf_ad_m1_2015.pdf
31 United Republic of Tanzania (2015) Toolkit no. 2: technical options for school water, sanitation and hygiene. Available at: www.wateraid.org/~/media/Files/Global/Publications-not-for-publications-library/toolkit_no2_technical_options_for_school_water_sanitation_and_hygiene.doc?la=en

32 MOET Viet Nam (2011) Decision # 4792/Q_-BGD_T by MOET Vice-Minister, 2 September. Available at: http://link.springer.com/article/10.1007/s10389-012-0515-x
33 WaterAid Madagascar (2010) Technical manual on community water supply, hygiene and sanitation facilities. Available at: www.wateraid.org/documents/plugin_documents/brochure_a5_wateraid_anglais_nov_bas.pdf
34 ADD International Bangladesh (2015) Disability friendly latrine: removing sanitation barriers of persons with disabilities. Action on Disability and Development (ADD).
35 Ministry of Drinking Water and Sanitation and WaterAid India (2015) *Handbook on Accessible Household Sanitation for Persons with Disabilities*. Ministry of Drinking Water and Sanitation Swachh Bharat Mission (Gramin) Government of India with WaterAid India, New Delhi.
36 Public Health Engineering Division (2011) *Handbook on Toilet Options for Rural Households in Bhutan*. Rural Sanitation & Hygiene Programme. Public Health Engineering Division, Department of Health, Royal Government of Bhutan, with technical assistance from SNV Bhutan.
37 Jones, H.E. and Reed, R.A. (2005) Water and sanitation for disabled people and other vulnerable groups: designing services to improve accessibility. WEDC, Loughborough University & DFID.
38 WASHplus (2015) WASHplus learning brief. Small doable actions: a feasible approach to behaviour change. FHI 360.
39 Wilbur, J. and Danquah, L. (2015) Undoing inequity: water, sanitation and hygiene programmes that deliver for all in Uganda and Zambia – an early indication of trends. Proceedings of 38th WEDC International Conference, Loughborough University.
40 Veromaminiaina, E. (2016) Rights to water and sanitation for people with disabilities in Madagascar. 7th RWSN Forum.
41 Wicken, J. (2016) Count me in. Partnering with the arts to get the message out about inclusive WASH. Available at: www.wateraid.org/news/blogs/2016/july/count-me-in-partnering-with-the-arts-to-get-the-message-out-about-inclusive-wash
42 Nwafor, A. and Ouangre, L. (2016) Achieving systemic change in WASH through the Human Rights Based Approach. 7th RWSN Forum.
43 WaterAid and WEDC (n.d.) Inclusive WASH: what does it look like? Available at: https://wedc-knowledge.lboro.ac.uk/collections/equity-inclusion/
44 Jones, H., Singini, W., Holm, R.H. and White, S. (2016) CLTS Plus – making CLTS ever more inclusive. Paper presented at the 39th WEDC International Conference, Kumasi, Ghana. WEDC, Loughborough University.
45 SAfAIDS and WaterAid (2014) Integrated approach to HIV and water, sanitation and hygiene in Southern Africa. A gap and needs assessment.
46 Age and Disability Consortium (2015) Minimum Standards for Age and Disability Inclusion in Humanitarian Action: pilot version.
47 Groce, N., Tramontano, C., Wilbur, J., Jones, H., Cavill, S., Gosling, L., Mamo and J. (2014). Undoing inequity: inclusive water, sanitation and hygiene programmes that deliver for all in Zambia. Baseline survey findings. LCD, WaterAid, WEDC.
48 Wapling, L. (2014) Undoing inequity: water, sanitation and hygiene programmes that deliver for all in Uganda and Zambia. Process review. WaterAid.
49 WaterAid and ATC (n.d.) A practical guide for inclusive WASH services at household and community levels in Uganda (hard copy only).
50 Michael, H. (2016) Identification and participation of people with disabilities and their access to WASH.
51 De Albuquerque, C. and Roaf, V. (2014) *Handbook on the Realisation of the Human Rights to Water and Sanitation*. Geneva: UNHCHR.
52 WEDC and WaterAid (2014) Accessibility and safety audits – various. Available at: https://wedc-knowledge.lboro.ac.uk/collections/equity-inclusion/general.html
53 WEDC and Plan (2015) Accessiblity and safety audits – market centre latrines. Available at: https://wedc-knowledge.lboro.ac.uk/collections/equity-inclusion/general.html

54 House, S., Ferron, S., Sommer, M. and Cavill, S. (2015) *Violence, Gender and WASH: A Practitioner's Toolkit*. London: WaterAid/SHARE.
55 DFAT (2015) Development for all: 2015–2020. Strategy for strengthening disability-inclusive development in Australia's aid program. Department of Foreign Affairs and Trade: Commonwealth of Australia.
56 AusAID (2013) Accessibility design guide: universal design principles for Australia's aid program. DFAT: Canberra.
57 DFID (2014) Disability framework – Leave No One Behind. London: DFID.
58 DFID (2015) Disability framework one year on – Leave No One Behind. London: DFID.
59 World Bank (2016) The environmental and social framework. Washington, DC: World Bank.
60 World Bank Group (2017) Including persons with disabilities in water sector operations: a guidance note. Washington, DC: World Bank.
61 WaterAid and SAFAIDS (2015) A field guide for integrating WASH and HIV programmes in Southern Africa.
62 DFID (2010) Disability, poverty and development. Available at: http://hpod.org/pdf/Disability-poverty-and-development.pdf. London: DFID.
63 Jones, H. (2013) Mainstreaming disability and ageing in water, sanitation and hygiene programmes: a mapping study carried out for WaterAid. Available at: www.wateraid.org/~/media/Publications/Mainstreaming-disability-and-ageing-in-water-sanitation-and-hygiene-programmes.pdf?la=en
64 CBM (n.d.) Tool: budgeting the inclusion of a disability perspective. Available at: www.inclusive-development.org/cbmtools/part3/1/Budgetingtheinclusionofadisabilityperspective.pdf
65 Heinicke-Motsch, K. and Sygall, S. (eds) (2003) *Building an Inclusive Development Community: A Manual on Including People with Disabilities in International Development Programs*. Mobility International, USA. Available at: http://pdf.usaid.gov/pdf_docs/Pnacy408.pdf
66 Coe, S. and Wapling, L. (2015) Review of equity and inclusion. Phase 2 report: country programme reviews and visits – Mali, Nepal, Bangladesh. Available at: www.wateraid.org/~/media/Publications/Equity_and_Inclusion_Review.pdf?la=en
67 WHO/UNICEF Joint Monitoring Programme for water supply and sanitation (2016) Task force on monitoring inequalities for the 2030 Sustainable Development Agenda. Meeting report.
68 UNICEF and WHO (2016) Core questions and indicators for monitoring WASH in schools in the sustainable development goals. New York: UNICEF.
69 Washington Group (2016) Washington Group on Disability Statistics. Available at: www.washingtongroup-disability.com/ (accessed 8 November 2016).
70 WHO (2016) International classification of functioning, disability and health (ICF). Available at: www.who.int/classifications/icf/en/
71 UNDESA (2014) United Nations expert group meeting on disability data and statistics, monitoring and evaluation: the way forward – a disability inclusive agenda towards 2015 and beyond. Paris. REPORT, 8–10 July.

10

ADDRESSING THE MENSTRUAL NEEDS OF WOMEN AND GIRLS IS NECESSARY TO ACHIEVE GENDER EQUALITY IN WATER AND SANITATION SERVICE DELIVERY

Bethany Caruso and Marni Sommer

Introduction

The onset and regular occurrence of menstruation is not only a normal part of life for women and adolescent girls, it is an indication of a healthy reproductive system.[1] Yet, while approximately 50% of the global population will experience, currently experiences, or previously experienced menstruation, menstruation itself is far from normalized. Rather, across the globe, women and girls experience fear and anxiety as they try to keep their menstrual status private and discretely access materials and facilities to manage their period; feel shame and embarrassment if they leak or their menstruation becomes known in another way; face restrictions on movement, ability to worship, food intake, where they can sleep, what they can touch, and which actions they can perform—potentially undermining their expected responsibilities as wives, mothers, and daughters.[2-5] They are expected to keep the normal and healthy biological experience of menstruation hidden, but face somewhat insurmountable obstacles to doing so, due to a lack of practical guidance, limited access to supplies, and insufficient facilities for safe and dignified management.[6] While keeping menstruation hidden is a burden that women and girls should not have to bear, what they need to maintain this socially proscribed status quo is not complex, but is often simply unavailable or inaccessible. The lack of attention to women's and girls' basic needs for a normal part of life is an indication that these needs are not considered to be equal to the basic needs of their male counterparts, and that women and girls, therefore, are not considered equal to their male counterparts. Further, that some women and girls have greater access to resources, facilities, and guidance for management compared to others indicates that menstruation can serve to further discriminate against already marginalized women and girls, including those who are displaced or have disabilities.[7,8]

In this chapter, we provide illustrative examples primarily from women's and girls' experience of menstruation in school settings in low- and middle-income countries (LMICs) given the extent of research available. Women's and girls' experiences out of school and in non-LMIC settings are equally important, and we highlight what is known while acknowledging where research is limited. We conclude with recommendations for research that could further existing understanding of what women and girls experience, and identify initiatives that have the potential to meet women's and girls' needs to enable them to pursue full, equal, and dignified lives.

Menstrual hygiene is an issue of equality

In their article "Taking the bloody linen out of the closet: Menstrual hygiene as a priority for achieving gender equality," Winkler and Rouf (2015) clearly situate menstrual hygiene within the human rights framework.[9] We draw on this foundational work as a means of framing this chapter. They note the various declarations, conventions, and articles through which the challenge of menstruation and its management can be understood as an issue of equality, of which we highlight three below:

- **Universal Declaration of Human Rights**. At the core of this declaration is dignity. Article 1 states: "All human beings are born free and equal in dignity and rights."[10] Menstruation is an issue of dignity and equality because of how women are treated simply for menstruating. As Winkler and Rouf note, "Dignity is difficult to maintain for women and girls when one of the signifiers of being female is a source of embarrassment and shame" (p. 14).[9]
- **Convention on the Elimination of All Forms of Discrimination against Women**. This convention requires states to take the actions necessary to guarantee women fully develop and advance so they may exercise and enjoy "human rights and fundamental freedoms on a basis of equality with men."[11] As Winkler and Rouf importantly clarify, the actions necessary for governing bodies to take need not be the same for men and women, but rather must reflect what is necessary for equality to be achieved. For menstrual hygiene, this requires addressing basic biological needs but also "transforming institutional and societal structures ... to eliminate underlying stereotypes and stigma and ... strengthen[ing] women's voice and participation" (p. 16).[9] In the spirit of strengthening women's voices, we include tables throughout the chapter with direct quotes from women and girls about their experiences of menstruation.
- **International Covenant on Economic, Social and Cultural Rights**. The various articles in this covenant and in other supporting documents guarantee education, work, health, water, and sanitation as human rights and emphasize

that human rights are guaranteed without discrimination, requiring states to actively address the needs of those who may be marginalized.[12] Barriers to education and work, negative health consequences, and discrimination due to menstruation as well as limited ability to manage menses in the face of poor water and sanitation environments have been documented, further supporting the claim that menstrual hygiene is an issue of equality.

Impacts of menstrual hygiene challenges in non-supportive social and physical environments

While the Declaration of Human Rights and other supporting documents call upon states to actively take measures to guarantee dignity for all with specific attention to women and girls to ensure that they are able to fully exercise their rights, these documents are not guarantees that women and girls will not suffer assaults to their dignity, that they will not face discrimination, and that their rights to education, health, work, water, and sanitation will be secured. On the contrary, women and girls have suffered grave assaults to dignity and health, been discriminated against, and have had their rights compromised for myriad reasons, including in regard to menstruation. The full range of dignity, health, education, and economic impacts of menstruation for women and girls who lack the knowledge, self-efficacy, resources, and enabling physical and social environments to manage their menstruation continues to emerge.

Impacts on dignity

Women and girls have voiced how the experience of menstruation has impacted their dignity. They describe shame, disgust, fear, embarrassment, and anxiety at menstrual onset and when managing their menses. These feelings can be borne out of a simple lack of understanding about what is going on in their body; menstruation is a taboo topic in many parts of the world, which prevents parents, family members, teachers, and others from informing girls about what menstruation is before it starts.[13,14] These feelings can also result if women and girls anticipate that their menstrual status may be revealed or if it already has been. They will actively isolate themselves from others in order to prevent potentially embarrassing situations. Secrecy becomes a tool with which girls hope to protect their dignity and privacy. They may modify their behaviors to cope in order to keep their reputations in tact. In a 2009 study involving 1,275 girls in urban Karachi Pakistan, 60% of girls avoided socializing with others and limited their movements.[15]

Women and girls who are not excluding themselves may be secluded, excluded or isolated by others to keep their potentially "polluting" or shameful status away. Among some cultures, women and girls may be secluded from the home for the duration of their period. In Nepal, women and girls may be relegated to sleeping in cow sheds or huts, a practice called Chhaupadi. In a study involving 672 women of menstrual age in the Kailali and Bariya districts, 21% of participants reported that their households used Chhaaupadi.[16] Exclusion can occur actively in the form of bullying or teasing, as was noted by girls in the Philippines and Bolivia.[3,4] Girls can potentially hide their menstrual status, but they may be teased more generally for going through puberty and changing physically, which cannot be easily hidden. This teasing may take the form of harassment (see Table 10.1).[17] Exclusion may come more passively in the form of socially imposed restrictions. Researchers have documented that menstruating women and girls have been restricted from going to places of worship or to markets; touching religious objects, food, water, or cooking utensils; eating certain types of food; bathing; participating in activities; or sleeping in certain locations.[14,18–22] Such restrictions, in turn, serve to make women's and girls' menstrual status public, hampering their dignity by denying them the ability to maintain secrecy and keep menstruation private. Moreover, restrictions can prevent women and girls from responsibilities they are expected to perform, and restrictions on touching water and on bathing have potential public health implications.

Restrictions imposed by parents may be intended to "protect" their daughters from being sexually assaulted by men, which becomes more impactful due to the risk of pregnancy after menarche. While these types of restrictions may aim to benefit girls, they require girls to bear the burden of a social environment where assault and harm to women and girls is normal. Echoing what has already been noted by Winkler and Rouf, social structures need transformation in order to ensure that women do not face discrimination. Table 10.1 provides quotes from women and girls from a range of studies, which demonstrate these various types of assaults to dignity.

Impacts on education

Article 26 of the declaration of human rights indicates that "everyone has the right to education."[10] Beyond being a right, decades of evidence support the importance of girls' education for improved population health outcomes, increased economic productivity, and other benefits for society.[23] A strong evidence base exists to support the positive association between girls' primary level education and increased contraceptive use, decreased fertility rates, and improved child health outcomes.[24,25] Educated girls are more likely to vaccinate their children, provide improved nutrition to their future families, and have improved sanitation practices.[26–28] Girls who achieve a threshold level of secondary school have lower rates of infection with HIV and lower rates of adolescent pregnancy.[23,29] Although girls' education is not a panacea for development,[30] there is evidence of additional social benefits from girls' education, including girls' increased engagement in civil society and their improved economic potential within their communities and the larger society.[23]

TABLE 10.1 From the voices of women and girls: impacts on dignity

---
Shame, embarrassment, fear

"The girl with her period is the one to hang her head." (Standard 7)

"Why would she hang her head?" (moderator) (silence)

"Children and boys will make fun of her." (Standard 7) (silence)

"The children have never seen this and they will start saying that she is dirty and people will start talking about her." (Standard 8)

(Kenya, school girls, McMahon et al., 2011)[35]

"When I first started menstruating I was shocked because I had not learned about it before . . . I was too embarrassed to tell my parents because I knew that they would not accept me and would say that I had bad behaviour. I could not tell them because they would say that I shamed the family and would shout at me."

(Ethiopia, rural out-of-school girl, Sommer et al., 2015)[36]

"She will be afraid, afraid . . . she's not going to want to play, neither will she want to go to the board . . . she's going to play only with her friends, with the women."

(Bolivia, school girl, Long et al., 2013)[14]

"If you tell people they will gossip about it in town. It will make you ashamed."

(Mali, rural school girl, Trinies et al., 2015)[37]

"Since the pad box is not there, if you put the pad in your pocket it may start smelling or it may fall down and you'll get embarrassed and ashamed."

(Kenya, FGD, urban private school, Girod et al., 2017)[17]

Secrecy

"We keep it secret so that no one would know."

(Kenya, girl pupil, Mason et al., 2013)[48]

Teasing

"I placed the pad in my pocket, so I could go and change, but the restroom was closed so I just went back downstairs. I immediately sat because there's already a teacher in front. Then a male classmate of mine was beside me so he got to see the brand of my pad peeping from my pocket. He then loudly exclaimed, "What's that?!" I just said, "It's nothing." But then he realized what it was and he laughed out so loud and he told our classmates. I was so embarrassed."

(Philippines, girl pupil, Haver *et al.*, 2013)[3]

"In primary school it was a problem because girls were so young, they could have accidents and did not know how to manage. Some [boys] tease them in primary – they tease them in secondary school too – it does not necessarily have to do with menstruation – they come and touch you to disturb you – so it has more to do with body changes in general."

(Tanzania, rural girl pupil, Sommer, 2010)[5]

"Girl 1: Some boys, they pretend that they're playing with you. Like, playing football. When they're playing, they come, and touch your breast. You think that it's just a play, but they have . . .

---

continued . . .

TABLE 10.1 Continued

Girl 2: Their intentions.
Girl 3: We would like it to stop.
Girl 1: We feel devastated."
(Kenya, FGD, urban public school, Girod et al., 2017)[17]

Restrictions

"She was told not to walk carelessly, meaning when she moves out of the house, she should always say where she is going and not go and do something else. And she was told to return to the house by 6pm (although the boys in the family are not restricted) – the reason being that boys are stubborn naturally and won't listen if they're given a curfew – and for the girls, they might get pregnant or raped if they are out late."
(Tanzania, rural girl pupil, Sommer, 2010)[5]

"If my grandmother is cooking she will not allow me to go closer there. And as I am a Muslim and now it is the month of fasting, I don't fast because I am menstruating and I don't go close to the mosque because it is not good."
(Sierra Leone, girl out-of-school, Caruso et al., 2013)[2]

In the last two decades, there have been remarkable achievements in narrowing or closing the gender gap in education in low-resource contexts around the world with particular progress made at the primary level.[31] These achievements have been largely inspired by Millennium Development Goal 2, which aimed to achieve universal access to primary education globally.[32] There remain myriad and significant barriers to girls completing their schooling, such as the demands of household chores on girls' time, parents' preference for educating sons, the distance from home to school, raising family fears about dangers to girls, the lack of female teachers in schools, early marriage and adolescent pregnancy, and family inability to pay for direct and indirect school fees.[33]

The onset of puberty presents particular challenges for girls' education in low-resource contexts.[5] In particular, girls' changing physiology and related societal expectations may interrupt her ability to participate regularly in school and/or cause her to drop out entirely.[13] For some girls, the timing of puberty aligns with the end of primary schooling and the start of secondary schooling, which may pose challenges to her continuation or transition to higher levels of schooling depending on cultural and social norms. In some cultural contexts, the onset of puberty and menarche in particular is a marker for early marriage within the family and society.[34] In other settings, the onset of puberty and menstruation raises family concerns around the potential for girls to become pregnant, which would negatively impact their marriageability and/or the family honor. In some countries, families proactively address these concerns by having their daughters marry shortly after menstrual onset.

There is increasing documentation of the ways in which the onset of menstruation and the subsequent need for girls to manage monthly menstrual flow at

TABLE 10.2 From the voices of women and girls: impacts on education

"It's like you can see that she is thinking something, that she has something urgent to share, but she will say nothing." (Teacher)   "Do you ask her what she is thinking? Do you ask why she's distracted?" (Interviewer)   "I know why she is distracted. This is something (teachers) know . . . when the session ends, she will not leave the room (until she is the last to leave) and then when she leaves, she will wrap sweaters around her middle and she will say, 'Teacher I am so sick' and then she will go from school and not come back all day or many days." (Teacher) (Kenya, school teacher, McMahon et al., 2011)[35]   "My menstruation started when I was in class and everyone started to laugh. This is the reason that I stopped going to school." (Ethiopia, rural out-of-school girl, Sommer et al., 2015)[36]   "No, I don't go [to the blackboard]. I will say I don't know what I am asked so that I cannot get up from my seat." (Sierra Leone, school girl, Caruso et al., 2013)[2]   "When your teacher is teaching, sometimes you cannot listen carefully because you are always bothered if you will get a leak . . ." (Philippines, girl pupil, Haver et al., 2013)[3]   "'Girls appear to do better pre- and post-pubescent, grades being only worse than boys around the menarche. Girls perform so well when they are in the lower primary, but when they reach class 5/6, they drop . . . you now find boys performing much better than girls." (Kenya, school teacher, Jewitt and Ryley, 2014)[47]

school may negatively impact their confidence, participation, and engagement in learning.[6] This includes evidence on the ways in which the inadequate provision of water, sanitation, and disposal facilities, menstrual hygiene management (MHM) guidance may hinder girls' ability to manage menstruation in school, and how the absence of inadequate materials (e.g. underwear, sanitary cloth or pad) and consumables (i.e. soap) may cause anxiety, discomfort, and potentially missed class time.[4,7,35–37] Table 10.2 provides quotes from women and girls from a range of studies, which demonstrate the intersection of menstruation and voiced impacts on girls' education, including distraction, school attendance, participation, and performance.

Qualitative research has enabled girls and teachers to voice their experiences of menstruation in the school setting and describe how they may be absent, distracted, reduce participation, or not perform as well. However, there is limited quantitative evidence that has found associations between girls' experiences of menstruation and these educational outcomes. A 2016 systematic review of eight menstrual hygiene interventions found that no interventions, whether providing menstrual materials or menstruation-related education, resulted in significant impacts on absenteeism.[40] A cluster quasi-randomized control trial of sanitary pad and puberty education (not included in the review) found declines in attendance for participants in both intervention and control arms, with significantly greater declines in the control.[41] While this study has some limitations, the results do suggest that material provision may be useful for girls' attendance and that further research is warranted to confirm findings.

There have been no studies that have specifically evaluated the impact of improved water, sanitation, and hygiene facilities on absenteeism among girls who are menstruating. A 2012 study evaluating a school-based water, sanitation and hygiene intervention found a 58% reduction in absenteeism among girls, but not among boys.[42] While this study does not focus on menstruation specifically, findings do highlight the need for appropriate facilities for girls regardless of their menstrual status.

Less well documented are the ways in which the absence of adequate water, sanitation and hygiene (WASH) facilities in schools may negatively impact the ability of female teachers to perform effectively during their monthly menstruation.[43] The absence of adequate sanitation facilities for female teachers may dissuade them from accepting or continuing in teaching positions, and the absence of female teachers in schools may hinder girls' perceptions of their own ability and potential to succeed or be eligible for opportunities after their schooling is complete, though more research is needed.[44]

Impacts on health

Article 12 of the International Covenant on Economic, Social and Cultural Rights "recognize[s] the right of everyone to the enjoyment of the highest attainable standard of physical and mental health."[12] The impacts of menstruation and menstruation-related experiences on women's and girls' health are not widely documented and further research is warranted. Yet evidence thus far indicates that the health impacts women experience related to menstruation are largely the result of needing to manage menses in unsupportive social and physical environments that do not enable them to meet their basic needs. A case control study exploring the association between menstrual practices and urogenital infections found that women were more likely to have symptoms of or be diagnosed with at least one urogenital infection (urinary tract infection or bacterial vaginosis) if they had used reusable pads to absorb menstrual blood compared to women using disposable pads.[43] They also found that increased wealth and having a space for personal hygiene in the house (compared to changing outside) were protective.

This research, along with research noted previously articulating the importance of WASH infrastructure in the school setting, highlights the importance of both access to resources and suitable physical environments for managing menses, both of which women and girls may not have control over simply because of their gendered inability to make decisions about purchases, to change the environment, or to exercise agency and the mobility they need to meet their needs. Article 22 of the Declaration of Human Rights indicates that:

everyone, as a member of society, has the right to social security and is entitled to realization, through national effort and international co-operation and in accordance with the organization and resources of each State, of the economic, social and cultural rights indispensable for his dignity and the free development of his personality.[10]

In the case of menstruation, women and girls are not always able to exercise their rights to manage menses with dignity so that their health and education remain uncompromised simply because what they need is not within their reach. Rather, women and girls may need to make decisions about how to cope with unsupportive environments, and these decisions may compromise health. For example, in the absence of a private and clean place to bathe, change, or wash their absorbents, girls may adapt their hygiene behaviors, choosing to carry out these behaviors less frequently. As one girl from Sierra Leone noted: "When I am in school I change once, because there is no soap and not enough water unless you buy some, but if at home I change several times and I bathe several times."[46]

Raising graver concerns, when girls have lacked access to the materials they need or prefer, they have reported engaging in sex to gain access[47,48] (see Table 10.3). In a cross-sectional survey, 3,418 menstruating females from rural Western Kenya, Phillips-Howard et al. (2015) found that two-thirds of pad users received them from a sexual partner. And while they found that overall only 1.3% engaged in sex for money to purchase pads, girls age 15 and under had significantly higher odds of engaging in this practice with 10% of 15-year-old girls reporting accessing pads in this manner.[49] In a follow-up feasibility study, Phillips-Howard et al. (2016) found that the provision of cups and pads over the course of one year was associated with a lower risk of sexually transmitted infections and that cup provision was associated with lower risk of bacterial vaginosis compared to girls who did not receive them.[50] These studies collectively demonstrate that managing menstruation can be risky to health when women and girls are not able meet their personal needs in a dignified, safe, and just manner. What remains unknown is how many women and girls are engaging in sex for pads, where this is happening, how often,

TABLE 10.3 From the voices of women and girls: impacts on health

"The fishermen are just living around us . . . If you have sex with me I'll give you everything you ask for" they say, then because you are in need of a pad, you will allow them. and in return they will give you money . . . they give around 200 shillings . . . It happens a lot . . . some just say yes 'cos they need that pad."
(Kenya, girl, Jewitt and Ryley, 2014)[47]

"Some people exchange sex for money. The money is used to buy pads. Maybe she is being given money then they have sexual intercourse . . . sometimes is good, sometimes it's not because you need help, so you will just engage yourself into sex."
(Kenya, girl pupil, Mason et al., 2013)[48]

and the extent of infections, pregnancy, and altered future trajectories that may occur as a result.

Finally, the shame and embarrassment that women and girls experience if their menstrual status is revealed, if they have a leak, or if they are seen tending to their needs, like washing a menstrual or drying cloth in an open space, may have more than ephemeral impact. The extent to which these experiences may accumulate to impact mental health, whether manifested as anxiety, depression, or overall well-being, is unknown but not implausible given how women and girls describe these reoccurring experiences.

Programmatic responses to menstruation and education

There are growing efforts around the world, and particularly in LMIC, to address the MHM barriers facing girls in school in particular.[6] Although girls and women out of school are equally in need of improved WASH facilities, information and materials, there have been few efforts to date to address their needs systematically. The increasing attention to MHM in schools can therefore serve as a blueprint for addressing the gender inequalities around menstruation beyond the school environment, including in households, workplaces, and for those who are in transit or displaced. The presence of adequate WASH facilities for adolescent girls and women is an issue of equality given that adolescent girls and women have unique water and sanitation-related needs compared to males, and require specific facilities and resources to meet those needs. The three programmatic areas highlighted below represent key areas for investment, and are embedded in the "MHM in Ten" agenda that was mapped out to enable improved global coordination for transforming schools for girls from 2014 to 2024.[51]

Adapted WASH infrastructure

Although all young people, teachers and school staff need adequate WASH infrastructure in schools, the importance of WASH infrastructure in schools has only recently been prioritized for boys and girls. This was exemplified by the lack of mention of the importance of WASH in schools in the MDGs, therefore limiting the prioritization of investment for national governments and donors. More recent evidence on school WASH has served to highlight the particular benefits of WASH infrastructure for schoolgirls in particular,[42,52–54] and with increased numbers of girls attending school in recent decades through the primary education for all efforts, there is growing attention to the need for separate girls' facilities in schools. More specifically, a body of research on MHM has indicated that separate facilities are only the starting place, with a need for improved WASH infrastructure that is more holistic (e.g. gender-segregated clean, safe toilets with soap and water nearby, doors with locks on the inside, hooks on the inside of walls, and disposal facilities of used menstrual materials). Examples of such efforts include the SPLASH program led by FHI360 in partnership with the Ministry of

Education in Zambia that aimed to improve school WASH facilities for girls, along with other MHM-related interventions; numerous non-governmental organizations are focusing on improving WASH facilities in schools alongside of other MHM interventions, such as Save the Children, WaterAid, Plan International, and World Vision; and national, regional and local governments are also focusing on transforming school WASH, through technical partnerships with UNICEF and other agencies.[55,56] However 50% of schools in the least developed countries still lack adequate water and sanitation,[57] let alone improved WASH infrastructure targeting the unique gendered needs of girls, female staff and teachers, and thus there is still much to be done in this area of programming. Additionally, there is a need for school WASH facilities to suit the needs of all girls; recent research from Kenya revealed that school toilets were not suitable for Muslim girls to practice ablution, forcing them to use dilapidated toilets that were more suitable for the practice over the newer facilities their non-Muslim counterparts enjoyed.[17]

Awareness raising and educational materials in schools

There has been a surge of awareness-raising efforts around the issue of menstruation in schools, with numerous organizations and campaigns (e.g. WSSCC, ZanaAfrica, WASH United's Menstrual Hygiene Day) pushing for "breaking the silence" on menstruation and the needs of girls in school. Efforts have included social media campaigns, educational gatherings focused on creating a safe space for girls and women to talk openly about menstruation (e.g. WSSCC's menstrual hygiene labs in India), and efforts to capture and convey girls' voiced experiences of their first menstruation and the barriers they face managing monthly menses in school. An important role of awareness raising can be the shifting of social norms around a given topic, and thus the menstrual advocacy efforts are serving to generate more open conversations and increased attention to the MHM needs of girls.

Along with awareness raising, however, there needs to be sustained efforts to inform and transform the learning environment, so that existing taboos and misconceptions around menstruation, along with ongoing shame and embarrassment, can be overcome. Two approaches for changing such behaviors or attitudes include the provision of menstrual educational materials to girls, along with sensitizing teachers to girls' unique needs. Assessment efforts of both aspects have found shy girls who are uncomfortable speaking to teachers, and teachers who skip curricula on menstruation and pubertal changes out of discomfort and embarrassment.[5,35] To address these challenges, girls' (and boys') puberty books developed by Grow and Know have been developed through careful participatory approaches with young people, and designed to be distributed directly to girls (and boys) to read on their own.[56] Similar efforts are being used by Save the Children, UNICEF and other organizations in development contexts (e.g. Sustainable Health Enterprises [SHE], BeGirl, ZanaAfrica), or those working in humanitarian response with displaced girls (e.g. Oxfam, IRC, WaterAid). However, engaging teachers is also important for improving the social environment of schools, thereby creating more enabling circumstances for girls' menstrual management. While some Ministries of Education, such as Uganda, Zambia and India, have developed guidelines for MHM in schools with attention to teacher training, there is still much to be done in strengthening teachers' comfort with the topic of menstruation, and knowledge about the content to deliver.

Menstrual management materials

Along with adequate WASH infrastructure, sensitized teachers and the provision of MHM guidance, women and girls require affordable, comfortable, hygienic materials for managing their menstruation. This might include a range of sanitary materials (e.g. disposable pads, reusable pads, cloths, menstrual cups) and underwear. Although many women and girls may be able to afford adequate supplies, there are large numbers who may lack the family or economic support to acquire sufficient materials. This in turn can negatively impact girls' ability to sit for long hours in the classroom, change soiled materials while at school, and feel confident enough to stand to respond to a question or write on the blackboard.[37,59] Women may also face challenges engaging in work.[60]

To address the challenge of materials, along with the question of whether the provision of materials can help girls to overcome the MHM barriers they face in schools, a growing number of studies have sought to evaluate the impact of material provision. Although some have been pilot efforts,[50,61] or been limited by resources to small sample sizes,[41] findings suggest that insufficient materials hinder girls' school-going in numerous ways, and that the provision of such materials – often in concert with MHM information – can improve their engagement in school. The opportunities enabled by ensuring women and girls not in school gain access remains unknown.

There have also been national level efforts to subsidize the provision of sanitary pads (e.g. India, Kenya) to girls in need. However, limited evaluation has been conducted on such efforts, hindering the ability to know the effectiveness and sustainability of such approaches. Qualitative research in Kenya has suggested that funding for materials is inconsistent and distribution of materials is not systematic, potentially leading some girls to go without materials despite having a need.[17]

Policy efforts to address menstruation and education

Both global and national level policy are essential to address the on-going gender inequities related to WASH and menstruation. There is significance, however, in noting that a sustained campaign was launched at the global level to bring attention to the unique gendered sanitation needs of girls and women during the development of the SDGs.[62] This in turn contributed to the inclusion in Goal 6 of attention to "the unique sanitation needs of girls and women," which is a starting point for identifying more specific targets and indicators needed at country level.[63]

Global level policy

To effectively address the WASH and gender inequities, global policy discussions should include attention to the creation and utilization of international targets that in turn are taken up by relevant initiatives and partnerships. These should be supported by the ongoing development of indicators and methods for global monitoring. Together, such efforts can help to mobilize global resources and action. Examples of such efforts in relation to schools include the "MHM in Ten" annual meeting organized by UNICEF and Columbia University, which brings together key stakeholders from across the relevant sectors (e.g. WASH, gender, education, health) with the aim of transforming school environments for girls by 2024.[51] Such global level dialogues can highlight the needs of diverse female student populations.

Further, though not explicit, several of the Sustainable Development Goals (SDGs) indirectly address issues related to menstruation and menstrual hygiene management. Prioritizing investment in associated targets may improve the circumstances in which women and girls need to manage menses and therefore their dignity, health, education and workforce engagement, and reduce their potential for shame, embarrassment, discrimination, and maltreatment (see Table 10.4).

National level policy

While global policy can provide a pathway for countries to achieve equity for girls in school and beyond, national level policy efforts should focus on the practical challenges to be addressed, such as the development of norms and standards for educational systems, and the integration of MHM approaches across Ministries of Education, Health and Water. These in turn will only succeed if budget line items are included in Education Sector Plans (or their equivalents), and the Ministry of Finance prioritizes monetary support.

A small number of national governments have developed (or are currently drafting) national level guidelines and indicators to improve MHM programming primarily through education systems, such as in India, Uganda and Zambia. Such efforts should be examined for their sensitivity to diverse cultural WASH practices.

Lastly, new movements are underway in both high and low-income countries to remove the value added tax on sanitary produces (when imported) and domestic taxes (when locally produced) in order to address the inequity created by girls and women having to pay tax on products inappropriately categorized as luxury items.

Research and intervention gaps

Understanding of girls' experiences of menstruation and what their needs for managing menses are in the school setting has increased over the past five years. However, a considerable amount of learning remains in order to ensure that all women and girls have equitable life chances compared to men and boys, specifically in schools.

TABLE 10.4 Examples of sustainable development goals and targets associated with menstrual hygiene management

---

Goal 3

Ensure healthy lives and promote well-being for all at all ages

Associated target
By 2030, ensure universal access to sexual and reproductive health-care services, including for family planning, information and education, and the integration of reproductive health into national strategies and programmes.

Goal 4

Ensure inclusive and quality education for all and promote lifelong learning.

Associated targets (not exhaustive)
By 2030, ensure that all girls and boys complete free, equitable and quality primary and secondary education leading to relevant and Goal 4 effective learning outcomes.

By 2030, eliminate gender disparities in education and ensure equal access to all levels of education and vocational training for the vulnerable, including persons with disabilities, indigenous peoples and children in vulnerable situations.

Build and upgrade education facilities that are child, disability and gender sensitive, and provide safe, nonviolent, inclusive and effective learning environments for all.

Goal 5

Achieve gender equality and empower all women and girls.

Associated targets
End all forms of discrimination against all women and girls everywhere.

Eliminate all forms of violence against all women and girls in the public and private spheres, including trafficking and sexual and other types of exploitation.

Ensure universal access to sexual and reproductive health and reproductive rights.

Enhance the use of enabling technology, in particular information and communications technology, to promote the empowerment of women.

Adopt and strengthen sound policies and enforceable legislation for the promotion of gender equality and the empowerment of all women and girls at all levels.

Goal 6

Ensure access to water and sanitation for all.

Associated targets
By 2030, achieve universal and equitable access to safe and affordable drinking water for all.

By 2030, achieve access to adequate and equitable sanitation and hygiene for all and end open defecation, paying special attention to the needs of women and girls and those in vulnerable situations.

continued . . .

TABLE 10.4 Continued

Goal 8
Promote inclusive and sustainable economic growth, employment and decent work for all. *Associated targets* By 2030, achieve full and productive employment and decent work for all women and men, including for young people and persons with disabilities, and equal pay for work of equal value. By 2020, substantially reduce the proportion of youth not in employment, education or training.

Underrepresented populations

Research needs to be carried out in populations with whom learning has yet to occur. Research carried out to date may inform understanding of MHM where it is not currently investigated, but cultural, social, environmental, and other differences influencing behaviors and experiences may not be appropriately accounted for if populations are not engaged directly. Countries that have yet to investigate experiences and needs related to menstruation should endeavor to research MHM to inform policy and programming needs, and to break the taboo of the topic in general. Too little evidence exists on the needs of women in general, and on the vast and growing population of displaced girls and women in particular, who represent a wide range of cultural backgrounds, socioeconomic statuses, and are displaced (in camps, host communities, informal settlements or in transit) in significantly different geographical contexts.

Countries that have carried out research on MHM should aim to identify if and where local gaps in learning exist. Specifically, differences in experiences between urban and rural populations, rich and poor, and among minority populations—whether ethnically or religiously distinct—and those with disabilities need to be understood. While girls are staying in school longer and enrollment is on the rise, girls out of school may be at a specific disadvantage if they have less access to education, materials and facilities for managing their menses compared to girls in a supportive education system. Female teachers, who are of particular benefit to girls' learning,[43] also need their menstrual hygiene needs met.

Evidence-based policies and programs

Further evidence assessing the effectiveness of school-based interventions or programs for addressing MHM in schools are needed in order to improve programming, scale-up, and inform policy.[6] Complex trials to assess health and education outcomes are important, but are not needed for many MHM programs. Rather, simple assessments should be carried out to assess whether or not programs are meeting the needs of girls and ameliorating the challenges they face in the school setting—for example, understanding if girls feel that the measures taken to assure their privacy are effective and safe, or if the new facilities created on their behalf enable them to address their needs as intended are valuable for assessing interventions. Qualitative research can be instrumental in answering these questions and resources are publically available to guide such inquiries.[39,64–66] It is imperative that the needs of all girls in a school are met, not just the majority or advantaged population, in order to prevent well-intended programs for creating inequities among the school population, as may be the case in Kenya.[17]

In addition, evidence is needed to better highlight how menstruation and vaginal bleeding more broadly are also issues of equity at home and in the workplace.[18,60,67–69] Although there exist some efforts to incorporate attention to menstrual health in the workplace (e.g. BSR/HER project), there is little documented evidence of the inequities related to WASH in informal and formal work environments, and of evidence-based solutions. In addition, limited evidence suggests that WASH facilities are also sites of violence for girls and women, and although a global toolkit has been developed for preventing such events, the sensitivity of both researching violence and sanitary practices hinders the knowledge of effective approaches.[70,71] Although there are differing menstrual-related challenges facing girls and women of different social, cultural and economic backgrounds, in development versus emergency contexts, and in rural versus urban settings documentation is needed on the ways in which program and policy can best meet their gendered needs and rights.

Conclusion

Although progress has been made in raising awareness about the gendered challenges facing girls and women in relation to WASH, there remains much to be accomplished in breaking the silence around their unique sanitation needs, building the evidence on the specific barriers they face at home, in the workplace, and in schools, and identifying effective interventions to address inequalities. The challenge for the WASH and equity community is that in order to guarantee protections, the assaults on their dignity need to be revealed, documented, and articulated to those with the resources to enact change and more equitable WASH.

Notes

1 Sommer, M., Sutherland, C., Chandra-Mouli, V. (2015) Putting menarche and girls into the global population health agenda. *Reproductive Health*, *12*(1): 24.
2 Caruso, B.A., Fehr, A., Inden, K., et al. (2013) WASH in Schools Empowers Girls' Education in Freetown, Sierra Leone: An Assessment of Menstrual Hygiene Management in Schools. New York: United Nations Children's Fund.
3 Haver, J., Caruso, B.A., Ellis, A., et al. (2013) WASH in Schools Empowers Girls' Education in Masbate Province and Metro Manila, Philippines: An Assessment of Menstrual Hygiene Management in Schools. New York: United Nation's Children's Fund, 2013.

4 Long, J., Caruso, B.A., Lopez, D., et al. (2013) WASH in Schools Empowers Girls' Education in Rural Cochabamba, Bolivia: An Assessment of Menstrual Hygiene Management in Schools. New York: United Nations Children's Fund.
5 Sommer, M. (2010) Where the education system and women's bodies collide: the social and health impact of girls' experiences of menstruation and schooling in Tanzania. *Journal of Adolescence*, 33(4): 521–9.
6 Sommer, M., Caruso, B.A., Sahin, M., et al. (2016) A time for global action: addressing girls' menstrual hygiene management needs in schools. *PLOS Medicine*, 13(2): e1001962.
7 Sommer, M., Schmitt, M.L., Clatworthy, D., Bramucci, G., Wheeler, E., and Ratnayake, R. (2016) What is the scope for addressing menstrual hygiene management in complex humanitarian emergencies? A global review. *Waterlines*, 35(3): 245–64.
8 Quint, E.H. and O'Brien, R.F. (2016) Menstrual management for adolescents with disabilities. *Pediatrics*, e20160295.
9 Winkler, I.T. and Roaf, V. (2014) Taking the bloody linen out of the closet: menstrual hygiene as a priority for achieving gender equality. *Cardozo Journal of Law & Gender*, 21: 1.
10 Assembly TUNG (1948) Universal declaration of human rights (217 [III] A). Available at: www.un.org/en/universal-declaration-human-rights/ (accessed 31 March 2017).
11 Nations TU (1988) Convention on the Elimination of All Forms of Discrimination against Women. Treaty Series, 1249, 13. Available at: www.un.org/womenwatch/daw/cedaw/recommendations/Generalrecommendation25%28English%29.pdf (accessed 5 April 2017).
12 Assembly TUNG (1966) International Covenant on Economic, Social, and Cultural Rights. Treaty Series, 999, 171. Available at: www.ohchr.org/EN/ProfessionalInterest/Pages/CESCR.aspx (accessed 23 October 2017 2017).
13 Sommer, M. and Sahin, M. (2013) Overcoming the taboo: advancing the global agenda for menstrual hygiene management for schoolgirls. *American Journal of Public Health*, 103(9): 1556–9.
14 Chandra-Mouli, V. and Patel, S.V. (2017) Mapping the knowledge and understanding of menarche, menstrual hygiene and menstrual health among adolescent girls in low- and middle-income countries. *Reproductive Health*, 14(1): 30.
15 Ali, T.S and Rizvi, S.N. (2009) Menstrual knowledge and practices of female adolescents in urban Karachi, Pakistan. *Journal of Adolescence*, 33(4): 531–41.
16 Ranabhat, C., Kim, C-B., Choi, E.H., Aryal, A., Park, M.B., and Doh, Y.A. (2015) Chhaupadi culture and reproductive health of women in Nepal. *Asia Pacific Journal of Public Health*, 27(7): 785–95.
17 Girod, C., Ellis, A., Andes, K.L., Freeman, M.C., and Caruso, B.A. (2017) Physical, social, and political inequities constraining girls' menstrual management at schools in informal settlements of Nairobi, Kenya. *Journal of Urban Health*, 1–12.
18 Caruso, B.A., Clasen, T.F., Hadley, C., et al. (2017) Understanding and defining sanitation insecurity: women's gendered experiences of urination, defecation and menstruation in rural Odisha, India. *BMJ Global Health*, 2(4): e000414.
19 Garg, S., Sharma, N., and Sahay, R. (2001) Socio-cultural aspects of menstruation in an urban slum in Delhi, India. *Reproductive Health Matters*, 9(17): 16–25.
20 Kumar, A. and Srivastava, K. (2011) Cultural and social practices regarding menstruation among adolescent girls. *Social Work in Public Health*, 26(6): 594–604.
21 Thakre, S., Reddy, M., Rathi, N., Pathak, K., and Ughade, S. (2011) Menstrual hygiene: knowledge and practice among adolescent school girls of Saoner, Nagpur District. *Journal of Clinical and Diagnostic Research*, 5(5): 1027–33.
22 van Eijk, A.M., Sivakami, M., Thakkar, M.B., et al. (2016) Menstrual hygiene management among adolescent girls in India: a systematic review and meta-analysis. *BMJ Open*, 6(3): e010290.
23 Herz, B.K. and Sperling, G.B. (2004) What works in girls' education: evidence and policies from the developing world. Council on Foreign Relations.

24 Klasen, S. (2000) Does gender inequality reduce growth and development? Evidence from cross-country regressions. Washington, DC.
25 Subbarao, K. and Raney, L. (1995) Social gains from female education: a cross-national study. *Economic Development and Cultural Change*, 44(1): 105–28.
26 Schultz, T.P. (2002) Why governments should invest more to educate girls. *World Development*, 30(2): 207–25.
27 Gage, A.J., Sommerfelt, A.E., and Piani, A.L. (1997) Household structure and childhood immunization in Niger and Nigeria. *Demography*, 34(2): 295–309.
28 Summers, L. (1992) Investing in all the people. World Bank.
29 De Walque, D. (2002) How does educational attainment affect the risk of being infected by HIV/AIDS? Evidence from a general population cohort in rural Uganda.
30 Vavrus, F.K. (2003) Desire and decline: schooling amid crisis in Tanzania. Peter Lang.
31 UNESCO (2012) *World Atlas of Gender Equality in Education*. Paris.
32 Nations U. (2000) GOAL 2: ACHIEVE UNIVERSAL PRIMARY EDUCATION. Available at: www.un.org/millenniumgoals/education.shtml (accessed 23 October 2017).
33 UNICEF (2016) The state of the world's children. New York.
34 Glynn, J.R., Kayuni, N., Gondwe, L., Price, A.J., and Crampin, A.C. (2014) Earlier menarche is associated with a higher prevalence of herpes simplex type-2 (HSV-2) in young women in rural Malawi. *Elife*, 3: e01604.
35 McMahon, S.A., Winch, P.J., Caruso, B.A., et al. (2011) 'The girl with her period is the one to hang her head': reflections on menstrual management among schoolgirls in rural Kenya. *BMC International Health and Human Rights*, 11: 7.
36 Sommer, M., Ackatia-Armah, N., Connolly, S., and Smiles D. (2015) A comparison of the menstruation and education experiences of girls in Tanzania, Ghana, Cambodia and Ethiopia. Compare: *A Journal of Comparative and International Education*, 45(4): 589–609.
37 Trinies, V., Caruso, B.A., Sogore, A., Toubkiss, J., and Freeman, M.C. (2015) Uncovering the challenges to menstrual hygiene management in schools in Mali. *Waterlines*, 34(1).
38 Ellis, A., Haver, J., Villasenor, J., et al. (2016) WASH challenges to girls' menstrual hygiene management in Metro Manila, Masbate, and South Central Mindanao, Philippines. *Waterlines*, 35(3): 306–23.
39 Long, J.L., Caruso, B.A., Freeman, M.C., Mamani, M., Camacho, G., Vancraeynest, K. (2015) Developing games as a qualitative method for researching menstrual hygiene management in rural Bolivia. *Waterlines*, 34(1): 68–78.
40 Hennegan, J. and Montgomery, P. (2016) Do menstrual hygiene management interventions improve education and psychosocial outcomes for women and girls in low and middle income countries? A systematic review. *PLOS One*, 11(2): e0146985.
41 Montgomery, P., Hennegan, J., Dolan, C., Wu, M., Steinfield, L., and Scott, L. (2016) Menstruation and the cycle of poverty: a cluster quasi-randomised control trial of sanitary pad and puberty education provision in Uganda. *PLOS One*, 11(12): e0166122.
42 Freeman, M.C., Greene, L.E., Dreibelbis, R., et al. (2012) Assessing the impact of a school-based water treatment, hygiene and sanitation programme on pupil absence in Nyanza Province, Kenya: a cluster-randomized trial. *Tropical Medicine and International Health*, 17(3): 380–91.
43 Muralidharan, K. and Sheth, K. (2016) Bridging education gender gaps in developing countries: the role of female teachers. *Journal of Human Resources*, 51(2): 269–97.
44 Pearson, J. and McPhederan, K. (2008) A literature review of the non-health impacts of sanitation. *Waterlines*, 27(1): 48–61.
45 Das, P., Baker, K.K., Dutta, A., et al. (2015) Menstrual hygiene practices, WASH access and the risk of urogenital infection in women from Odisha, India. *PLOS One*, 10(6): e0130777.
46 Caruso, B.A., Freeman, M., Long, J., et al. (2013) Going global: a systematic approach for investigating girls' experiences of menstruation across a range of contexts. UNICEF-Columbia University Menstrual Hygiene Management Virtual Conference, 29 October. UNICEF House, New York.

47 Jewitt, S. and Ryley H. (2014) It's a girl thing: menstruation, school attendance, spatial mobility and wider gender inequalities in Kenya. *Geoforum*, 56: 137–47.
48 Mason, L., Nyothach, E., Alexander K., et al. (2013) 'We keep it secret so no one should know': a qualitative study to explore young schoolgirls attitudes and experiences with menstruation in rural western Kenya. *PLOS One*, 8(11): e79132.
49 Phillips-Howard, P.A., Otieno, G., Burmen, B., et al. (2015) Menstrual needs and associations with sexual and reproductive risks in rural Kenyan females: a cross-sectional behavioral survey linked with HIV prevalence. *Journal of Women's Health*, 24(10): 801–11.
50 Phillips-Howard, P.A., Nyothach, E., ter Kuile, F.O., et al. (2016) Menstrual cups and sanitary pads to reduce school attrition, and sexually transmitted and reproductive tract infections: a cluster randomised controlled feasibility study in rural western Kenya. *BMJ Open*, 6(11): e013229.
51 'MHM in Ten': advancing the MHM agenda in WASH in schools (2014) In UNICEF CUa, editor. New York.
52 Garn, J.V., Greene, L.E., Dreibelbis, R., Saboori, S., Rheingans, R.D., Freeman, M.C. (2013) A cluster-randomized trial assessing the impact of school water, sanitation and hygiene improvements on pupil enrolment and gender parity in enrolment. *Journal of Water, Sanitation and Hygiene for Development*, 3(4): 592–601.
53 Garn, J.V., Caruso, B.A., Drews-Botsch, C.D., et al. (2014) Factors associated with pupil toilet use in Kenyan primary schools. *International Journal of Environmental Research and Public Health*, 11(9): 9694–711.
54 Dreibelbis, R., Greene, L.E., Freeman, M.C., Saboori, S., Chase, R.P., Rheingans, R. (2012) Water, sanitation, and primary school attendance: a multi-level assessment of determinants of household-reported absence in Kenya. *International Journal of Educational Development*.
55 Sommer, M., Hirsch, J.S., Nathanson, C., Parker, R.G. Comfortably, safely, and without shame: defining menstrual hygiene management as a public health issue. *American Journal of Public Health*, 0: e1-e10.
56 Sommer, M., Robles, P., Comey, D., et al. (2017) WASH in schools empowers girls' education: proceedings of the menstrual hygiene management in schools virtual conference, 2016.
57 UNICEF (2013) Call to action, WASH in Schools. New York.
58 Blake, S., Boone, M., Yenew, Kassa A., Sommer, M. (2017) Teaching girls about puberty and menstrual hygiene management in rural Ethiopia: findings from a pilot evaluation. *Journal of Adolescent Research*, 0743558417701246.
59 Sommer, M., Ackatia-Armah, N.M. (2012) The gendered nature of schooling in Ghana: hurdles to girls' menstrual management in school. *JENdA: A Journal of Culture and African Women Studies*, 20.
60 Sommer, M., Chandraratna, S., Cavill, S., Mahon, T., Phillips-Howard, P. (2016) Managing menstruation in the workplace: an overlooked issue in low-and middle-income countries. *International Journal for Equity in Health*, 15(1): 1.
61 Montgomery, P., Ryus, C.R., Dolan, C.S., Dopson, S., Scott, L.M. (2012) Sanitary pad interventions for girls' education in Ghana: a pilot study. *PLOS One*, 7(10): e48274.
62 JMP (2012) Consultation on draft long list of goal, target and indicator options for future global monitoring of water, sanitation and hygiene. WHO/UNICEF. Joint Monitoring Programme.
63 UN (2016) SUSTAINABLE DEVELOPMENT GOAL 6: Ensure availability and sustainable management of water and sanitation for all. Available at: https://sustainabledevelopment.un.org/sdg6 (accessed 7 December 2016).
64 Caruso, B.A. (2014) WASH in dchools empowers girls' education: tools for assessing menstrual hygiene management in schools. New York: United Nations Children's Fund.
65 Caruso, B.A., Ellis, A., Sahin, M. (2015) WASH in schools for girls e-course: increasing national capacity to conduct research on menstrual hygiene management in schools. New York: United Nations Children's Fund.

66 The WinS4Girls e-course (2015) Available at: http://washinschoolsmapping.com/the-wins4girls-e-course/ (accessed 23 October 2017).
67 Hulland, K.R., Chase, R.P., Caruso, B.A, et al. (2015) Sanitation, stress, and life stage: a systematic data collection study among women in Odisha, India. *PLOS One*, *10*(11): e0141883.
68 Sahoo, K.C., Hulland, K.R., Caruso, B.A., et al. (2015) Sanitation-related psycho social stress: a grounded theory study of women across the life-course in Odisha, India. *Social Science & Medicine*, *139*: 80–9.
69 Sommer, M., Phillips-Howard, P.A., Mahon, T., Zients, S., Jones, M., and Caruso, B.A. (2017) Beyond menstrual hygiene: addressing vaginal bleeding throughout the life course in low- and middle-income countries. *BMJ Global Health*, *2*(2): e000405.
70 Sommer, M., Ferron, S, Cavill, S., and House, S. (2015) Violence, gender and WASH: spurring action on a complex, under-documented and sensitive topic. *Environment and Urbanization*, *27*(1): 105–16.
71 House, S., Ferron, S., Sommer, M., and Cavill, S. (2014) Violence, gender and WASH: a practitioner's toolkit. London.

11

INTERLOCKING INEQUALITIES RELATED TO WATER AND SANITATION, NUTRITION AND HEALTHCARE ACCESS

John Anderson and Oliver Cumming

Introduction

In most low- and middle-income countries (LMIC) there are significant subnational disparities in water and sanitation hygiene (WASH) service access, as discussed in Chapter 1. Summary evaluations of the progress achieved during the MDG era show mixed results: the drinking water target was met early while the sanitation target was missed by a significant margin.[1] In 2015, at the close of the MDG period (1990–2015), over 90% of the world's population were estimated to have access to an improved water source, and approximately 70% had access to improved sanitation. Despite significant progress in extending water and sanitation services, with billions gaining access during the MDG period, in 2015, 663 million people still lacked access to improved water and 2.4 billion lacked access to improved sanitation.[1]

MDG progress was unequal and many regional, national and subnational populations remain under served with low rates of progress. Sub-Saharan Africa, Central Asia and Oceania all fell short of the improved drinking water target.[1] Overall, progress on sanitation lagged behind water, with access to improved sanitation coverage remaining lower than 50% in 47 countries. Most of these countries were located in sub-Saharan Africa and Southern Asia and overlap with the shortfalls in progress in improved water coverage. Urban and rural disparities declined worldwide due to higher rates of progress in rural areas, yet, both water and sanitation access is still significantly higher in urban areas. Significant gaps remain between the richest and poorest households in improved water and sanitation access, but these gaps are typically greater for improved sanitation.

The water and sanitation MDG is not unique in the unequal progress achieved between 1990 and 2015. Other related MDGs, such as undernutrition (MDG 1) and child mortality (MDG 4), saw similar patterns of disparity between regions and countries, and within countries. While large global reductions were achieved in rates of stunting and child mortality, only three regions met the MDG 1 target to reduce stunting by half or more, and only two regions met the MDG 4 target to reduce child mortality by two-thirds.[2] Of all underweight children, 90% live in just two regions – South Asia and sub-Saharan Africa – and, while both these regions saw significant reductions during the MDG period, the MDG targets were missed by a large margin. For many low-income countries, the gap in stunting between the wealthiest and the poorest has increased, and children in rural areas, where most progress in stunting reductions were made, are still twice as likely to be stunted than urban children.[2]

This inequality in progress is a key feature of the MDG era, which cuts across specific MDG goals or development sectors. In response to this, the new Sustainable Development Goals (SDGs) place the reduction of inequalities as both a stand-alone goal (SDG 10) and as cross-cutting theme which features in most of the other SDGs, including for water and sanitation.[3] In addition, and in contrast to many of the MDG targets, many SDGs are universal, thereby aiming to ensure that access to services and health, and other social benefits are enjoyed by all. The water and sanitation SDG (6) aims to "ensure availability and sustainable management of water and sanitation for all," specifically by achieving universal and equitable access to drinking water (6.1), sanitation and hygiene (6.2). The nutrition SDG (2) references "ending hunger," and more specifically targeting "the poor and people in vulnerable situations" (2.1). The health SDG (3) aims to "ensure healthy lives and well-being for all" by achieving universal healthcare coverage (3.8).

In this chapter, we explore if, and how, inequalities in access to water and sanitation are co-distributed with other inequalities that may interact with or compound the public health and development impact of poor water and sanitation access. To do this, we consider three SDG sectors – water and sanitation (SDG 6), nutritional status (SDG 2) and healthcare (SDG 3) – and explore patterns of inequality by socioeconomic status (SDG 1) and urban/rural settings (SDG 10) for six low-income countries. For each of these sectors, we select basic indicators and use freely available Demographic and Health Surveys (DHS) (Figure 11.1). For SDG 6, to ensure availability of water and sanitation for all, we use child-level data on household access to basic improved water and sanitation facilities, as defined by the Joint Monitoring Programme (JMP),[1] but did not include sharing by households in our classification. For SDG 2, to eliminate hunger we used moderate to severe stunting as defined by height-for-age measurements that were less than two standard deviations below mean z-scores, standardized to WHO growth reference standards[4] as an indicator for undernutrition.[5] For SDG 3, to ensure healthy lives and promote well-being for all, we used access to a full course (three-dose) of Diphtheria, Pertussis and Tetanus (DPT) vaccination as an indicator for access to healthcare, that was also recommended as a core impact indicator for MDG 4.[5]

We used a descriptive analysis of these indicators to address the following three questions: 1) do the same patterns of inequality occur in water and sanitation, nutrition and healthcare across countries; 2) at a national level, what proportion of children in each of these six countries have unimproved, unsafe water and sanitation, poor nutritional status and poor access to healthcare; 3) to what extent are these inequalities concentrated within subpopulations (e.g. SES and urban/rural children)? We follow this analysis with a review of literature on the links between these sectors, the social factors underlying interlocking inequalities, and suggest how policy can be shaped to address inequalities in the SDG era.

Patterns of inequalities for water and sanitation, nutrition and healthcare

The DHS household surveys, like the Multiple Indicator Cluster Surveys (MICS),[6] are implemented approximately every five years, in most low- to middle-income countries (LMICs) in order to obtain nationally representative data for a broad range of demographic and health indicators.[7] We use DHS surveys here for two reasons. First, because these same datasets, along with others, are used by the United Nations Joint Monitoring Programme (JMP) to produce estimates of progress towards the MDGs, and now the SDGs are consistent with existing global monitoring efforts. Second, these datasets are publicly available, meaning they can be accessed and used by national actors from across all three sectors of interest – WASH, nutrition and healthcare.

These surveys provide important information for all three sectors and, more specifically, provide nationally representative child-level data on our factors of interest: access to drinking water source and sanitation facility, receiving a third dose of DPT, and stunting (Table 11.1). In this chapter, we analyze the most recently available surveys for six LMICs: Bangladesh,[8] the Democratic Republic of Congo (DRC),[9] Ethiopia,[10] Mozambique,[11] Nigeria,[12] and Pakistan.[13] These countries are not intended to be globally or LMIC representative, but do include a diverse range of LMIC contexts, all of which carry a relatively high water and sanitation-related disease burden. Table 11.2 presents 2015 estimates of a range of key demographic and SDG health indicators for these six countries.

All estimates were calculated with survey weights provided by DHS that account for the sampling methods. We replicated DHS methods for estimating socioeconomic status using observations of household assets. Household assets, including characteristics of housing, sources of drinking water, access and type of sanitation facilities, possession of durable goods and owned agricultural land, are analyzed using principal component analysis (PCA).[17] PCA results are used to assign weights to each asset, which are used to rank each household by their composite household score. We repeated this calculation, but excluded water and sanitation as assets to avoid potential confounding,[18] and then divided each into five equal "wealth quintiles" where the poorest quintile represents the lowest 20% of household asset scores and the richest the highest 20%.

Below, we present out results by the three questions posed above concerning if, and how, inequalities related to water and sanitation, access to healthcare and

TABLE 11.1 Indicator definitions and descriptions for indicators of water and sanitation, healthcare and nutrition used in analyses

Input	2030 goal	Description	Source
Nutritional status	**SDG 2**		**DHS child recode**
Child stunting	SDG 2.2	Height-for-age (HFA) measurements	HW8
Not stunted		HFA z-score > −2 standard deviations (SD) from the mean	
Moderate to severe		HFA z-score < −2 SD from the mean	
Access to Care	**SDG 3**		**DHS child recode**
Received DPT 3 dose	SDG 3.8	Child immunization card or mother recall	H7
Water and sanitation access	**SDG 6**		**DHS household recode**
Drinking water source	SDG 6.1		
Unimproved		"Dug well: Unprotected Well", "Unprotected Spring", "Tanker Truck", "Cart with Small Tank", "Surface Water (River, Dam, Lake, Stream, Canal, Irrigation Channel)", "Bottled Water"	HV201
Improved		"Piped Water to Neighbour", "Public Tap/Standpipe", "Tube Well or Borehole", "Protected Well", "Protected Spring" and "Rainwater", "Piped into Dwelling" or "Piped to Yard/Plot", and "On Premises" improved water source	HV201, HV235
Sanitation access	SDG 6.2		
None and unimproved		"Flush or pour flush toilet: Flush to somewhere else", "Pit Latrine: without slab/open pit", "Bucket Toilet", "Hanging Toilet/Hanging Latrine", "No Facility/Bush/Field"	HV205
Improved (includes shared facility)		"Flush or pour flush toilet: Flush to septic tank/pit	HV205, HV225

continued ...

TABLE 11.1 Continued

Input	2030 goal	Description	Source
		latrine", "Flush or pour flush: don't know where", "Pit Latrine: VIP/with slab", "Composting toilet", "Flush or pour flush toilet flush to piped sewer system"	

undernutrition are co-distributed in these six LMICs. In surveys, there is often incomplete data – that is, data on a given child may be missing one or more values for a factor of interest. In figures displaying data by subpopulation, children with data for any of the indicators of coverage or status are included in the analysis. However, when considering child-level overlapping risk, we only include children for which there are data on all indicators of access and nutritional status.

Question 1: Do the same patterns of inequality occur in water and sanitation, nutrition and healthcare across countries?

Patterns in child access to improved water, sanitation, and DPT 3 vary by country and differ across indicators. For all countries, except Bangladesh, access to water and sanitation, DPT 3 coverage and the likelihood of not being stunted are all higher for children in the richest households in each country (Figure 11.1). In Bangladesh, and only for access to water, coverage is approaching 100% for children in all quintiles. The proportion of children stunted is at least twice as high for children in the poorest quintiles as compared to those living in the richest households. There are consistently large disparities in access to improved sanitation with much higher coverage for children in the richest quintiles. Improved sanitation access is very low (< 25%) for all quintiles in DRC and Ethiopia and for every quintile in Mozambique except for the richest. Only the richest in Pakistan have improved sanitation coverage over 75%.

Nigeria and Bangladesh represent contrasting patterns of inequalities for access to improved drinking water, but inequalities in access to improved sanitation are similar. In Nigeria, access to improved water is twice as high for children in the richest quintile as compared to the poorest households. In both countries, access to sanitation remains inequitable and coverage is below 50% for all wealth quintiles in Nigeria. Patterns in access to healthcare contrast, with much higher and more equitable coverage for children living in Bangladesh than children in Nigeria.

In Figure 11.2, the proportional distribution of indicators is displayed for children by wealth quintile, and urban and rural settings. Children living in the rich urban households have higher access to improved water, improved sanitation and DPT 3 vaccination, and also have the lowest prevalence of stunting. In most countries, access to DPT 3 vaccination, and improved water and sanitation in rural settings lags those in urban settings. The proportion of children who are moderately

TABLE 11.2 Country demographics and health indicators for 2015

Country	Population (1000s)[a]	Proportion of Population Urban[b]	GDP[c] (billions 2017 US$)	Literacy[f]	Under 5 Mortality[d] (deaths/1000 births)	Improved Sanitation Coverage[e]	Improved Water Coverage[e]	DPT 3 Coverage[d]	Proportion of moderately to severely stunted children[d]
Bangladesh	160,996	34%	195	62%	37.6	61%	87%	94%	36%
Democratic Republic of Congo	77,267	43%	35	77%	98.3	29%	52%	81%	43%
Ethiopia	99,391	20%	62	49%	59.2	28%	57%	86%	40%
Mozambique	27,978	32%	15	59%	78.5	21%	51%	80%	43%
Nigeria	182,202	48%	487	60%	108.8	29%	69%	56%	33%
Pakistan	188,925	39%	271	56%	81.1	64%	91%	72%	45%

a UN Population Data[14]
b UN Urbanization Data[15]
c World Bank Data[16]
d WHO Global Health Observatory Data
e JMP Estimates[1]

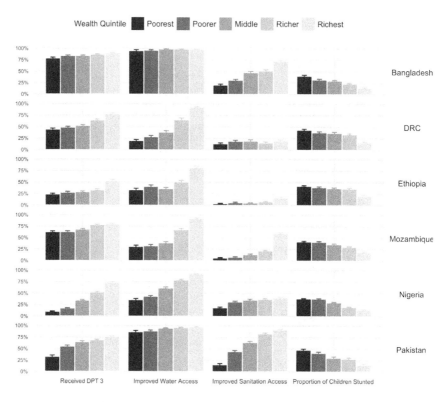

FIGURE 11.1 Distribution of access to healthcare, water and sanitation, and nutritional status disaggregated into wealth quintiles. Error bars represent standard errors for estimated proportions.

to severely stunted is generally higher in rural areas, but levels are similar when comparing the poorest urban quintile to the poorest rural children. Proportions of stunting in the urban richest are below 15% across countries, the lowest across all subpopulations. Bangladesh has extended high DPT 3 coverage and, along with Pakistan, access to improved water equitably for wealth, and for urban and rural children.

Despite living in highly populated cities with closer proximity to urban infrastructure, access for the urban poor lags progress among higher urban wealth quintiles along with many rural subpopulations. The most concerning example is access to improved sanitation for the urban poor, which is below 50% for five out of the six countries and below 25% for half of the countries included in the analysis. Lacking access to improved sanitation in densely populated urban settings may pose a greater risk than in low-density rural areas. Fecal contamination risk overlaps with poor access to DPT 3, particularly in Nigeria and Ethiopia, where coverage is well below 50% for the urban poor. In Mozambique, risk from the lack of improved sanitation also overlaps with access to improved water, where coverage is just above 50%.

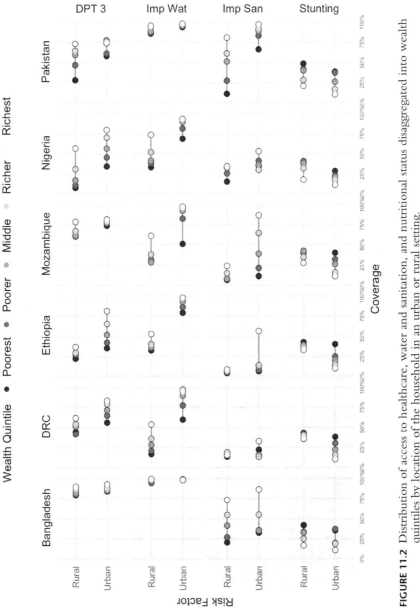

FIGURE 11.2 Distribution of access to healthcare, water and sanitation, and nutritional status disaggregated into wealth quintiles by location of the household in an urban or rural setting.

Question 2: At a national level, what proportion of children in each of these six countries have unimproved water and sanitation, poor nutritional status and poor access to healthcare?

In Figure 11.3, we present the scenarios that individual children face between countries by stacked bars displaying the proportion of children in each combined category of receiving DPT 3, access to improved sanitation, and stunting. The proportion of children who were stunted, not vaccinated with DPT 3, and lived-in households without access to improved sanitation are represented by the lighter portions of the stacked bar. In Ethiopia, almost 25% of children faced all three risks. In all countries, nearly 20% of children with complete data are stunted and lack access to either DPT 3, improved water or sanitation. Bangladesh and Pakistan stand out from the four sub-Saharan African countries, with over 25% of children not stunted and with full access to the three indicators, and over 75% had access to either DPT 3 vaccination or improved sanitation.

Question 3: To what extent are these inequalities concentrated within certain groups?

Figure 11.4 uses the same stacked bar format as Figure 11.3, but presents patterns in urban and rural children in panel A and panels B and C that focus on children

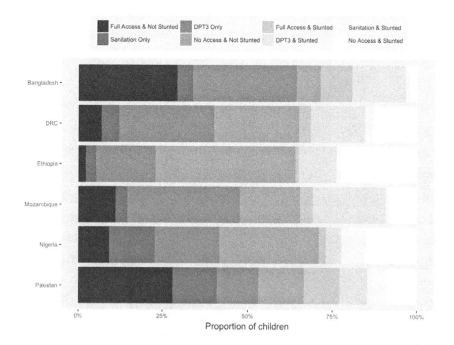

FIGURE 11.3 Access to healthcare, water and sanitation, and nutritional status, stacked by the scenarios of coverage and status for each child included in DHS surveys for each country

Interlocking inequalities **205**

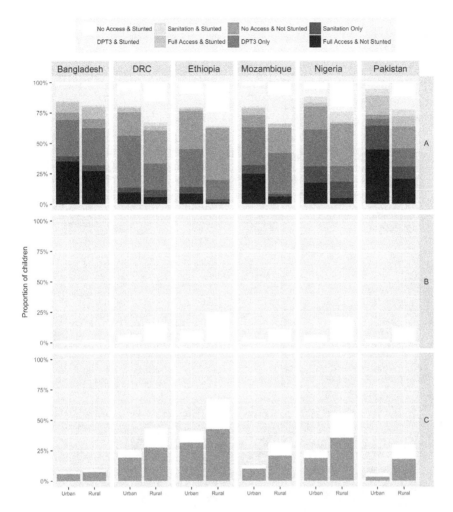

FIGURE 11.4 Access to healthcare, water and sanitation indicators, and nutritional status, stacked by the scenarios of coverage and status for each child surveyed by country DHS, disaggregated for urban and rural subpopulations. All scenarios are displayed in panel A, while panels B and C display a subset of select scenarios from panel A.

lacking both DPT 3 vaccination and improved sanitation. In all countries except Bangladesh, proportions of stunted children without access to both improved sanitation and DPT 3 vaccinations in rural areas are more than double the proportions for urban children (Figure 4B). Over 50% of rural children in Ethiopia and Nigeria lack access to both improved sanitation and DPT 3, whereas less than 40% of urban children face the same circumstances in poor access (Figure 4C). In contrast, only about 10% or less of urban and rural children lack access to improved sanitation and DPT 3 in Bangladesh.

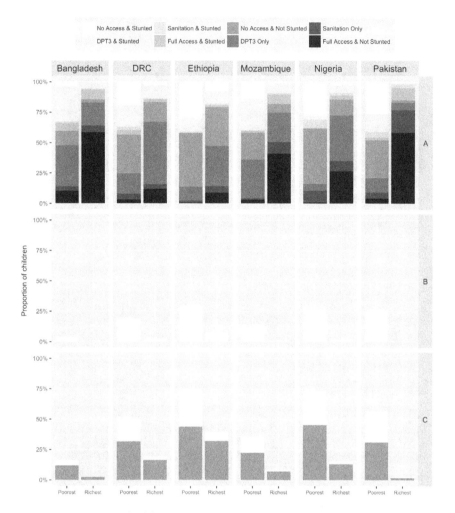

FIGURE 11.5 Access to healthcare, water and sanitation indicators, and nutritional status, stacked by the scenarios of coverage and status for each child surveyed by country DHS, disaggregated for the poorest and richest subpopulations. All scenarios are displayed in panel A, while panels B and C display a subset of select scenarios from panel A.

Across all countries, children in the poorest households face much higher levels of overlapping risks of stunting, no access to improved sanitation and DPT 3 vaccination than in the richest households (Figure 11.5B). Only the richest urban children in Pakistan and Bangladesh have children who are not stunted and have access to both DPT 3 vaccination and improved sanitation that are higher than 50% (Figure 11.5A). These disparities are most striking in Pakistan, Ethiopia and Nigeria, where over 25% of the poorest children face overlapping poor access as compared to less than 15% (Ethiopia) and much less than 10% (Pakistan and

Nigeria) of the richest children. In considering all children lacking access to both improved sanitation and DPT 3 coverage, disparities in lack of access are most extreme Nigeria and Pakistan (Figure 11.5C).

The health and social consequences of multiple inequalities

Our analysis shows that similar patterns of inequality regarding water and sanitation, nutrition and healthcare exist across the six countries (Figure 11.1), that significant proportions of children in each country who lack access to water and/or sanitation also lack access to adequate healthcare and nutrition (Figure 11.3) and that there are stark differences in the concentration of these deprivations between children in the poorest and richest quintiles (Figure 11.5). A failure to tackle these inequalities perpetuates discrimination against, and exclusion of, certain groups, but also limits overall progress whether at the global, regional, national or subnational levels. It has been observed that the countries that achieved the most rapid improvements in child health under the MDGs were those that succeeded in reaching these underserved populations.[19,20]

These inequalities are often co-distributed so that the same households or same children suffer not one deprivation, such as poor access to water and sanitation, but multiple deprivations that plausibly interact negatively (Figure 11.6). Access to preventive care that promotes immune system function and timely diarrheal treatment is more critical for children with poor water and sanitation access who are more likely to suffer more frequent and more severe bouts of diarrhea. Poor access to water and sanitation contributes via different mechanisms to chronic

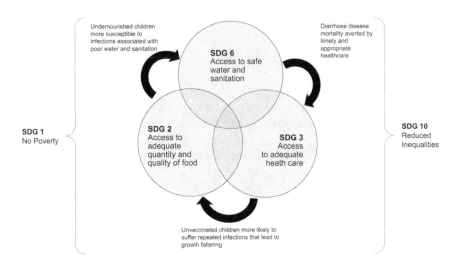

FIGURE 11.6 Conceptual diagram tying relationships between Sustainable Development Goals (SDG) and linkages to poor child health outcomes

undernutrition, manifested in low height-for-age or stunting,[21] and low vaccination rates increase individual and population level risk of multiple infectious diseases that contribute to child mortality.[22] Despite the most rapid reductions in under-five mortality being among the poorest children in most regions, mortality risk for both the poorest and for rural children remains 1.9 and 1.7 times higher than for the richest and urban children, respectively.[2] Below, we consider how and to what extent these multiple inequalities might interact negatively, both biologically and socially, and contribute to poor overall progress in health and development indicators.

Water, sanitation and undernutrition

There is growing evidence that water and sanitation influence the nutritional status of children in multiple ways, both directly through biological mechanisms and indirectly through social mechanisms.[21] Undernutrition is a condition that occurs when the body lacks the calories or nutrients necessary for normal function, growth and development, causing wasting, underweight and chronic stunting. Food insecurity and suboptimal breastfeeding, and frequent disease are known causes of undernutrition,[23] as well as a more recently characterized subclinicial condition known as Environmental Enteric Dysfunction (EED).[24]

EED is associated with poor sanitary conditions and chronic enteric pathogen exposure and is characterized by immune responses that cause inflammation and alter gut structure and function. These changes occur at the cellular level of the small intestine wall, including broadened villi structure, increased permeability, and mucosal inflammation.[25] In addition to loss of fluids from diarrhea, the child's body is not able to absorb the nutrients necessary for growth or for full immune system function, resulting in higher severity of future infection and increased risk of mortality.[26] Muscosal inflammation is a defense against enteropathogen colonization, but it can also prevent growth of beneficial microbes, allowing enteropathogens with survival mechanisms to thrive.[22] Proinflammatory cytokines are also directly linked to inhibition of the growth hormone–insulin-like growth factor (GH–iGF-i) axis, which is critical for linear growth.[27,28]

Access to safely managed, improved sources of drinking water and sanitation facilities along with sustained hygiene practices may protect children from EED.[29] A recent review of 18 risk factors of child stunting attributed the second largest fraction of stunting cases to unimproved sanitation (7.2 million) and water (1 million).[30] While observational studies have found strong associations between unimproved sanitation and unimproved drinking water sources,[31] results from more rigorous studies have been mixed.[32]

Healthcare, water and sanitation

Access to healthcare is also important for mitigating the impacts from poor access to water and sanitation by providing preventive care and treatment of diarrheal diseases. Oral Rehydration Therapy (ORT) is highly effective at preventing mortality from diarrheal diseases[37] and can be provided at health facilities, or health workers can explain how the solution can be made at home. Zinc and vitamin A supplements reduce morbidity and mortality from diarrheal disease.[38,39] Access to diarrhoeal disease vaccines[35] are more critical to children lacking access to improved water and sanitation.

Undernutrition and healthcare

Access to healthcare is important for obtaining preventive care (e.g. nutritional supplements and vaccines), health education (e.g. exclusive breastfeeding, child nutrition, and the importance of hygiene during child care), and treatment for diseases and malnutrition. Zinc supplements are effective in promoting linear growth and preventing stunting.[33] Zinc and vitamin A supplements have been linked with decreased intestinal permeability, a contributor to malabsorption in EED.[34] Access to routine immunizations, rotavirus, cholera and new ETEC and Shigella vaccines could be especially critical for undernourished children by preventing diarrhea,[35] although the impact on EED on vaccine effectiveness needs further investigation.[36]

Social linkages between water and sanitation, nutrition and health

Ecosocial theory recognizes that a human is simultaneously both a social and biological being whose physiology reflects both biological and social circumstances experienced throughout their lifetime.[40] A child who grows up in poverty is more likely to reflect social conditions caused by global and local disparities that result from unequal distribution of power, resources and access to basic human rights. Poor access to water and sanitation, nutrition and health services result in co-occurring or syndemic enteric disease and malnutrition that physically manifests itself in poor growth and development.[41]

SDG 1 – to end poverty in all its manifestations by 2030 – embraces a comprehensive approach to ending poverty and extending the definition of poverty beyond income and wealth to include other dimensions such as deprivation of formal education, reliable employment, food security, safety and physical security and access to services, such as healthcare and water and sanitation.[42] This framework explicitly links underlying poverty to the other SDGs. Living in poverty inflicts psychosocial stress linked to both acute and chronic health issues and is exacerbated by illnesses of other household members.[43] At a societal level, the poor embody institutionalized inequalities or structural violence[44] driven by discrimination based on race, ethnicity, class, religion, political views or cultural background.[45–48] Lack of access to basic rights such as access to health services and water and sanitation infrastructure disproportionately concentrates infectious disease and malnutrition in impoverished communities.

In general, urban populations benefit from higher concentrations of resources, health services and economic opportunities than in rural populations.[49] However, the urban poor, who make up the majority of an estimated 880 million people living in informal settlements and slums worldwide,[50] are deprived of the benefits of urban life and instead live in unhealthy conditions in the most overcrowded places in the world.[51] Surveys of urban communities in Kenya and Zambia correlated population growth with declining immunization coverage and access to clean water[52] and children living in slums are left more vulnerable by lower rates of breastfeeding and higher rates of undernutrition.[53] Low urban sanitation coverage can increase disease risk due to higher population densities than in rural populations.[54] Access to water and sanitation is heavily influenced by larger institutions charged with building and maintaining expensive infrastructure, including piped sewage and drinking water for rapidly growing populations, particularly in urban centers in sub-Saharan Africa and Southern Asia.[55] Financial constraints, invisibility and exclusion by social institutions are barriers for the urban poor and all those living in informal settlements and slums.[56–58]

Although not addressed in this chapter in detail, reduction of gender inequalities is a critical step in reducing overall inequality in child health and is addressed in more detail in Chapters 6 and Chapter 11. One analysis of over 30 LMICs found that women and children living in the poorest 20% of households lagged behind the wealthier 80% in a composite index developed from coverages of eight preventative and curative interventions.[59] A recent study comparing GDP and a gender inequality index in 96 countries indicated that reductions in gender inequality may have greater impacts than rising GDP on child malnutrition and mortality.[60]

Implications for policy

Our analysis of six countries across South Asia and sub-Saharan Africa identified overlapping poor coverage for indicators of water, sanitation and healthcare, both in subpopulations and individual children. We found that patterns and inequalities in access differ across countries, urban and rural settings and wealth, reflecting variation in health challenges, strategies and investment used to address diarrheal disease burden. In every country, children living in the poorest households face the largest disadvantages from lack of access and poor nutritional status. In most countries, rural children are more likely to experience overlapping deprivations, but in many cases the urban poor struggle with similar circumstances, despite closer proximity to services.

The results showing that the poorest people in rural and in some urban subpopulations are facing overlapping deprivations has important implications for addressing SDG goals, including overarching goals of eliminating poverty (SDG 1) and reducing inequalities (SDG 10). This requires going beyond focusing efforts on low-income or high-burden regions, or countries to more effective subnational targeting of interventions to the most vulnerable rural and urban subpopulations within LMICs,[61] as many of the world's poor now reside in middle-income countries.[62] More effective surveillance and higher resolution data will facilitate identification and monitoring of concentrations of vulnerable children on intra-regional and intra-urban scales as urbanization and global economic trends lead to population shifts. The use of free and publically available health and demographic data, such as the DHS or MICS surveys, as demonstrated here, provides a simple tool for understanding and monitoring these population-level distributions.

The largest gains in child health can be realized by pro-poor targeting of investments in health, nutrition and WASH interventions. Recommendations by the Lancet Commission on Investing in Health[63] included steps toward progressive universalism as the most promising way to achieve universal access to healthcare (SDG 3). Proposed pathways include public investment in healthcare interventions packages aimed at reducing maternal and child infectious diseases and essential non-communicable diseases with financing options that disproportionately benefit the poor. Combining universal health coverage with geographic, pro-poor targeting of WASH (SDG 6) and nutrition (SDG 2) sector investments would have the largest impacts on reducing disparities and achieving SDGs.

A collective and cross-sectoral effort is critical to extending access to services to those that remain unreached by efforts during the MDG era.[64] The breadth of these relationships creates an urgent need to coordinate and pool resources across sectors, including health, agriculture, urban and rural development. One deliberately multisectoral intervention, combining health, education and agricultural interventions, that was evaluated rigorously, reported a significant reduction in child mortality and improvements in chronic stunting, immunization, use of bed nets, improved water and sanitation.[65] Measuring progress toward reducing overlapping deprivations in addition to tracking individual indicators may be an effective way to promote cross-sectoral planning and delivery.

Comparing progress between countries can provide lessons about what strategies are most successful and inform solutions across diverse settings. High and equitable coverage for healthcare and water are just two indicators of the exemplary progress that Bangladesh has made in meeting many MDGs. The underlying reasons behind these impressive health gains are complex; however, a large force of community health workers and a pluralistic health system brought high priority interventions directly to all households, successfully reducing inequalities.[66] Much of this was achieved despite unremarkable health system inputs[67] and with persistent malnutrition and poverty, a pattern reflected in this study (Figure 11.2). In contrast, Nigeria made very poor progress across multiple MDGs despite having a GDP that is nearly 2.5 times higher than Bangladesh (Table 11.2). Analysis of healthcare delivery showed poor healthcare performance and community health workers that spent little time engaging communities.[68]

It is encouraging that sub-Saharan Africa and South Asia made significant progress in expanding and maintaining levels of both water and sanitation during the MDG era. However, efforts were undermined by the highest global rates of urbanization and population growth. In many of these settings, governments do not have the resources to build housing, health and infrastructure at rates fast enough to service population growth. The result is often unplanned unexpansion and results in informal settlements that are not recognized as within the metropolitan or municipal boundary, nor as part of any adjoining rural administrative authority. As a result, large intra-urban disparities in access and nutrition persist and concentrate poor health outcomes into neglected communities.[54] Coordinated efforts to engage communities in collective action around low-cost condominial sewerage systems, designed and installed by community members and government agencies, have shown promise for providing sanitation solutions to resource-limited and heterogeneous urban communities in Pakistan[69] and cities in Brazil.[70–73] In Marikina City, Philippines, a cross-sectoral approach that involved community members and health workers in the Healthy Cities Initiatives resulted in reductions in dengue disease prevalence as well as improved WASH and healthcare access for poor urban communities.[74]

The consequences of interlocking inequalities from failures to achieve universal access to healthcare and adequate WASH concentrates syndemic burdens of poverty, disease, and malnutrition into the most vulnerable children. The failure of social institutions to ensure access to basic services magnifies the frequency and severity of disease, contributing to chronic malnutrition, and denying many the opportunity of a healthy and productive adult life. These interlocking inequalities are not the same across and within countries, reflecting differences in economic growth, investments in health and built environments, urbanization, culture, geography and climate. Policy must be tailored to the demands and challenges of each country in order improve the health and well-being for all, meeting SDG goals. Thus, it is important to understand how and where these inequalities overlap, so that investment by health, nutrition and WASH sectors can target the most deprived and vulnerable children in a given setting.

Notes

1. UNICEFWHO (2015) Progress on sanitation and drinking water – 2015 update and MDG assessment, 1–90. World Health Organization.
2. UNICEF (2015) Progress for children: beyond averages – learning from the MDGs, 1–72.
3. United Nations (2015) Transforming Our World: the 2030 Agenda for Sustainable Development.
4. Assaf, S., Kothari, M. T., & Pullum, T. (2015) An assessment of the quality of DHS anthropometric data, 2005–2014, 1–82. ICF International.
5. Requejo, R., Bryce, B., Victora, V., & Deixel, D. (2013) Accountability for maternal newborn and child survival: the 2013 update.
6. UNICEF (2015) Monitoring the Situation of Children and Women for 20 Years: The Multiple Indicator Cluster Surveys (MICS) 1995–2015, 1–96. UNICEF.
7. Rutstein, S. O. & Rojas, G. (2006) Guide to DHS Statistics, 1–168. Demographic and Health Surveys/ORC Macro.
8. National Institute of Population Research and Training (NIPORT) (2016) Mitra and Associates, Mitra and ICF International. Bangladesh Demographic and Health Survey 2014. NIPORT, Mitra and Associates, and ICF International.

9. Ministère du Plan et Suivi de la Mise en œuvre de la Révolution de la Modernité (MPSMRM), Ministère de la Santé Publique (MSP)ICF International (2014) Democratic Republic of Congo Demographic and Health Survey 2013–14. MPSMRM, MSP and ICF International.
10. Central Statistical Agency ICF International (2012) Ethiopia Demographic and Health Survey 2011. Central Statistical Agency and ICF International.
11. Ministério da Saúde (MISAU), Instituto Nacional de Estatística (INE)ICF International (2011) Mozambique Demographic and Health Survey 2011. MISAU, INE and ICF International.
12. National Population Commission (NPC)ICF International (2014) Nigeria Demographic and Health Survey 2013. NPC and ICF International.
13. National Institute of Population Studies (NIPS)ICF International. Pakistan Demographic and Health Survey 2012–13. NIPS and ICF International.
14. United Nations (2015) World Population Prospects: The 2015 Revision, Volume II: Demographic Profiles (ST/ESA/SER.A/380), 1–875. Department of Economic and Social Affairs, Population Division.
15. United Nations (2014) World Urbanization Prospects: The 2014 Revision, CD-ROM edition. Department of Economic and Social Affairs, Population Division.
16. World Bank (2015) World development indicators.
17. Rutstein, S. O. & Johnson, K. (2004) The DHS Wealth Index. DHS Comparative Reports 1–77. ORC Macro.
18. Rheingans, R., Anderson, J. D., Luyendijk, R., & Cumming, O. (2013) Measuring disparities in sanitation access: does the measure matter? *Tropical Medicine & International Health*, 19, 2–13.
19. Victora, C.G. et al. (2012) How changes in coverage affect equity in maternal and child health interventions in 35 countdown to 2015 countries: an analysis of national surveys. *The Lancet*, 380, 1149–1156.
20. Victora, C.G. et al. The contribution of poor and rural populations to national trends in reproductive, maternal, newborn, and child health coverage: analyses of cross-sectional surveys from 64 countries. *Lancet Global Health*, 5, e402–e407.
21. Smith, L.C. & Haddad, L. (2015) Reducing child undernutrition: past drivers and priorities for the post-MDG Era. *World Development*, 68, 180–204.
22. Prendergast, A.J. & Kelly, P. (2016) Interactions between intestinal pathogens, enteropathy and malnutrition in developing countries. *Current Opinion in Infectious Diseases*, 29, 229–236.
23. Black, R.E. et al. Maternal and child undernutrition and overweight in low-income and middle-income countries. *The Lancet*, 382, 427–451 (2013).
24. Keusch, G.T. et al. (2014) Environmental enteric dysfunction: pathogenesis, diagnosis, and clinical consequences. *Clinical Infectious Diseases*, 59, S207–S212.
25. Prendergast, A.J. et al. (2015) Assessment of environmental enteric dysfunction in the SHINE trial: methods and challenges. *Clinical Infectious Diseases*, 61, S726–S732.
26. Caulfield, L., de Onis, M., Blossner, M. & Black, R. (2004) Undernutrition as an underlying cause of child deaths associated with diarrhoea, pneumonia, malaria, and measles. *American Journal of Clinical Nutrition*, 80, 193–198.
27. Crane, R.J., Jones, K.D.J., & Berkley, J.A. (2015) Environmental enteric dysfunction: an overview. *Food and Nutrition Bulletin*, 36, S76–S87.
28. Walters, T.D. & Griffiths, A.M. Mechanisms of growth impairment in pediatric Crohn's disease (2009) *Nature Reviews Gastroenterology and Hepatology*, 6, 513–523.
29. Humphrey, J.H. (2009) Child undernutrition, tropical enteropathy, toilets, and handwashing. 374, 1032–1035.
30. Danaei, G. et al. (2016) Risk factors for childhood stunting in 137 developing countries: a comparative risk assessment analysis at global, regional, and country levels. *PLOS Medicine*, 13.
31. Trehan, I., Kelly, P., Shaikh, N., & Manary, M.J. (2016) New insights into environmental enteric dysfunction. *Archives in Disease in Childhood*, 101, 741–744.

32. Cumming, O. & Cairncross, S. (2016) Can water, sanitation and hygiene help eliminate stunting? Current evidence and policy implications. *Maternal and Child Nutrition 12* Supplement 1, 91–105.
33. Imdad, A. & Bhutta, Z.A. (2011) Effect of preventive zinc supplementation on linear growth in children under 5 years of age in developing countries: a meta-analysis of studies for input to the lives saved tool. *BMC Public Health*, 11.
34. Syed, S., Ali, A., & Duggan, C. (2016) Environmental Enteric Dysfunction in Children. *Journal of Pediatric Gastroenterology and Nutrition*, 63, 6–14.
35. Das, J.K. et al. (2013) Vaccines for the prevention of diarrhoea due to cholera, shigella, ETEC and rotavirus. *BMC Public Health*, 13.
36. Prendergast, A.J. (2015) Malnutrition and vaccination in developing countries. Philosophical Transactions of the Royal Society London, B: *Biological Sciences, 370*, 20140141–20140141.
37. Munos, M.K., Walker, C.L.F., & Black, R.E. (2010) The effect of oral rehydration solution and recommended home fluids on diarrhoea mortality. *International Journal of Epidemiology*, 39, 75–87.
38. Yakoob, M.Y. et al. (2011) Preventive zinc supplementation in developing countries: impact on mortality and morbidity due to diarrhoea, pneumonia and malaria. *BMC Public Health*, 11, S23.
39. Imdad, A. et al. (2011) Impact of vitamin A supplementation on infant and childhood mortality. *BMC Public Health*, 11.
40. Krieger, N. (2005) Embodiment: a conceptual glossary for epidemiology. *Journal of Epidemiology & Community Health*, 59, 350–355.
41. Singer, M. & Bulled, N. (2013) Interlocked Infections: the Health Burdens of Syndemics of Neglected Tropical Diseases. *Annals of Anthropological Practice*, 36.2, 328–345.
42. Alkire, S. (2007) The missing dimensions of poverty data: introduction to the special issue. *Oxford Development Studies*, 35, 347–359.
43. Sapolsky, R. (2005) Sick of poverty. *Scientific American*, 293, 92–99.
44. Farmer, P. E., Nizeye, B., Stulac, S., & Keshavjee, S. (2006) Structural violence and clinical medicine. *PLOS Medicine*, 3, e44.
45. Dressler, W.W., Oths, K.S., & Gravlee, C.C. (2005) Race and ethnicity in public health research: models to explain health disparities. *Annual Review of Anthropology*, 34, 231–252.
46. Dressler, W.W. (2004) Culture and the risk of disease. *British Medical Bulletin*, 69, 21–31.
47. Gravlee, C.C. (2009) How race becomes biology: embodiment of social inequality. *American Journal of Physical Anthropology*, 139, 47–57.
48. Krieger, N. (2003) Does racism harm health? Did child abuse exist before 1962? On explicit questions, critical science, and current controversies: an ecosocial perspective. *American Journal of Public Health*, 93.
49. WHOUN-Habitat (2016) Global report on urban health: equitable, healthier cities for sustainable development. 1–242. World Health Organization.
50. UN-Habitat (2016) Urbanization and development: emerging futures. UN Habitat.
51. Save the Children (2015) State of the world's mothers 2015: the urban disadvantage. 1–18. Save the Children Federation.
52. Fotso, J.-C., Ezeh, A. C., Madise, N. J., & Ciera, J. Progress towards the child mortality millennium development goal in urban sub-Saharan Africa: the dynamics of population growth, immunization, and access to clean water. *BMC Public Health*, 7, 218 (2007).
53. Ezeh, A. et al. (2017) The history, geography, and sociology of slums and the health problems of people who live in slums. *The Lancet, 389*, 547–558.
54. Alirol, E., Getaz, L., Stoll, B., Chappuis, F., & Loutan, L. Urbanisation and infectious diseases in a globalised world. *The Lancet Infectious Diseases, 11*, 131–141 (2011).
55. McGranahan, G. (2015) Realizing the right to sanitation in deprived urban communities: meeting the challenges of collective action, coproduction, affordability, and housing tenure. *World Development*, 68, 242–253.
56. Wong, J. (2015) Achieving universal health coverage. *Bulletin of the World Health Organization*, 93, 663–664.

57 Taffa, N. & Chepngeno, G. (2005) Determinants of healthcare seeking for childhood illnesses in Nairobi slums. *Tropical Medicine & International Health*, 10, 240–245.
58 Matthews, Z. et al. (2010) Examining the "Urban Advantage in Maternal Healthcare in Developing Countries". *PLOS Medicine*, 7.
59 Requejo, J. H. et al. (2015) Countdown to 2015 and beyond: fulfilling the health agenda for women and children. *The Lancet*, 385, 466–476.
60 Marphatia, A.A., Cole, T.J., Grijalva-Eternod, C., & Wells, J.C.K. (2016) Associations of gender inequality with child malnutrition and mortality across 96 countries. *Global Health Epidemiology*, 1, 178.
61 Global health 2035: a world converging within a generation (2013), 382, 1898–1955l.
62 Sumner, A. (2011) The new bottom billion: what if most of the world's poor live in middle-income countries? Institute of Development Studies.
63 Jamison, D.T., Summers, L.H., Alleyne, G., et al. (2013) Global health 2035: a world converging within a generation. *The Lancet*, 382, 1898–1955.
64 Rheingans, R., Cumming, O., Anderson, J., & Showalter, J. (2012) Estimating inequities in sanitation-related disease burden and estimating the potential impacts of pro-poor targeting. 1–49. SHARE: Sanitation and Hygiene Applied Research for Equity.
65 Pronyk, P.M. et al. (2012) The effect of an integrated multisector model for achieving the Millennium Development Goals and improving child survival in rural sub-Saharan Africa: a non-randomised controlled assessment. *The Lancet*, 379, 2179–2188.
66 Ahmed, S.M., Evans, T.G., Standing, H., & Mahmud, S. (2013) Harnessing pluralism for better health in Bangladesh. *The Lancet*, 382, 1746–1755.
67 Chowdhury, A.M.R. et al. (2013) The Bangladesh paradox: exceptional health achievement despite economic poverty. *The Lancet*, 382, 1734–1745.
68 Kress, D.H., Su, Y., & Wang, H. (2016) Assessment of primary healthcare system performance in Nigeria: using the primary healthcare performance indicator conceptual framework. *Health Systems & Reform*, 2, 302–318.
69 Sinnatamby, G., Mara, D., & McGarry, M. (1986) Shallow systems offer hope to slums. *World Water*, 39–40.
70 Mara, D., Lane, J., Scott, B., & Trouba, D. (2010) Sanitation and health. *PLOS Medicine*, 7, e1000363.
71. Satterthwaite, D. & McGranahan, G. (2006) Overview of the global sanitation problem. *Human Development Report*, 27, 289–306.
72 Barreto, M.L. et al. (2007) Effect of city-wide sanitation programme on reduction in rate of childhood diarrhoea in northeast Brazil: assessment by two cohort studies. 370, 1622–1628.
73 Genser, B. et al. (2008) Impact of a city-wide sanitation intervention in a large urban centre on social, environmental and behavioural determinants of childhood diarrhoea: analysis of two cohort studies. *International Journal of Epidemiology*, 37, 831–840.
74 WHO (2008) Our cities, our health, our future: acting on social determinants for health equity in urban settings. World Health Organization.

12

INEQUALITY BEYOND THE TOILET

Fecal sludge management and the community-level dimensions of sanitation

David Berendes and Joe Brown

Introduction

The primary purpose of sanitation facilities is to provide safe separation of feces from human contact.[1] To accomplish this goal, human waste must be safely contained along the entire sanitation chain, including at the sanitation facility itself using onsite storage, emptying of the storage and transport, and downstream treatment before disposal or reuse.[2] However, in the world's poorest countries, the sanitation sector has to-date invested more on delivery of household-level sanitation facilities (e.g. slab or toilet and associated superstructure) and improvement of toilet coverage than wastewater and sludge management.[3,4] Historically the investment in downstream sanitation infrastructure has been highly subsidized, large public works.[4] The majority of households with sanitation, even urban households, are served by pit latrines, septic tanks, or other on-site systems that retain biosolids (sludge) that accumulates and must be safely managed.[5,6] Thus, fecal sludge management (FSM) services are critically important for reducing exposure risks among communities. Many of the world's poorest people lack available, accessible, and affordable ways to manage fecal sludge, making them, their communities, and neighboring communities disproportionately more vulnerable to diarrheal disease, enteric infection, and longer term sequelae. Notably, those living in areas with high population density, annual flooding, or nearby dumpsites are the most at risk from poor management of fecal wastes. This chapter will describe the inequalities in availability, accessibility, and affordability of fecal waste management services and their consequences for the poorest of the poor. We conclude with a discussion of policy and measurement needs, in the context of the sustainable development goals (SDGs), to ensure successful delivery of safely managed sanitation in an equitable fashion.

Wastewater management, fecal sludge management, and the SDGs

Though sanitation facilities vary worldwide, all require management of human waste beyond the user interface ("fecal waste management" or FWM). FWM can take a variety of forms, including sewerage, emptying and transport by trucks, open drains, on-site composting, and others. Broadly, FWM can be subdivided into "wastewater management" and "fecal sludge management". Wastewater management, a term originally encapsulating all FWM, has recently been limited to downstream management within sewered systems.[3,7] In these systems, combined (with runoff) or separate sewer systems transport human waste to a treatment facility or otherwise outside of the neighborhood. The waste is separated from human contact during this transport, as pipes are buried in the ground. Traditionally, these systems were centralized, rather than decentralized, for historical reasons associated with planning and financing; however, this is beginning to change in higher income settings.[8] Notably, even in high-income countries, access to these systems has traditionally been restricted to communities with sufficient income to make the extension revenue neutral, often excluding the poorest and most marginalized groups.[9]

FSM also concerns the containment of human waste generated from onsite sanitation.[3] "Onsite sanitation" constitutes any form of non-sewered sanitation, including toilets with septic tanks and pit latrines. In many cases, this has been managed by manual emptying of pits or sealing old pits and redigging new pits. FSM generally involves transporting human waste from full septic tanks, pits, or other containment systems to treatment facilities or designated disposal sites, though offsite dumping of untreated waste occurs frequently. Notably, containment of waste in FSM systems has been more varied, with many cities turning to open drains as an interim or long-term FSM strategy.[5]

Though conceptually included in the definition of "improved sanitation" in the Millennium Development Goals (MDGs), FWM was not explicitly monitored in the MDG era. MDGs focused on monitoring sanitation indicators that represented reduced exposure of users at their sanitation facility. Improved sanitation constituted the highest explicitly measured category of sanitation, defined as a private (one household per toilet) sanitation facility connected to sewerage and onsite sanitation options like flush or pour flush toilets leading to a septic tank or pit latrine, ventilated improved pit (VIP) latrines, composting toilets, and pit latrines with a slab.[1] Though private, improved household sanitation facilities have been associated with reduced prevalence of diarrhea in the household when compared with unimproved sanitation and shared sanitation using DHS metrics,[10,11] some aspects of improved sanitation safety were not effectively measured using household sanitation conditions. Many of the FWM options associated with these sanitation facilities did not safely treat human waste before it entered the environment, and thus did not prevent human contact with waste beyond the latrine in the public domain, where these exposures and risk of transmission may result in even larger public health burdens than those in the household itself.[12] Recent estimates suggest that up to 1.5 billion people classified as using improved sanitation in 2010 actually had a sewerage connection where excreta was not treated prior to disposal.[13]

In the SDG framework, the addition of the category of "safely managed" sanitation explicitly reflects the need for continuity of containment along the entire sanitation chain. "Safely managed" sanitation is the new, highest rung of the sanitation ladder, referring to the quality of containment and/or emptying and treatment services. It sits above "basic sanitation," which corresponds to the older definition of "improved sanitation".[14] Conceptually and practically, this separation in evaluating the quality of FWM vs. that of the sanitation facility alone is an advancement in global monitoring policy in that it focuses on understanding of excreta management at the household and community levels. As with the MDGs, the quality of containment at the household level is evaluated through questions and observation.[15] However, the criteria for "safely managed" dictate that human waste transported to an unknown location, or worse, to be dumped somewhere inside or outside the community without treatment or effective containment in a dedicated facility is not safely managed, and is therefore a public health concern. With its inclusion, these critera compel community members and government leaders to understand where their excreta go.

Inequalities in FWM services for the poor

Though FWM has been added to sanitation monitoring in the SDGs, there are still important inequalities and barriers to consider with regard to service provision for the poor. Inequalities exist in the availability, accessibility, and affordability of these services. Those areas that are the poorest are also 1) the most in need of FWM services; 2) the least able to access and afford the services, and 3) the most vulnerable to the effects of poor FWM within their own or from other communities. Many of these inequalities stem from both historical factors (e.g. current urban expansion exceeding the scope of historical city planning projections) and modern-day decisions made in the implementation of household sanitation interventions and current infrastructure planning. The following section will review both historic and current data on inequalities in FWM services, and discuss the health and other implications.

Need for FWM services: The need for FWM services—based on the type of sanitation facility present—is high overall in low- and middle-income countries (LMIC), and increases disproportionately as household wealth decreases. Evidence from Accra, Ghana. suggests that socioeconomic status and waste disposal—both non-sewered and sewered—are inherently linked.[16] A recent analysis of Demographic and Health Survey (DHS) data from 58 countries between 2003–2015[17] indicated that facilities used by about 63% of households in those countries— constituting almost 1.8 billion people—were not connected to sewerage and thus required FSM for sustained use. The proportion of toilets that needed some form of FSM for sustained use increased exponentially with increasing levels of poverty: adjusting for onsite piped water infrastructure and urban or rural location of the household, the rich, middle, poor, and poorest wealth quintiles had 2.7, 7.1, 31, and 170 times higher likelihood of using a facility needing FSM than one that was connected to sewerage, respectively, than those in the richest wealth quintile.[17]

Further, an equal, if not larger, number of households in rural areas used sanitation facilities that would require FSM services to continue to function than households in urban areas. This finding held when compared by wealth quintile. Overall, in urban areas, residents not using facilities that would need FSM generally used toilets connected to sewerage, while in rural areas, residents not falling into the FSM category generally did not have a toilet.[17] This finding is notable given that so much of the current and previous focus of FSM service planning has been concentrated in cities.[3,18,19]

The disparity in type of facility by wealth status results from a combination of limitations associated with funding mechanisms and targets. Until recently, short-term funding mechanisms placed little emphasis on sustainability, meaning that implementers had been more concerned with funding the construction of as many sanitation facilities as possible and not on the means to support emptying, transport, and treatment over time.[2,20] "Coverage" targets, which often failed to account for the entire sanitation chain, were instead focused solely on household access, did not provide motivation to ensure that excreta was safely contained. The emphasis on sanitation coverage metrics as part of the MDGs and the relative costs of sanitation technologies presented further challenges, with little funding going to the provision of infrastructure or services beyond the user interface itself.[20-23] In some respects, this emphasis was justifiable given the enormous gaps in sanitation services and the immediate need to improve the living conditions and dignity of people, preceding the need for FWM.

Early efforts by implementers in the MDG era to emphasize "equal" technology provision for the poor (as for the rich) restricted technologies to expensive, conventional sewerage, ignoring other options like simplified condominial sewerage (a piped network relying on gravity-based flow, but with smaller pipe diameters, eased regulations on pipe gradients and depths, and more flexibility in where pipes are laid) or emptying services. The benefits of emptying services mostly accrue to the relatively poor.[3] Given that onsite systems cost 50–75% less than conventional sewerage (and yet not appreciably less than simplified sewerage), they became the norm in many areas, leaving a gap in services.[24] The effect of these shortcomings was that the necessary support for sanitation facilities for the poorest households was not present years later when containment systems filled, needed maintenance or emptying, or worse, when facilities failed altogether. When selecting sanitation technology or infrastructure, future users were unaware of the costs, training (self-maintenance), and logistics of maintaining the facility.[18] Many may have discounted future costs associated with emptying and maintenance for a variety of reasons.[25]

Infrastructure expansion by local government can fill some of the sanitation gap in cities, but there are challenges. Municipalities may choose not to fund infrastructure expansion into poor neighborhoods whose tax base or revenue collection cannot offset the costs of service provision.[9] Further complicating matters, implementation of piped infrastructure is accompanied by challenges beyond cost when considering poor neighborhoods, especially in cities. Logistical and political concerns limit the installation of sewer pipes; specifically, the need to remove excreta for the poorest of the poor often is complicated by issues of land ownership. The common practice of renting households may mean that landlords are unwilling to fund such projects for their poorer tenants, seeing this work as outside of their responsibilities.[23,25] The destruction or upheaval of property for the installation of sanitary infrastructure also complicates matters for both landlords and tenants. Political issues often arise with the installation of permanent infrastructure in informal settlements, an action that may be interpreted as implicit recognition of the informal settlement when the government does not desire it to be there.[26] Both of these issues are of particular concern in urban areas, as discussed in Chapter 8.

Affordability of FWM: The high prevalence of facilities requiring emptying and transport—rather than sewerage—means that FWM is often more difficult for poorer users to access and financially afford because of differential payment structures between sewered sanitation and facilities requiring FSM. On the whole, governments and public finance mechanisms retained a $16 billion annual gap in funding for basic sanitation to meet the MDG coverage goals, and $56 billion for sufficient wastewater treatment.[23] At the city-level, richer neighborhoods with sewers therefore have FWM services built-in, lowering monthly costs as the initial high implementation costs have already been paid.[27] Often, the initial investments in sewerage have been financed by a public utility, deferring costs from the users themselves.[27] Use of sewerage systems also puts a water cost on the user, as water must be available for this type of system, although onsite water connections have been growing in prevalence at a higher rate than sanitation facilities.[17,28]

In contrast, the poor often live in neighborhoods without existing sewerage and therefore require FSM services, which differentially distribute costs to the users themselves. Per an example from a recent case study in Dakar, Senegal, implementation and use of sewerage distributed approximately 6% of the cost to the users, while FSM services passed on approximately 84% of costs.[27] In all, sewer-based sanitation cost the utility approximately 40 times more than FSM services and thus, under FSM service models, costs to the user total close to 5% of household income and often must be paid in a lump sum, rather than being able to be distributed in monthly instalments.[27,28] In areas of Ghana, the situation is far worse, with the cost of FSM services making up to 32% of the poorest households' annual income.[22] Shifting from a "per use" to a regular schedule of annual or monthly costs has the potential to significantly reduce the cost of emptying (in some cases by up to 97%) per month and enable users to pay more easily to use the service.[29]

The high costs and "pay-per-use" structure associated with emptying means that households use these services as infrequently as possible.[30] In Dakar, most households (65–96%) reported emptying their onsite excreta containment at most once per year, only when full and overflowing.[28] In areas where public toilets are the only option, the costs of emptying a single stall within a public toilet may encompass more than an entire month's budget for the public toilet itself, forcing closures of the toilet.[21]

Non-governmental organizations (NGOs) may subsidize the costs of sanitation provision themselves or help to support private providers and entrepreneurs, but often cannot bear full costs for FSM services. Some NGOs—for example, Sustainable Organic Integrated Livelihoods (SOIL) in Haiti—have included emptying as well as composting of latrine waste for reuse as fertilizer into their cost models in an attempt to recover expenses earlier in the sanitation chain and sustain their business model.[31–34] However, a recent evaluation of NGOs providing public sanitation facilities in Kibera—a slum in Nairobi, Kenya—noted that funders provided for the costs of infrastructure, but not administration, for the toilet and that the length of funding was not sufficient to include FSM services, even when users were bearing much of the day-to-day costs.[21]

At the city, regional, and even national levels, the absence of effective financial and regulatory strategies to promote and sustain emptying services contribute to the high costs for the poorest of the poor and reduce the availability of services. Like sewerage systems, emptying services require planning and oversight at the municipal level.[35] Regulating sanitation—and particularly unsewered FSM—as a service and implementing the corresponding tariffs, subsidies, and infrastructure to ensure its success remains a challenge for governments, especially when sanitation is a privately operated service. Thus, they often lack organization in this capacity, leading to an absence of regulation to ensure safe FSM services.[5] Further, the centralized wastewater treatment systems present in many countries may actually increase the costs of FSM services, as much of these costs come in the form of fuel and truck maintenance from excessive mileage.[30] The transfer stations needed to facilitate decentralized treatment systems and minimize mileage for the trucks themselves are not common currently.[22,36] This overall lack of governmental support to facilitate public or even private emptying services forces operators to bear the burden of costs themselves, leaving prices high in a complete free market and putting services out of reach of the poor.[30,37]

The burden of these high prices is borne by both service providers and users: service providers often cannot afford multiple truck fleets and ensure consistent business, while the prevalence of single truck companies means that users receive inconsistent service. In the example from Dakar, ratios of emptying trucks to households ranged from 1:1,000 to greater than 1:50,000, with similarly high ratios observed in Kampala, Uganda.[28,30] In these circumstances, unreliable services mean that poorer residents may be forced to abandon the toilet (and usually defecate in the open), or use often illegal, manual emptiers who may dispose of waste in the local environment, putting the users and their neighbors at increased health risks.[18,22]

Accessibility of FWM: In addition to the financial burden, because FSM services are not built in to the neighborhood like piped sewerage, physical barriers to the service exist, including those associated with the geography of a neighborhood, as well as the density and construction of the housing and sanitation facilities present.

The geography of a neighborhood can greatly influence how easy or difficult it is for FSM services, like trucks, to get into neighborhoods and physically access the households that require their services. In urban areas, poorer neighborhoods and informal settlements are often densely populated, with household structures close to one another and narrow streets, which prevent trucks from entering. Recent surveys of FSM in major urban centers of Africa and Asia found that about one-third (34%) of households reported using manual, rather than mechanical, emptiers.[28] In many locations, manual emptying is illegal with little or no regulatory oversight such that so-called informal emptiers are often the poorest of the poor themselves, use little to no protective equipment, make little for their services, and dispose of waste in nearby open areas or drains.[28,38] Geography influences rural areas in different ways than urban neighborhoods. Private sector provision of emptying services for poorer rural users of facilities requiring FSM have traditionally been non-existent, as major cities have been viewed as the only potentially viable market for them.[35] While this absence necessitates government involvement in providing these services, especially where water-based sanitation is the norm, in reality household users remain responsible for the desludging of filled toilets and/or the construction of new ones.[4]

The choice of sanitation technology itself, which differs between low- and high-income populations, can compound the problems of FSM. For example, household systems in some of the poorest areas may not be equipped to be easily maintained. In low-income urban areas of Vellore, India, pour-flush toilets that do not empty to open drains are discharged into a holding tank under the household. However, in contrast to richer portions of the city, many of the older tanks in the poorest neighborhoods do not have outflow or access pipes to connect with emptiers. Instead, emptiers must break open the floor of the household to access the tank, increasing the costs of FSM services for the household as they must pay to both break open the floor and have it replaced.[39,40] Subsequent contamination of the household living environment is also a possibility. Septic tanks and other water-based containment, common in India (as discussed above) and other areas of Asia for cultural reasons,[41] also challenge FSM due to the higher water volume of sludge. These high liquid volumes increase the frequency with which tanks must be emptied, raising the logistic and financial burdens on users (in addition to costs associated with water usage). In contrast, many areas of sub-Saharan Africa do not use septic tanks and rather use dry sanitation systems due to insufficient water quantity at the point of use. While these technologies save households in water costs and therefore may be more suitable for poorer and denser areas where water supply is a problem, the sludge in these pits becomes more compacted, dense, and thereby more difficult to remove, often requiring the addition of water to fluidize the sludge for removal.[2,18] This creates an additional waste stream that requires safe management to reduce environmental contamination.

Vulnerability: In addition to having their own difficulties with respect to the availability, accessibility, and affordability of quality FSM services, the poorest communities in urban areas are often the most vulnerable to the health consequences of poor FSM and FWM services from their own neighborhood and the city at large. These vulnerabilities exist because of risk factors, including increased population density, poor environmental conditions, social or cultural inequalities, geography, prevalence of co-morbidities, and poorer access to care.

Poor urban communities tend to have higher population densities and to live 'downstream'—in areas more susceptible to flooding—when compared to the higher income areas of cities.[42] Higher population densities lead to easier transmission of infectious diseases, including those transmitted via the fecal-oral route.[43] Further, in many low-income urban areas, the population density is so high that the only sustainable sanitation solution are public toilets or communal (private) facilities.[44,45] While an effective solution for increasing sanitation coverage for large, dense populations, these toilets fill quickly due to the high volume of users and must be maintained. Management of these facilities may be community-based (by users) or run by local governments or NGOs. In the latter case, these management models take the decision-making power away from the users themselves, leaving those poorest most susceptible to risk associated with the toilets if full (and unusable) or when flooded.[21]

The risks associated with unavailable or poor quality FSM services are often exacerbated by the geography of poor urban neighborhoods, which may be informal settlements and may include semi-permanent housing in locations susceptible to flooding.[42] In combination with high population density, flooding can contaminate the local environment with excreta, increasing risks of diseases like typhoid fever and enteric infections.[16,46–49] The high prevalence of open drains, acting as a substitute for proper FSM in these areas, exacerbates flood risks and leaves children and others exposed to high concentrations of enteric pathogens.[39,50–53]

Poor rural communities are also disproportionately more vulnerable to health consequences associated with poor FSM and FWM services based on their geography, though primarily for reasons of isolation. The absence of access to emptying services means that the rural poor often must conduct their own onsite maintenance, emptying, and safe containment of biosolids. For households who choose to dig a new pit or construct a new tank, rather than emptying the current one, those poorest may lack 1) the resources to purchase new construction materials (or those for ongoing maintenance) and 2) the training to dig sufficiently deep pits that are not susceptible to collapse.[4] Many rural households may choose to empty the current pit, collecting the fecal sludge for reuse as fertilizer. The rural poor have the most use for this end product; however, by emptying the facilities themselves, they also put themselves at higher risk for exposure to fecal pathogens.[54] Further, economic stressors may result in these populations reusing both human and animal waste before pathogens can be properly inactivated, adding to potential personal exposures, as well as contamination of crops.[55]

Future directions and needs

There is a need to create "safely managed" sanitation that effectively contains fecal pathogens in waste and yet is also logistically, financially, and culturally acceptable. Solutions that meet this criterion range from simple, onsite systems to reticulated sewerage networks that convey waste to a treatment works. Further, safe management of sanitation systems needs to be included in project and program-level monitoring and evaluation to allow progress to be measured in the context of the SDGs. The cause–effect relationship between increased access to toilets and the need for FWM needs to be explicitly recognized as critical to delivering health gains potentially achievable by ascending the sanitation ladder. With the rapid expansion of water networks and increasing coverage of onsite sources in the post-MDG era come increasing wastewater volumes and, therefore, needs for wastewater management, thus FWM is an immediate and ever-growing issue in the sanitation sector.

Creating safely managed sanitation. Creation of safely managed sanitation to reach the poorest of the poor will likely require alternatives to conventional sewerage, which may not be financially and logistically feasible in many settings. Instead, consideration of fecal sludge management needs to include systems approaches with the end goal of reducing community-level risks of exposure to excreta. Such approaches must involve policymakers and local governments, community members, non-governmental organizations, and private-sector service providers in order to create an enabling environment with economic incentives for FSM emptying and treatment services.[56]

Policymakers and local and national governments should consider the effects that regulatory and economic policies have on the institutional framework for FSM. Government personnel and institutions may hold enormous power to promote these systems, both through financing and through awareness building and dissemination of key information. At the same time, these entities must also account for the private sector in creating regulatory frameworks that promote cost-effective solutions and enable sustainable investments. Government remains an important regulator of not only the financing, but also the health and environmental implications of FSM services, and thus must be engaged to effectively enforce regulations on national and local levels.[2,5]

Community members, both as consumers and providers of FSM services, may be most able to help governments in designing effective regulatory conditions. As consumers, they are most primed to address the gap in information about emptying practices that is frequently observed when governments first attempt to address the problem.[3,5] Further, targeted approaches to generate representative community engagement may be the most effective way to reach the poorest of the poor, who often lack a voice in negotiations.[24] This outreach may also serve as an opportunity to educate household residents about management of fecal sludge in toilets and general toilet maintenance, an oft-forgotten arm of sustaining sanitation use, and to promote consistent use.[23,57]

Important entities that can drive services are the donors themselves, whether local, national, or international, through their structuring of contracts. Traditionally, funding has heavily favored the installation of infrastructure through short, time-dependent allocations on discrete projects. Sustained funding for services, in contrast, may better enable sustained FSM services through the promotion of and support for regular payment structures, which may be more feasible and sustainable than lump sum or "pay-per-use" structures, especially with subsidies for the poorest residents.[22,27] Infrastructural investments should be focused on strategically placed transfer stations for trucks hauling fecal sludge to reduce distances driven and maximize system efficiency.[22,36] Those infrastructure investments that are for the toilets themselves should consider future servicing costs (or construction of new pits, etc.) for the toilet to promote sustained use.[23,56]

However, the private sector may also be critical for innovation in delivery of cost-sustainable service systems in some settings, as well as improving the capacity for innovation of the market and innovating to keep emptying and service costs in a reasonable range, whether through public–private partnerships or by itself.[23] Cooperation between governments and private operators can improve efficiency and expand services while ensuring that the market remains profitable for private investment and innovation. Leveraging existing private operators may provide an initial, on-the-ground network for service delivery with minimal effort on the government's part, and can play an important role in ensuring sustainable service models.[23]

Monitoring and evaluating "safely managed" sanitation. The challenge of monitoring and evaluating the safe management of sanitation is a key step, though difficult in practice to conduct, in ensuring equity for the poorest of the poor. While current efforts to quantify fecal sludge through rough mass-flow diagrams provide an approximation of the problem and are a useful tool for advocating for these services at a city-level,[3,5] more detailed household, community, and downstream data collection is needed. At the household, integration of questions around emptying practices may provide a baseline assessment of knowledge (and potentially regular use) of emptying practices, though questions need to be standardized and tested.[39] Within the community, government engagement to standardize and regulate the emptying industry can normalize emptying services, mitigating the taboo associated with them in many cities and encouraging the participation of such service providers in data collection.[2] This participation will not only improve data quality for government and SDG purposes, but may also improve record-keeping and standardize practices for the service providers themselves. Although models for how this integration and data sharing might occur have yet to be developed, the involvement of service providers in quantifying the "final fate" of fecal sludge, combined with downstream efforts to account for fecal sludge intake at transfer stations, treatment plants, and reuse sites, is important and can help to reduce the environmental and health burdens in the community, and especially for those poorest. Because of the inclusion of many of these criteria in the SDGs,[58] best practices for collection of these data and for systems-level monitoring are just now beginning to be considered. They represent an important intersection of the research and practice communities to ensure community health.

Conclusions

Effective fecal waste management services for the poorest of the poor are essential to ensuring the health and dignity of communities. For those poorest, fecal waste management may mean fecal sludge management, which requires community implementers, governments, the private sector, and practitioners to think beyond the toilet itself and invest in community-level service models. Otherwise, in the absence of safely managed sanitation, poor onsite containment of feces can contaminate the local environment, leaving users and nearby residents exposed to excreta in the short term. In the long term, infrequent and expensive FSM services may cause users to abandon unserviced toilets and dump untreated excreta into drains or rivers, or other environments that put neighbors and downstream residents at even more risk. Addressing these short- and long-term aspects is essential to ensure sustained use of sanitation. For the poorest of the poor specifically, these effects are observed at a disproportionately higher rate, and have dire consequences for their health and well-being. Affordable and accessible containment and FSM services must accompany the provision of household toilets to prevent additional health risks to the community at large.

Notes

1 WHO and UNICEF (2015) Update and MDG assessment, 2015. Available at: www.wssinfo.org/
2 Strande, L., Ronteltap, M., and Brdjanovic, D. (2014) *Faecal Sludge Management Systems Approaches*. IWA Publishing.
3 Peal, A., Evans, B., Blackett, I., Hawkins, P., and Heymans, C. (2014) Fecal sludge management (FSM): analytical tools for assessing FSM in cities. *Journal of Water, Sanitation and Hygiene for Development*, 4: 371.
4 Nelson, K.L. and Murray, A. (2008) Sanitation for unserved populations: technologies, implementation, challenges, and opportunities. *Annual Review of Environment and Resources*, 33: 119–51.
5 Peal, A., Evans, B., Blackett, I., Hawkins, P., and Heymans, C. (2014) Fecal sludge management: a comparative analysis of 12 cities. *Journal of Water, Sanitation and Hygiene for Development*. 4: 563–75.
6 Blackett. I., Hawkins, P., and Heymans, C. (2014) The missing link in sanitation service delivery: a review of fecal sludge management in 12 cities. Washington, DC. WSP-World Bank.
7 Parkinson, J. (2003) Decentralized wastewater management in peri-urban areas in low-income countries. *Environment and Urbanization*, 15, 75–90.
8 Burian, S.J, Nix, S.J., Pitt, R.E., and Durrans, S.R. (2000) Urban wastewater management in the United States: past, present and future. *Journal of Urban Technology*, 7: 33–62.
9 Stillo, F. and MacDonald Gibson, J. (2016) Exposure to contaminated drinking water and health disparities in North Carolina. *American Journal of Public Health*, 107: e1–6.
10 Fuller, J.A., Clasen, T., Heijnen, M., and Eisenberg, J.N.S. (2014) Shared sanitation and the prevalence of diarrhea in young children: evidence from 51 countries, 2001–2011.

American Journal of Tropical Medicine and Hygiene, published online May 27. DOI:10.4269/ajtmh.13-0503.
11　Fuller J.A., Westphal, J.A., Kenney, B., Eisenberg, J.N.S. (2015) The joint effects of water and sanitation on diarrhoeal disease: a multicountry analysis of the Demographic and Health Surveys. *Tropical Medicine & International Health*, 20: 284–92.
12　Cairncross, S., Blumenthal, U., Kolsky, P., Moraes, L., and Tayeh, A. (1996) The public and domestic domains in the transmission of disease. *Tropical Medicine & International Health*, 1: 27–34.
13　Baum, R., Luh, J., and Bartram, J. (2013) Sanitation: a global estimate of sewerage connections without treatment and the resulting impact on MDG progress. *Environmental Science & Technology*, 47: 1994–2000.
14　WHO, UNICEF (2015) JMP green paper: global monitoring of water, sanitation and hygiene post-2015. Available at: www.wssinfo.org/fileadmin/user_upload/resources/JMP-Green-Paper-15-Oct-2015.pdf
15　UNICEF, WHO (2017) Progress on drinking water, sanitation and hygiene. DOI:10.1111/tmi.12329.
16　Fobil, J., May, J., and Kraemer, A. (2010) Assessing the relationship between socioeconomic conditions and urban environmental quality in Accra, Ghana. *International Journal of Environmental Research and Public Health*, 7: 125–45.
17　Berendes, D.M., Sumner, T.A., and Brown, J.M. (2017) Safely managed sanitation for all means fecal sludge management for at least 1.8 billion people in low and middle income countries. *Environmental Science and Technology*, 51: 3074–83.
18　Koné, D. (2010) Making urban excreta and wastewater management contribute to cities' economic development: a paradigm shift. *Water Policy*, 12: 602–10.
19　Ingallinella A.M., Sanguinetti, G., Koottatep, T., Montanger, A., and Strauss, M. (2002) The challenge of faecal sludge management in urban areas – strategies, regulations and treatment options. *Water Science and Technology*, 46: 285–94.
20　van der Hoek, W., Evansm B, Bjerrem J., Calopietro, M., and Konradsen, F. (2010) Measuring progress in sanitation. Available at: http://eprints.whiterose.ac.uk/42846/
21　Schouten, M. and Mathenge, R. (2010) Communal sanitation alternatives for slums: a case study of Kibera, Kenya. *Physics and Chemistry of the Earth*, Parts A/B/C, 35: 815–22.
22　Boot, N.L.D. and Scott, R.E. (2009) Faecal sludge in Accra, Ghana: problems of urban provision. *Water Science and Technology*, 60: 623–31.
23　Mehta, M. and Knapp, A. (2004) The Challenge of Financing Sanitation for Meeting the Millennium Development Goals. Ministry of the Environement, 12th session of the United Nations Commission on Sustainable Development, New York.
24　Paterson, C., Mara, D., and Curtis, T. (2007) Pro-poor sanitation technologies. *Geoforum*, 38: 901–7.
25　Chunga, R.M., Ensink, J.H.J., Jenkins, M.W., and Brown, J. (2016) Adopt or adapt: sanitation technology choices in urbanizing Malawi. *PLOS One*, 11: 1–16.
26　Nallari, A. (2015) 'All we want are toilets inside our homes!': The critical role of sanitation in the lives of urban poor adolescent girls in Bengaluru, India. *Environment and Urbanization*, 27: 1–16.
27　Dodane, P.-H., Mbéguéré, M., Sow, O., and Strande, L. (2012) Capital and operating costs of full-scale fecal sludge management and wastewater treatment systems in Dakar, Senegal. *Environmental Science and Technology*, 46: 3705–11.
28　Chowdry, S. and Kone, D.D. (2012) Business analysis of fecal sludge management: emptying and transportation services in Africa and Asia. Available at: www.susana.org/en/resources/library/details/1662
29　Balasubramanya, S., Evans, B., Hardy, R., et al. (2017) Towards sustainable sanitation management: establishing the costs and willingness to pay for emptying and transporting sludge in rural districts with high rates of access to latrines. *PLOS One*, 12: 1–20.
30　Murungi, C. and van Dijk, M.P. (2014) Emptying, transportation and disposal of feacal sludge in informal settlements of Kampala, Uganda: the economics of sanitation. *Habitat International*, 42: 69–75.

31 Preneta, N., Kramer, S., Magloire, B., and Noel, J.M. (2013) Thermophilic co-composting of human wastes in Haiti. *Journal of Water, Sanitation and Hygiene for Development*, 3: 649.
32 Berendes, D., Levy, K., Knee, J., Handzel, T., and Hill, V.R. (2015) Ascaris and Escherichia coli inactivation in an ecological sanitation system in Port-au-Prince, Haiti. *PLOS One*. DOI:10.1371/journal.pone.0125336
33 Russel, K., Tilmans, S., Kramer, S., Sklar, R., Tillias, D., and Davis, J. (2015) User perceptions of and willingness to pay for household container-based sanitation services: experience from Cap Haitien, Haiti. *Environment and Urbanization*, 27: 525–40.
34 Tilmans, S., Russel, K., Sklar, R., Page, L., Kramer, S., and Davis, J. (2015) Container-based sanitation: assessing costs and effectiveness of excreta management in Cap Haitien, Haiti. *Environment and Urbanization*, 27: 89–104.
35 Evans, B., Haller, L., and Hutton, G. (2004) Closing the sanitation gap: the case for better public funding of sanitation and hygiene. Available at: eprints.whiterose.ac.uk/42860/9/EvansBE13.pdf
36 Kennedy-Walker, R., Holderness, T., Alderson, D., Evans, B., and Barr, S. (2015) Network modelling for road-based faecal sludge management. *Proceedings of the Institution of Civil Engineers*, 167: 157–65.
37 Chaggu, E., Mashauri, D., van Buuren, J., Sanders, W., and Lettinga, G. (2002) Excreta disposal in Dar-es-Salaam. *Environmental Management*, 30: 609–20.
38 Hawkins, P. and Muximpua, O. (2015) Developing business models for fecal sludge management in Maputo. Maputo, Mozambique. Available at: www.wsp.org/sites/wsp.org/files/publications/WSP-Developing-Business-Models-for-Fecal-Sludge-Management-Maputo.pdf
39 Berendes, D., Kirby, A., Clennon, J.A., et al. (2017) The influence of household- and community-level sanitation and fecal sludge management on urban fecal contamination in households and drains and enteric infection in children. *American Journal of Tropical Medicine and Hygiene*, 96: 1404–14.
40 John, S.M., Thomas, R.J., Kaki, S., et al. (2014) Establishment of the MAL-ED birth cohort study site in Vellore, Southern India. *Clinical Infectious Diseases*, 59, Suppl. 4: S295–9.
41 Coffey, D., Gupta, A., and Hathi, P. (2014) Culture and the health transition: understanding sanitation behavior in rural north India. Available at: www.theigc.org/wp-content/uploads/2015/04/Coffey-et-al-2015-Working-Paper.pdf
42 Turley, R., Saith, R., Bhan, N., Rehfuess, E., and Carter, B. (2013) Slum upgrading strategies involving physical environment and infrastructure interventions and their effects on health and socio-economic outcomes (Cochrane Review). Available at: www.ncbi.nlm.nih.gov/pubmed/23440845
43 Alirol, E., Getaz, L., Stoll, B., Chappuis, F., and Loutan, L. (2011) Urbanisation and infectious diseases in a globalised world. *The Lancet Infectious Diseases*, 11: 131–41.
44 Biran, A., Jenkins, M.W., Dabrase, P., and Bhagwat, I. (2011) Patterns and determinants of communal latrine usage in urban poverty pockets in Bhopal, India. *Tropical Medicine & International Health*, 16: 854–62.
45 Kwiringira, J., Atekyereza, P., Niwagaba, C., et al. (2014) Descending the sanitation ladder in urban Uganda: evidence from Kampala slums. *BMC Public Health*, 14: 624.
46 Akullian, A., Ng'eno, E., Matheson, A.I., et al. (2015) Environmental transmission of typhoid fever in an urban slum. *PLOS Neglected Tropical Diseases*, 9: 1–14.
47 Carlton, E.J., Eisenberg, J.N.S., Goldstick, J., Cevallos, W., Trostle, J., and Levy, K. (2014) Heavy rainfall events and diarrhea incidence: the role of social and environmental factors. *American Journal of Epidemiology*, 179: 344–52.
48 Carrel, M.A., Emch, M., Streatfield, P.K., and Yunus M. (2009) Spatio-temporal clustering of cholera: The impact of flood control in Matlab, Bangladesh, 1983–2003. *Health & Place*, 15: 741–52.
49 Osei, F.B., Duker, A.A. (2008) Spatial and demographic patterns of cholera in Ashanti region – Ghana. *International Journal of Health and Geographics*, 7: 44.

50 Labite, H., Lunani, I., van der Steen, P., Vairavamoorthy, K., Drechsel, P., and Lens, P. (2010) Quantitative microbial risk analysis to evaluate health effects of interventions in the urban water system of Accra, Ghana. *Journal of Water Health*, 8: 417–30.
51 Katukiza, A.Y., Ronteltap, M., van der Steen, P., Foppen, J.W.A., and Lens, P.N.L. (2014) Quantification of microbial risks to human health caused by waterborne viruses and bacteria in an urban slum. *Journal of Applied Microbiology*, 116(2): 447–63.
52 Katukiza, A.Y., Temanu, H., Chung, J.W., Foppen. J.W.A., and Lens, P.N.L. (2013) Genomic copy concentrations of selected waterborne viruses in a slum environment in Kampala, Uganda. *Journal of Water and Health*, 11: 358–70.
53 Gretsch, S.R, Ampofo, J.A, Baker, K.K., et al. (2015) Quantification of exposure to fecal contamination in open drains in four neighborhoods in Accra, Ghana. *Journal of Water and Health*, 14(2).
54 Thye, Y.P., Templeton, M.R., and Ali, M.A. (2011) Critical review of technologies for pit latrine emptying in developing countries. *Critical Reviews in Environmental Science and Technology*, 41: 1793–819.
55 Julian, T.R. (2016) Environmental transmission of diarrheal pathogens in low and middle income countries. *Environmental Sciences: Process & Impacts*, 0: 1–12.
56 Tilley, E., Strande, L., Lüthi, C., et al. (2014) Looking beyond technology: an integrated approach to water, sanitation and hygiene in low income countries. *Environmental Science and Technology*, 48: 9965–70.
57 O'Reilly, K. and Louis, E. (2014) The toilet tripod: understanding successful sanitation in rural India. *Health & Place*, 29: 43–51.
58 United Nations (2015) Transforming our world: the 2030 agenda for sustainable development. DOI:10.1007/s13398-014-0173-7.2.

PART 4

Enhanced monitoring of inequalities in water and sanitation

13
MONITORING INEQUALITIES IN WASH SERVICE LEVELS

Tom Slaymaker and Rick Johnston

Introduction

The Sustainable Development Goals (SDGs) include ambitious targets for 'universal access' to drinking water, sanitation and hygiene (WASH) by 2030. These targets apply to all countries and not only aim to end open defecation and extend access to basic services for all, but also to progressively improve service levels over time. This reflects a growing concern within the WASH sector with the equity, safety and sustainability of services provided (see Chapter 3). This chapter discusses some of the conceptual and practical challenges associated with monitoring inequalities in service levels and provides an overview of emerging proposals for enhancing global monitoring of WASH during the SDG period.

The WHO/UNICEF Joint Monitoring Programme for Water Supply Sanitation and Hygiene (JMP) has played a leading role in developing global norms to benchmark progress on drinking water, sanitation and hygiene since it was established in 1990. It reported on global, regional and national progress towards MDG target 7c and is responsible for global monitoring of the new 2030 SDG targets related to WASH. Towards the end of the MDG period (1990–2015), WHO and UNICEF convened a series of international consultations on future WASH monitoring, establishing technical working groups on drinking water, sanitation, hygiene, and equity and non-discrimination. This led to a broad consensus that SDG monitoring should build on established indicators and datasets used during the MDG period (see Chapter 1) and introduce new indicators that address the normative criteria of the human rights to safe water and sanitation. As such, a key principle guiding emerging proposals for SDG WASH monitoring has been the concept of progressive achievement of universal access while reducing and eliminating inequalities in service levels.

Different lenses for thinking about improvements in service levels

Emerging approaches are grounded in the idea of a 'service ladder' whereby users can gradually progress from a lower level of service (or no service at all) to a higher level of service characterised by multiple criteria. While this idea is not new,[1,2] it has recently gained greater traction within the WASH sector.[3,4,5] The MDG targets simply focused on reducing absolute inequalities in access but, as coverage has increased, attention has increasingly focused on inequalities in drinking water and sanitation service levels. While the JMP has increasingly disaggregated sub-categories of 'improved' and 'unimproved' drinking water and sanitation facilities (see Chapter 1), it has long been recognised that households using the same type of infrastructure may experience different levels of service. The current focus on improving service levels is influenced by several different schools of thought, including human rights theory, public health theory, and business theory.

The relevance of human rights theory has been outlined in Chapter 2. The general principles of 'universality' and 'progressive realisation' of social and economic rights are now well established and commit states to allocate the 'maximum available resources' towards improving outcomes across all population groups.[6,7] These concepts have also influenced the 2030 Agenda for Sustainable Development which reflects a number of key human rights principles in that it seeks to be universal, transformative, comprehensive and inclusive.[8] Indeed, the 2015 Transforming our World declaration sets out the vision of 'a world where we reaffirm our commitments regarding the human right to safe drinking water and sanitation and where there is improved hygiene'.[9]

Initially recognised in a General Comment by the UN Committee on Economic, Social and Cultural Rights in 2002,[10] the human rights to safe water

TABLE 13.1 Normative criteria of the human rights to safe water and sanitation

Criterion	UNCESCR, General Comment 15 (November 2002)[11]	Independent Expert Report to Human Rights Council (July 2010)[13]
Sufficient quantity	Availability	Availability
Continuity of service		
Safe for health	Quality	Quality/safety
Aesthetically acceptable		
Time/distance required to collect	Accessibility (physical)	Accessibility
Suitable for use by all, including disabled and older people		
Affordable	Accessibility (economic)	Affordability
Non-discrimination	Accessibility	(cross-cutting)

and sanitation were further elaborated under the mandate of an Independent Expert. Following resolutions by the Human Rights Council and General Assembly of the United Nations in 2010,[11] they are now widely recognised by UN member states and increasingly referenced in national policies and legislation.[12]

The UNCESCR General Comment identified three main criteria – availability, quality, accessibility– and three subcategories of accessibility – physical, economic and non-discrimination. The Independent Expert subsequently proposed five normative criteria similar to GC 15, but separated acceptability from quality and considered non-discrimination as a cross-cutting concern rather than a normative criterion[13] (see Table 12.1). The importance of safe water and sanitation for the realisation of other human rights related to poverty, food, health, housing, education, gender equality and environment has also been recognised.[14,15]

Another defining feature of the human rights approach is that it combines aspirational targets for universal access with an explicit focus on reducing and eliminating inequalities. To this end, the JMP post-2015 working group on equity and non-discrimination[6] recommended simultaneously tracking both overall rates of progress and progress in reducing the 'gap' between advantaged and disadvantaged groups (Figure 13.1; see Figure 2.1). This concept was subsequently reflected in formulation of the SDG targets for WASH, which call for 'universal and equitable' access to safe water, sanitation and hygiene for all.

Public health theory provides another important lens for thinking about progressive improvements in service levels. Improvements in water, sanitation and hygiene are widely recognised to be an essential foundation for better nutrition and health (see Chapter 11) but the relationship is complex.[16,17,18] Inadequate drinking water, sanitation and hygiene services account for a significant share of the global burden of disease and remain a leading cause of death among children under five. Studies have shown that even basic interventions to reduce open defecation, increase handwashing or provide basic water and sanitation facilities can reduce the burden of disease by up to 30%.[19] But while upgrading to higher levels of service is likely to further reduce pathogen exposure, the resulting improvements in health will depend on several factors and may be non-linear.

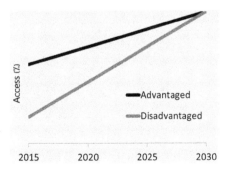

FIGURE 13.1 Progressively reducing and eliminating inequalities (Satterthwaite, 2012[6])

Howard and Bartram[3] argue that a public health perspective to categorise water service levels needs to take account of interlinkages between the proximity of the source and the quality and quantity of water consumed. This is supported by research suggesting that consumption decreases as water collection time increases[20,21] and that handwashing and food hygiene are often first to be compromised.[22] Furthermore, water quality has been shown to deteriorate rapidly during transit and storage.[23,24] This suggests that securing potential health gains will require incremental improvements across all three dimensions.

When it comes to reducing disease, incremental improvements in community-level sanitation coverage may be at least as important as sanitation at the household level.[25] Even when people have good sanitation practices themselves, if they live in communities where poor sanitation is prevalent, their health remains at risk. This concept is in line with the theory that chronic exposure to enteric pathogens negatively impacts gut structure and function. The damaged tissue is unable to absorb nutrients effectively, leading to malnutrition and increased vulnerability to infectious diseases, such as diarrhoea[26,27] (see Chapter 11). One analysis drawing on 29 national datasets from developing countries found that when neighborhood-level sanitation coverage was below 60% there was a modest protective effect against diarrhoeal disease (reducing risk by 18%), but that above this threshold the protective effect sharply increased, so that at 100% neighbourhood scale coverage, the risk of diarrhoea was 56% lower.[25] Similarly, a recent World Bank study in Indonesia[28,29] found that increasing Open Defecation-Free (ODF) status at the village level from 20% to 60% would have no impact on stunting, but an increase from 60% to 100% would significantly increase height-for-age z-scores (see Figure 13.2).

Business management theory sets out from a very different starting point – the aim being to maximise profit – but arrives at a similar conclusion that an effective

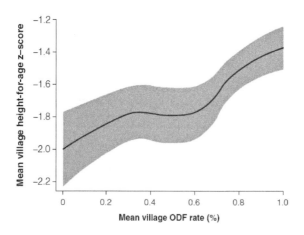

FIGURE 13.2 Non-linear health gains from improved sanitation (World Bank, 2017)

strategy is to progressively improve the quality of systems. Quality Improvement (QI) frameworks were first developed to systematically reduce deviations and errors in the manufacturing industry,[30] but have since been applied in customer service,[31] healthcare[32] and financial services sectors.[33] A wide range of quality improvement systems have been proposed, including continuous quality improvement (QCI), total quality management (TQM), statistical process control (SPC), plan-do-study-act (PDSA) cycles, and Lean Six Sigma, highlighting the effectiveness of systematic approaches to quality improvement.

A common premise underlying these various frameworks is that all work is done through systems and that all systems can be improved. Most of these QI frameworks follow a standard sequence:

- Identify areas for potential improvement.
- Continuously collect and analyse high-quality data on processes and outputs related to the targeted areas.
- Identify actions that can marginally reduce variation or improve quality
- Apply improvement packages based on the results of the analysis

A characteristic of QI frameworks is that they encourage the identification and addressing of problems and inefficiencies, rather than stigmatising them. This approach is applied iteratively, with the result that small changes are progressively introduced and continuously reduce unwanted variation in outcomes, eventually yielded substantial improvements over time. QI approaches differ from conventional monitoring and evaluation in their systematic approach to using data to identify and address root causes of complex issues, rather than simply documenting progress over time.

Benchmarking service levels

While the concept of progressive improvement in WASH services is well established, benchmarking and comparing service levels between and within countries presents a number of challenges. First, there is no universally agreed minimum acceptable package of WASH services. Second, it is difficult to combine the multiple different criteria used to assess service levels into a single composite measure. Third, efforts to assess progress must take into account both current status and trends over time. Finally, efforts to compare progress must consider both absolute inequalities in access and relative inequalities in the type and level of service provided to population subgroups. The following section discusses these challenges and considers emerging approaches to addressing them.

Since 2000, the JMP has used a simple system for classifying household drinking water and sanitation facilities into improved and unimproved types. Improved drinking-water sources are those designed to protect against contamination, whereas improved sanitation facilities are those designed to hygienically separate excreta

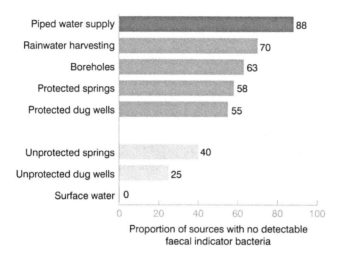

FIGURE 13.3 Improved sources are not always safe (WHO, 2017[35])

from human contact (see Chapter 1). While the binary improved/unimproved classification can be applied in almost all contexts, it has long been recognised that the type of infrastructure that households use is an inadequate proxy for the level of service provided.[34]

Studies have confirmed that while improved drinking-water sources are less likely to be contaminated than unimproved sources[35] (see Figure 13.3), contamination is often widespread and varies between improved types.[24,36] While some households use sources located on premises, others use distant sources where water collection represents a significant burden.[37] There is clearly a big difference between having water available 24 hours per day and having a supply that is intermittent or available for 2–3 hours each day, and there is evidence to suggest that discontinuous supplies are more likely to be contaminated.[38] Similarly, an improved sanitation facility may be private or shared with other households. It may flush to a sewer that leads to a treatment plant, or it may simply flush to an open drain or into the street. In countries that only have information on the type of infrastructure used, these disparities in service levels remain invisible. Information on service levels is available for a growing number of countries, but the indicators and thresholds used to assess service levels vary.

The human rights to water and sanitation focus attention on the following dimensions of inequalities in service levels.

Accessibility

Most countries aspire to having piped water supplies on premises, but there is less agreement on the minimum acceptable standards for those that rely on sources located off-site. Some countries set standards for the maximum amount of time spent collecting water (e.g. <1 hour per trip), whereas others relate to distance travelled (<1 km from household to source). There is evidence that consumption starts to decrease if a round trip to collect water exceeds 30 minutes, but the effect also depends on terrain and other factors.[39] The fact that household survey responses to questions on time and distance are sometimes unreliable makes it even more difficult to establish a precise threshold. Sanitation facilities may be located off premises, presenting a physical barrier to access, but accessibility is also determined by whether or not they are shared with other households. Relatively few countries consider sharing to be acceptable and, among those that do, minimum standards for the number of people allowed to share different types of facilities vary making it difficult to benchmark and compare.[40]

Availability

Minimum acceptable standards for water availability are also context specific. The term 'availability' is sometimes used to refer to the quantity of water supplied. WHO has developed normative guidance on the minimum quantities of water required for drinking, cooking, personal hygiene (at least 20 litres per person per day) and other essential domestic uses such as bathing and laundry (at least 50 lpcpd).[3] But the actual amounts of water consumed vary widely, from as little as 5–10 lpcpd in the Horn of Africa to over 400 lpcpd in parts of North America, depending on culture, wealth and geography. A more meaningful comparison therefore is the continuity or reliability of the service and whether the water supplied is sufficient to meet basic needs. Many countries record the number of hours per day that services are typically available and, while such data are often restricted to urban populations using regulated networks, this can be benchmarked against national standards, which range from 4 hours per day to 24 hours per day. Many surveys also ask households whether their main water source is currently functioning and whether the water supplied is sufficient to meet their needs. In some countries, both types of data are available, revealing that while many households have discontinuous supplies, they may still be sufficient to meet their needs.[35]

Quality

The importance of water safety for health is well documented and there has been a progressive harmonisation of national standards for drinking-water quality, many of which are now aligned with the WHO Guidelines for Drinking Water Quality.[41] There is broad agreement on the contaminants that pose the greatest risk to human health globally, but the development of water safety plans and systems for surveillance and testing of drinking-water quality varies across countries.[42] While very few countries have comparable data on the coverage and effectiveness of water safety plans, many collect information on the quality of drinking water.[43] The frequency, location and methods used for testing vary from country to country, but a core set of standard microbial and chemical parameters are increasingly widely measured. Sanitary water safety can be assessed by inspecting the adequacy of sanitation systems and measures to protect drinking-water sources and delivery systems, as well as direct testing of water samples for faecal contamination. Chemical contamination (particularly fluoride and arsenic) is also known to present a significant risk to human health.[41] A wide range of other parameters may also be monitored at national and subnational levels.

Acceptability

Acceptability of drinking water (taste, colour, odour) can be an important determinant of the source that households choose to use and the amount of water they consume.[44] Acceptability is closely related to accessibility, availability and quality, but can be quite subjective and often highly variable, making it difficult to measure and to compare within and between countries. Acceptability of sanitation facilities has also been shown to be a key determinant of whether people are prepared to stop defecating in the open and start using latrines. Key concerns include safety and comfort, privacy, cleanliness and ease maintenance. These also tend to be highly context specific and difficult to measure and compare when facilities may be acceptable to some people but not others. Importantly, a sanitation facility should not only be acceptable to the people who use it, but also to those who are affected by arrangements for the treatment and final disposal of excreta produced.[14]

Affordability

The affordability of drinking water and sanitation services is a longstanding concern and a potential economic barrier to access.[45] It is identified as a normative criterion of the human rights to water and sanitation and is explicitly referenced in SDG target 6.1 which calls for 'universal and equitable access to safe and affordable drinking water'.[46] The WHO/UNICEF JMP normative interpretation is that payment for services should not present a barrier to access or prevent people meeting other basic needs.[47] Many countries conduct surveys of household income and expenditure, but these tend to focus on water expenditures rather than sanitation and hygiene, and on tariffs and recurrent costs rather than on the capital investments required to establish a piped water supply or install a new sanitation system. While it is possible to estimate the share of annual household income or expenditure going to WASH, there is currently no commonly agreed threshold above which costs are considered unaffordable, nor can it be assumed that households that make no payment have affordable services. The question of how WASH expenditure impacts other basic services is even more complex and is explored further in Chapter 15.

Discrimination

Human rights prohibit direct discrimination of individuals or groups on the grounds of race, colour, sex, language, religion, political or other opinion, national or social origin, property, birth, disability or other status.[15] The Special Rapporteur has also identified a number of specific types of stigmatisation associated with realisation of the human rights to safe water and sanitation.[48] Sociocultural barriers to access are very widespread, but the particular combination of factors tends to be highly context specific. Where disaggregated data are available, it is possible to identify evidence of discrimination by income, education, race, ethnicity, disability and other generic characteristics.[49] However, the specific nature of discrimination will be different in each setting and is unlikely to be captured in mainstream survey instruments. As such, local forms of discrimination are more likely to be identified through national and subnational participatory processes and qualitative assessments.[7]

International consultations on future indicators for WASH monitoring recommended building on established indicators relating to the types of infrastructure people use and integrating information on the level of service received, taking into account the normative criteria of the human rights to safe drinking water and sanitation outlined above. However, the integration of data on technology and service levels is technically challenging, especially in countries where these are drawn from different data sources. While national household surveys and censuses remain the primary source of data on the types of technology people use, administrative and regulatory data coverage is increasing rapidly and expected to be the main future source of data on service levels. Most countries, though, which already collect service-level data only report average levels of compliance and very few produce disaggregated statistics for population subgroups.

Furthermore, the availability and quality of data relating to service criteria and the way in which they are combined can significantly determine the assessment of service levels. Every new criterion that is introduced increases the data required for monitoring compliance. If data for one or more criteria are unavailable for part of the population, the resulting service-level assessments will be incomplete and difficult to compare. It is also important to consider the relationship between variables before trying to integrate them. For example, improvements in the accessibility, availability and quality of drinking water are often interdependent and should therefore arguably be considered together.[3] Affordability, on the other hand, is primarily a function of the socioeconomic characteristics of the user group, and should therefore be assessed independently from the type and level of service provided.[47]

Another key consideration when developing global benchmarks is ensuring that they are universally applicable and relevant to all countries. The use of service ladders with multiple different rungs enables comparison of progress across countries at different stages of development. In addition to providing a set of norms against which countries can benchmark existing services, it focuses attention on whether or not countries are making progress, regardless of their position on the ladder.

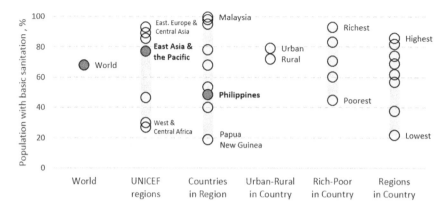

FIGURE 13.4 Population using at least basic sanitation services, by SDG region, country, rural-urban, wealth quintile and subnational region, Philippines[50] (author's analysis based on WHO/UNICEF JMP, 2017 (permission granted))

The JMP service ladders have been gradually refined over the years to better distinguish inequalities in services. At the bottom they seek to distinguish between those who have suboptimal services and those that have no service at all and rely on surface water or practise open defecation. But in principle there is no limit to the number of rungs that could potentially be added on top because there is always room for improvement. The challenge for national and global monitoring is rather to establish benchmarks that are suitably ambitious but also achievable.

Finally, there is an inherent tension between efforts to continuously improve existing services and efforts to progressively reduce inequalities in WASH services. While there is broad agreement that priority should be given to ending open defecation and ensuring that everyone has access to at least a basic level of service, in line with the Delhi principle of 'some for all, not all for some' (see Chapter 4), governments have to strike a balance between investing in keeping existing services running and investing in extending services to those who remain unserved. The 2030 agenda commits member states to reduce inequalities within and between countries, and reflects an increased focus on indicators of inequality. In addition to monitoring overall trends in coverage, JMP updates have increasingly highlighted inequalities between rural and urban areas, between rich and poor, and between other groups and the general population (Figure 13.4).

To date, the focus of 'gap analysis' has been on monitoring absolute inequalities in access, but as basic service coverage increases and data on service levels become more widely available, the focus will shift to monitoring inequalities in service levels.

Drinking water

The WHO/UNICEF JMP has developed a new service ladder to facilitate enhanced monitoring of drinking water. It builds on the established improved facility-type classification and introduces new rungs with additional criteria relating to service levels. Improved drinking-water sources are those that by nature of their design and construction have the potential to deliver safe water and include piped water, boreholes or tubewells, protected dug wells, protected springs, rainwater and packaged or delivered water. For global monitoring purposes, the population using improved sources is divided into three groups according to the level of service received.

Safely managed drinking-water services represent an ambitious new rung at the top of the service ladder. In order to meet the criteria for a safely managed service people must use an improved source that meets three criteria: it should be accessible on premises, water should be available when needed, and the water supplied should be free from contamination. If the improved source does not meet any one of the three criteria, but a round trip to collect water takes 30 minutes or less, it will be categorised as a basic drinking-water service. If water collection from the improved source exceeds 30 minutes, then it will be classified as a limited drinking-water service. The bottom rungs continue to distinguish those populations using unimproved sources that are not designed to protect against contamination, such as unprotected dug wells or unprotected springs, and those with no service at all who rely on drinking water directly from surface water sources (Table 13.2).

The new ladder therefore provides continuity with existing monitoring systems, while introducing new information on the level of service received based on the normative criteria of the human rights to safe water and sanitation – i.e. accessibility, availability and quality. Household surveys and censuses remain the primary source of information on the different types of facilities that households use, but information on service levels is available from both household surveys and administrative sources, including regulators. Household surveys are typically carried out every three to five years and provide disaggregated information for the entire population. Administrative data tend to be collected more frequently, but may not

TABLE 13.2 The new JMP ladder for drinking-water services

Service level	Definition
Safely managed	Drinking water from an improved water source that is located on premises, available when needed and free from faecal and priority chemical contamination
Basic	Drinking water from an improved source, provided collection time is not more than 30 minutes for a round trip, including queuing
Limited	Drinking water from an improved source for which collection time exceeds 30 minutes for a round trip, including queuing
Unimproved	Drinking water from an unprotected dug well or unprotected spring
Surface water	Drinking water directly from a river, dam, lake, pond, stream, canal or irrigation canal

Note: Improved sources include: piped water, boreholes or tubewells, protected dug wells, protected springs, rainwater, and packaged or delivered water.

cover all population groups. Identifying the best source for each indicator and, where appropriate, integrating data from different sources is a key challenge for national and global monitoring.

Accessible on premises. Household surveys and censuses routinely collect information on the population with household connections, the location of non-piped sources and the time taken to collect water from sources located off premises. Sources located on premises (within the dwelling, yard or plot) are not limited to piped water but include boreholes, rainwater, protected wells and springs.[47] Households without water on premises are typically asked to estimate the time required to travel to the water source, queue, fill containers and return. Administrative data sources may also include information on the proportion of the population with piped household connections and the proportion using public taps, but are often limited to urban areas and exclude private supplies. Many countries have established minimum standards for time spent collecting water and 30 minutes per round trip is a widely used upper limit. Others have standards relating to the distance travelled which are broadly comparable – e.g. no more than 500 metres each way. While household estimates of time or distance are not always precise, they nevertheless provide a useful indication of the relative burden of water collection. The vast majority of countries have data available on the accessibility of drinking-water services. It is estimated that in 2015, while three out of four people use improved sources accessible on premises and nine out of ten spend less than 30 minutes, over a quarter of a billion people still spent more than 30 minutes collecting water.[47]

Available when needed. National statistical offices, regulators and utilities all collect information on availability, but use a wide range of different measures. While many countries have established normative standards expressed in litres per capita per day, very few have reliable data on the actual quantities of water consumed. Information on the amount of time when water is available is more widely available. Regulators often collect information on the number of hours of service per day as well as the frequency and duration of interruptions reported by utilities. Household surveys and censuses sometimes collect information on hours of service per day, but also frequently ask households whether they are able to access sufficient water to meet their needs. While hours of service per day is a more objective measure, the quantity of water supplied per hour varies according to context. From a human rights perspective, it is important to assess whether supplies are sufficient relative to needs. While this is a more subjective measure, it is still broadly comparable. For global monitoring, the JMP combines data on the availability of drinking water when needed and data on the number of hours of service, and uses 12 hours per day as the global minimum benchmark for 'available when needed'. On this basis, it is estimated that in 2015, eight out of ten people used improved sources with water available when needed.

Free from contamination. To be considered safe, drinking water must be free from pathogens and elevated levels of harmful substances at all times.[41] Direct testing of drinking-water quality provides an important measure of 'safety' and can be used to verify the effectiveness of existing arrangements for managing contamination risks. Most countries have national standards aligned with the WHO guidelines for drinking-water quality that identify faecal contamination, arsenic and fluoride as the highest priority parameters for global monitoring. Data on water quality primarily come from administrative sources, including regulators that collect information from utilities on the number of tests conducted and percentage microbial and chemical compliance. Regulatory data coverage varies, but is generally better for urban than for rural populations.[43] A growing number of nationally representative household surveys have also integrated water-quality testing in recent years, enabling risks to be assessed for different subgroups and linked to other socioeconomic characteristics such as wealth.

Faecal contamination is usually identified through the detection of indicator bacteria such as *E. coli* or thermotolerant coliforms in a 100 mL sample of water although the frequency of testing and the methods used vary across country. The results may vary, depending on the location of tests within the distribution system,[51] but for the purpose of global monitoring the JMP uses data on the quality of water at the point of delivery/collection, which may be a household tap, community stand-post, borehole or well. Contamination can be highly variable, so brief events may escape detection even with regular testing. Effective water treatment should deactivate indicator bacteria along with other microbes, but certain pathogens such as *Cryptosporidium parvum* may be more resistant to some disinfection processes such as chlorination.[52] Furthermore, indicator bacteria may attenuate more rapidly in the environment than some pathogens. So, while the presence of *E. coli* is considered a reliable indicator that drinking water is faecally contaminated and unsafe, the absence of *E. coli* does not guarantee safety. In 2015, water-quality data were available for less than half the global population. It was estimated that three out of four people used improved sources free from contamination, but low levels of compliance were reported in many low- and middle-income countries with data.[47]

Sanitation

Global norms for the safe management of excreta date back at least 60 years. The third edition of the WHO *Guidelines for Drinking Water Quality* shifted the focus of the guidelines from monitoring for compliance with drinking water standards to a risk-management framework in which monitoring is secondary to a systematic identification of hazards that could lead to compromising water safety, and the implementation of control measures to prevent such system failures. This approach, embodied in the Safe Drinking Water Framework and Water Safety Plans (WSP), is now being adapted to the sanitation subsector.

Sanitation Safety Planning (SSP) draws on the same risk-management framework to assess, manage and monitor risks from the point of generation (e.g. the toilet) to the waste's final use and/or disposal.[53] SSP differs from WSPs in several ways:

- SSP considers multiple exposure groups for hazards.
- SSP often operates without a clear regulatory framework, with roles and responsibilities shared among different sectors and levels.
- SSP aims to reduce negative health impacts, but may also aim to increase positive benefits of wastewater use (e.g. valorising water, nutrients, or energy in wastes).

Like Water Safety Plans, the first generation of Sanitation Safety Planning tools focuses mainly on formal networked services, but already adaptations are being made for on-site sanitation systems including septic tanks and container-based sanitation systems.

This focus on identifying and preventing system failures underpins the forthcoming WHO *Guidelines for Sanitation and Health* that are expected to be published in 2018. The guidelines call for a progressive improvement in sanitation services, with an initial focus on elimination of open defecation, which represents the most egregious risk to public health. There is less epidemiologic evidence regarding the health impacts of moving from basic sanitation to higher levels of service, but the limited studies that have examined such transitions point to potentially large health gains.[19]

The WHO/UNICEF JMP has introduced elements of levels of service in the new global monitoring ladder for sanitation services (Table 13.3). The ladder builds on the classification used in MDG monitoring of the population using 'improved' or 'unimproved' sanitation facilities. Those who use no sanitation facilities at all are classified as having no services and practising open defecation, while those who use sanitation facilities that lack design measures for isolating faeces from human exposure are considered to use unimproved facilities. The population using improved sanitation facilities, as defined during the MDG period, will now be divided into three groups on the basis of the quality of the service. Those who use improved facilities that are public or shared with other households are considered to have limited sanitation services, while those who use facilities that are not shared are classed as having at least basic sanitation services.

TABLE 13.3 The new JMP ladder for sanitation services

Service level	Definition
Safely managed	Use of improved facilities that are not shared with other households and where excreta are safely disposed of in situ or transported and treated offsite
Basic	Use of improved facilities that are not shared with other households
Limited	Use of improved facilities shared between two or more households
Unimproved	Use of pit latrines without a slab or platform, hanging latrines or bucket latrines
Open defecation	Disposal of human faeces in fields, forests, bushes, open bodies of water, beaches or other open spaces, or with solid waste

This population can potentially qualify as having safely managed sanitation services, if the excreta are either safely disposed of in situ or are transported and treated off-site.

Data for the bottom four rungs of the sanitation ladder are normally available from household surveys and censuses. These types of data sources give information on what type of facilities people use, which may be different from the types of facilities that people theoretically have access to on the basis of infrastructure coverage. There are numerous examples of sanitation facilities that are built through government or non-/government programmes, but are not used by the intended beneficiaries.[54]

The information required for classifying services as safely managed is not always available with the household. A survey might be able to collect information on the proportion of on-site sanitation systems in which excreta are safely disposed in situ, but cannot provide information about the kind of off-site treatment wastes receive. Data on transport and treatment of excreta, both from on-site systems (e.g. latrines, septic tanks, container-based sanitation) and households with sewer connections, must come from service providers or authorities that oversee their work. Collecting such data in a consistent and harmonised way, and integrating this information with data from households about the use of sanitation facilities, represents one of the main technical challenges for monitoring SDG 6.

Shared sanitation. Well-designed and operated shared sanitation facilities can effectively isolate faeces from human exposure and could be considered as 'safe' from a health perspective. However, other aspects of service drawn from the human rights framework such as 'accessibility' may be compromised when sanitation facilities are shared. Shared facilities may not be safely accessible during the night or outside certain hours, and women may face harassment when using such facilities.[46] For these reasons, use of shared facilities is considered a limited service, and it is estimated that in 2015 8% of the population had limited sanitation services.

Wastewater treated off-site. For the purposes of global monitoring of SDG target 6.2, excreta are considered to be safely managed when transported through sewer networks to a wastewater treatment plant that delivers at least secondary (biological) treatment. Treatment plants that deliver only primary treatment are not considered as qualifying for safely managed services, unless the effluent is discharged in a way that precludes further human exposures – e.g. through a long ocean outfall. Most countries have at least some data on the type of treatment that wastewater treatment plants deliver, and it is estimated that in 2015, 73% of wastewater receives at least secondary treatment and 27% of the population uses toilets that are not shared. and are connected to such treatment plants.

Excreta transported and treated off-site. Excreta that are removed from on-site storage facilities can be transported and treated at appropriate treatment facilities, typically through trucking services. Wastewater treatment plants treating sewage may be able to receive and treat such wastes, but as wastes from on-site systems are much more concentrated than sewage, there is a risk that the plant can be overwhelmed. As for wastewater, treatment plants that deliver at least secondary treatment (for both the solid and liquid fractions) are counted as safely managed. Many countries, including high-income countries, lack data on the amount of excreta that is transported and treated off-site. Insufficient data were available to estimate the global population whose excreta were safely transported and treated off-site in 2015.

Excreta treated and disposed of in situ. On-site storage represents a kind of treatment, and if such systems are appropriately designed and operated, they can safely isolate and inactivate faecal pathogens. Household surveys can provide information about the emptying of such on-site storage facilities, and where excreta are not emptied, they are considered to be disposed of in situ and qualify as safely managed. It is estimated that in 2015, 13% of the global population used on-site sanitation systems that were not shared with other households and had not been emptied, and thus were counted as safely managed.

Hygiene

While the health benefits of improved hygiene are well established, hygiene was not considered in the MDG framework. International consultations during planning for post-MDG targets considered different types of hygiene, including handwashing, menstrual hygiene and food hygiene, and recommended handwashing with soap as a priority indicator for health in all settings.

Measuring actual handwashing behaviour is notoriously difficult.[55] Self-reported behaviours do not yield reliable data, as respondents are likely to give the 'correct' response rather than reflect actual practice. The most accurate method of measuring handwashing practice is structured observation, which involves a surveyor spending many hours closely following people and recording their handwashing practices after key events such as defecation or food preparation. Modelled estimates based from 42 structured observation studies suggest that just 19% of people worldwide wash their hands with soap after contact with excreta.[56]

This intensive method is appropriate for research studies, but not for routine national monitoring. The most reliable proxy indicator of handwashing practice has been found to be the presence of handwashing facilities, including soap and water, in the home.[57] Clearly, without soap and water readily available, effective handwashing can't take place, and evidence suggests that having facilities in the home helps to establish a social norm around handwashing, leading to behaviour change.

Many household surveys include a section on hygiene practices where the surveyor visits the handwashing facility and verifies the availability of soap and water in order to classify a household as having basic handwashing facilities. Households with a handwashing facility that lacks either soap or water are classified as having limited handwashing facilities. In 2015, data were available for 70 countries, which was not sufficient to make a global estimate, but regional estimates of basic handwashing ranged from 17% in sub-Saharan Africa to 76% in Western Asia and Northern Africa.

Conclusion

Enhanced national and global monitoring of drinking water, sanitation and hygiene implies going beyond tracking the types of facilities that people use and assessing the levels of service provided. The normative criteria of the human rights to water and sanitation provide a useful framework for monitoring inequalities in WASH service levels, but applying these criteria is challenging and requires integrating data from multiple sources. The updated JMP service ladders provide a framework that enables countries to benchmark and compare progress, but it will take time to harmonise the indicators used to assess the accessibility, availability and quality of services at national and subnational levels. As more data become available, it will be possible not only to assess the level of service received by different population groups, but also to monitor the progressive reduction of inequalities in WASH service levels over time. Improvements in monitoring systems represent an important first step towards addressing inequalities in WASH services, but need to be coupled with a focused effort by national stakeholders to understand and address the underlying causes of inequality that are often highly context specific.

Notes

1 White, G.F., Bradley, D.J., and White, A.U. (1972) Drawers of water: domestic water use in East Africa. University of Chicago Press, Chicago.
2 Lloyd, B. and Bartram, J. (1991) Surveillance solutions to microbiological problems in water quality control in developing countries. *Water Science and Technology*, 24(2): 61–75.
3 Howard, G. and Bartram, J. (2003) Domestic water quantity, service level and health. World Health Organization, Geneva.
4 Lockwood, H. and S. Smits (2011) *Supporting Rural Water Supply: Moving toward a Service Delivery Approach*. Practical Action Publishing: Rugby.
5 Kayser, G.L., Moriarty, P., Fonseca, C. and Bartram, J. (2013) Domestic water service delivery indicators and frameworks for monitoring, evaluation, policy and planning: a review. *International Journal of Environmental Research and Public Health*, 10: 4812–4835.
6 Satterthwaite, M. (2012) JMP working group on equity and non-discrimination final report. WHO/UNICEF Joint Monitoring Programme for Water Supply and Sanitation.
7 UN OHCHR (2012) Human rights indicators: a guide to measurement and implementation. New York and Geneva: UN OHCHR.
8 Danish Institute for Human Rights (2015) Human rights and the 2030 Agenda for Sustainable Development.
9 United Nations (2015). Transforming Our World: The 2030 agenda for sustainable development. Geneva: United Nations, Department of Economic and Social Affairs.
10 United Nations Committee on Economic, Social and Cultural Rights (2002) General Comment No.15: The Right to Water (Articles 11 and 12 of the Covenant).
11 United Nations (2010) Resolution on Human Right to Water and Sanitation, UN General Assembly Research, A/64/292.
12 WHO/UN-Water (2017) UN-Water Global Analysis and Assessment of Sanitation and Drinking-Water (GLAAS) 2017 report. Financing universal water, sanitation and hygiene under the Sustainable Development Goals.
13 De Albuquerque, C. (2010) Report of the independent expert on the issue of human rights obligations related to access to safe drinking water and sanitation. Geneva.
14 Zimmer, A., Winkler, I. and Albuquerque, C. (2014) Governing wastewater, curbing pollution, and improving water quality for the realization of human rights. *Waterlines*.

15 De Albuquerque (2014) *Realising the Human Rights to Water and Sanitation: A Handbook by the UN Special Rapporteur.*
16 Bartram, J. and Cairncross, S. (2010) Hygiene, sanitation, and water: forgotten foundations of health. *PLOS Medicine*, 7(11): e1000367. Available at: https://doi.org/10.1371/journal.pmed.1000367
17 Brown, J., Cairncross, S. and Ensink, J.H.J. (2013) Water, sanitation, hygiene and enteric infections in children. *Archives of Disease in Childhood*, 98: 629–634.
18 Cumming, O. and Cairncross, S. (2016) Can water, sanitation and hygiene help eliminate stunting? Current evidence and policy implications. *Maternal & Child Nutrition*, 12, 91–105.
19 WHO (2014) Preventing diarrhoea through better water, sanitation and hygiene: exposures and impacts in low- and middle-income countries.
20 Cairncross, S. and Feachem, R. (1993) *Environmental Health Engineering in the Tropics: An Introductory Text* (2nd edn). John Wiley, Chichester.
21 Thompson, J., Porras, I.T., Tumwine, J.K., Mujwahuzi, M.R., Katui-Katua. M., Johnstone, N. and Wood, L. (2001) *Drawers of Water II: 30 years of Change in Domestic Water Use and Environmental Health in East Africa*. IIED, London.
22 Gautam, O.P, Esteves-Mills, J., Chitty, A. and Curtis, V. (2015) *Complementary Food Hygiene*. London School of Hygiene and Tropical Development, London.
23 Clasen, T.F. and Bastable, A. (2003) Faecal contamination of drinking water during collection and household storage: the need to extend protection to the point of use. *Journal of Water and Health*, 1(3): 109–115.
24 UNICEF (2014) Nepal 2014 Multiple Indicator Cluster Survey Final Report. United Nations Children's Fund. Government of Nepal. National Planning Commission Secretariat.
25 Jung, Y.T., Hum, R.J., Lou, W. and Cheng, Y. (2017) Effects of neighbourhood and household sanitation conditions on diarrhea morbidity: systematic review and meta-analysis. *PLOS One*, 12(3).
26 Humphrey, J.H. (2009) Child undernutrition, tropical enteropathy, toilets, and handwashing. *The Lancet*, 374: 1032–1035.
27 Keusch, G.T., Denno, D.M., Black, R.E. et al. (2014) *Environmental Enteric Dysfunction: Pathogenesis, Diagnosis, and Clinical Consequences. Clinical Infectious Diseases.* An official publication of the Infectious Diseases Society of America. 59 (Suppl. 4): S207–S212. doi:10.1093/cid/ciu485.
28 Cameron, L.C., Chase, C., Joseph, G. and Pinto, R. (2017) Child stunting and cognitive impacts of water, sanitation and hygiene in Indonesia. Policy Research Working Paper, World Bank, Washington, DC.
29 World Bank (2017) Improving service levels and impact on the poor: a diagnostic of water supply, sanitation, hygiene, and poverty in Indonesia. WASH Poverty Diagnostic. World Bank, Washington, DC.
30 Maani, K., Putterill, M. and Sluti, D. (1994) Empirical analysis of quality improvement in manufacturing. *International Journal of Quality & Reliability Management*, 11(7): 19–37.
31 Ramaswamy, R. (1996) *Design and Management of Service Processes: Keeping Customers for Life.* Addison-Wesley, Reading, MA.
32 Nicolay, C., Purkayasta, S., Greenhalgh, A., Benn, J. et al. (2012) Systematic review of the application of quality improvement methodologies from the manufacturing industry to surgical healthcare. *British Journal of Surgery*, 99(3): 324–335.
33 Leseure, M., Hudson-Smith, M. and Delgado, C. (2010) The implementation of lean Six Sigma in financial services organizations. *Journal of Manufacturing Technology Management*, 21(4): 512–523.
34 WHO and UNICEF (2000) Global Water Supply and Sanitation Assessment 2000 Report, WHO/UNICEF, Geneva/New York.
35 WHO (2017) Thematic Report on Safely Managed Drinking Water Services. WHO/UNICEF Joint Monitoring Programme for Water Supply and Sanitation. Geneva.

36 Bain, R., Cronk, R., Wright, J., Yang, H., Slaymaker, T. and Bartram, J. (2014) Fecal contamination of drinking-water in low- and middle-income countries: a systematic review and meta-analysis. *PLOS Medicine*, 11(5).
37 UNSD (2015) The world's women 2015: trends and statistics. United Nations Statistical Division.
38 Kumpel, E. and Nelson, K.L. (2013) Comparing microbial water quality in an intermittent and continuous piped water supply. *Water Research*, 47: 5176–5188.
39 Cairncross, S. and Kinnear, J. (1992) Elasticity of demand for water in Khartoum, Sudan. *Social Science and Medicine*, 34(2): 183–189.
40 Evans, B., Hueso, A., Johnston, R., Norman, G., Pérez, E., Slaymaker, T. and Trémolet, S. (2017) Limited services? The role of shared sanitation in the 2030 Agenda for Sustainable Development. *Journal of Water, Sanitation and Hygiene for Development*, 7(3): 349–351.
41 WHO (2011) *Guidelines for Drinking Water Quality* (4th edn). World Health Organization, Geneva.
42 WHO and IWA (2017) Global status report on water safety plans: a review of proactive risk assessment and risk management practices to ensure the safety of drinking-water. World Health Organization; International Water Association.
43 Peletz, R., Kumpel, E., Bonham, M., Rahman, Z. and Khush, R. (2016) To what extent is drinking water tested in sub-Saharan Africa? A comparative analysis of regulated water quality monitoring. *International Journal of Environmental Research Public Health*, 13: 275.
44 Nekesa, J., Casey, V., Brown, L., and Carpenter, J. (2016) Is it time for the problem of corrosion and subsequent pump failure to be eliminated? 7th Rural Water Supply Network Forum, July. Abidjan, Côte d'Ivoire.
45 Hutton, G. (2012) Monitoring "affordability" of water and sanitation services after 2015: review of global indicator options. United Nations Office of the High Commissioner for Human Rights, Geneva.
46 Heller, L. (2015) *Report of the Special Rapporteur on the human right to safe drinking water and sanitation to the UN Human Rights Council*, 5 August. A/HRC/30/39.
47 WHO and UNICEF (2017) Progress on drinking water, sanitation and hygiene: 2017 update and SDG baselines. WHO/UNICEF Joint Monitoring Programme for Water Supply, Sanitation and Hygiene, Geneva.
48 De Albuquerque, C. (2012) Stigma and the realization of the human rights to water and sanitation. Report of the Special Rapporteur on the human right to safe drinking water and sanitation to the Human Rights Council, 2 July. A/HRC/21/42.
49 UNICEF and WHO (2016) Inequalities in sanitation and drinking water in Latin America and the Caribbean. WHO/UNICEF Joint Monitoring Programme for Water Supply and Sanitation, Geneva.
50 UNICEF and WHO (2017) Snapshot of progress on drinking water, sanitation and hygiene in East Asia and Pacific Region. UNICEF, Bangkok.
51 Howard, G. (2002) *Water Supply Surveillance: A Reference Manual*. Water, Engineering and Development Centre, Loughborough University, Loughborough.
52 Driedger, A.M., Rennecker, J.L. and Marinas, B.J. (2001) Inactivation of Cryptosporidium parvum oocysts with ozone and monochloramine at low temperature. *Water Research*, 35, 41–48
53 WHO (2015) *Sanitation Safety Planning: Manual for Safe Use and Disposal of Wastewater, Greywater and Excreta*. World Health Organization, Geneva.
54 Evans, B., van der Voorden, C. and Peal, A. (2009) Public funding for sanitation: the many faces of sanitation subsidies. Water Supply and Sanitation Collaborative Council, Geneva.
55 Luby, S.P., Halder, A.K., Huda, T., Unicomb, L. and Johnston, R.B. (2011) Using child health outcomes to identify effective measures of handwashing sciences. *American Journal of Tropical Medicine and Hygiene*, 85(5): 882–892. doi:10.4269/ajtmh.2011.11-0142

56 Freeman, M.C., Stocks, M.E., Cumming, O., Jeandron, A., Higgins, J.P.T., Wolf, J., Prüss-Ustün, A., Bonjour, S., Hunter, P.R., Fewtrell, L. and Curtis, V. (2014) Systematic review: hygiene and health: systematic review of handwashing practices worldwide and update of health effects. *Tropical Medicine and International Health*, *19*: 906–916. doi:10.1111/tmi.12339.

57 Ram, P. (2013) Practical guidance for measuring handwashing behavior. Water and Sanitation Program. World Bank, Washington, DC.

14
BENCHMARKING PROGRESS ON REDUCING INEQUALITIES OVER TIME

Jeanne Luh and Jamie Bartram

Introduction

Sustainable Development Goal (SDG) 6 to "ensure access to water and sanitation for all" includes targets that aim to achieve "universal and equitable access to safe and affordable drinking water for all" and "access to adequate and equitable sanitation and hygiene for all" by 2030.[1] The focus on access for all aligns with the human rights to water and sanitation[2,3] and General Comment 15,[4] which were adopted by the United Nations (UN) in 2010 and by the United Nations Committee on Economic, Social and Cultural Rights (CESCR) in 2003, respectively. In the former, the UN "recognizes the right to safe and clean drinking water and sanitation as a human right that is essential for the full enjoyment of life and all human rights",[2] and in the latter, General Comment 15 holds countries responsible and legally accountable to use the maximum resources available to ensure that "sufficient, safe, acceptable, physically accessible and affordable water" is progressively realized for all, without discrimination.[4] The core human rights concept of progressive realization recognizes that countries differ in both resources available and constraints faced, and thus compliance is attained when countries take deliberate, concrete steps towards achieving universal access as quickly and effectively as possible.[5]

Current estimates of access to "improved" water and sanitation services, as defined by the WHO/UNICEF Joint Monitoring Programme (JMP) for Water Supply and Sanitation, show that despite significant progress during the 1990–2015 period, the global population is far from achieving access for all, with disparities in access within and between countries.[6]

To monitor inequality in water and sanitation access between two or more populations, existing and proposed approaches include the Concentration Index, the Index of Equality Betterment, Gap Analyses, and looking at patterns of inequality. We briefly describe below each approach and examples from the literature when applicable. Concentration indices are adapted from the Lorenz curve and are a standard measure used to assess wealth-related inequalities in health.[8] For our purposes, the concentration index measures the inequality in access to water and sanitation across different wealth quintiles.[9,10] Values range from −1 to +1, where a value of zero indicates an absence of wealth-related inequality in access to water and sanitation, and positive and negative values indicate inequality. Specifically, negative values suggest higher coverage among the poor, and positive values suggest higher coverage among the rich.[9] Roche et al. (2017) calculated separate urban and rural concentration indices for 25 sub-Saharan African countries and showed that all countries had index values that were high, positive numbers (i.e., high inequality favouring the rich) for both 1) access to water and sanitation and 2) access to water with collection time under 30 minutes, plus sanitation and a handwashing facility with soap.[9] It should be noted that the concentration index can only be calculated when the groups being compared have an intrinsic order (e.g., wealth quintiles, education level) and cannot be used for groups with no order (e.g., gender).[11]

The Index of Equality Betterment (IEB) was developed by Rutstein[11] and measures the total improvement needed to achieve equality in water or sanitation. The IEB can be calculated for any equality variable as long as data is available using the following equation:

$$IEB = \frac{\left(\sum n_g \times \left(i_{high} - i_g\right)\right)}{\sum n_g} \quad (1)$$

where n is the number of categories in the equality variable (e.g., for wealth quintiles, $n = 5$), g is the equality group category, i_{high} is the coverage for the equality group category with the best value, and i_g is the coverage for equality group category g. IEB values can then be compared across countries and different equality variables.[11]

Various types of gap analyses have been proposed as simple metrics to assess inequality. The 2014 JMP report[7] uses one type of gap analysis to assess inequalities between urban and rural populations, and between the richest and poorest quintiles (see pp. 270–271 for more details). In addition, three other gap analyses proposed include assessing the 1) gap between the coverage between the best and worst-off groups, 2) coverage ratio between the best and worst-off groups, and 3) ratio of the proportion of the unserved population in the best and worst-off groups.[11] As an example, if the richest and poorest quintiles in a country had 80% and 20% access to safe water, the three-gap analyses measures would be gap of 60 percentage points, coverage ratio of 4:1, and ratio of 20%:80%, respectively.

Patterns of inequality were first used by Victora et al.[12] when analyzing the proportion of children that received six or more child-survival interventions such as measles vaccination. Visual inspection was used to define a 'top', 'bottom', and 'linear' inequality pattern for the shape of the curves when the percentage of children receiving six or more child-survival interventions was plotted against wealth quintile. A 'top' inequality pattern corresponded to countries where coverage in the richest group was significantly higher than coverage in other groups, while a 'bottom' inequality pattern indicated that coverage in the poorest group was disproportionately lower than coverage in the other groups. A "linear" pattern corresponded to countries where coverage steadily increased from the poorest to the richest group, without disproportionately large jumps. These patterns of inequality can also be applied when looking at access to water and sanitation as a function of wealth quintile in a country. Roche et al.[9] found that of the 25 sub-Saharan African countries examined, the majority of countries had a "top" inequality pattern for both urban and rural populations, indicating that the richest quintile had substantially greater coverage in water and sanitation, as compared to the other four quintiles.

Despite the differences in these existing methods to assess inequality in water and sanitation access, all four methods focus on assessing inequality using data from only one time point, and is similar in approach to the methodology used in determining whether a country met its MDG targets. Specifically, the focus is on the status of a country in terms of whether it has reached its target (e.g., is the concentration index 0 which would signify equality; is the gap coverage ratio between the best and worst-off groups equal to 1 which would signify equality), without consideration of the different starting points that countries have. The risk associated with this approach is that countries with a low starting point that have made significant steps towards achieving universal access may be condemned for not reaching universal access. As an example, for both the left and right panels in

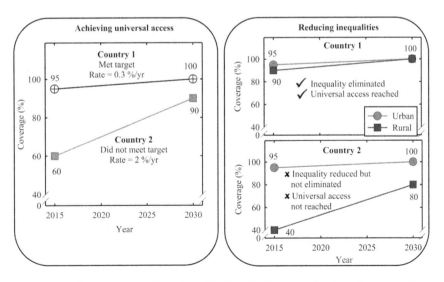

FIGURE 14.1 Country comparison for achieving SDG target of universal access and eliminating inequalities

Figure 14.1, Country 2 would be classified as a failure in meeting its 2030 target even though its increase in coverage per year in panel a) and reduction in rural–urban disparities in panel b) is greater than Country 1.

A comparative analysis is thus needed to put into perspective the actual progress that countries have made. Frontier analysis offers an alternative tool to measure the progressive reduction of inequalities that takes into account the starting point of a country and compares its performance against the historically best-performing countries at similar starting points. As such, its advantage over other approaches is that it uses the "maximum feasible output" historically achieved as the basis for a realistic, meaningful, and reasonable benchmark of performance. For example, to evaluate progress towards reducing rural–urban inequalities, countries would be compared to other countries that had a similar rural–urban disparity. In addition, this analysis can be performed using rates of change data, instead of coverage data, thus allowing trends in progress (e.g., progression, regression, stagnation) to be evaluated. The concept of frontier analysis can be applied to various scenarios and can be modified according to different needs, such as comparison of progress across time for a single country. In this chapter, we discuss the principles of frontier analysis and apply this method to assess the progress towards the reduction of rural–urban inequalities and the relative progress between the higher served and lesser served populations, respectively, for countries with available data.

Frontier analysis as an alternative approach

General principles

Frontier analysis is based on the principles of data envelopment analysis (DEA), which is used to define the "best-practice frontier" or "benchmarks" for operations management (e.g., defining the best-performing bank, hospital, school, etc.).[13] DEA was first used to estimate the efficiency of decision-making units (e.g., banks, hospitals, countries, etc.) in the 1970s[14] and is similar to the stochastic frontier approach, in that both methods estimate the best-practice frontiers; however, the

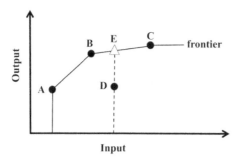

FIGURE 14.2 Definition of best-practice frontier for single input–single output case (taken from Luh et al.;[16] modified from Pascoe et al.[15])

way in which the frontier is defined and thus how efficiency is measured, differs. In DEA, all possible input–output combinations are used to define the best-practice frontier, while in the stochastic frontier approach, a relationship between the inputs and outputs is first estimated and used to define the frontier.[15] Figure 14.2 illustrates how the best-practice frontier is defined for a single input-single output case. Points A, B, C, and D represent different decision-making units. The best-practice frontier is defined as the upper boundary of these points (i.e., envelops the data) and in Figure 14.2 is constructed of points A, B, and C. As points A, B, and C are best-performers, their efficiency is 100%. For point D, which lies below the frontier, its efficiency is less than 100%; for the same input x as point D, point E would correspond to the output that would result in 100% efficiency.

Use of frontier analysis to assess performance in public health goals and targets

A common method used in operations research, DEA has also been used to assess country performance in the fulfillment of social and economic rights. Fukuda-Parr et al. (2009) proposed the use of an Achievement Possibility Frontier (APF) to calculate an index that measures economic and social rights fulfillment using indicators in the dimensions of education, food, health, housing, and decent work.[17] While "data envelopment analysis" is not explicitly mentioned, the APF approach draws on the principles of DEA in defining a best-practice frontier. For each economic and social rights indicator, the achievement of a country (i.e., output) is plotted as a function of its gross domestic product (GDP) per capita (i.e., input), which is an indicator of resource capacity. The APF is then defined as the maximum level historically achieved by any country at each GDP per capita value and is constructed by fitting a curve through the frontier points. For example, one economic and social rights indicator assessed by Fukuda-Parr et al. was primary school completion rate. A country's performance (or efficiency) is then based on the primary school completion rate achieved as compared to the maximum rate historically achieved by countries at the same GDP per capita.[17]

Luh et al. (2013) further modified this concept in two ways by: 1) defining the output as historically achieved rates of change instead of historically achieved levels (i.e., status); and 2) defining the input as the status of a country instead of a resource capacity indicator.[18] Through these two changes, the focus is directed towards whether countries are making progress, which aligns with the human rights principle of progressive realization, while taking into account a country's level of development (given by the initial status of the country). Luh et al. (2013) applied this modified DEA approach to the water and sanitation sector to assess countries' performance towards providing equitable access (e.g., examining the disparity in access between rural and urban locations) and this was further used to create a water and sanitation performance index.[19] In this chapter, we draw on these published results, update the analyses with the most recent data available, and describe the results in further detail.

Frontier analysis applied to drinking water coverage

We use drinking water coverage to provide a simple illustration of how frontier analysis can be used in the water and sanitation sector, before examining its use in assessing inequalities. Step-by-step details on how to perform frontier analysis can be found in Luh et al.[16] For drinking-water coverage, SDG 6.1 target is to achieve universal access to safe water,[1] and thus we are interested in whether a country is making progress towards 100% coverage. We note that while SDG 6.1 seeks to ensure access to safe water for all, at present there is insufficient data available on whether water sources are actually safe, with most available data focusing on access to improved services. As such, we focus on using the indicator of access to improved water, of which data is available from the JMP 2015 Country Files[21] (see p. 262). We select our metric of interest to be the percentage of the population with access to improved water. We also set our target to be 100% coverage, which means that in order for countries to demonstrate progress (i.e., have a positive performance), coverage should be moving towards 100% and not away from 100%.

To construct the best-practice frontier, we select our output of interest to be the rate of change in coverage. The rate of change provides information on whether a country is moving towards a target, the degree to which it is progressing or regressing over time, and goes beyond determining whether a country has met its target. For example, from 2000 to 2010, the total improved drinking-water coverage in the Dominican Republic decreased from 90.1% to 76.4%, while during a similar time period (2000–2011), Ethiopia increased its coverage from ~26% to ~50%. Despite the overall lower coverage in Ethiopia, it is moving faster towards increasing access, as compared to the Dominican Republic during the same time frame. To obtain the rate of change, coverage data are plotted as a function of time and the rate of change is calculated as the slope of the best fit line. Depending on the objective of the study, the criteria for data inclusion can vary, although we suggest a minimum of five data points spanning a minimum of three different years to minimize variability from the survey data. For studies in which data availability is limited, researchers may choose to use a minimum of three points, instead of five, in order to have as many historical rates of change as possible. On the other hand, for studies interested in looking at progress over a specific time period, all data points within that time period may be used to calculate the rate of change. Additional criteria such as visual inspection to ensure that all data points used follow a linear fit, the requirement that data points do not span more than ten years, decisions on how to address multiple data points from the same year, or exclusion of data points during years of internal or external conflict may also be imposed. For each calculated rate of change, we also determine the corresponding coverage value (input parameter) as the average coverage during the time span with which the rate of change was calculated.

Figure 14.3a presents all calculated rates of change as a function of their corresponding coverage for countries with available data. Using the FEAR[22] software package in R,[23] outliers were removed and the frontier points were identified as

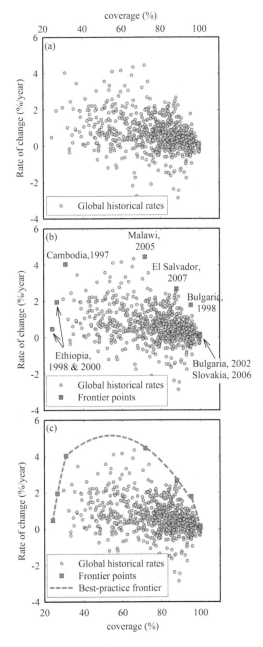

FIGURE 14.3 Identification and construction of the best-practice frontier for total improved drinking water coverage

those points that form the "envelope". These frontier points correspond to Bulgaria 1998 and 2002, Cambodia 1997, El Salvador 2007, Ethiopia 1998 and 2000, Malawi 2005, and Slovakia 2006 and are shown in Figure 14.3b as black squares. Frontier points represent the maximum achievable rate of change, or benchmark rate, that has been historically obtained by a country at that specific level of coverage. We use historical rates of change to define the benchmark rates, as these are rates that have been achieved in the past by countries at that level of coverage, and thus are realistic and attainable. A polynomial equation is then fit to the frontier points to obtain the best-practice frontier (i.e., the line that sits on top of all other points, see Figure 14.3c), which allows "virtual" frontier points to be calculated for every coverage level.

Country performance in increasing access to water can then be assessed through a performance index that compares a country's rate of change to the benchmark (maximum achievable) rate (obtained from the best-practice frontier) using Equation 14.2:

$$index = \frac{rate_{i,j} - min\ rate_j}{max\ rate_j - min\ rate_j} \qquad (2)$$

where $rate_{i,j}$ is the actual rate of change for country i at coverage level j; maximum $rate_j$ is the maximum rate achievable by any country at coverage level j (obtained from the best-practice frontier) and the minimum $rate_j$ is set at zero (no progress). Equation 14.2 produces a scoreless index that assesses country performance and allows countries to be compared against each other. The most recent performance indices for all countries with available data are available in Appendix 14.1.

Performance indices can be used to compare across different countries or for a country to perform self-assessments over time, as seen in Figures 14.4a and 14.4b, respectively. In Figure 14.4a, performance indices for six countries are shown for the average year of 2011, where each country is paired with another at the same level of coverage or same rate of change. For example, both South Africa and El Salvador had total improved drinking-water coverage of ~92%. However, the rate of change was decreasing for South Africa and increasing for El Salvador, resulting in performance indices of −0.50 and 0.54, respectively. In addition, while the rate of change indicates whether a country is progressing or regressing; two countries with the same rate of change can have different performance indices depending on their level of coverage, as seen with Honduras and Kazakhstan in Figure 14.4a. Both countries have rates of change of ~0.49%/year, however Kazakhstan has a higher performance index of 0.27 as compared to 0.18 of Honduras. When performance indices are calculated across time, a country can assess whether they are maintaining a consistent performance. In Figure 14.4b, Mali shows a consistently positive index throughout the years, indicating that the country is increasing its coverage. The increase in performance index from 1998 to 2007 indicates that Mali has effectively used its available resources to increase coverage. On the other hand, Figure 14.4b indicates that country performance in increasing access to total

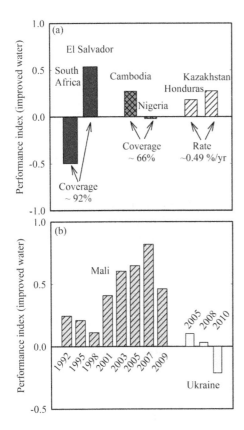

FIGURE 14.4 Comparison of performance indices (a) across countries in 2011 and (b) across time for Mali and Ukraine

improved water has decreased in Ukraine, with index scores of 0.10, 0.03, and −0.21 for the average years of 2005, 2008, and 2010, respectively. In fact, the most last negative index shows that total improved drinking-water coverage decreased in recent years in Ukraine.

Frontier analysis applied to inequalities in water and sanitation

Identifying frontier points and constructing a best-practice frontier can be applied for any variable with sufficient data (see p. 261). In addition to assessing progress towards increasing access to total improved water and sanitation, frontier analysis can also be used to assess progress towards reducing inequalities in water and sanitation. In the following pages, we discuss the use of frontier analysis to assess progress towards reducing two types of inequalities: 1) inequality in access between two population groups (e.g., rural and urban populations in a country) and 2) inequality in the rate of change between a higher served and a lesser served population (e.g., population using unimproved water and population using non-piped improved sources). These two types of inequalities represent different ways in which inequality can be considered, from both the standpoint of comparing coverage between groups, and also considering the rate at which they move up the water and sanitation service ladder. The two examples discussed below were selected because the analyses have already been performed in previous studies.[18] In this chapter, we simply update the analyses using the most recent data available from the JMP 2015 Country Files.[21] While not discussed in this chapter, frontier analysis can also be used to assess inequalities in access for different wealth quintiles, age groups, ethnicities, and religions, among other variables, as long as data is available. In the case where several subgroups are possible (e.g., wealth quintiles, religions, etc.), two subgroups must be selected for comparison. For wealth quintiles, we recommend comparison between the richest quintile and the poorest quintile, which would be in alignment with existing analysis from the JMP.[7]

Data requirements

In order to perform frontier analysis, time series data for many countries are needed. In the case of water and sanitation, data on national coverage, rural and urban coverage, and coverage by wealth quintiles can be obtained from data that is already collected and made publicly available and free of charge, specifically the WHO/UNICEF JMP Country Files, which are a compilation of nationally representative surveys including the Demographic and Health Survey (DHS), Multiple Indicator Cluster Surveys (MICS), Living Standards Measurement Study (LSMS), World Health Survey (WHS), and national census data.[21] If a specific indicator is desired that is not yet available in the JMP Country Files, one can also obtain the DHS and MICS questionnaires to determine if they have the indicator of interest and access these surveys for the information. Time series data is needed in order to calculate rates of change and a large number of countries is desired as the best-practice frontier, and thus benchmark rates are defined based on historical data. As mentioned on p. 258, rates of change can be calculated following different criteria such as a minimum number of data points, a minimum and/or maximum time span and number of years, visual inspection to ensure that all data points used follow a linear fit, decisions on how to address multiple data points from the same year, and inclusion or exclusion of data points during years of internal or external conflict. At present, there is currently not enough data available to perform frontier analysis for safely managed drinking water and sanitation services, which is the target and indicator of SDG targets 6.1 and 6.2; however, as estimates become available, frontier analysis can eventually be used.

Reduction of rural-urban water and sanitation inequalities

To assess progress towards reducing inequalities between two populations, we use the example of total improved drinking water between urban and rural populations.

Inequality between rural and urban populations is reduced when the inequality gap in coverage between urban and rural populations decreases, and this decrease in difference cannot be due to a reduction in coverage (i.e., coverage for urban population decreases with time and converges with that of the rural population). The inequality gap between urban and rural populations can be evaluated in different ways, such as the ratio between rural access and urban access to improved water or the difference between urban and rural coverage. For the purposes of this chapter, we use the former metric, which we define as the RU Ratio, where equality is achieved when the RU Ratio is 1 (i.e., coverage for urban and rural populations is the same). RU Ratios lower and higher than 1 indicate the presence of inequality in coverage, where RU Ratio < 1 occurs when urban coverage is greater than rural coverage and RU Ratio > 1 indicates the opposite. Figure 14.5 illustrates a) the urban and rural coverage for Mauritania during 1992 to 2000 and b) the corresponding RU Ratio. As seen in Figure 14.5, urban and rural coverage converged and then diverged, which is reflected in RU Ratios less than 1 for 1992, 1993, and 1995, and RU Ratios greater than 1 for 1996 and 2000.

While the RU Ratio provides the level of inequality at a specific time point, it does not indicate whether the inequality gap is decreasing or increasing with time (i.e., whether there is progress towards reducing inequality). To assess progress, we calculate the rate of change of the RU Ratio, similar to the method and data inclusion criteria for total improved drinking-water coverage. Both the sign of the rate of change in RU Ratio and the value of the RU Ratio determine whether a country is progressing or regressing. For example, when the RU Ratio is less than 1, a positive rate of change indicates that a country is reducing the inequality

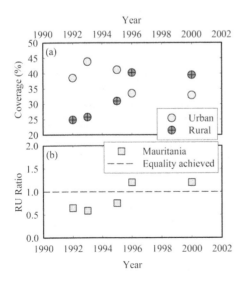

FIGURE 14.5 a) Urban and rural improved water coverage as a function of time; b) corresponding RU Ratio for Mauritania.

in coverage between the two populations. However, if the RU Ratio is greater than 1, a positive rate of change reflects an increasing disparity in coverage between the two populations. The construction of an index to measure progress towards reducing rural urban inequalities is similar to that described above for drinking-water coverage. RU rates of change are plotted as a function of RU Ratio, and frontier analysis is used to identify frontier points and construct a best-practice frontier. The best-practice frontier allows benchmark rates of change to be calculated for all RU Ratio values, and these benchmark rates are then used to calculate an index of performance following Equation 14.2.

Figure 14.6 presents rural and urban coverage data for a) Chad and b) Ghana from 1988 and 2013. As seen in Figure 14.6a for Chad, from 1997 to 2000, rural coverage remained relatively unchanged at 42%, while urban coverage increased from 50% to 67%, thus increasing the inequality gap between the two populations. In contrast, Figure 14.6b for Ghana showed that rural and urban access was converging, with urban access slowly increasing from 84% to 90% while rural access had a significant increase from 28% to 74% from 1988 to 2013. The corresponding RU Ratios for Chad and Ghana are presented in Figure 14.6c and illustrate the decreasing and increasing trend, respectively, towards an RU Ratio of 1. Rates of change of the RU Ratio are calculated for every five data points shown in Figure 14.6c as well as for all countries with available data.

To construct the best-practice frontier, we plot the rates of change from all countries against the RU Ratio. We define the rate of change to be dependent on the RU Ratio because it becomes increasingly difficult to address the disparity in coverage between the two populations as the RU Ratio approaches 1. As such, we expect that rates of change will begin to decrease for RU Ratios close to 1 and that the rate of change will be zero when the RU Ratio is 1 (when coverage is the same in both rural and urban populations). Figure 14.6d shows the global historical rates of change of the RU Ratios for all countries (plotted as circles), with rates of change for Chad and Ghana shown as well. Data envelopment analysis was used to identify eight frontier points corresponding to Armenia 2005, Bulgaria 1998, Ethiopia 2000, Malta 1995, Nigeria 2010, Peru 2008, Slovakia 2006, and Zambia 1996, which were used to construct the best-practice frontier shown in the solid line. The best-practice frontier allows benchmark rates to be calculated at all RU Ratios, so that the progress of a country in reducing the rural–urban inequality is calculated based on the best performing country at the same RU Ratio.

The most recent performance indices for all countries with available data, calculated using Equation 14.2, are presented in Appendix 14.2. Figure 14.7 demonstrates how the indices can be used for comparison purposes for six countries in 2011. As seen in Figure 14.7a for the pairing of Kazakhstan and Paraguay, and the pairing of Cambodia and Nigeria, countries with the same RU Ratio can have very different index values. In the case of the latter pairing, while both countries have an RU Ratio of 0.69, Cambodia has an index value of 0.06, indicating very little progress towards reducing the inequality between rural and urban coverage.

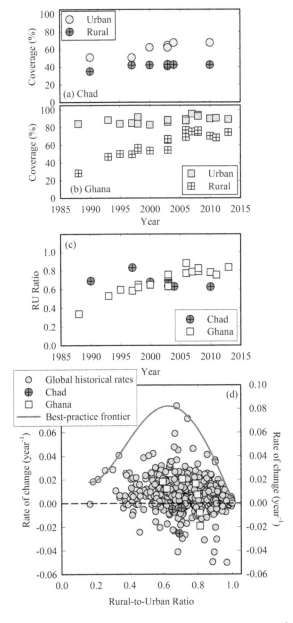

FIGURE 14.6 Urban and rural improved water coverage for a) Chad and b) Ghana; c) corresponding RU Ratios for Chad and Ghana; d) frontier plot showing all global historical data for rates of change of the RU Ratio.

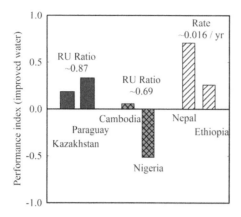

FIGURE 14.7 Performance indices in 2011 for Kazakhstan, Paraguay, Cambodia, Nigeria, Nepal, and Ethiopia

However, Nigeria actually showed a negative index value of −0.51, signifying regression, or, in other words, an increase in inequality between rural and urban populations. If we consider two countries with the same rate of change in RU Ratio, we see that the performance index is affected by the initial RU Ratio. Both Nepal and Ethiopia have rates of change of RU Ratio ~0.016/year; however, their RU Ratios were 0.94 and 0.44, respectively. The corresponding benchmark rates, calculated using the best-practice frontier, were determined to be 0.024 and 0.062/year, which resulted in index values of 0.71 and 0.26 for Nepal and Ethiopia, respectively. Use of variable benchmark rates for different RU Ratios takes into account the difficulty in reducing the rural–urban inequality gap as the rural coverage approaches urban coverage.

Comparison of progress between two populations

To examine the relative progress between two populations, we use the example of a higher served and lesser served population. From 1990 to 2015, the JMP has country data for three categories of water and sanitation: unimproved, other improved (i.e., non-piped/non-sewerage improved services), and piped/sewerage. In this example, we look at the population using an unimproved water source and the population using a non-piped improved water source. We chose to compare progress between these two populations because both can be upgraded. While it is desired that both populations achieve access to piped water, we define equality to be achieved when the population using an unimproved source is upgraded to an improved source at a faster rate than the population using a non-piped improved source is upgraded to a piped source. Specifically, countries should focus on ensuring that 100% of the population has access to some sort of improved source rather than focusing only on delivering piped water to subpopulations that already have access to an improved source. Moving forward, as data on access to safe water becomes available, this analysis can be applied where "basic" and "safe" sources are used instead of "non-piped improved" and "piped" sources.

Relative progress is assessed by calculating the rates of change for 1) the proportion of the population using an unimproved water source (ΔU) and 2) the proportion of the population using a non-piped other improved source (ΔOI). Instead of a direct comparison between the two rates, we compare the rates of change normalized against their respective proportion of the population that still remains to be upgraded (i.e., $\Delta U/U$ compared to $\Delta OI/OI$). We expect that over time, as both populations are upgraded, $\Delta U/U$ will be negative as the proportion of the population using an unimproved source decreases.

Depending on whether the population using an unimproved source is upgraded to a non-piped improved source or a piped source, $\Delta OI/OI$ may also be a negative value. Specifically, we define equality to be achieved when $\Delta U/U$ decreases at a faster rate than $\Delta OI/OI$ (i.e., $\Delta U/U$ is more negative than $\Delta OI/OI$, so $\Delta U/U \leq \Delta OI/OI$). As such, the metric used to assess progress towards reducing inequalities between these two groups is given by $\Delta OI/OI - \Delta U/U$, where positive values indicate progression and negative values indicate regression. For the purposes of this analysis, we do not differentiate between an upgrade from unimproved to non-piped other improved versus an upgrade from unimproved to

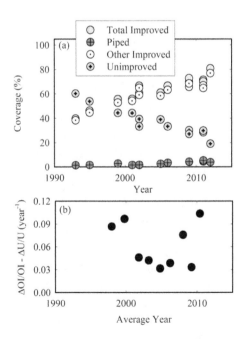

FIGURE 14.8 a) Coverage for total improved, piped, other improved, and unimproved water for Uganda. b) Corresponding values for the difference between the normalized rate of change of other improved access and the normalized rate of change of unimproved access.

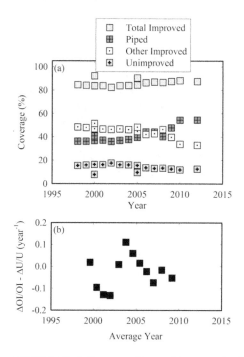

FIGURE 14.9 a) Coverage for total improved, piped, other improved, and unimproved water for Republic of Moldova. b) Corresponding values for the difference between the normalized rate of change of other improved access and the normalized rate of change of unimproved access.

piped services. We also note that similar results would be obtained if we chose to compare the normalized rates of change between the population using total improved (TI, equal to piped and other improved) sources and the population using piped sources (P), where normalization would be against proportion of the population that still remains to be upgraded (i.e., ØTI is normalized against the proportion of the population using an unimproved source and ØP is normalized against the proportion of the population using a non-piped source). In such a case, equality would be achieved when the population using total improved source has a faster rate of increase than the population using a piped source.

Using JMP data, panel a) of Figures 14.8–14.10 present data for the proportion of the population using total improved, piped, other non-piped improved, and unimproved sources for Uganda, Republic of Moldova, and Republic of Korea, with their corresponding ØOI/OI − ØU/U values presented in panel (b) of Figures 14.8–13.10, respectively. As seen from the coverage data in Figures 14.8–14.10, from 1993 to 2012, Uganda increased the proportion of its population using a non–piped other improved source, with little change in the proportion of the population using a piped source. This indicates that funds for water and sanitation were almost all directed towards upgrading the population using an unimproved source, and thus progress towards equality is achieved, which is reflected in

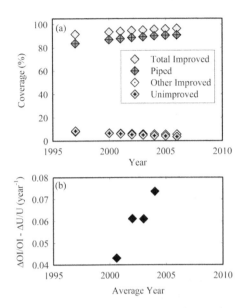

FIGURE 14.10 a) Coverage for total improved, piped, other improved, and unimproved water for Republic of Korea. b) Corresponding values for the difference between the normalized rate of change of other improved access and the normalized rate of change of unimproved access.

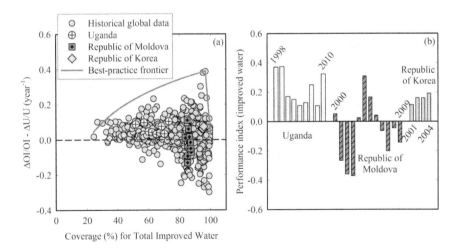

FIGURE 14.11 a) Global historical data for the difference between the normalized rate of change of other improved access and the normalized rate of change of unimproved access. b) Performance indices for Uganda, Republic of Moldova, and Republic of Korea.

the positive $\Delta OI/OI - \Delta U/U$ values. On the other hand, Republic of Moldova showed the opposite trend, with little decrease in the proportion of the population using an unimproved source (corresponding to little increase in the population using an improved source) during 1998 and 2012. However, the proportion of the population using a piped source increased with time, particularly from 2008 to 2012, indicating that almost all funds were directed towards upgrading the population using a non-piped improved source to a piped source, which shows regression towards achieving equality. For the Republic of Korea, from Figure 13.10a alone, the coverage data is not enough to determine whether the Republic of Korea is making progress towards reducing inequality between the higher served and lesser served populations. Both populations using a piped source and total improved source increase almost in parallel from 1989 to 2011, where most of the population using an improved source is due to piped sources, and the total population with access to improved sources is greater than 95%. Using the normalized rates, the $\Delta OI/OI - \Delta U/U$ values shown in Figure 14.10b are all positive, indicating progression.

To calculate performance index values, the metric $\Delta OI/OI - \Delta U/U$ can be calculated for all countries with available data and plotted as a function of total improved coverage to identify frontier points as shown in Figure 14.11a. The best-practice frontier, shown as a solid line, was constructed using four points corresponding to Belarus, 2012, Costa Rica, 2006, and Ethiopia, 1998 and 2000. Using Equation 14.2, the most recent performance indices for all countries with available data are presented in Appendix 14.3. Performance indices for Uganda, Republic of Moldova, and Republic of Korea as a function of time are shown in Figure 14.11b, where all indices are positive for Uganda and Republic of Korea, and most indices are negative for Republic of Moldova.

Application of performance index results

As explained above, the calculated performance indices can be used for comparisons across time within a country (see Figures 14.11a and b) and comparisons across different countries (see Figure 14.7). The performance indices provide an additional metric of assessing the elimination and reduction of inequalities and complement conventional monitoring from the JMP. For example, in the 2014 JMP progress report that highlighted inequalities, inequalities were visualized using equity trees, trend analyses, and gap analyses.[7] The equity tree focuses on coverage of different subpopulations within a country (e.g., rural, urban, poorest 20%, richest 20%), and is key in unmasking disparities in coverage that are hidden when averages are used. Trend analysis shows how coverage for different subpopulations in a country have changed with time and can be used to describe different typologies – for example, in the case of rural and urban sanitation, the JMP report demonstrated uneven progress, equitable progress, levelling up, and stagnation between 1995 and 2010 for rural Pakistan, rural Peru, urban Cambodia, and rural Burkina Faso, respectively.[7] Finally, urban–rural gap analysis (or quintile gap analysis) plots the change in inequality against the change in coverage in four-quadrant graphs. This type of analysis allows for tracking progress on eliminating inequalities by determining where a country falls into one of four-quadrants: increasing coverage and increasing equality, reducing coverage and increasing equality, reducing coverage and reducing equality, and increasing coverage and reducing equality (see Chapter 1).

The performance index described in this chapter provides an additional step beyond assessing trends (through the calculated rate of change) and determining whether equality is increasing or decreasing. By using historically maximum achievable rates as benchmark rates, the index also provides information on whether a country is reaching its maximum potential in terms of efforts used to reduce inequality. A performance index of 0.5 means that the country has progressed at a rate that was at least half of their maximum achievable rate and that the country has unfulfilled potential to more effectively use its resources to achieve the greatest possible progress. As such, the performance index aligns with the principle of the progressive realization for the human rights to water and sanitation.

In addition, this approach can be used to assess progress towards the reduction of inequalities in other sectors such as access to healthcare, so that comparisons might be drawn between sectors. Progress towards eradicating extreme poverty for all, achieving universal coverage for primary school completion, and reduction of maternal mortality ratio was previously illustrated using frontier analysis in Luh et al.[16] However, the focus was only on national populations and did not look at the reduction of inequalities between subgroups (e.g., rural versus urban). Further analysis can be carried out to determine whether countries that are making progress towards reducing inequalities in access to water and sanitation are also making progress in reducing inequalities in other sectors.

Limitations and future direction

Limitations of this approach fall into two main categories: limitations related to the data and limitations related to the methodology. In the first category, we used publicly available data from the JMP, which is household survey data. This data does not include extra-household settings such as healthcare facilities, workplaces, or schools, and therefore does not capture all aspects of water and sanitation access. As our frontier analysis is conducted using rates of change, time series data is needed for many countries. Currently, there is limited data available to assess the reduction of inequalities for many axes of discrimination such as gender, race, and ethnicity, among others.

With respect to the methodology, the rates of change used to construct the frontier plot are calculated using a linear fit to the data points. The assumption is that progress during the time period of the five data points used is linear; however, this may not be the case as non-linear progress can also occur as demonstrated in Fuller et al.[24] By using a linear fit for all data points, this may affect the rate of change and therefore the identification of frontier points. Misidentification of frontier points can result in inaccurate estimates of the benchmark rates used to calculate the performance index. In addition, further work is needed to determine the number of data points that should be used to calculate the rates of change and whether there is a minimum range of years that the data points should span. In the examples discussed in this chapter, we did not have a minimum time span and we used groups of five data points, the latter of which resulted in the exclusion of countries with only three or four time points.

The computations required to calculate performance indices are more complicated than other methods to assess progress that rely on status, trends, or examining gaps. We identified frontier points using the free software R, although STATA, SAS, and specialized software packages for data envelopment analysis are also available. Use of these software may be considered too much work and may deter one from this approach.

Despite these limitations, this approach provides a new dataset that allows country performance to be assessed. Luh and Bartram used this approach to determine whether an association exists between specific national indicators and progress.[25] Future studies can focus on evaluating how enabling environment characteristics are associated with this indicator of progress.

Notes

1. United Nations General Assembly (2015) Resolution adopted by the General Assembly on 25 September 2015. Transforming our world: the 2030 Agenda for Sustainable Development. A/RES/70/1. 21 October.
2. United Nations General Assembly (2010) Resolution on Human Right to Water and Sanitation. A/RES/64/292. 3 August 2010. United Nations, New York.
3. United Nations General Assembly (2016) The Human Rights to Safe Drinking Water and Sanitation. A/RES/70/169. 22 February. United Nations, New York.
4. United Nations Committee on Economic, Social, and Cultural Rights (2003) General Comment No. 15: The Right to Water. E/C.12/2002/11. 20 January.
5. United Nations General Assembly (2013) Report of the Special Rapporteur on the human right to safe drinking water and sanitation, Catarina de Albuquerque. A/HRC/24/44. 11 July.
6. WHO/UNICEF Joint Monitoring Programme for Water Supply and Sanitation (2015) Progress on sanitation and drinking water – 2015 update and MDG assessment. World Health Organization, Geneva.
7. WHO/UNICEF Joint Monitoring Programme for Water Supply and Sanitation (2014) Progress on sanitation and drinking water – 2014 update. World Health Organization, Geneva.
8. Wagstaff, A., Paci, P., and van Doorslaer, E. (1991) On the measurement of inequalities in health. *Social Science & Medicine, 33*(5), 545–557.
9. Roche, R., Bain, R., Cumming, O. (2017) A long way to go: estimates of combined water, sanitation and hygiene coverage for 25 sub-Saharan African countries. *PLOS One, 12*(2): e0171783.
10. Yang, H., Bain, R., Bartram, J., Gundry, S., Pedley, S., and Wright, J. (2013) Water safety and inequality in access to drinking-water between rich and poor households. *Environmental Science & Technology, 47*, 1222–1230.
11. Satterthwaite, M. (2012) JMP Working Group on Equity and Non-Discrimination Final Report. Available at: www.wssinfo.org/fileadmin/user_upload/resources/JMP-END-WG-Final-Report-20120821.pdf (accessed 24 November 2012).

12 Victora, C.G., Fenn, B., Bryce, J., and Kirkwood, B.R. (2005) Co-coverage of preventive interventions and implications for child-survival strategies: evidence from national surveys. *The Lancet*, *366*(9495), 1460–1466.
13 Cook, W.D., Tone, K., and Zhu, J. (2014) Data envelopment analysis: prior to choosing a model. *Omega 44*, 1–4.
14 Charnes, A., Cooper, W.W., and Rhodes, E. (1978) Measuring the efficiency of decision making units. *European Journal of Operational Research*, *2*, 429–444.
15 Pascoe, S., Kirkley, J.E., Greboval, D., and Morrison-Paul, C.J. (2003) Measuring and assessing capacity in fisheries. 2. Issues and methods. FAO Fisheries Technical Paper. No. 433/2. Rome, Food and Agriculture Organization of the United Nations, 130pp.
16 Luh, J., Cronk, R., and Bartram, J. (2016) Assessing progress towards public health, human rights, and international development goals using frontier analysis. *PLOS One*, *11*(1): e0147663.
17 Fukuda-Parr, S., Lawson-Remer, T., and Randolph, S. (2009) An index of economic and social rights fulfillment: concept and methodology. *Journal of Human Rights*, *8*, 195–221.
18 Luh, J., Baum, R., and Bartram, J. (2013) Equity in water and sanitation: developing an index to measure progressive realization of the human right. *International Journal of Hygiene and Environmental Health*, *216*, 662–671.
19 Cronk, R., Luh, J., Meier, B.M., and Bartram, J. (2015) The Water, Sanitation, and Hygiene Performance Index: A comparison of country performance in realizing universal WaSH. Available at: https://waterinstitute.unc.edu/wash-performance-index-report/ (accessed 21 December 2016).
20 WHO/UNICEF Joint Monitoring Programme for Water Supply and Sanitation (2017) Safely managed drinking water – thematic report on drinking water 2017. World Health Organization, Geneva.
21 WHO/UNICEF Joint Monitoring Programme for Water Supply and Sanitation (2015) Country File documents. Available at: www.wssinfo.org/documents/?tx_display controller[type]=country_files (accessed 19 October 2016).
22 Wilson, P.W. (2013) FEAR: Frontier Efficiency Analysis with R. R package version 2.0.
23 R Development Core Team (2011) R: A Language and Environment for Statistical Computing. R Foundation for Statistical Computing, Vienna. Available at: www.r-project.org/
24 Fuller, J.A., Goldstick, J., Bartram, J., and Eisenberg, J.N.S. (2016) Tracking progress towards global drinking water and sanitation targets: a within and among country analysis. *Science of the Total Environment*, *541*, 857–864.
25 Luh, J. and Bartram, J. (2016) Drinking water and sanitation: progress in 73 countries in relation to socioeconomic indicators. *Bulletin of the World Health Organization*, *94*(2), 111–121A.

APPENDICES

APPENDIX 14.1 Performance indices of the most recent year available for progress towards achieving universal access to improved water and sanitation

Country	Water Average Year	Water Coverage (%)	Water Rate (%/year)	Water Index	Sanitation Average Year	Sanitation Coverage (%)	Sanitation Rate (%/year)	Sanitation Index
Afghanistan	2008	43.2	2.20	0.45	2008	37.6	1.14	0.20
Albania	2009	95.7	−0.37	−0.23	2009	97.1	0.08	0.07
Andorra	2007	100.0	0.00	0.00	2007	100.0	0.00	0.00
Angola					2008	42.5	1.97	0.33
Argentina	2008	97.8	0.21	0.22	2008	96.6	0.63	0.50
Armenia	2009	97.8	0.25	0.27	2003	92.3	0.12	0.05
Austria					2004	100.0	0.00	0.00
Azerbaijan	2005	78.5	0.85	0.22				
Bangladesh	2011	85.0	0.10	0.03	2011	84.6	0.42	0.10
Belarus	2012	99.7	0.07	0.35	2012	99.1	0.13	0.29
Belgium	2007	100.0	0.00	0.00	2001	100.0	0.00	0.00
Belize	2006	92.6	0.98	0.49	2006	93.3	0.68	0.31
Benin	2008	73.3	0.32	0.07	2008	32.3	1.18	0.23
Bhutan	2007	93.4	1.03	0.55				
Bolivia	2009	86.1	0.53	0.18	2009	65.0	1.80	0.29
Bosnia and Herzegovina	2004	98.2	0.17	0.22	2004	95.5	−0.01	−0.01
Botswana	2009	95.6	−0.33	−0.20	2006	66.1	−0.74	−0.12
Brazil	2010	96.6	0.11	0.08	2010	82.7	0.70	0.16
Bulgaria	2009	99.4	−0.02	−0.06	2008	100.0	0.00	0.00
Burkina Faso	2008	73.1	0.80	0.18	2008	30.0	1.45	0.30
Burundi	2007	73.4	0.25	0.06	2007	54.4	0.87	0.14
Cambodia	2011	65.8	1.33	0.27	2011	42.7	3.30	0.54
Cameroon	2007	68.2	0.87	0.18	2007	57.9	0.37	0.06
Cape Verde	2005	85.4	0.60	0.20	2006	55.4	1.38	0.21
Central African Republic	2001	63.0	0.47	0.09	2001	27.7	0.58	0.13
Chad	2004	47.0	0.16	0.03	2004	14.8	0.08	0.04
Chile	2006	96.9	0.45	0.36	2006	95.5	0.59	0.37
China	2007	87.3	0.90	0.32	2009	73.8	1.06	0.19
Colombia	2010	90.4	−1.25	−0.53	2009	89.3	0.81	0.26
Comoros	2001	90.1	0.00	0.00	2003	31.9	0.93	0.18
Congo	2007	72.6	0.51	0.11	2007	41.4	0.54	0.09
Congo, Democratic Republic of	2007	49.1	0.57	0.11	2008	44.1	−0.95	−0.15
Costa Rica	2009	97.1	0.04	0.04	2009	97.7	−0.17	−0.19
Côte d'Ivoire	2004	78.6	−0.48	−0.12	2004	44.4	0.72	0.12
Czech Republic					2005	100.0	0.00	0.00
Denmark					2001	100.0	0.00	0.00

continued . . .

APPENDIX 14.1 Continued

Country	Water				Sanitation			
	Average Year	Coverage (%)	Rate (%/year)	Index	Average Year	Coverage (%)	Rate (%/year)	Index
Djibouti	2003	84.4	0.69	0.21				
Dominican Republic	2010	84.3	2.34	0.73	2010	93.2	0.33	0.15
Ecuador	2004	81.5	0.29	0.08	2004	84.6	0.72	0.17
Egypt	2007	97.9	0.07	0.08	2007	98.3	0.36	0.50
El Salvador	2011	92.2	1.12	0.54	2011	77.7	0.77	0.15
Estonia	2008	99.4	0.11	0.34	2010	99.7	−0.01	−0.04
Ethiopia	2011	49.6	1.46	0.29	2011	35.6	2.56	0.46
Fiji					2002	79.8	2.14	0.44
Finland					2003	100.0	0.00	0.00
Gambia	2005	85.5	0.27	0.09	2003	81.6	0.03	0.01
Georgia	2007	95.0	0.38	0.23	2007	93.3	−1.00	−0.45
Germany	2004	100.0	0.00	0.00	2005	100.0	0.01	0.08
Ghana	2010	82.2	−0.61	−0.17	2008	66.1	−0.51	−0.08
Greenland					1998	100.0	0.00	0.00
Guatemala	2006	89.2	−0.45	−0.17	2006	71.1	0.75	0.13
Guinea	2009	71.1	0.76	0.17	2009	36.9	1.28	0.23
Guinea Bissau	2002	55.8	1.92	0.37				
Guyana	2004	91.2	0.50	0.22	2004	89.2	0.48	0.15
Haiti	2004	62.3	−0.29	−0.06	2003	43.2	0.66	0.11
Honduras	2011	88.4	0.48	0.18	2010	83.6	0.40	0.09
Hungary					2003	100.0	0.00	0.00
Iceland	2009	100.0	0.00	0.00	2009	100.0	0.02	0.16
India	2010	88.3	0.74	0.28	2010	45.0	3.00	0.48
Indonesia	2011	85.5	−0.38	−0.12	2008	66.2	2.19	0.36
Iran, Islamic Republic of	2004	94.6	0.19	0.11	2004	92.0	1.04	0.41
Iraq	2006	82.4	0.90	0.26	2004	88.2	0.88	0.26
Jamaica	2008	93.6	0.47	0.25	2008	98.0	0.47	0.58
Japan	2003	100.0	0.00	0.00				
Jordan	2008	96.7	0.28	0.21	2007	99.5	0.09	0.29
Kazakhstan	2011	93.8	0.50	0.27	2003	99.1	0.05	0.11
Kenya	2009	59.4	0.70	0.14	2009	53.8	0.97	0.15
Korea, Republic of	2004	95.6	0.43	0.26	2004	100.0	0.00	0.00
Kyrgyzstan	2008	85.0	0.45	0.14	2007	96.8	0.10	0.08
Lao, People's Democratic Republic	2007	60.6	2.20	0.43	2007	51.4	3.05	0.48
Lesotho	2007	80.1	0.29	0.08	2007	37.5	0.69	0.12
Liberia	2010	71.1	0.13	0.03	2010	37.0	0.88	0.16
Lithuania	2010	95.4	0.31	0.18	2008	91.8	0.67	0.26
Luxembourg					1996	100.0	0.00	0.00

continued . . .

APPENDIX 14.1 Continued

Country	Water Average Year	Coverage (%)	Rate (%/year)	Index	Sanitation Average Year	Coverage (%)	Rate (%/year)	Index
Madagascar	2010	47.6	0.76	0.15	2010	32.3	0.57	0.11
Malawi	2011	81.3	0.58	0.16	2011	17.1	0.82	0.34
Malaysia					2003	96.3	0.47	0.35
Mali	2009	65.8	2.24	0.46	2009	41.3	1.73	0.29
Malta	2005	100.0	0.00	0.00	2005	100.0	0.00	0.00
Mariana Islands, Northern	2004	96.1	0.20	0.13	2000	91.2	0.62	0.23
Marshall Islands	2001	93.2	0.13	0.07	2001	81.7	0.61	0.13
Mauritania	2005	49.9	0.70	0.14	2005	40.0	2.22	0.38
Mexico	2010	95.5	−0.09	−0.05	2010	91.8	1.14	0.44
Moldova, Republic of	2009	87.4	0.18	0.06	2009	82.5	−0.28	−0.06
Mongolia	2008	59.9	1.81	0.36	2007	83.0	1.31	0.30
Morocco	2007	83.5	0.33	0.10	2006	81.0	1.17	0.25
Mozambique	2008	46.4	2.22	0.44	2008	22.5	2.12	0.58
Myanmar	2006	73.2	1.44	0.33	2006	81.6	1.45	0.31
Namibia	2007	86.0	−0.65	−0.22	2009	42.4	0.28	0.05
Nepal	2011	87.0	2.30	0.80	2009	48.1	3.91	0.62
Netherlands	2006	100.0	0.00	0.00	2006	100.0	0.00	0.00
Nicaragua	2007	83.2	−0.09	−0.03	2006	69.1	1.05	0.17
Niger	2009	51.3	3.57	0.69	2007	14.1	0.65	0.40
Nigeria	2012	69.2	0.06	0.01	2012	53.6	3.21	0.50
Norway					2005	100.0	0.00	0.00
Pakistan	2009	91.1	0.14	0.06	2009	59.7	3.66	0.57
Palau	2001	93.0	0.31	0.16	2001	83.1	3.92	0.89
Palestine	2007	75.1	−2.10	−0.50	2007	98.8	−0.02	−0.05
Panama	2009	92.6	0.35	0.17	2009	78.5	0.75	0.15
Paraguay	2011	90.6	1.53	0.65	2011	88.2	0.74	0.22
Peru	2012	88.2	1.59	0.59	2011	79.5	1.69	0.34
Philippines	2007	89.6	0.28	0.11	2007	84.2	0.32	0.08
Russian Federation	2010	96.3	0.04	0.03	2010	86.3	0.89	0.23
Rwanda	2011	73.6	3.55	0.82	2011	72.0	−2.09	−0.36
Saint Lucia	2005	94.9	0.17	0.11				
Samoa	2007	96.0	0.89	0.57	2005	97.8	−0.06	−0.06
Samoa, American	1995	95.7	0.42	0.25				
Senegal	2010	74.9	1.51	0.36	2010	67.0	2.06	0.34
Serbia	2007	99.3	−0.01	−0.02	2007	98.0	−0.01	−0.02
Sierra Leone	2010	58.2	0.67	0.13	2011	44.1	0.28	0.05
Slovakia	2010	100.0	0.00	0.00	2010	100.0	−0.02	−0.15
Slovenia					2005	100.0	0.00	0.00

continued ...

Benchmarking progress on reducing inequalities **277**

APPENDIX 14.1 Continued

Country	Water				Sanitation			
	Average Year	Coverage (%)	Rate (%/year)	Index	Average Year	Coverage (%)	Rate (%/year)	Index
South Africa	2011	93.2	−1.75	−0.91	2009	85.0	3.56	0.88
Spain					2006	100.0	−0.01	−0.04
Sri Lanka	2009	89.6	0.31	0.12	2008	92.8	1.30	0.55
Swaziland	2006	63.0	1.20	0.24	2006	74.3	0.64	0.12
Sweden					2005	100.0	0.00	0.00
Switzerland					2004	100.0	0.00	0.00
Tajikistan	2007	66.5	1.32	0.27	2006	95.2	0.45	0.27
Tanzania, United Republic of	2010	55.3	0.98	0.19	2010	22.9	2.31	0.63
Thailand	2006	94.5	0.44	0.26	2005	99.1	0.04	0.09
Timor Leste	2006	64.0	0.76	0.15	2006	47.5	−0.07	−0.01
Togo	2004	55.1	0.68	0.13	2004	32.2	0.02	0.00
Trinidad and Tobago	2001	93.2	0.28	0.15	2001	98.0	0.10	0.12
Tunisia	2002	91.3	0.52	0.23	2001	85.9	0.89	0.23
Turkey	2007	96.2	0.54	0.36	2007	92.1	0.66	0.26
Uganda	2010	73.1	2.02	0.46	2011	32.1	−0.80	−0.16
Ukraine	2010	97.0	−0.26	−0.21	2005	97.7	0.09	0.10
Uruguay	2011	99.2	0.11	0.29	2011	96.2	0.92	0.66
Viet Nam	2010	90.8	0.30	0.13	2010	74.8	1.92	0.35
Yemen	1999	60.2	−0.69	−0.14	2002	45.0	1.51	0.24
Zambia	2006	58.8	0.40	0.08	2006	54.1	0.70	0.11
Zimbabwe	2011	76.3	0.63	0.15	2010	63.2	−1.13	−0.18

APPENDIX 14.2 Performance indices of the most recent year available for progress towards reducing inequalities in access between rural and urban populations for improved water and sanitation

Country	Water				Sanitation			
	Average Year	Average RU Ratio	Rate (1/year)	Index	Average Year	Average RU Ratio	Rate (1/year)	Index
Afghanistan	2008	0.53	0.01	0.18	2008	0.54	0.00	0.00
Albania					2009	0.95	0.00	0.02
Andorra	2007	1.00	0.00	0.00	2007	1.00	0.00	0.00
Angola					2008	0.22	0.01	0.12
Argentina	2008	0.91	0.02	0.53	2008	0.95	0.01	0.37
Armenia	2009	0.95	0.01	0.33	2003	0.82	0.00	0.05

continued ...

APPENDIX 14.2 Continued

Country	Water				Sanitation			
	Average Year	Average RU Ratio	Rate (1/year)	Index	Average Year	Average RU Ratio	Rate (1/year)	Index
Austria					2004	1.00	0.00	0.00
Azerbaijan	2005	0.72	0.01	0.14				
Bangladesh	2011	0.99	0.00	−0.61	2011	0.97	−0.02	−1.00
Belarus	2012	0.99	0.00	0.08	2012	0.98	0.00	0.18
Belgium	2007	1.00	0.00	0.00				
Belize	2006	0.95	0.00	0.12	2006	0.95	0.01	0.20
Benin	2008	0.81	0.00	0.02	2008	0.23	0.00	0.02
Bhutan	2007	0.91	0.01	0.45				
Bolivia	2008	0.69	0.05	0.56	2009	0.35	0.00	0.02
Bosnia and Herzegovina	2004	0.98	0.00	0.27	2004	0.94	0.00	−0.03
Botswana	2004	0.92	0.00	−0.10	2004	0.60	0.02	0.21
Brazil	2010	0.85	0.00	0.09	2010	0.57	0.01	0.11
Bulgaria	2004	1.00	0.00	0.00	2008	1.00	0.00	0.00
Burkina Faso	2008	0.73	0.00	0.04	2005	0.16	0.00	0.13
Burundi	2007	0.78	0.00	−0.03	2007	0.71	0.00	−0.06
Cambodia	2011	0.69	0.00	0.06	2011	0.36	0.04	0.59
Cameroon	2007	0.53	0.01	0.07	2005	0.40	−0.01	−0.07
Cape Verde	2005	0.95	0.00	−0.02	2006	0.55	0.00	−0.04
Central African Republic	2001	0.59	0.00	0.02	2001	0.30	−0.02	−0.25
Chad	2004	0.65	−0.01	−0.06	2004	0.17	−0.01	−0.27
Chile	2006	0.81	0.02	0.32	2006	0.82	0.02	0.26
China	2007	0.82	0.01	0.18	2007	0.66	0.00	0.01
Colombia	2000	0.70	0.01	0.09	2009	0.72	0.01	0.17
Comoros					2003	0.55	0.01	0.14
Congo	2007	0.37	0.01	0.13	2007	0.25	0.00	−0.04
Congo, Democratic Republic of	2007	0.34	0.00	0.12	2003	0.58	0.05	0.58
Costa Rica	2006	0.91	0.00	0.15	2006	0.96	0.00	0.16
Côte d'Ivoire	1997	0.76	0.00	0.06	2004	0.31	0.01	0.08
Czech Republic					2005	1.00	0.00	−0.15
Denmark					2001	1.00	0.00	0.00
Djibouti	2003	0.69	0.00	−0.05				
Dominican Republic	2010	0.93	0.00	−0.06	2010	0.90	0.00	0.10
Ecuador	2004	0.80	0.00	−0.06	2004	0.72	0.01	0.14
Egypt	2007	0.98	0.00	0.09	2004	0.96	0.01	0.50
El Salvador	2011	0.85	0.02	0.43	2011	0.69	0.01	0.15
Estonia	2008	0.98	0.00	0.30	2008	0.99	0.00	0.11

continued . . .

APPENDIX 14.2 Continued

Country	Water				Sanitation			
	Average Year	Average RU Ratio	Rate (1/year)	Index	Average Year	Average RU Ratio	Rate (1/year)	Index
Ethiopia	2011	0.44	0.02	0.26	2011	0.48	0.04	0.51
Fiji					2002	0.72	0.03	0.37
Finland					2003	1.00	0.00	0.00
Gambia	2005	0.87	0.00	−0.03	2003	0.80	−0.01	−0.11
Georgia	2007	0.92	0.01	0.18				
Germany	2004	1.00	0.00	0.00	2002	1.00	0.00	0.00
Ghana	2008	0.81	−0.02	−0.32	2007	0.60	0.03	0.33
Greenland					1998	1.00	0.00	0.00
Guatemala	2004	0.86	0.00	−0.06	2006	0.60	0.00	0.04
Guinea	2009	0.66	0.00	−0.02	2009	0.27	0.00	0.03
Guinea Bissau	2002	0.63	−0.01	−0.11				
Guyana	2004	0.94	0.00	0.07	2004	0.92	0.01	0.13
Haiti								
Honduras	2011	0.82	0.00	−0.05	2009	0.79	0.01	0.20
Hungary					2003	1.00	0.00	0.00
Iceland	2009	1.00	0.00	0.00	2009	1.00	0.00	−0.19
India	2007	0.89	0.00	−0.01	2010	0.37	0.01	0.14
Indonesia	2009	0.81	0.02	0.35	2008	0.67	0.03	0.33
Iran, Islamic Republic of					2004	0.94	0.00	0.15
Iraq	2006	0.61	0.02	0.24	2004	0.76	0.02	0.29
Jamaica	2008	0.92	0.00	−0.09	2008	0.99	0.00	0.47
Japan	2003	1.00	0.00	0.00				
Jordan	2008	0.94	0.00	0.17	2007	0.99	0.00	0.25
Kazakhstan	2011	0.87	0.01	0.18	2000	0.99	0.00	0.06
Kenya	2009	0.62	0.01	0.07	2009	0.62	0.01	0.12
Korea, Republic of	2004	0.83	0.02	0.29	2004	1.00	0.00	0.00
Kyrgyzstan	2008	0.82	0.01	0.09	2003	0.97	0.00	0.11
Lao, People's Democratic Republic	2007	0.68	0.02	0.22	2007	0.44	0.03	0.33
Lesotho	2003	0.81	0.00	−0.02	2007	0.40	0.01	0.10
Liberia	2010	0.70	0.00	−0.05	2008	0.39	−0.03	−0.41
Lithuania	2010	0.90	0.00	0.12	2008	0.83	0.01	0.17
Luxembourg					2000	1.00	0.00	−0.18
Madagascar	2010	0.42	−0.01	−0.13	2010	0.50	−0.02	−0.22
Malawi	2010	0.84	0.01	0.15	2011	0.32	−0.03	−0.45
Malaysia					2003	0.96	0.00	0.15
Mali	2009	0.63	0.01	0.10	2009	0.31	0.00	0.06
Malta	2005	1.00	0.00	0.00	2005	1.00	0.00	0.00

continued . . .

APPENDIX 14.2 Continued

Country	Water				Sanitation			
	Average Year	Average RU Ratio	Rate (1/year)	Index	Average Year	Average RU Ratio	Rate (1/year)	Index
Mariana Islands, Northern								
Marshall Islands					2001	0.64	0.01	0.08
Mauritania	2005	0.88	0.02	0.38	2005	0.23	0.01	0.20
Mexico	2010	0.90	−0.02	−0.58	2010	0.81	0.00	−0.06
Moldova, Republic of	2007	0.82	−0.01	−0.23	2008	0.73	0.01	0.10
Mongolia	2008	0.66	0.05	0.58	2007	0.59	0.02	0.22
Morocco	2003	0.60	0.01	0.14	2006	0.63	0.02	0.23
Mozambique	2008	0.42	0.02	0.37	2008	0.21	0.03	0.66
Myanmar	2006	0.77	0.00	0.06	2006	0.82	0.01	0.20
Namibia	2000	0.74	0.02	0.34	2006	0.23	0.00	−0.04
Nepal	2011	0.94	0.02	0.71	2009	0.48	0.03	0.44
Netherlands	2006	1.00	0.00	0.00	2004	1.00	0.00	0.00
Nicaragua	2005	0.67	0.00	−0.03	2004	0.66	0.01	0.09
Niger	2008	0.43	0.01	0.12	2007	0.10	0.00	0.14
Nigeria	2012	0.71	−0.03	−0.39	2012	0.56	−0.02	−0.21
Norway	2007	0.93	0.00	−0.15	2005	1.00	0.00	0.00
Pakistan	2001	0.84	0.01	0.11	2009	0.53	0.03	0.36
Palau					2001	0.75	0.04	0.56
Palestine					2007	0.99	0.00	−0.13
Panama	2009	0.85	0.00	0.06	2009	0.66	0.00	0.05
Paraguay	2011	0.87	0.01	0.33	2011	0.78	0.01	0.08
Peru	2012	0.82	−0.01	−0.09	2011	0.55	0.02	0.28
Philippines	2007	0.94	−0.01	−0.31	2005	0.83	0.00	0.02
Russian Federation	2010	0.91	0.00	−0.14	2010	0.76	−0.01	−0.18
Rwanda	2011	0.79	0.00	−0.05	2009	0.81	0.00	0.04
Saint Lucia	2005	0.96	0.00	0.03				
Samoa	2007	0.99	0.00	0.69				
Samoa, American								
Senegal	2010	0.67	0.03	0.33	2010	0.56	0.01	0.12
Serbia	2007	0.99	0.00	−0.08	2007	0.97	0.00	−0.11
Sierra Leone	2005	0.41	0.01	0.12	2011	0.43	0.00	−0.05
Slovakia	2010	1.00	0.00	0.00	2009	1.00	0.00	0.00
Slovenia					2005	1.00	0.00	0.00
South Africa	2011	0.84	−0.03	−0.58	2009	0.76	0.04	0.62
Spain								
Sri Lanka	2007	0.89	0.01	0.22	2008	0.97	0.01	0.61
Swaziland	2006	0.61	0.01	0.14	2001	0.71	0.01	0.10

continued ...

APPENDIX 14.2 Continued

	Water				Sanitation			
Country	Average Year	Average RU Ratio	Rate (1/year)	Index	Average Year	Average RU Ratio	Rate (1/year)	Index
Sweden					2005	1.00	0.00	0.00
Switzerland					2001	1.00	0.00	0.00
Tajikistan	2007	0.62	0.02	0.22	2006	0.96	0.00	0.19
Tanzania, United Republic of	2010	0.55	0.00	0.00	2010	0.23	−0.03	−0.57
Thailand	2006	0.97	0.00	0.13	2003	0.99	0.00	−0.13
Timor Leste	2006	0.68	−0.01	−0.16	2006	0.49	−0.03	−0.33
Togo	2004	0.45	0.00	−0.02	2004	0.19	−0.01	−0.18
Trinidad and Tobago								
Tunisia	2002	0.80	0.01	0.20	2001	0.69	0.02	0.21
Turkey	2007	0.94	0.01	0.30	2007	0.81	0.01	0.18
Uganda	2009	0.73	0.00	−0.01	2011	0.36	−0.02	−0.23
Ukraine					2005	0.95	0.00	0.08
Uruguay	2011	0.94	0.00	−0.12	2011	0.95	0.01	0.29
Viet Nam	2010	0.91	0.00	−0.01	2009	0.69	0.03	0.38
Yemen					2002	0.33	0.02	0.22
Zambia	2001	0.42	0.01	0.10	2004	0.46	0.01	0.12
Zimbabwe	2007	0.70	−0.01	−0.11	2007	0.52	−0.01	−0.14

APPENDIX 14.3 Performance indices of the most recent year available for relative progress between higherserved and lesser served populations

	Water				Sanitation			
Country	Average Year	Average Coverage (%)	∅OI/OI −∅U/U (year^{-1})	Index	Average Year	Average Coverage (%)	∅OI/OI −∅U/U (year^{-1})	Index
Afghanistan	2006	41.4	0.07	0.40				
Albania	2009	95.7	−0.07	−0.18	2009	97.1	−0.03	−0.09
Andorra								
Angola					2008	42.5	0.08	0.26
Argentina	2008	97.8	−0.06	−0.22	2008	96.6	0.16	0.41
Armenia	2009	97.8	0.07	0.26				
Austria								
Azerbaijan	2005	78.5	0.02	0.07				
Bangladesh	2010	83.8	0.08	0.22	2005	72.7	0.12	0.27

continued ...

APPENDIX 14.3 Continued

Country	Water Average Year	Water Average Coverage (%)	Water $\emptyset OI/OI$ $-\emptyset U/U$ (year^{-1})	Water Index	Sanitation Average Year	Sanitation Average Coverage (%)	Sanitation $\emptyset OI/OI$ $-\emptyset U/U$ (year^{-1})	Sanitation Index
Belarus	2012	99.7	0.07	1.00	2011	99.1	−0.10	−0.81
Belgium								
Belize	2006	92.6	0.09	0.24	2006	93.3	0.11	0.28
Benin	2007	73.1	0.00	0.01	2006	28.9	0.02	0.14
Bhutan	2007	93.4	0.18	0.48				
Bolivia	2009	86.1	0.04	0.11	2009	65.0	0.06	0.13
Bosnia and Herzegovina	2004	98.2	0.08	0.37	2004	95.5	0.00	−0.01
Botswana	2008	95.8	−0.16	−0.40				
Brazil	2010	96.6	−0.10	−0.27	2010	82.7	0.06	0.14
Bulgaria	2006	99.0	−0.10	−0.74	2002	99.4	0.17	1.00
Burkina Faso	2008	73.1	0.03	0.09	2005	26.6	0.05	0.39
Burundi	2007	73.4	0.01	0.03	2007	54.4	0.04	0.09
Cambodia	2011	65.8	0.04	0.15	2011	42.7	0.16	0.51
Cameroon	2007	68.2	0.05	0.16	2004	57.5	0.01	0.03
Cape Verde	2005	85.4	0.00	0.01				
Central African Republic	2001	63.0	0.02	0.08				
Chad	2004	47.0	0.00	−0.01	2003	14.0	0.01	0.17
Chile	2006	96.9	−0.04	−0.10	2006	95.5	0.15	0.39
China	2007	87.9	0.02	0.05	1997	58.0	0.06	0.15
Colombia	2010	90.4	−0.60	−1.00	2009	89.6	0.09	0.20
Comoros	2001	90.1	−0.01	−0.04				
Congo	2007	72.6	0.03	0.11				
Congo, Democratic Republic of	2007	49.1	0.04	0.16				
Costa Rica	2009	97.1	0.02	0.05	2009	97.7	−0.07	−0.24
Côte d'Ivoire	2004	78.6	−0.04	−0.12	2001	43.6	0.03	0.09
Czech Republic								
Denmark								
Djibouti	2003	84.4	0.06	0.18				
Dominican Republic	2010	84.3	0.16	0.46	2001	90.7	0.09	0.21
Ecuador	2004	81.5	−0.06	−0.17	2004	84.6	0.04	0.09
Egypt	2007	97.9	−0.03	−0.13	2007	98.3	0.19	0.85
El Salvador	2011	92.2	0.12	0.33	2011	77.7	−0.06	−0.14
Estonia	2008	99.3	0.06	0.60	2002	99.5	−0.03	−0.36
Ethiopia	2011	49.6	0.06	0.26	2006	24.7	0.13	1.00
Fiji								
Finland								

continued ...

APPENDIX 14.3 Continued

Country	Water Average Year	Water Average Coverage (%)	Water $\varnothing OI/OI -\varnothing U/U$ (year^{-1})	Water Index	Sanitation Average Year	Sanitation Average Coverage (%)	Sanitation $\varnothing OI/OI -\varnothing U/U$ (year^{-1})	Sanitation Index
Gambia	2005	85.5	0.01	0.02				
Georgia	2007	95.0	0.05	0.12	2004	95.0	−0.21	−0.53
Germany								
Ghana	2010	82.2	−0.04	−0.10	2008	66.8	−0.03	−0.08
Greenland								
Guatemala	2006	89.2	−0.09	−0.25	2006	71.1	0.05	0.11
Guinea	2009	71.1	0.03	0.10				
Guinea Bissau	2002	55.8	0.08	0.33				
Guyana	2004	91.2	0.06	0.17	2004	89.2	0.05	0.12
Haiti	2004	62.3	−0.02	−0.06				
Honduras	2010	88.0	0.21	0.58	2010	83.6	0.05	0.10
Hungary								
Iceland								
India	2010	88.3	0.05	0.14	2008	42.1	0.07	0.24
Indonesia	2011	85.7	−0.01	−0.03	2002	53.7	0.08	0.20
Iran, Islamic Republic of	2004	94.6	0.00	0.00				
Iraq	2006	82.4	0.18	0.52				
Jamaica	2008	93.6	0.08	0.22	2004	97.4	0.06	0.21
Japan								
Jordan	2008	96.7	0.12	0.31				
Kazakhstan	2011	93.8	0.09	0.23	2003	99.1	0.06	0.45
Kenya	2009	59.4	0.02	0.07	2007	53.2	0.03	0.07
Korea, Republic of	2004	95.6	0.07	0.19				
Kyrgyzstan	2005	83.3	0.03	0.09				
Lao, People's Democratic Republic	2007	60.6	0.08	0.30				
Lesotho	2007	80.1	0.01	0.04	2007	37.5	0.03	0.11
Liberia	2010	71.1	0.01	0.04	2009	39.2	0.01	0.04
Lithuania	2010	95.4	0.00	0.00				
Luxembourg								
Madagascar	2010	47.6	0.03	0.16	2005	30.2	0.02	0.12
Malawi	2011	81.3	0.03	0.08	2010	16.9	0.18	0.96
Malaysia								
Mali	2009	65.8	0.10	0.34				
Malta								
Mariana Islands, Northern	2004	96.1	0.05	0.14				
Marshall Islands								

continued . . .

APPENDIX 14.3 Continued

	Water				Sanitation			
Country	Average Year	Average Coverage (%)	∅OI/OI −∅U/U (year⁻¹)	Index	Average Year	Average Coverage (%)	∅OI/OI −∅U/U (year⁻¹)	Index
Mauritania	2005	49.9	−0.01	−0.04				
Mexico	2010	95.5	−0.12	−0.32	2010	93.5	−0.11	−0.27
Moldova, Republic of	2009	87.4	−0.05	−0.14	2008	82.8	0.04	0.09
Mongolia	2006	58.9	0.02	0.08				
Morocco	2007	83.5	0.02	0.05	2005	78.9	0.13	0.28
Mozambique	2008	46.4	0.07	0.35	2006	19.9	0.11	1.00
Myanmar	2003	72.0	0.06	0.18	2005	79.3	0.14	0.31
Namibia	2007	86.0	−0.09	−0.26	2004	39.9	0.02	0.06
Nepal	2009	84.6	0.09	0.25	2008	44.0	0.13	0.39
Netherlands								
Nicaragua	2006	82.6	−0.01	−0.02	2006	69.1	0.04	0.10
Niger	2008	52.9	0.09	0.38				
Nigeria	2012	67.8	0.08	0.26	2012	53.6	0.15	0.38
Norway								
Pakistan	2008	89.5	0.08	0.21	2006	47.0	0.01	0.04
Palau								
Palestine	2004	80.9	−0.25	−0.72	2004	97.3	0.18	0.56
Panama	2009	92.6	0.08	0.22	2006	75.5	0.03	0.08
Paraguay	2011	90.6	0.15	0.40	2011	88.2	0.07	0.16
Peru	2012	88.2	0.04	0.10	2010	78.8	0.17	0.37
Philippines	2007	88.8	0.04	0.12	2007	85.0	0.01	0.02
Russian Federation	2010	96.3	−0.10	−0.27	2009	86.6	−0.04	−0.09
Rwanda	2011	73.6	0.16	0.51				
Saint Lucia	2005	94.9	−0.03	−0.09				
Samoa	2003	94.8	0.09	0.22				
Samoa, American	1995	95.7	0.06	0.16				
Senegal	2010	74.8	0.02	0.07	2009	65.6	0.04	0.09
Serbia								
Sierra Leone	2010	58.2	0.03	0.11				
Slovakia								
Slovenia								
South Africa	2011	93.2	−0.05	−0.14	2009	84.1	0.29	0.65
Spain								
Sri Lanka	2006	86.4	0.11	0.29				
Swaziland								
Sweden								
Switzerland								
Tajikistan	2007	66.5	0.08	0.26	2005	95.2	0.08	0.21

continued ...

APPENDIX 14.3 Continued

	Water				Sanitation			
Country	Average Year	Average Coverage (%)	$\varnothing OI/OI$ $-\varnothing U/U$ (year^{-1})	Index	Average Year	Average Coverage (%)	$\varnothing OI/OI$ $-\varnothing U/U$ (year^{-1})	Index
Tanzania, United Republic of	2010	55.3	0.03	0.11	2010	22.7	0.13	1.00
Thailand	2006	94.5	0.06	0.16				
Timor Leste	2005	60.9	0.05	0.17				
Togo	2004	55.1	0.03	0.10	2001	32.7	−0.03	−0.13
Trinidad and Tobago	2001	93.2	0.00	0.01	2001	98.0	0.04	0.18
Tunisia	2002	91.3	0.05	0.12				
Turkey	2007	96.2	0.06	0.16	2007	92.1	0.00	−0.01
Uganda	2010	73.1	0.10	0.32				
Ukraine	2010	97.0	−0.10	−0.27	2005	97.7	0.05	0.18
Uruguay	2011	99.2	0.12	1.00	2011	96.2	0.24	0.61
Viet Nam	2009	90.3	0.03	0.07	2008	69.4	0.13	0.30
Yemen	1999	60.2	−0.08	−0.28	2002	45.0	0.07	0.21
Zambia	2006	58.5	0.02	0.09	2003	53.7	0.00	0.00
Zimbabwe	2010	77.2	−0.06	−0.18	2005	66.3	−0.04	−0.08

15

COUNTING THE COSTS AND BENEFITS OF EQUITABLE WASH SERVICE PROVISION

Guy Hutton and Luis Andres

Introduction

The 2030 Agenda has set ambitious targets for water supply, sanitation and hygiene (WASH), as part of Sustainable Development Goal (SDG) number 6. Faced with a global vision of universal access (in both households and institutions) to 'safely managed' WASH services, countries need to set their own targets and develop a roadmap for how these targets will be achieved. One central element of national planning, priority-setting and budgeting is an understanding of the costs, benefits and affordability of achieving national coverage targets. Also, an understanding is needed of the distribution of the costs and benefits to enable conclusions about the equity implications of reaching different population groups.

Raising the funds to meet the investment needs, as well as Operations and Maintenance (O&M) costs, will be a major challenge to achieving the SDG WASH targets.[1] Determining the mix of public and private financing is a key policy decision that will determine the effectiveness, equity, efficiency and sustainability of WASH services. Cost-benefit analysis, which explicitly assesses the population incidence of costs and benefits, is therefore particularly important for ensuring that inequalities in service coverage at the start of the SDG period are reduced.[2] Making progress on inequalities will be a major challenge, as well as an indicator of the success of the 2030 Agenda, as to how much the needle can be shifted for poor and vulnerable groups.

While significant progress was made during the Millennium Development Goal (MDG) period on target 7C, the nature of the target made it possible to achieve the target without significantly impacting poor and vulnerable groups. Indeed, in many countries the water and sanitation coverage of poorer wealth quintiles increased at a slower rate than better-off wealth quintiles.[3] Hence, the aspiration of sector stakeholders in the discussions that led to the adoption of SDG WASH targets was that coverage rates for poor and vulnerable groups should increase at a faster rate than other unserved populations.[4] Subsequently, the importance of reaching poor and vulnerable groups with WASH services was established in the wording of the SDG WASH targets themselves, to "achieve universal and equitable access to safe and affordable drinking water for all" (target 6.1) and "achieve access to adequate and equitable sanitation and hygiene for all, and end open defecation, paying special attention to the needs of women and girls and those in vulnerable situations" (target 6.2).

Population categories deserving greater attention include those living in poverty as well as those who are marginalized or disadvantaged for different reasons.[4] While poverty is commonly determined at household level (taking into account both income-earners and dependents), the terms 'marginalized' or 'disadvantaged' can be applied at community, household or individual levels. For example, ethnicity, degree of geographical remoteness from commercial centres, and the slum population are identified at the household and community levels. Some vulnerable groups are identified at the individual level, such as women, young children, the sick and the elderly, to reflect intra-household variations in access to WASH services. Other vulnerable groups are defined according to their temporary (but sometimes long-term) status, such as victims of natural disasters, refugees or prisoners. Hence, given the large range in vulnerable and marginalized population groups, the targeting of WASH services will be different depending on the nature and level of vulnerability.

Some attributes of WASH services makes their provision different from other services in a country or a community. One key characteristic is what is known in economics as the 'externalities' associated with WASH. In this case the lack of WASH services for one population group causes a negative externality for another population group, such as caused by the transmission of fecal-oral diseases. This is especially true in areas with high population density, such as the case of the impacts of open defecation on child height (stunting) in developing countries.[5] Conversely, improved WASH services for some populations can lead to health and environmental benefits for all.[6] A second characteristic of WASH is that in many circumstances the solutions require organization at community level or above to be successfully implemented. This can happen in two ways: 1) the improvement of individual sanitation and hygiene behaviour through changing social norms, and 2) the construction and management of large infrastructure (e.g. wells, pipelines, treatment plants) to provide WASH access, which necessarily happens at community level or above. This can lead to scale economies for infrastructure provision – with falling unit costs per household reached when more households are reached with services.[7] On the other hand, the costs of reaching the 'last mile' (the last few per cent of unreached population), often in difficult topographies, can be significantly greater than the average unit costs. These two attributes of WASH services outlined have major implications for how services are financed. Most key is that poor and vulnerable populations cannot or should not be left behind, and that some form of cross-subsidization is usually required.

The SDG indicators 6.1.1 (on drinking water) and 6.2.1 (on sanitation and hygiene) both define a 'safely managed' service level. This service level is higher than the 'improved' definition used during the MDG period (see Chapter 1). The WHO and UNICEF, who manage the Joint Monitoring Programme (JMP) and are custodian agencies for SDG targets 6.1 and 6.2, have also defined a 'basic' level of drinking water and sanitation services, which is similar to the previous 'improved' definition during the MDG period. In examining the normative criteria of the human rights to water and sanitation (accessibility, quality, availability, acceptability and affordability), there is necessarily a key trade-off between the first four criteria (which define the service type and level) and the fifth criterion. Affordability of a service will therefore be challenged by raising the service level, and will depend on the capacity and willingness of poor and vulnerable populations to pay, and the availability of subsidies.

In the spirit of progressive realization stated in the human rights to water and sanitation, governments need to show that they are implementing improved policies and mobilizing additional resources to realize the human rights for all. Hence, given the higher ambitions of the SDG WASH targets, planning authorities will need to base their programming on what service level can be achieved with the available funding from both public funds and tariffs recovered from households. In settings with greater resource constraints, it will not be feasible to achieve 'safely managed' services in the short or medium term. Planning authorities will also face difficult decisions about whether to allocate funds to upgrade those with a basic service to a safely managed service, or to extend basic services to those with no or limited service.

To advance the understanding of how poor and vulnerable groups can be better targeted with WASH services in national (and subnational) policies, plans and programmes, this chapter aims to:

- understand the (differential) costs and benefits of reaching different population groups, which will have implications for policies and programme implementation;
- provide a framework in which costs and benefits of reaching different groups of society can be better analysed;
- assess the financing requirements for reaching these groups, in terms of both volumes as well as financing mechanisms and new funding sources;
- provide recommendations for sector policies and programmes.

Costs

Global cost estimates

A study conducted by the World Bank has estimated the costs of achieving SDG targets 6.1 and 6.2.[1] The study focused on household WASH in 140 low- and middle-income countries, with cost results presented for rural and urban areas, for water, sanitation and hygiene, and for basic and safely managed services. Overall, and at global level, the capital expenditure required is greater than has been historically spent during the MDG period – for basic WASH the capital cost for extending services to the unserved is 0.12 per cent of gross product of the 140 countries, while for safely managed WASH it is 0.39 percent. The study showed significant variation between regions, with the African region and some parts of Asia requiring a multiple of these cost numbers, as shown in Figure 15.1. Also, the costs of operating and maintaining new and existing services need to be factored into infrastructure investment decisions – given that a major share of the public funds are currently allocated to operations and maintenance (O&M) costs. If O&M costs paid by households are too high (i.e. do not justify the private benefits), populations might abandon use of the service.

The main conclusion of the World Bank study is that the cost of reaching a basic level of WASH service still represents a major challenge for many regions and countries, given the annual spending required exceeds current spending. While major costs remain in rural areas due to the size of current populations unserved and often higher costs of reaching the 'last mile', costs of serving urban areas are increasing due to urbanisation and the tendency for more technology-intensive solutions in urban areas with higher unit costs. Furthermore, the study concluded that public funding will be needed to expand access to WASH services given that O&M costs often exceed commonly used affordability thresholds of 3–5 per cent of annual income, a finding supported by evidence presented on affordability by WHO/UNICEF JMP.[2] The implication of these findings is that emphasis should be on policies and public budgets to reach a basic WASH service for all.

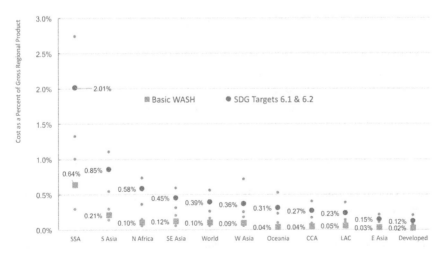

FIGURE 15.1 Costs of basic and safely managed services as a percentage of Gross Regional Product (GRP) by MDG region, with uncertainty range

Source: Hutton and Varughese, 2016. Reproduced with permission of The World Bank.

National studies on WASH cost and affordability

A growing number of studies have been conducted in countries that present the unit costs of WASH services as well as the affordability of costs paid by households. Many of these studies were used in generating global numbers (see Appendix D of Hutton and Varughese[1]). Multi-country initiatives assessing the costs of WASH services include the following:

- FEASIBLE model, implemented by COWI Denmark and OECD. This tool has been applied mainly in countries of Central Asia and North Africa.[8] The model estimates national costs of WASH investment and O&M costs based on representative subnational unit cost estimates and multiplies these by the population sizes to be served with new and existing services.
- WASHCost, implemented by IRC International Water and Sanitation Center (Netherlands). The initiative estimated WASH costs in four countries and focused on estimating life- cycle costs, identifying six comprehensive categories of cost and giving greater focus to capital maintenance and capacity building.[9]
- Economics of Sanitation Initiative (ESI), implemented by the World Bank. Cost-benefit studies covered six countries in Southeast Asia and estimated annual equivalent costs of providing different types of sanitation service to calculate cost-benefit ratios and annual economic rates of return.[10]
- Service Delivery Assessments, implemented by the World Bank. These studies measured indicators to adequacy of policies, regulations, institutions and financing to reach national WASH targets across 50 countries in Africa, Asia and Latin America.[11] The studies estimated the costs of achieving national WASH targets and compared costs with financing available.
- Plan International implemented a global study that included estimating the unit costs of water and sanitation services delivered by its own programmes in 45 countries.[12]
- International Benchmarking Network for Water and Sanitation Utilities (IBNET), implemented by the World Bank, provides the tariffs and costs of service provision for utilities submitting data from a large number of countries.[13]

It is not the purpose of this chapter to comprehensively review these initiatives or other costing studies. Further reading on economic approaches to investment appraisal can be found in World Bank (2013),[14] while guidance specific to the water sector can be found in Cameron et al. (2011).[15] The first step is to decide which unit costs are to be measured. Second, the cost items to be included should be identified, bearing in mind that policy makers need to know all the related costs to implementing a service. Third, the disaggregation of costs to capture the equity perspective should be made relevant to influence policy decisions that favour the poor and vulnerable groups. Fourth, the data analyses to be conducted should be planned in advance, as it has implications for data collection.

When estimating costs, a decision needs to be made on whether costs are valued using existing financial or using economic prices. Financial prices reflect what providers at different parts of the supply chain and what customers actually pay. Financial prices do not always fully reflect the costs of the service – some tariffs are set under the service provision cost, while other tariffs might include a profit element. For example, a connection fee charged by a utility to receive piped water or sewerage rarely covers the full capital costs. To make up for this 'loss', a utility might charge (some customers) higher monthly tariffs than the operational costs and/or it might receive a subsidy from a government agency. Hence, in the WASH sector the prices customers face are rarely indicative of the cost of provision.

Economic prices, on the other hand, reflect the opportunity cost of the resources and help identify the best use of resources from a societal perspective. This is particularly relevant for economies in which prices are fixed by government or affected by trade restrictions, and hence are not entirely determined by market conditions. Economic prices are also relevant when some inputs (such as household labour costs) are not included in the financial price. Economic prices therefore provide a truer picture of the actual total costs of a service from an overall societal, rather than a single stakeholder, perspective.

A second question concerns the valuation of future costs. Given the time preference for money (as indicated by the existence of real interest rates that are usually greater than 0 per cent), it is necessary to express costs incurred in different periods in common terms. Hence, it is necessary to choose a base year, and value past and future costs in the same year using the discount rate.

Framework for the assessment of affordability

The concept of affordability is not new,[16,17] but no consensus has been reached on methodology for measuring it[2] and various options have been proposed for measuring affordability in the SDG era.[18] There has been limited exploration of WASH affordability that distinguishes different contexts, such as urban versus rural, connected versus unconnected households, and service levels. Also, the literature tends to focus on water affordability and less commonly encompasses sanitation and hygiene aspects. Furthermore, there has been limited study of how higher WASH expenditure drives down the availability of disposable income for other non-water consumption; and the inverse, how non-water expenditure crowds out funds available for WASH. Indeed, the relative shares of WASH and other expenditures reflect the underlying price and the availability of services and their impact on overall welfare. At the same time, a higher monetary expenditure on WASH does not necessarily imply a higher quantity, or for that matter quality, of service level as this depends on its price, source, type of use, distance, and other factors. This suggests that the role of WASH in household welfare should also be examined not only from the demand for WASH services, but also from the supply side.

According to the WHO/UNICEF JMP, affordability of water and sanitation services is an important cross-cutting concern, which affects the ability to deliver on the human rights to water and sanitation.[2] The Human Right to Water and Sanitation places obligations on states and utilities to regulate payments for services and make provision to ensure that all members of the population can afford to access basic services. Expenditure on drinking water and sanitation typically includes infrequent large capital investments as well as more regular recurrent costs, both of which need to be taken into account in any affordability threshold set. Rigorous assessments of affordability would also need to take account of wealth or income, including WASH sector subsidies or other social transfers provided by the state.

Evidence from willingness-to-pay studies, however, points to the limitations of setting rigid benchmarks that define what is and what is not affordable to (poor) households. Households are often willing to pay significantly more than current tariffs if they are guaranteed a level of service that meets their expectations. Some households are willing to pay more than 3 to 5 per cent of their monthly income for a utility service, while others would refuse to pay that much. In this sense, the affordability threshold analysis does not help determine how many households in a particular utility service area would see cost recovery prices as a barrier to continuing to use WASH services, nor whether affordable prices would be enough to induce unconnected households to use the services.[19]

An alternative way of defining water affordability is to establish a normative WASH poverty line based on an affordability threshold which is based on a monetary value of the subsistence WASH basket. This basket can accommodate, for instance, the service level that has been mandated by the SDG targets 6.1 and 6.2, but the affordability line could also be adapted based on the level on access and quality set in national policy or standards. The spirit of the assessment is that populations should, at a minimum, have access to WASH at the defined levels – i.e. that the defined price of the minimum standard within the WASH poverty basket can be paid for, based on each group's income level.

Given the lack of data on costs for different population groups, from an affordability perspective it is useful to categorize populations as falling into one of four main groups depending on the service level and financing mechanism. This categorization is based on what minimum service level populations are being targeted for, and not the current level of service that might be below the minimum standard.

An affordability framework is presented in Figure 15.2. Populations are distributed based on their affordability threshold in four quadrants, with connection status along the Y-axis and degree of service affordability along the X-axis. The population segment along the Y-axis is based on access or quantity of water available to them, whereas the population segment along the X-axis is based on their level affordability based on the price of the WASH basket and level of poverty (poor or extreme poor). This framework helps unbundle the policy implications based on whether the population is connected or not connected to the system, and if the level of service is affordable or unaffordable. As a result, it links WASH access, affordability and poverty.

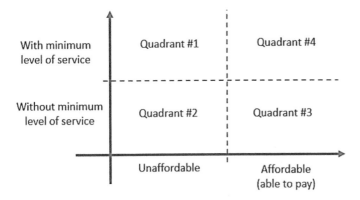

FIGURE 15.2 Populations fall into four affordability quadrants when accessing a targeted minimum level of service

Source: Andres et al. (2017).[20]

Quadrant 1: includes population groups that have access to the minimum targeted service level but cannot afford it. What is interesting here is that although they are served, the level of water service or connection is somewhat unaffordable to them or they may be paying more than 5 per cent of their income. It may therefore be judged that there are equity/fairness concerns. This group is of interest from a poverty and affordability threshold. To understand the impediments this group faces, it is a supply- or demand-side problem.

Quadrant 2: consists of population groups that cannot afford to pay for the minimum targeted service level. The population in this quadrant is of greatest interest for many reasons from a policy point of view. This population cannot afford to pay for the basket (access to water, quality access), they do not have the basket and hence they are a candidate either for the subsidy or lowering the standards to make the service more affordable, to transition to Quadrant 3.

Quadrant 3: can afford to pay, but do not have minimum service level. Even though they are able to pay, they are not connected to the network. This quadrant represents the population that should be able to pay for the minimum service level (i.e. within the affordability threshold). The policy implications for this population are varied, depending on why they do not have access to the service: is it lack of information, supply side issues, or location?.

Quadrant 4: includes population groups who can afford to pay and are served. A high proportion of the population would likely be situated in the fourth or the fifth quintile of the income distribution, and the income and demand curve of this population is highly inelastic. However, what may be of interest about the population in this quadrant are their characteristics, such as what percentage of their income they are spending on water. This population can be further broken into those who are paying tariffs that would cover system operation and maintenance only, and those who cover both O&M and capital costs.

There are some additional considerations when applying the above framework. First, affordability at the household level is not only a function of the interplay between population income, willingness to pay and the cost of providing the service – it is also dependent on the level of subsidy. Hence, a costly service can be made affordable by providing targeted assistance to lower income population groups. Second, given that available expenditure data are based on the existing service levels and not the targeted service levels, it is difficult to build up a full picture of affordability. Hence, the existing data show that many populations – especially rural – do not spend much on WASH and this is because their level of

TABLE 15.1 Example policy recommendations for different population groups based on existing service levels

Group	Subgroup	Policy recommendation
Populations currently facing no direct financial cost	Limited or no service such as drawing water from surface sources or open defecation	Prioritize those who are poor and vulnerable to receive intervention and subsidies.
	WASH service has a financial cost which is entirely subsidized by government, community or other agency	Maintain in category for poorest and most vulnerable groups. Other groups should be shifted to paying affordable tariffs for the service.
Populations currently facing direct financial costs that are affordable	Lower level of service, entirely financed by household contributions	Provide higher level of service, with subsidies for poor and vulnerable population.
	Higher level of service that is partially financed by the government, community or other agency, and the household contribution is considered affordable	Maintain status quo (bring more population to this category).
Populations currently facing direct financial costs that are unaffordable	Higher level of service, which is largely or fully paid for by the household, or	Shift to paying affordable tariffs for the service.
	Lower level of service but has high associated costs either for natural reasons (e.g. water scarcity) or lack of efficiency or competition in service provision (e.g. vendor-supplied water).	If for natural reasons, shift to paying affordable tariffs for the service. If for market reasons, provide appropriate (and differentiated) subsidy level to make tariff affordable.

service is low (e.g. households drawing surface water or practising open defecation). Urban populations accessing water vendor services, on the other hand, might be shown to be spending high amounts – even higher than those accessing piped water with associated better service level.

For policy makers, it is important to think through the financing implications and socioeconomic impacts of each of these quadrants, and how different population groups can be optimally moved from conditions of lower affordability to better affordability. Table 15.1 shows the policy recommendations for each population group.

Assessment of affordability considerations for different populations groups

Given that each population group with different vulnerabilities will require finetuned policy recommendations, this section explores the issues faced for each. Table 15.2 summarises the findings.

Poor households are classified as those living below the national poverty line. For the purpose of global estimations and comparisons, a poverty threshold of US$1.90 (year 2015) has been defined by the World Bank. Also, as part of its Twin Goals, the World Bank has focused on the bottom 40 per cent (B40) of households according to income (defined per country) as being deserving of increased policy and financial support. 'Poor people' is a broad category that includes many of the categories covered below. On the other hand, not all of the population falling in the categories below would necessarily be poor, and some may be deserving of support despite not being categorized as poor.

Analysis across countries analyzed in World Bank (2017)[21] suggests that among the studied factors, wealth is the most important determinant of WASH status. Some countries have made laudable progress in expanding access to improved drinking water and sanitation among households in the B40 of national wealth distribution. However, the gap between these and households in the top 60 per cent (T60) of the wealth distribution persists. Meanwhile, in other countries, B40 households are gaining access in urban but not rural areas. In short, the global gap in access to improved WASH between the B40 and T60 remains large, although access patterns vary widely in and between countries (Figure 15.3). On average, 78 per cent of households in the T60 have access to improved water, compared with only 43 of the households in the B40; 33 percent of households in the T60 have access to piped water on premises, compared with only 17 percent of the B40.

For sanitation, access is far lower among the B40 than the T60. Some 37 percent of people in the B40 practice open defecation, compared with 17 percent of households in the T60. However, the number of people practicing open defecation is distributed across these groups. Two in three (64 percent) of people in the T60 have access to shared or unshared improved sanitation facilities, compared with close to one in three (40 percent) among the B40. Finally, only

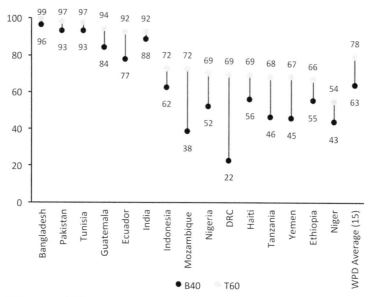

(a) Improved Water

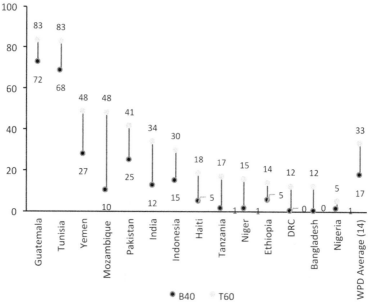

(b) Piped Water on Premise

FIGURE 15.3 Access to any improved, piped water on premises only, and sanitation indicators, by wealth level in selected countries

Note: B40 = bottom 40 percent of asset wealth distribution; T60 = top 60 percent of asset wealth distribution; DRC = Democratic Republic of the Congo; WPD = WASH Poverty Diagnostic.

Source: Andres et al. (2017).[22]

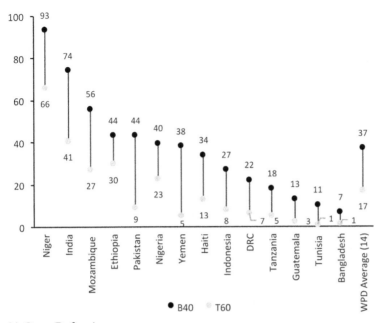

(c) Open Defecation

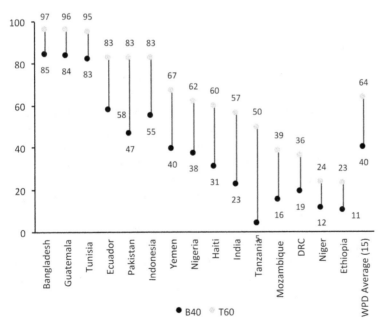

(d) Shared and Unshared Improved Facilities

FIGURE 15.3 Continued

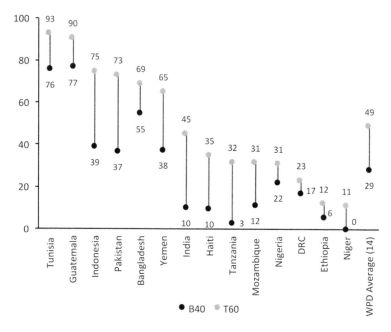

(e) Improved Sanitation

FIGURE 15.3 Continued

half of the population in the T60 has access to improved sanitation, while 29 percent of the population in the B40 does.

Poor households are often faced with the same theoretical choice of WASH service options and prices as any household. However, in reality those choices might be limited because some providers are unable to provide, or choose not to provide, services in poor neighborhoods. For example, a utility network might not service a poor area due to concerns about financial viability or lack of land tenure. A sludge truck might not be able to access houses down long narrow streets, or might not operate outside its service area due to fuel costs. Hence, other solutions are needed for these households and these can lead to higher unit costs. Poor households are furthermore less likely to invest in or consume WASH services for non-financial reasons, such as lower education level, lack of exposure to basic or safely managed WASH options, more ingrained social norms that deprioritize improved WASH practices or because they are renting their dwelling.

Slum-dwellers are among the worst-served population with public services, including health, education, social services and environmental services (such as solid waste management). Inadequate WASH in newly urbanized/periurban areas reflect a lack of capacity–at both the local and national level—to plan for rapid development and expand service networks as needed.[22]

Remote or isolated populations pose a major challenge to achieving universal access of WASH services. Remoteness is a function of both distance and

TABLE 15.2 Summary of costs, affordability and other constraints of poor and vulnerable groups from accessing WASH services

Population category	Affordability of accessing WASH services	Other constraints to accessing WASH services
The poor (below national poverty line or in the bottom 40%)	The poor face higher proportional costs to access WASH services when compared with their cash incomes	Lower education level; lack of exposure to WASH options; ingrained social norms; more likely to rent their dwelling
Slum-dwellers	Low levels of service might be free or cost little, while higher service levels either cannot be offered or are unaffordable.	Lack of land or house tenure; lower education level; more ingrained social norms; more likely to rent their dwelling
Remote and isolated populations	Non-cash based economies makes paying for services very challenging; small dispersed population can increase unit costs	Lack of access to markets; multiple homes; lower education level; lack of exposure to WASH options; ingrained social norms
Ethnic groups	Non-cash based economies makes paying for services very challenging; small dispersed population can increase unit costs	Intervention from outside groups and government seen as coercion; ingrained social norms; lower education level; lack of exposure to WASH options
Women	Women have limited access to cash, but might prioritize WASH with what they have	Women have less power decision making in the household to spend on WASH
Female-headed households	Likely to have a lower income than in households with two or more adults	Women have been shown to prioritize WASH spending when they have control over household finances
Children	Same as entire household – but impact of cost on family depends on dependency ratio	Customs might prioritize adult use of toilet. Children likely to suffer poor institutional WASH when at schools
Elderly, the sick and physically disabled	Need for targeting technologies with specific features can increase unit costs; sick need to spend more money on medical care; elderly do not benefit from safety nets/pension	Limited role in decision making on household priorities
Emergency contexts (e.g. natural disasters) and refugees	Limited cash to pay for WASH; generally not expected to pay for WASH	Lack of availability of WASH options; distance from population centres; high vulnerability of population
Prison population	Not expected to pay for WASH	Dependent on prison facilities

accessibility in terms of paths, roads and air. Isolation is more likely in mountainous areas, difficult terrain and seasonally flooded areas. For nomadic populations, large distances, multiple resting spots, as well as unpredictability makes it difficult to reach these people. Remote populations have limited access to markets, and, due to higher distribution costs, the goods and services available to them are often higher (when left to the market). Furthermore, ingrained norms and presence of taboos makes it more difficult to bring about behaviour change and knowledge transfer than in other populations. Furthermore, these populations tend to be poorer and more likely to operate in a non-cash economy for making contributions to WASH services.

Ethnic group is a category of people who identify with each other based on similarities, such as common language, ancestral, social, cultural, or national experiences, and is typically an inherited status based on the society in which a person lives. The sense in which the term "ethnic group" is understood in this chapter is related to any disadvantages an ethnic group may face based on its ethnicity, whether they be of an economic, geographical (e.g. remoteness), social (beliefs or customs that reduce the likelihood that members will demand or consume WASH services), or discriminatory nature.[22]

Such groups need to be dealt with sensitively, as programmatic interventions from outside groups can be perceived as uninvited coercion, with the promotion and even forcing of interventions that reflect a different cultural standpoint or world view. Hence, any interventions that do occur, including both software and hardware components, need to be adapted to the understandings and preferences of the specific ethnic groups and further refined based on preliminary experience. For this reason, and also due to the typically low density and remote nature of many ethnic groups, unit costs tend to be higher than for the general population. Conversely, if done in the right way and gaining the trust of traditional leaders, behaviour change can be achieved relatively quickly and with high compliance due to the social cohesion of many ethnic groups. Furthermore, the acceptability of "simple" technological solutions can lead to lower average costs per household compared with the general population.

Women and female-headed households form an important and large group that is often considered vulnerable. The majority of household chores and childcare fall on women and girls, and in the case of water collection it falls on them in 71 percent of cases.[23] Such tasks are often very time-consuming. Where paths to water sources are long and through remote areas, this may put women at risk of physical and sexual violence.[21]

In terms of sanitation and hygiene, women have different needs than men, where having a private nearby place to perform sanitation and menstrual hygiene management (MHM) and other hygiene are particularly important, and not having these exposes them to potential harm (see Chapter 10). These needs are heightened even more during pregnancy and in the postpartum period. In some societies, women are not allowed to use the household latrine even if there is one, which is reserved for men and/or for the elderly household members (see Chapter 5).

Looking after young children also requires convenient and hygienic facilities to reduce the incidence of disease and save time. Women who head a household might only have one income, plus all the duties normally performed by two adults, hence making them a vulnerable group.

Children form an important vulnerable group, especially when combined with other characteristics covered in this section. Children, especially young children, are more vulnerable to fecal-oral disease, and are subject to the WASH practices of the family, before they have adopted their own practices. Young children need a different sanitation solution (e.g. nappy, potty) until they are able to use a latrine/toilet, and JMP numbers show safe disposal of child feces to be lower than other population groups. Furthermore, the quality of water used in weaning products is especially important. The level of cost for children to access WASH services will be determined more by the location and family characteristics (see above) than by age. Large families investing in WASH facilities will generally face lower unit costs per individual. However, large families with a low ratio of income-earners to dependents are more likely to face affordability constraints, with limited cash income needed for other priorities (food, education and healthcare).

The elderly, the sick and the physically disabled form three distinct but often overlapping groups that are very sensitive to the availability of WASH services. Having access in the household/plot is especially important for these groups. In addition, for many of these groups, special fittings are required for them to access water and toilet facilities, which will cost extra. In the case of sanitation, some may not be able to use the household toilet and might need a mobile toilet of some kind. Even if affordable, these fittings or different hardware options are not available in many contexts. In particular, people with disabilities face significant barriers to WASH access.[21]

Emergencies brought about by natural events and conflicts represent a particular challenge to WASH. According to data published by WHO and UNICEF, populations in fragile states are four times more likely not to have a basic water service and two times more likely not to have basic sanitation.[22] Many governments and agencies are well prepared to respond to the emergency phase of disasters. However, several issues are still not dealt with when the immediate necessities of the emergencies subside, such as disposal of fecal waste and low-cost water provision. Constraining factors include the distance of the affected population from WASH and health infrastructures, the high vulnerability of the population, economic distress, and contexts where people are ready to suspend social norms (e.g. revert to open defecation, use of surface water for drinking-water supply).

Refugees represent a growing problem globally, a large proportion of which result from the emergency situations discussed above. The refugee crisis is both cross-border as well as of a national nature (called internally displaced people (IDP)). The majority of refugees in the developing world are given temporary shelter, and hence temporary solutions also need to be found for their WASH needs. Most of these refugees have limited cash and possessions, and many do not have an income, hence they are left to rely on donors and NGOs that support refugee settlements.

The prison population is also a growing one globally, and one in which people are often subjected to poor WASH access, which leads to indignities and suffering. The issue of affordability relates not to the prisoners' income or willingness to pay, but the budgets and willingness of the government to fund better WASH services for prisons.

Benefits

Types of benefit

There are many proven benefits for populations gaining access to WASH services. The benefits are shown for water and sanitation in Table 15.3. Overall, the strongest evidence is on the health, environmental, and gender impacts, available from many surveys and field studies. There is moderate evidence for the time savings, educational benefits, value of resource reuse, and socioeconomic benefits associated with improved WASH, where primary data from surveys and field studies is more limited. It should be noted that some of these benefits are related, hence all the benefits listed are not fully additive.

Evidence on economic benefits

Studies have been conducted in over 60 countries that quantify the economic impacts of poor sanitation, also known as "damage cost" studies. Figure 15.4 presents a summary of these estimates. These studies are largely based on modelling of different impacts using data from a variety of sources as well as a number of economic assumptions. Health costs account for up to the equivalent of 5 percent of GDP of some countries, while in countries where non-health impacts were assessed, they account for up to 4 percent of GDP. None of the studies presented the impacts specifically for poor and vulnerable groups, although they are likely to account for a significant proportion of the damage costs.

Economic evaluation studies compare the costs with the benefits to estimate benefit-cost ratios or percentage annual rates of return. The evidence generally shows high returns to spending on WASH both from global [24,25] as well as country studies.[26] However, studies have tended to present costs and benefits for the general population, with limited evidence on subpopulations based on income or other characteristic.

Exploring benefits for vulnerable groups

While these studies indicate that health costs are more burdensome for poorer households, there are few studies that explore the full range of economic and social benefits of improved WASH. Hence, it is likely that the benefits of improved

TABLE 15.3 Benefits of drinking-water and sanitation services

Benefit	Drinking-water	Sanitation
Health	Averted cases of diarrhoeal disease Malnutrition-related diseases Health-related quality of life impacts Dehydration from lack of access to water Less flood-related health impacts (better water management) Averted premature deaths related to the above	Averted cases of diarrhoeal disease Averted cases of helminths Malnutrition-related diseases Health-related quality of life impacts Dehydration from not drinking due to poor latrine access (especially women) Less flood-related health impacts Averted premature deaths related to the above
Living environment		Reduction in untreated fecal waste in the immediate environment, giving unpleasant sights and odours With less bacteriological contamination of drinking-water sources, there will be less household time and costs treating drinking water
Convenience and time savings	Travel and waiting time averted for collecting water from community sources	Travel and waiting time averted for using communal toilet facilities or practising open defecation
Leisure and quality of life/intangibles	Avoided effort from water hauling with benefits going disproportionately to women, children, the sick and the elderly	Safety, privacy, dignity, comfort, status, prestige, aesthetics, with benefits going disproportionately to women, the sick and the elderly
Educational gains	Improved educational levels due to higher school enrolment and attendance rates Impact of childhood malnutrition on education	Improved educational levels due to higher school nrolment and attendance erates Impact on education of childhood malnutrition
Reuse: nutrients		Use of human feces or sludge as soil conditioner and fertilizer in agriculture
Reuse: energy		Use of human (and animal) waste as input to biogas digester leading to fuel cost savings and income opportunities

continued . . .

TABLE 15.3 Continued

Benefit	Drinking-water	Sanitation
Reuse: water security		Safely treated wastewater for use in agriculture
Economic and financial value	Health economic gains (less health expenses, less health-related absence from productive activities, lower mortality) Value of time savings Increased incomes due to more tourism income and business opportunities Productive uses of water Value associated with improved education outcomes Rise in value of property Reduced payments to high cost services (e.g. water vendors)	Health economic gains (less health expenses, less health-related absence from productive activities, lower mortality) Value of time savings Increased incomes due to more tourism income and business opportunities Value of safely treated fecal matter and wastewater for safe reuse in agriculture Value associated with improved education outcomes Rise in value of property Reduced payments for public toilets with a fee

Source: Adapted from Hutton (2012b).[23]

WASH services for population groups suffering social exclusion would give a more favourable benefit-cost ratio through the greater gain in dignity it gives these populations and self-perceived social status, among others. A growing number of studies evaluate the barriers to WASH services faced to by vulnerable groups vis-à-vis the general population (see Chapter 10). Jones et al. (2002)[27] present a literature review to document the various problems faced by disabled people in accessing WASH. Table 15.4 provides an indication of the strength of direction of selected impacts for various poor and vulnerable population groups. At this stage, greater quantification is not possible, and further evidence is needed.

Funding and financing

Global cost-benefit studies have demonstrated that WASH services provide good social and economic returns when compared with the cost of the services.[25,24] This is true for all population groups, but especially for poor and vulnerable groups who are more likely to have no or very poor services. However, despite these economic returns, there is insufficient investment in WASH services for these population groups. This is partly a question of information asymmetry – households and communities are not aware of some of the benefits they will enjoy as a result of a better WASH service, or cannot act on the information due to system inertia. Insufficient investment also reflects the persistence of traditional practices and

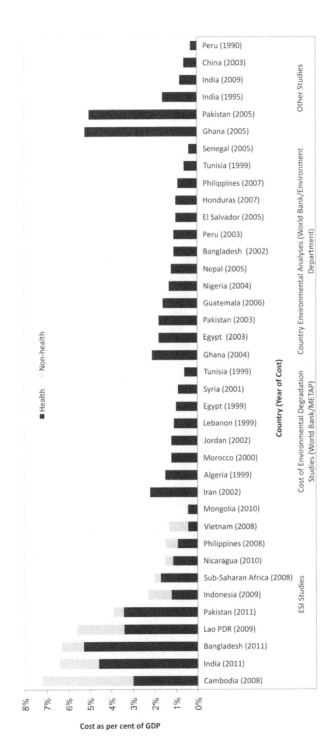

FIGURE 15.4 Economic costs of poor water and sanitation in selected countries, as a percent of Gross Domestic Product, disaggregated by health and non-health

Source: Hutton and Chase (2016).[25] Reproduced with permission of the *International Journal of Environmental Research and Public Health*.

TABLE 15.4 Potential to gain for different population groups from sanitation interventions[1,2]

Population group	Health	Living environment	Convenience and time savings	Dignity (social)	Educational outcomes[3]
The poor (below national poverty line)	↑↑↑	↑↑	↑	↑↑	↑
Slum-dwellers	↑↑↑	↑↑↑	↑↑	↑↑	↑
Remote and isolated populations	↑	↑	↑	↑	↑
Ethnic groups	↑	↑	↑		↑
Women and female-headed households	↑↑	↑	↑↑	↑↑↑	↑↑
Children	↑↑↑	↑	↑	↑↑	↑↑↑
Elderly, the sick and physically disabled	↑↑↑	↑	↑↑↑	↑↑↑	↑↑[4]
Emergency contexts	↑↑↑	↑↑↑	↑↑	↑	↑
Refugees	↑↑	↑↑	↑↑	↑	↑
Prison population	↑↑	↑↑	↑	↑↑	

Notes
1 Some benefits are not included, such as reuse and property values, as the benefits are unlikely to vary with the general population.
2 Water will have similar health and convenience impacts, and also educational outcomes.
3 From both reduced stunting, less illness time (health-related absenteeism), and higher enrolment and completion rates (especially being girl-friendly) due to better WASH facilities.
4 Educational gains for disabled children.

Source: Assessment by the authors.

preferences, which are dictated by social customs as to what is considered normal or desirable. A third factor supporting the status quo is that these populations would like to improve their condition, but do not have the means to pay for the service, with a greatest constraint being on raising the up-front costs of investment.

Hence, lack of funding and financing mechanisms are critical bottlenecks to achieving the SDG WASH targets. Recommendations are provided under three major sets of policy instrument – financing mecanisms, subsidies and supply-side efficiencies.

Financing mechanisms for poor and vulnerable groups

A financing mechanism essentially changes the availability of funds so that different options can be considered. For households, a common bottleneck is the availability of funds to pay up-front costs of capital hardware, including a connection fee for piped services. Hence, many households are willing to take a repayable loan which can be paid off over subsequent years.

However, the micro-finance market until now has not provided solutions for a large proportion of households either due to unavailability in rural areas, especially those distant from commercial centres; financial institutions not lending for water (and especially sanitation) investments; high interest rates; or the lack of collateral that households can offer against the loan. Given poor households are particularly challenged by these barriers, different initiatives have successfully made loans accessible to poor households. The Grameen Bank in Bangladesh has successfully reached rural populations with affordable loans for WASH, specifically targeting women. Repayment rates are reportedly very high. Also, Water.org has leveraged hundreds of millions of dollars of loans to rural households by providing funding to NGOs and microfinance providers for capacity building and technical assistance, who then leverage funding from banks and capital markets to disburse loans to people in need.[27] An alternative to commercial loans is small-group (community) savings schemes and revolving funds.

Delivering subsidies

Providing WASH services to the poor will require rethinking the financial instruments for achieving universal coverage. Subsidies are a subset of financial flows between governments, utilities, and customers. National governments provide budget allocations to subnational government entities that play either a direct or indirect role in water and sanitation service delivery. These fiscal transfers may be used to fully or partially finance capital projects, cover operation and maintenance (O&M) expenses not met by utility revenues, and to finance capacity building for utility staff. These fiscal transfers may flow through subnational government entities or less commonly be provided directly to utilities.[20]

Two arguments can be used for public subsidies to WASH. The first is the externality argument – that the WASH behaviours and service choices of poor and vulnerable households can negatively impact others. Thus there is a justification for WASH services to be financially supported to increase equality and to provide benefits for all. The second is the ethical and human rights argument, that society and/or the state has a duty to help the poor and vulnerable access essential services.

If providing subsidies is an option, there are various choices that need to be made. First, which cost or programme components should be subsidized? Policy makers need to choose between subsidizing activities to promote household WASH investment and change social norms and behaviours versus subsidizing the costs of the service, with a broad distinction between subsidizing capital investment versus O&M costs.

Second, should subsidies be targeted or provided to the entire population accessing a given service? Generalized subsidies have the advantage of having lower transaction costs, but with the consequence that the better-off populations will capture some of the subsidies. Targeted subsidies work best when it is mainly a poorer group accessing the subsidized service (e.g. location-specific), or when vouchers or cash distribution can piggy-back on robust mechanisms that identify deserving households or individuals. There are also a number of options to design programs to reduce elite capturing and increase the power of impoverished groups to allocate resources toward their priorities.

Third, what is the subsidy level and therefore what proportion of the service cost is being paid for by (poor) households? This will vary in each context, depending on whether the facilities are private or communal facilities, the funds available and the proportion of population that is targeted. In contexts where a service area covers both poor and non-poor households, the pricing mechanism can be defined to allow for cross-subsidization between population groups,

In general, the literature on subsidies is dominated by studies that examine various forms of usage subsidies. This is reflected both in the cases documented in Komives et al. (2005)[18] and Andres and Fuente (2017).[20] The broader literature on usage subsidies focuses largely on subsidies that rely on self-selection via quantity, particularly increasing block tariffs (IBTs). This reflects the widespread implementation of IBTs in low and middle-income countries.

Reducing unit costs

It is often the case that service costs can be reduced, without any impact on the service level. This can be achieved in several ways – four alternatives are detailed here.

First, technological innovation and dissemination can lead to major cost reductions over time. For example, as water and wastewater treatment technologies advance, greater efficacy is achieved. Also, the falling price and increasing performance of plastic products enables lower cost latrines to be produced – not only latrine slabs but also superstructure. Hence, producers can save costs at different parts of their production process by investing in new technologies.

Second, many markets are highly regulated, monopolistic and hence there is very limited competition. In some cases, such as piped water or wastewater networks, it does not make economic sense to have alternative networks competing for the same customers. While some regulations are essential to maintain, such as wastewater discharge standards, other regulations (such as on market entry) can be reduced. By enabling more producers and suppliers in the marketplace will therefore increase competition, with impacts on costs, innovation and product availability.

Third, there exist many production inefficiencies due to poor planning, lack of accountability, product wastage and leakage. By institutionalizing modern management practices and identifying cost-beneficial interventions to undertake, costs can eventually be cut back and lower prices delivered to the consumer. This is helped by opening markets up to competition, to increase incentives for good performance.

Fourth, there remains significant potential in some contexts to reduce unit costs by identifying better-priced factors of production and through exploiting economies of scale – which involves spreading relatively fixed costs over a larger production base. While the evidence is mixed on the optimal size of a utility's service area, authorities need to make evidence-based decisions when dividing up cities or districts into service zones, considering among other things the factors that are driving costs.

Final remarks

Given that poor and vulnerable population groups are not homogeneous, WASH financing policies need to distinguish different populations and specific actions for dealing with each of them. First, a realistic policy is needed on what minimum service levels are to be aimed for (for vulnerable groups) that meets the human rights to water and sanitation. This policy needs to be backed up with a service costing, financing strategy and implementation plan to ensure the service level is affordable to poorer populations. While affordability of water services needs to be understood in the light of the impact of WASH expenditure on the consumption of other essential goods, there are challenges to assessing this with the currently available data. Hence, benchmarks are needed for easily measuring whether WASH services of a minimum level are likely to be unaffordable for specific population groups. There are many different strategies for making WASH services more affordable to poor and vulnerable population, and the optimal strategy will depend on the effectiveness of targeting mechanisms, availability of subsidies and strength of local financial (loan) markets, among other things. While there are already many examples of public actions to make WASH services more affordable, more evaluations are needed on their successes and weaknesses, and conditions under which they do or do not work.

Notes

1 Hutton, G. and Varughese, M. (2016). The costs of meeting the 2030 Sustainable Development Goal targets on drinking water, sanitation, and hygiene. Washington, DC: World Bank, Water and Sanitation Program.
2 WHO/UNICEF (2017). Progress on drinking water, sanitation and hygiene: 2017 update and SDG baseline. Joint Monitoring Programme. Geneva: World Health Organization, and New York: UNICEF.
3 WHO/UNICEF (2015). Progress on drinking water and sanitation: 2015 update and MDG assessment. Joint Monitoring Programme. Geneva: World Health Organization, and New York: UNICEF.
4 WHO/UNICEF (2013). Post 2015 WASH targets and indicators. Joint Monitoring Programme. Geneva: World Health Organization, and New York: UNICEF.
5 Hathi, P., Haque, S., Pant, L., Coffey, D., and Spears, D. (2017). Place and child health: the interaction of population density and sanitation in developing countries. *Demography*, 54: 337–360. doi 10.1007/s13524–016–0538-y
6 Andres. L., Briceño, B., Chase, C., and Echenique. J.A. (2014). Sanitation and externalities. Evidence from early childhood health in rural India. Policy Research Working Paper 6737. Washington, DC: World Bank.
7 Ferro, G., Lentini, E.J., Mercadier, A.C. (2011). Economies of scale in the water sector: a survey of the empirical literature. *Journal of Water, Sanitation and Hygiene for Development*, 1(3): 179–193.

8 Organisation for Economic Cooperation and Development (2007). Feasible Financing Strategies for Water Supply and Sanitation. Paris: OECD.
9 International Water and Sanitation Center (IRC). IRC WashCost projects for India, Ghana, Mozambique and Burkina Faso. The Hague: IRC, 2008–13.
10 Hutton, G., Rodriguez, U-P., Winara, A., Nguyen, V.A., Kov, P., Chuan, L., Blackett, I., Weitz, A. (2014). Economic efficiency of sanitation interventions in Southeast Asia. *Journal of Water, Sanitation and Hygiene in Development*, 4(1): 23–36.
11 World Bank (2015). Service delivery assessments for water supply and sanitation in East Asia and the Pacific. Washington, DC: World Bank, Water and Sanitation Program.
12 Robinson, A. (2009). Global expenditure review: water supply and environmental sanitation. Woking: Plan International.
13 Danilenko, A., van den Berg, C., Macheve, B. and Moffitt, J. (2014) *The IBNET Water Supply and Sanitation Blue Book 2014: The International Benchmarking Network for Water and Sanitation Utilities Databook*. World Bank, Washington, DC.
14 World Bank (2013). Investment project financing: economic analysis guidance note. Washington DC, World Bank.
15 Cameron, J., Hunter, P., Jagals, P., and Pond, K. (2011). Valuing water, valuing livelihoods. Guidance on social cost-benefit analysis of drinking-water interventions, with special reference to small community water supplies. Geneva: World Health Organization, and London: IWA Publishing.
16 Smets, H. (2009). Access to drinking water at an affordable price in developing countries. In: El Moujabber, M., Mandi, L., Trisorio-Liuzzi, G., Martín, I., Rabi, A., and Rodríguez, R. (eds.). Technological perspectives for rational use of water resources in the Mediterranean region. Bari: CIHEAM. pp. 57–68 (Options Méditerranéennes: Série A. Séminaires Méditerranéennes; n. 88).
17 Smets, H. (2012). Quantifying the affordability standard. In: *The Human Right to Water: Theory, Practice and Prospects*. Cambridge: Cambridge University Press.
18 Hutton, G. (2012). Monitoring "Affordability" of water and sanitation services after 2015: Review of global indicator options. Geneva: United Nations Office of the High Commissioner for Human Rights.
19 Komives, K., Foster, V., Halpern, J., and Wodon, Q. (2005). Water, electricity, and the poor: who benefits from utility subsidies? Washington, DC: World Bank.
20 Andres, L. and Fuente, D. (2017). Scoping study for subsidies in water. Washington, DC: World Bank.
21 World Bank (2017). WASH inequalities in the era of the Sustainable Development Goals: rising to the challenge. Global Synthesis Report of the Water Supply, Sanitation, and Hygiene (WASH) Poverty Diagnostic Initiative. Washington DC, World Bank.
22 Andrés, L., Loughnan, E., and Li, S. (2017). Navigating the shifting international MDG to SDG frameworks to assess WASH coverage in 18 countries in a meaningful way. Background paper for the WASH Poverty Diagnostics Initiative, World Bank, Washington, DC.
23 WHO/UNICEF (2012). Progress on drinking water and sanitation: 2012 update. Joint Monitoring Programme. Geneva: World Health Organization and New York: UNICEF.
24 Hutton, G. (2012). Global costs and benefits of drinking-water supply and sanitation interventions to reach the MDG target and universal coverage. WHO/HSE/WSH/12.01. Geneva: World Health Organization.
25 Whittington, D., Jeuland, M., Baker, K., and Tuen, Y. (2012). Setting priorities, targeting subsidies among water, sanitation, and preventive health interventions in developing countries. *World Development*, 40(8): 1546–1568.
26 Hutton, G. and Chase, C. (2016). The knowledge base for achieving the sustainable development goal targets on water supply, sanitation and hygiene. *International Journal of Environmental Research and Public Health*, 13(6).

27 Jones, H., Parker, K.J., and Reed, R. (2002). Water supply and sanitation access and use by physically disabled people: a literature review. Loughborough: Water, Engineering and Development Centre, Loughborough University.
28 World Bank (2015). Financing water and sanitation for the poor: the role of microfinance institutions in addressing the water and sanitation gap. Washington, DC: World Bank, Water and Sanitation Program.

INDEX

Note: The index uses UK spelling. Page numbers in *italic* refer to figures; page numbers in **bold** refer to tables; and page numbers in ***bold italic*** refer to boxes.

"3Es" (effectiveness, equity and efficiency) 141
"3Ts" framework (tariffs, taxes and transfers) 141–142

ability to pay *see* ATP
acceptability *see* water acceptability
accessibility: drinking water 3, 9, 11, 16, 64–65, 94–95, 200, 241, 244; FWM 221–222; sanitation 9, 11, 118, 197, 200, **202**, **203**, 207, 253; sanitation services 3–4, 32–33, 63, 140–141, 238–239; water services 32–33, ***72–73***, 110–111, 140–141, 238–239
Accessibility and Safety Audit **165**, 169
accessible facilities 161–162, **163**, **165**, 169; disabled people 157–158, 159, **163**, 170, 301; marginalised groups 159, **163**, **165**; schools 83, 170, 183, 185–186
affordability 40, 42, 140, 240, 288, 289, 291–295, **299**, 309; FSM 154, 220, 226
Afghanistan ***8***
Africa ***10***, 52, 97, 105, 289; FSM 222; groundwater 101, *102*; handwashing *18*; water availability 99–101, *103*; water supply 100, 108, 109–110
ageing *see* older people

Agenda for Sustainable Development (2030) 26, 39, 43, 46–47, 54, 234, 242, 286; universality 47–48, 49, 54
APF (Achievement Possibility Frontier) 257
arsenic 98
Asia 11, 196, 211, 289; children 197, 210; FSM 222; safe drinking water 98, 100; water supply 108
ATP (ability to pay) 64, 226; *see also* WTP
Australia 161, 166
availability *see* water availability

B40 households 295, 298
Bain, R. 254–255
Bakker, K. 67
Bangladesh ***13***, 98, 198, 200, 211, 307; DPT 3 vaccinations 202, 205, 206; healthcare access **201**, **202**, **203**; nutrition access **202**, **203**; sanitation access **202**, **203**, 205, 206; water access **202**, **203**
Bartram, J. 236, 257, 258, 272
basic capabilities 69
basic sanitation 46, 63, 71, 158, 218, 220, 246, 301
Batchelor, C. 139
best-practice frontiers 256–257, 261, 264, 270; drinking water coverage 258, *259*

Biekens, M.F.P. 96
Bolivia 86, 179
Brazil *19*, 212
Bryce, J. 254–255
budgets **168**, 307
Burkina Faso 163
Burmen, B. 184

Calow, R. 101
Cambodia 163, 264, *266*
capabilities 68, 69–70
Castro, J.E. 66, 67
Cavill, S. 145–146
CCI (Center for Community Initiatives) 126, 127
CEDAW (Convention on the Elimination of All Forms of Discrimination Against Women) 28, 32, 177
censuses 6, 8–9, 11, 15, 19, 22, 241, 243
Central Human Capabilities List 69–70
CESCR (Committee on Economic, Social and Cultural Rights) 30, 33, 234–235, 253
Chad 264, *265*
child mortality 15, 196–197, 208, 210, 211
children 17, 210, 212, 301; DPT 3 vaccinations 204, 205, 206–207; health 207, 210, 211; healthcare access 200, 204, 207–208, *209*; inequalities 254–255; nutrition access 207–208; poverty 209; rural areas 197, 202, 204–205, 208, 210; sanitation access 200, 204, 205, 206–207; stunted growth 200, 202, 204, 205, 206; undernutrition 208, 210; urban areas 197, 204–205, 206, 208; water access 200, 204
China **10**, 97, 98, 108, 110
chronic illnesses 157, 158, 161, 170, 172, 236
cities 84, 98, 108
climate change 50, 53–54, 97, 101, 104–106, **107**
Committee on Economic, Social and Cultural Rights *see* CESCR
Concentration Index 253, 254
conflicts 86–87
contamination 4, 16, 238, 240, 244–245; *see also* pollution
Convention on the Elimination of All Forms of Discrimination Against Women *see* CEDAW
costs *see* economic costs; service costs
CRC (Convention on the Rights of the Child) 28

Cronk, R. 257, 258
CRPD (Convention on the Rights of Persons with Disabilities) 28, 159, **160**
Cumming, O. 254–255

Dar es Salaam, Tanzania 121–123, 124, 126; sanitation services 123, 124, **125**, 126–127, 129, **130–131**; water services 122, 124, **125**, 126–129
data analysis 22–23
data collection 22; *see also* censuses; household surveys
data disaggregation 11, 52, 170, 241
data integration 22, 241
DEA (data envelopment analysis) 256–257, 272
de Albuquerque, C. 26
Delhi, India **72**
Democratic Republic of Congo *see* DRC
Demographic and Health Surveys *see* DHS
developing countries 40, 50, 101, 104, 105, 236, 287
development cooperation 33, 35, 38–40, 41, 43
DFID (Department for International Development, UK) 164, 166
DHS (Demographic and Health Surveys) 4, 16, 18, 197, 198, 200, 211, 218, 262
difference principle 68
dignity 35, 81, 177, 178, 179, **180–181**
Diphtheria, Pertussis and Tetanus vaccinations *see* DPT
disabled people 21, 50, **160**, 161, 163, 166, 172; accessible facilities 157–158, 159, *163*, 170, 301; discrimination 30, 31; inclusion **167**, **168**
Disabled Persons' Organisations *see* DPO
disadvantaged groups 20, 22, 37, 38, 41, 50–51, 157–158, 159, 161, *163*; *see also* marginalised groups
disaggregated data *see* data disaggregation
disaggregation 170
discrimination 28, 29–31, 33–34, 41, 43, 241
disparities in access 37–38; rural areas 38, 117, 119–120, 196, 256; urban areas 38, 117, 119–120, 196, 256
Dominican Republic 258
DPO (Disabled Persons' Organisations) 163
DPT (Diphtheria, Pertussis and Tetanus) vaccinations 197, 198, 202; children 204, 205, 206–207

DRC (Democratic Republic of Congo) 198, 200; DPT 3 vaccinations 205; healthcare access **201**, **202**, **203**; nutrition access **202**, **203**; sanitation access **202**, **203**, 205; water access **202**, **203**

drinking water 4, 16, 98, 138, 139, 243–245; accessibility 3, 9, 11, 16, 64–65, 94–95, 200, 241, 244; equality 63, 71; household water treatment 16; improved 4, **5**; MDGs 9, 13, 46, 71, 73, 81, 157; SDGs 21, 64, 73, 94–95; service ladder 242–243; sustainability 97; water quality 16, 106, 241, 244–245

drinking water coverage 3, 258–261

drinking water services 6, 19, **303–304**

drinking water sources 5, 16, 76, 81, 111–112; contamination 4, 16

droughts 99, 104, 105

East Asia 11

economic costs 302, *305*

Economics of Sanitation Initiative *see* ESI

education 15, 179, 181, **182**

EED (Environmental Enteric Dysfunction) 208, 209

effectiveness, equity and efficiency ("3Es") 141

El Salvador 260

emergencies 301

England 161

Environmental Enteric Dysfunction *see* EED

environmental protection 4, 50, 53–54

equality 28, 29, 32, 39, 43, 54, 70, 137, 159, 266; budgets *168*; drinking water 63, 71; legislative frameworks 40–41; sanitation access 35, 41, 63, 76; service levels 64–66; water access 35, 41, 63, 76; water supply 67, 73, 76

equity 28–29, 138

ESI (Economics of Sanitation Initiative) 290

Ethiopia **13**, 86, 106, 198, 200, 258, 266; DPT 3 vaccinations 205, 206; healthcare access **201**, **202**, **203**; nutrition access **202**, **203**; sanitation access 202, **203**, 205, 206; water access 202, **203**; water supply 109–110

ethnic groups 300

exclusion 28, 31, 172, 304

faecal sludge management *see* FSM
faecal waste management *see* FWM

FEASIBLE model 290

fecal sludge management *see* FSM

fecal waste management *see* FWM

Fenn, B. 254–255

financing 42–43, 137–139, 142–143, 153–154, 304, 306–307, 309; Kenya 143–145; *see also* investment

financing mechanisms 306–307

floods 52, 99, 104, 105, 223

Fonseca, C. 139

food 27

formal settlements 11

Franceys, R. 139, 145–146

Free Basic Water Policy 67

frontier analysis 256–257, 258–262, 271–272

FSM (faecal sludge management) 108, 112, 140, 149, 150, 216, 217, 219, 221–223, 224; affordability 154, 220, 226; rural areas 219, 223; urban areas 219, 222, 223

Fukuda-Parr, S. 257

funding 34, 40–41, 42–43, 137–139, 141–143, 145–146, 149–150, 153–154, **168**, 289, 304, 306, 309; Nakuru, Kenya 150–152, 153, 154; Tunisia 146–149; *see also* investment

FWM (faecal waste management) 217–222, 223, 224–225, 226

gap analyses 242–243, 253, 254, 270–271

gender 30, 50–51, 90; WASH insecurity 80, 81, 82–84, 88, 89; WASH security 80, 81, 82–83, 84, 89; *see also* girls; women

gender equality 16, 36

gender inequalities 50–51, 89, 187–188, 191, 210; *see also* girls; menstruation; water collection; women

general capabilities 69

geographic disparities 38

Ghana 53, 218, 220–221, 264, *265*

girls 30, 50, 80, 81, 82–83, 178, 185–186; climate change 53–54; education 179, 181, **182**; health 84–85, 183; inequalities 176, 185; menstruation 30, 176, 178–179, **180–181**, 181–182, 183, 184, 186–187; MHM 188, 190–191; water collection 50, 53

GLAAS (Global Analysis and Assessment of Sanitation and Drinking-Water) 39, 47, 50, 142–143

Gleeson, T. 96

Global Action Plan (WHO/UNICEF) 86

global costs 288–289
global monitoring 3, 15, 37, 242, 249
global policies 64, 167, 188
GRACE data 97
groundwater 95, 96, 98, 99–100, 105, 110, 111; Africa 101, *102*; Dar es Salaam 122, 127
groundwater storage 96, 100, *102*, 104
group-related inequalities 38
Guidelines for Drinking Water Quality (WHO) 239, 245
Guidelines for Sanitation and Health 246
Gujarat, India 68–69, 75

handwashing 18, 248
health 27, 84–86, 89, 98, 118, 141, **184**, 287; children 207, 210, 211; girls 84–85, 183; menstruation 183, 184; women 84–86, 89, 183
healthcare access 49, 86, 197, 200, **201, 202, 203**, 207–209, 210–212
health financing strategies 141
Heller, L. 26
high-income countries 5, 48, 150, 154, 217
HIV (PLHIV) 157, 158, 159, 166–167, 170, 172
homeless people 31
Honduras 260
household surveys 4, 6, 8–9, 11, 15, 19, 22, 120, 241, 243–244, 248, 271
household water treatment 16
housing 27, 30–31, 198, 220, 221–222, 223
Howard, G. 236
Human Development Report (UNDP) 70, 99
human rights 27, 35, 41, 48, 178, 234; drinking water 64, 65; non-discrimination 28, 29, 159; sanitation 21, 26–27, 36–37, 39, 43, 49, 65, 159, 233–235, 249, 288, 292; sanitation access 32–33, 165, 238–241, 253; water 21, 26–27, 36–37, 39, 43, 49, 67, 159, 233–235, 249, 288, 292; water access 32–33, 165, 238–241, 253
human rights laws 28, 29, 42
hygiene 4, 18, 21, 248

IBNET (International Benchmarking Network for Water and Sanitation Utilities) 290
IBTs (increasing block tariffs) 147, 308
ICCPR (International Covenant on Civil and Political Rights) 28

ICERD (International Convention on the Elimination of All Forms of Racial Discrimination) 28
ICESCR (International Covenant on Economic, Social and Cultural Rights) 28, 33, 38–39, 178, 183
ICF (International Classification of Functioning, Disability and Health) 170
IDP (internally displaced persons) 31, 52, 301–302
IDWSSD (International Drinking Water Supply and Sanitation Decade) 64, 66, 117
IEB (Index of Equality Betterment) 253, 254
improved drinking water 5, 9, 11, 20, 234, 237, 238
improved sanitation 9, 11, 20, 208, 217, 218, 234, 237, 238, *298*
improved/unimproved classification 4, *5, 10*, 237–238
improved water access 266–270, *296*
inclusion 28, 29, 163–164, 166, 167–170
increasing block tariffs *see* IBTs
Index of Equality Betterment *see* IEB
India **72–73**, 86, 97, 98, 112, 161, 222; Gujarat 68–69, 75; MHM 187, 188; water supply 83–84, 99, 108; women 83, 84, 85, 86
Indonesia 161, 166, 236
inequalities 3, 11–16, 20–21, 33, 36, 46, 50, 160, 212, 235, 253–256; discrimination 29, 31; education 15; frontier analysis 261–262; FWM 218–219; gender 50–51, 89, 187–188, 191, 210; girls 176, 185; JMP 12, 20, 170, 242, 270; MDGs 3, 11–12, 234; monitoring 3, 15, 22–23, 172; regulatory frameworks 41; rural areas 262–266, 270–271; sanitation access 33, 34, 35, 36–37, 39, 43, 71, 197–198; SDGs 15, 21–22, 50–54, 76, 157, 170, 172, 235, 253, 255–256; service levels 64, 238–241; urban areas 262–266, 270–271; water access 33, 34, 35, 36–37, 39, 43, 71, 197–198; water supply 70, 76; women 176, 185
informal settlements 11, **13**, 31, 41, 52, 54, **72**, 84, 120, 210, 212; Dar es Salaam 122, 123, 126, 127, 129
interconnectedness 48–50, 54
internally displaced persons *see* IDP

International Benchmarking Network for Water and Sanitation Utilities *see* IBNET
International Classification of Functioning, Disability and Health *see* ICF
International Convention on the Elimination of All Forms of Racial Discrimination *see* ICERD
International Convention on the Protection of All Migrant Workers and their Families 28
International Covenant on Civil and Political Rights *see* ICCPR
International Covenant on Economic, Social and Cultural Rights *see* ICESCR
International Disability Alliance 163
International Drinking Water Supply and Sanitation Decade *see* IDWSSD
international monitoring 3, 117, 118, 120, 123, 129, 131
International Year of Sanitation (2008) 6
intersectionality 83, 159–161
intra-household inequalities 38, 76
intra-urban areas 38
investment 33, 41, 42–43, 46, 51, 113, 142, 304, 306; sanitation services 33, 36, 40; water services 33, 36, 40, 95–96, 110–111
invisible power 71
irrigation 68, 96, 97
isolated populations 298, 300
Israel 71

JMP (Joint Monitoring Programme, WHO/UNICEF) 3–4, *14*, 47, 118, 121, 234, 235, 237, 288; affordability 240, 289, 291–292; drinking water 6, 8–9, 244; inequalities 12, 20, 170, 242, 270; MDGs 13, 71, 198, 233; sanitation 6, *10*, 197, 253; SDGs 21, 47, 198; service ladders 6, 7, *8*, *9*, 12, 73, 118, 140, 233–234, 241–243, 246–247, 249; water access 197, 253
JMP Country Files (WHO/UNICEF) 258, 262, 266
Jones, H. 167

Kazakhstan 260, 264, *266*
Kenya 53, 86–87, 143–145, 184, 186, 210, 221; Nakuru 150–152, 153, 154
Kirkwood, B.R. 254–255
Korea, Republic of 268, *269*, 270

Lancet Commission on Investing in Health 211
Lawson-Remer, T. 257
LDCs (Least Developed Countries) 119, 185–186
legislative frameworks 40–41, 161
LICs (low-income countries) 5, 120, 138, 142, 197, 288; health facilities 49, 86; safely managed water and sanitation 138; sanitation services 52–53; stunting 197
LMICs (low- and middle-income countries) 138, 177, 185, 196, 198, 200, 210–211; FWM (fecal waste management) 218; healthcare access 210
LSMS (Living Standard Measurement Study) 4
Luh, J. 257, 258, 272

MacDonald, A. 101
Madagascar 163
Maji ni Maisha (MnM), Kenya 144
Malawi 126
Mali 260, *261*
marginalised groups 29–30, 31, 37, 41, 46, 50–51, 170, 287; accessible facilities 159, **163**, **165**; inclusion 164, **167**, 169, 172; *see also* disadvantaged groups
maternal health 85–86
maximin principle 68
MDGs (Millennium Development Goals) 4, 46, 118, 137, 196–197, 198, 211, 286; drinking water 9, 13, 46, 71, 73, 81, 157; education 181; FWM 217; hygiene 18; inequalities 3, 11–12, 234; monitoring 6, 8, 73, 75; sanitation access 11, 71, 73, 157; sanitation coverage 9, 219; schools 185
MDS (Model Disability Survey, WHO) 170, 171
Mehta, L. 64, 71
menstrual hygiene 177, 178
menstruation 30, 85, 176, 178, 181–183, 184–185, 187
MHM (menstrual hygiene management) 85, 176, 182–183, 185, 186–187, **189–190**, 190–191
"MHM in Ten" 185, 188
MICs (middle-income countries) 48, 52, 120, 138, 142, 288; healthcare access 49, 86
MICS (Multiple Indicator Cluster Surveys, UNICEF) 4, 16, 18, 198, 211, 262
Middle East *10*

Millennium Declaration (UN, 2000) 46
Millennium Development Goals *see* MDGs
Millennium Summit on Sustainable Development 4
Mnif, M. 149
Mobility International **168**
Moldova, Republic of 268, *269*, 270
Mombassa, India 20
monitoring systems 168–170; global 3, 15, 37, 242, 249; inequalities 3, 15, 22–23, 172; international 3, 117, 118, 120, 123, 129, 131; MDGs 6, 8, 73, 75; SDGs 22, 73, 172, 233; *see also* JMP; WASH monitoring
Movik, S. 64
Mozambique 21, 167, 198, 200; DPT 3 vaccinations 205; healthcare access **201**, **202**, **203**; nutrition access **202**, **203**; open defecation *20*; sanitation access 202, **203**, 205; water access 202, **203**
Mujica, A. 149
Multiple Indicator Cluster Surveys *see* MICS

Nakuru, Kenya 150–152, 153, 154
national governments 22, 37, 48, 49, 117, 154, 166–167, 188, 224, 307
national policies 19, 33–34, 37, 39, 40–41, 48, 50–51, 65, 212; MHM 167, 188; *see also* WASH policies
neighbourhoods 217, 220, 221–222, 223
Nepal 142–143, 179, 266
New Delhi Statement 66, 242
NGOs (non-governmental organizations) 39, 88; FSM 221, 223
Nigeria 198, 200, 211, 264, 266; DPT 3 vaccinations 205, 206, 207; healthcare access **201**, **202**, **203**; nutrition access **202**, **203**; sanitation access 202, **203**, 205, 206, 207; water access 202, **203**
non-discrimination 28, 29, 34, 39, 40–41, 43, 159, 163
North Africa 100
Nussbaum, M. 69, 70
nutrition access 197, 200, **202**, **203**, 207–208
Nyothach, E. 184

O&M (Operations and Maintenance) costs 286, 289, 293
ODF (Open Defecation-Free) status 52, 236

OECD (Organisation for Economic Cooperation and Development) 47, 138, 146
older people 157–158, 159, 161, 166, *167*, 170, 172, 301
open defecation 6, 11, *12*, *20*, 41, 48, 52, 98, 149, 235, 287, 295, *297*
open drains 217, 222, 223
O'Reilly, K. 89
ORT (Oral Rehydration Therapy) 209
Otieno, G. 184

Pakistan 178, 198, 200, 202, 212; DPT 3 vaccinations 205, 206, 207; healthcare access **201**, **202**, **203**; nutrition access **202**, **203**; sanitation access **202**, **203**, 205, 206, 207; water access **202**, **203**
Palestine 71
Papua New Guinea 160
periurban areas 11, **13**
Philippines 179, 212
Phillips-Howard, P.A. 184
piped water 4, *19*, 48, **72**, 122, 238–239, 295, *296*, 308
Plan International 290
PLHIV (people living with HIV) *see* HIV
pollution 98, 101, 111; *see also* contamination
poor households 295, 298, **299**, 302, 304, 309
population subgroups 20–21
poverty 31, 36, 209, 210, 287, 292
primary goods 67–68
prisoners 31, 287, 302
private sector participation 40, 67
progressive realisation 33, 38–39, 41, 234
public health 235–236
public services 27, 36, 148, 150, 169
public subsidies 307
public toilets 32, 52, 84, 221–222, 223

QI (Quality Improvement) frameworks 236–237

Randolph, S. 257
Rapid Assessments of Drinking-Water Quality studies 16
Rawls, J. 67–68
refugees 31, 52, 287, 301–302
regulatory frameworks 40, 41, 161
remote populations 298, 300
repayable finance 141–143
Robeyns, I. 69
Roche, R. 254–255

Roma people 29, 31
Ross, I. 149
Rouf, V. 177
rural areas 11, *12*, **13**, 20, 41, 106, 138, 210, 289; children 197, 202, 204–205, 208, 210; disparities in access 38, 117, 119–120, 196, 256; FSM 219, 223; inequalities 262–266, 270–271
RU Ratio 263–266

safe drinking water 3, 46, 64, 71, 98, 100, 243
safely managed sanitation 21, 118–120, 137, 138, 140–141, 216, 224–226, 247, 248, 287–288
safely managed water 21, 118–120, 137, 138, 140–141, 287–288
safety 81, **165**, 266–267
Said, F. 149
sanitation 4, **10**, 17, 18, 21, 245–248; accessibility 9, 11, 118, 197, 200, **202**, **203**, 207, 253; human rights to 21, 26–27, 36–37, 39, 43, 48, 65, 159, 233–235, 249, 288, 292
Sanitation and Water for All (global partnership) 6
sanitation coverage 9, *10*, 119, 120–121, 219
sanitation facilities 3–4, **5**, **6**, 18, 83, 84, 87, 216, 219, 239
sanitation infrastructure 140, 219–220, 225, 238
sanitation security 81, 86
sanitation services 6, 19, 27, 46–47, 66–67, 138, 142, 219–220, 236, **303–304**, *306*; accessibility 32–33, 63, 140–141; investment 33, 36, 40
sanitation technologies 219, 222
SBA (Strengths Based Approaches) 89
schools 50, 179; accessible facilities 83, 170, 183, 185–186; menstruation **182**, 182, 183, 184, 186–187; MHM 177, 185, 188, 190–191
SDG 1 *see* poverty
SDG 2 *see* nutrition access
SDG 3 *see* healthcare access
SDG 6 27, 35, 43, 46–47, 48, 52, 53–54, 197, 247, 253, 286; *see also* girls; inequalities; safe drinking water; safely managed sanitation; universal access; vulnerable groups; women
SDG 10 *see* inequalities
SDG 11 *see* sustainability
SDG 13 *see* climate change

SDG indicators 21–22, 46, 138, 198, **199–200**, 287–288
SDGs (Sustainable Development Goals) 3, 26–27, 34–36, 40, 46, 94, 197, 198, 286–287; climate change 53–54; drinking water 21, 64, 73, 94–95; environmental protection 53–54; inequalities 15, 21–22, 49–53, 54, 76, 157, 170, 172, 235, 253, 255–256; interconnectedness 48–50; MHM 187, 188, **189–190**; monitoring 22, 73, 172, 233; safely managed sanitation 21, 112, 118, 218, 225–226; safely managed water 21, 112, 118; sanitation access 35, 48, 73, 80, 81, 253, 255–256; sustainable management 46–47, 94, 118; universal access 43, 76, 80, 137–138, 197, 233, 235; universality 47–48, 49; water access 35, 48, 73, 80, 81, 253, 255–256
SDI (Slum Dwellers International) 126
Sen, A. 68, 69
Senegal 220
septic tanks 108, 216, 217, 222
service costs 289–290, **299**, 308–309
Service Delivery Assessments 290
service ladders 6, 7, **8**, *9*, 12, 73, 118, 140, 233–234, 241–243, 246–247, 249
service levels 5, 16, 22, 64–66, 153, 233, 237–241, 249, 287–288, *294*, 309; affordability 291–295; inequalities 64, 238–241; service ladders 6, 7, **8**, *9*, 12, 73, 118, 140, 233–234, 241–243, 246–247, 249
service providers 41, 145–146
service sustainability 40, 42, 48, 54, 153, 164, 233
sewer connections networks 18
shared sanitation *10*, 17, 120–121, 247, 295, *297*
Sierra Leone 106
slums 20, 31, 210, 298
social exclusion 172, 304
social inclusion 29
social model of inclusion **160**, 172
Some for All Rather than More for Some *see* New Delhi Statement
South Africa 67, 71, 85, 260
South Asia 11, 98, 100, 211; children 197, 210
South Eastern Asia 11
Southern Africa 10, 100, 105, 158, 166, 196
Southern Asia 196, 210

Sri Lanka *74*
SSP (Sanitation Safety Planning) 245–246
structural violence 71
stunted growth 197, 198, 200, 287
subnational regions 19, 22
sub-Saharan Africa 11, 197, 210, 211; children 210; drinking water 13, 16, *17*, 71, 95, 196; FSM 222; handwashing 18; hygiene 18; inequalities 254, 255; water availability 99, 100, 112; water supply 109
subsidies 307–308, 309
substantive equality 32
sustainability 46–47, 49, 52, 70, 75, 97, 219
sustainable cities 50, 51–53
Sustainable Development Goals *see* SDGs
sustainable management 46–47, 94, 118
SWA (Sanitation and Water for All) 6, 64
Swaziland 167

T60 households 295, 298
tanker trucks 4, *10*, 120
Tanzania 123–124; *see also* Dar es Salaam, Tanzania
tariffs 154, 290
tariffs, taxes and transfers ("3Ts" framework) 141–142
Taylor, R. 96
ter Kuile, F.O. 184
Timor-Leste 165
TrackFin (WHO) 143
Transforming our World declaration (2015) 234
Trémolet, S. 149
Trevett, A. 145–146
Truelove, Y. *72*
Tunisia 146–149, 153–154
TUPF (Tanzania Urban Poor Federation) 126, 127

Uganda *163*, 164, 221, *267*, 268, *269*, 270; MHM 187, 188
UK (United Kingdom) 71, 164
Ukraine 260–261
UN (United Nations) 29, 39, 66, 117, 235, 253
UNCESCR *see* CESCR
undernutrition 196–197, 200, 208
UNECE (United Nations Economic Commission for Europe) 35
UNICEF (United Nations Children's Fund) 49–50, 97, 301
unimproved sanitation 208, 234

unimproved water access 234, 266–270
universal access 35, 66–67, 95, 118, 140, 197, 233–234, 253, 258; SDGs 43, 76, 80, 137–138, 197, 233, 235
Universal Declaration of Human Rights (1948) 28, 177, 178, 179, 183
universality 47–49, 50, 54
UN-Water GLAAS *see* GLAAS
urban areas 11, *12*, **13**, 20, 52, 53, 84, 106, 119–120, 202, 210; children 197, 204–205, 206, 208; disparities in access 38, 117, 119–120, 196, 256; FSM 219, 222, 223; inequalities 262–266, 270–271; service costs 289; water supply 108–110
urogenital infections 85, 183

van Beek, L.P.H. 96
Victora, C.G. 254–255
violence 71, 87, 191
vulnerable groups 35, 43, 50–51, 157–158, 161, 286–287, 288, **299**, 300–301, 304, 309

Wada, Y. 96
WASHCost 290
WASH expenditure 240
WASH infrastructure 46, 89, 161, 183, 185–186, 287
Washington Group (WG) questions 170, 171
WASH insecurity 80, 81, 82–87, 89, 90
WASH interventions 54, 87
WASH monitoring 3–4, 13, 15, 22–23, 37, 233, 241
WASH policies 50–51, 52–53, 66–67, 80, 88–89, 90, 161, 168, 309; *see also* global policies; national policies
WASH Poverty Index 88–89
WASH security 80, 81, 82–83, 84, 86, 89
WASH services 3, 87–88, 196, 233; service costs 288–289, 290–291; service levels 3, 237–238
WASH stakeholders 4, *10*, 22
wastewater management 217, 224, 247–248, 308
water, human rights to 21, 26–27, 36–37, 39, 43, 48, 67, 159, 233–235, 249, 288, 292
water acceptability 240; *see also* water quality
water access 118, 197, 200, **202**, **203**, 207, 253
WaterAid 163, 169

water availability 95–97, 98, 101, 105, 110, 239; Africa 99–101, *103*; drinking water 241, 244
water collection 50, 52–53, 81, 83, 85, 106, 239, 243, 300
water coverage 119, 120–121; drinking water 3, 258–261
water demand 101, 104
water infrastructure 108
Water.org 307
water quality 16, 41, 48, 73, 97, 98, 106, 111–112, 236, 239–240; drinking water 16, 106, 241, 244–245
water resources 36, 54, 75, 95–96, 98, 101, 104–106, **107**
water resources management 99, 110, 112–113
Water Safety Plans *see* WSP
water scarcities 70, 96, 97, 99
water security 81
water services 4, 27, 29–30, 41, 46–47, 75, 138, 235–236; accessibility 32–33, **72–73**, 110–111, 140–141; Dar es Salaam 122, 124, **125**, 126–129; investment 33, 36, 40, 95–96, 110–111
water supply 63–64, 66–69, 70–71, 76, 95–97, 106, 108–110, 120, 138, 139–140; Africa 100, 108, 109–110; India 83–84, 99, 108
water tariffs 146, 154
water technologies 54, 308
water withdrawals 95, 96–97, 101

wealth analysis 37–38
wealth quintiles 11–12, 16, 21, 22
Welle, K. 75
WHO (World Health Organization) 30, 46, 70, 117, 141, 157, 301; Guidelines for Drinking Water Quality 239, 245; MDS 170, 171; TrackFin 143
willingness to pay *see* WTP
Winkler, I.T. 177
women 30, 50, **72**, 82–83, 87, 178, 300–301; climate change 53–54; education **182**; health 84–86, 89, 183; inequalities 176, 185; menstruation 30, 85, 176, 178–179, **180–181**, 184, 186, 187; MHM 190; WASH insecurity 80, 81, 83–84, 89; WASH security 80, 82–83, 84, 89; WASH services 87, 88, 90; water collection 50, 52–53, 81, 82, 85, 300
World Bank 66, 67, 98, 138, 145, 157, 166, 236, 288, 289, 290, 295
World Inequality Database on Education 15
world's population 52, 81, 96, 106, 108, 157, 196
World Summit on Sustainable Development 4, 46, 118
WSP (Water Safety Plans) 53, 239, 245
WTP (willingness to pay) 139–140, 292

Zambia 126, **163**, 164, 185–186, 210; MHM 187, 188

CPSIA information can be obtained
at www.ICGtesting.com
Printed in the USA
BVHW040439220119
538317BV00005B/25/P